Introducing Microsoft SQL Server 2019

Reliability, scalability, and security both on premises and in the cloud

Kellyn Gorman, Allan Hirt, Dave Noderer, Mitchell Pearson, James Rowland-Jones, Dustin Ryan, Arun Sirpal, and Buck Woody

Introducing Microsoft SQL Server 2019

Authors: Kellyn Gorman, Allan Hirt, Dave Noderer, Mitchell Pearson, James Rowland-Jones, Dustin Ryan, Arun Sirpal, and Buck Woody

Additional material: Mitchell Pearson

Managing Editor: Alexander Mazonowicz

Acquisitions Editor: Alicia Wooding

Production Editor: Nitesh Thakur

Editorial Board: Shubhopriya Banerjee, Bharat Botle, Ewan Buckingham, Mahesh Dhyani, Taabish Khan, Manasa Kumar, Alex Mazonowicz, Pramod Menon, Bridget Neale, Dominic Pereira, Shiny Poojary, Erol Staveley, Ankita Thakur, Nitesh Thakur, and Jonathan Wray

First Published: April 2020

Production Reference: 1160420

ISBN: 978-1-83882-621-5

Published by Packt Publishing Ltd.

Livery Place, 35 Livery Street

Birmingham B3 2PB, UK

About the Authors

Kellyn Gorman is an Azure Data Platform Architect for Microsoft with a long history in multi-platform technology. She spends a 60/40% split between Oracle on Azure and Analytics with her present team at Microsoft. A recent Idera ACE, a current friend of Redgate in the Microsoft community and an Oracle ACE Director alumnus, she has been awarded numerous awards over the years for her technical contributions and community volunteerism. She is one of only six women part of the Oak Table, a network for the Oracle scientist. She has extensive experience in environment optimization, automation and architect of robust environments, specializing in multi-terabyte management of OLAP/DSS systems. A consistent advocate for logical tuning of code and design before hardware solutions. She's recently become known for her expertise in DevOps, Enterprise Manager, AWR, (Automatic Workload Repository) Warehouse and virtualization of database environments with complex cloud management. The technical knowledge required to support these features offers great educational opportunities to learn by attending her technical presentations, engaging with her on social media presence as DBAKevlar or reading her blog, https://dbakevlar.com/.

Boston-based Cloud and Data Center and Data Plaform Dual MVP **Allan Hirt** has been working with SQL Server since 1992 and clustering in Windows Server since the days just after Wolfpack. He got his start with databases as an intern at SQL Solutions, which then got purchased by Sybase where he remained an intern until the end of college. Allan has used every version of SQL Server that Microsoft has released for Windows. He founded his own company, Megahirtz, in 2007 and is now partners with Max Myrick in SQLHA.

You will often find Allan speaking at local user groups, SQL Saturdays, and various conferences like PASS Summit, SQLBits, and TechEd as well as doing various webcasts during the years. He has authored quite a bit of content over the years including articles for SQL Server Magazine and whitepapers for Microsoft that are up on TechNet and MSDN. He is the author or co-author of a quite a few books, and is working on his latest, *Mission Critical SQL Server*, which will be due out soon.

Dave Noderer is the CEO / President and founder of Computer Ways, Inc., a software development company in Deerfield Beach, FL. Dave is an electrical engineer by training, designed computers for 20 years and has been writing software since founding Computer Ways, Inc. in 1994. Dave spent three years as an officer and director of INETA (International .NET Association) where he oversaw the enrollment and support of hundreds of user groups worldwide and 16 years as a Microsoft MVP. He co-founded Florida .NET User groups in 2001 and has been holding meetups in South Florida ever since. Since 2005, he has led the annual, free South Florida Code Camp. This event attracts over 1000 developer attendees. Dave is involved in local community activities as a board member of the Deerfield Beach Historical Society, the Hillsboro Lighthouse Society, and TechLauderdale.org.

James Rowland-Jones (JRJ) is a Principal Program Manager at Microsoft. He is currently part of the SQL Server team working on SQL Server 2019 Big Data Clusters and data virtualization. Prior to joining SQL Server, JRJ worked extensively on Azure SQL Data Warehouse. He helped the team launch Gen 1 of the service and led the product management effort to bring Gen 2 into preview.

JRJ is passionate about delivering highly scalable solutions that are creative, simple and elegant. He is also a keen advocate for the worldwide SQL community; previously serving on the Board of Directors for PASS while also helping to build SQLBits–Europe's largest data event. JRJ was awarded Microsoft's MVP accreditation from 2008 to 2015 for his services to the community.

> *For Jane, Lucy, Kate, and Oliver. Forever x.*

Dustin Ryan is a Senior Cloud Solution Architect at Microsoft. Dustin has worked in the business intelligence and data warehousing field since 2008, has spoken at community events such as SQL Saturday, SQL Rally, and PASS Summit, and has a wide range of experience designing and building solutions featuring SQL Server and Azure. Prior to his time at Microsoft, Dustin worked as a business intelligence consultant and trainer for Pragmatic Works. Dustin is also an author, contributor, and technical editor of books.

Dustin resides outside Jacksonville, Florida with his wife, three children, and a three-legged cat and enjoys spending time with his family and serving at his local church.

Arun Sirpal is a SQL Server consultant and currently a Microsoft Data Platform MVP. Specializing in both SQL Server and Microsoft Azure, he has over 12 years' experience architecting, designing, and performance tuning physical and virtualized SQL Servers and has a wealth of experience with designing solutions using the Azure Data Platform including Azure SQL Database, Azure SQL Database Managed Instances, elastic pools, and hybrid concepts. Arun is also a frequent writer, speaker, and technical reviewer and a member of Microsoft's Azure Advisors and SQL Advisors groups.

Buck Woody works on the Azure Data Services team at Microsoft and uses data and technology to solve business and science problems. With over 35 years of professional and practical experience in computer technology, he is also a popular speaker at conferences around the world; author of over 700 articles and eight books on databases, machine learning, and R, he also sits on various Data Science Boards at two US Universities, and specializes in advanced data analysis techniques.

Table of Contents

Chapter 3: High Availability and Disaster Recovery   81

Chapter 4: Hybrid Features – SQL Server and Microsoft Azure 111

Chapter 9: SQL Server 2019 Big Data Clusters   249

Chapter 11: Data Warehousing   319

Chapter 13: Power BI Report Server — 389

Chapter 14: Modernization to the Azure Cloud — 423

Preface

About

This section briefly introduces the coverage of this book, the technical skills you'll need to get started, and the hardware and software required to complete the book.

About Microsoft SQL Server 2019

From its humble beginnings in OS/2 with version 1.1, SQL Server has proved over and over that it is a database that data professionals love to use. The engine is reliable, and the T-SQL dialect has everything the developer needs to quickly write resilient, high-performing applications.

With every release, SQL Server has improved on performance, functions, reliability, and security. As the releases progressed, more features were added, and then entirely new capabilities—a job engine, a reporting server, business intelligence, and data mining systems. Groundbreaking technologies, such as in-memory databases and columnstore indexes, made SQL Server one of the most installed Relational Database Management Systems (RDBMSes) in the world.

In Spring of 2016, Microsoft announced that SQL Server would be made available on the Linux operating system—something unbelievable to many technical professionals. Addition of Platform Abstraction Layer (PAL) in SQL Server allowed it to run on Linux operating systems such as Ubuntu, Red Hat Enterprise Linux, and SUSE. It also added support for Linux containers, opening up amazing new possibilities for deployment and operation.

SQL Server 2019 represents not only an evolutionary release, but a revolutionary release. The promise of containers is completely realized with support for Kubernetes. The new SQL Server 2019 Big Data Clusters leverages Kubernetes as the deployment platform and adds the power of Spark and Apache Hadoop File System (HDFS). Additionally, SQL Server 2019 supports Data Virtualization and workloads with deployable applications running on-premises, in the cloud, and even in hybrid configurations. This allows SQL Server 2019 to modernize your data estate and applications with intelligence over any data—structured and unstructured.

Like the releases before it, SQL Server 2019 isn't limited to just the Windows platform. In addition to SQL Server 2019 on Windows, Linux, and containers, Microsoft has also announced a new product—Azure SQL Database Edge—which is a small-footprint SQL Server engine that runs on Edge devices and the ARM platform. This allows a consistent developer experience from the ground to the cloud and the edge. Add to this the choice of platform and the choice of programming languages such as T-SQL, Java, C/C++, Scala, Node.js, C#/VB.NET, Python, Ruby, and .NET Core. Need more? You can add your own languages as well.

SQL Server 2019 supports machine learning and extensibility with R, Python, Java, and Microsoft .NET. You're able to operationalize your machine learning models close to the data, and developers can leverage Java and other languages server-side.

But it's not just about new features. SQL Server maintains its high standards in performance and security. This release boasts industry-leading performance. It has the #1 OLTP performance benchmarks, and #1 DW performance on 1 TB, 3 TB, and 10 TB non-clustered DW workloads. It supports in-memory across all workloads and is the most consistent on-premises data platform—in both IaaS and PaaS. SQL Server 2019 has intelligent query processing features that improve the performance of mission-critical queries. They also support in-memory transactions and in-memory analytics for hybrid transactional and analytical processing.

Security is essential in any data storage and processing system, and SQL Server has prided itself on being the most secure database over the last eight years according to the National Institute of Standards and Technology's (NIST's) Comprehensive Vulnerability Database. SQL Server supports enterprise security and compliance with security features such as Transparent Data Encryption, Auditing, Row-Level Security, Dynamic Data Masking and Always Encrypted. SQL Server 2019 adds support for secure enclaves in Always Encrypted to enable rich computations on encrypted data.

SQL Server 2019 allows you to solve modern data challenges. Data virtualization with PolyBase allows you to use SQL Server 2019 as a data hub, directly querying data from data sources. These sources include Oracle, SAP HANA, MongoDB, Hadoop clusters, Cosmos DB, and SQL Server—all using T-SQL, and without separately installing client connection software. SQL Server 2019 also gives you insights and rich new reports, even for mobile BI with Power BI Report Server.

SQL Server 2019 improves reliability with several features in the High Availability and Disaster Recovery architecture and works with the built-in availability features in Kubernetes. It recovers faster with Accelerated Database Recovery.

This book covers these features, giving you a tour of each of them and diving in with real-world examples and sample code you can try out on your own. Put together by recognized experts and members of the team that wrote the software, we'll get you up to speed quickly and ready to start your own adventure with this latest release of the world's best data platform.

About the chapters

Chapter 1, Optimizing for performance and real-time insights, explains how SQL Server 2019 gets the most out of your hardware and empowers your analytics with features such as Hybrid Buffer Pool, and hybrid transactional and analytical processing.

Chapter 2, Enterprise Security and Compliance, covers the essential elements in SQL Server 2019 to ensure your operations are not compromised and that they stay compliant with industry regulations for data usage.

Chapter 3, High Availability and Disaster Recovery, covers SQL Server 2019's built-in methods to increase availability, minimize downtime for maintenance, and assist when outages occur.

Chapter 4, Hybrid Features—SQL Server and Microsoft Azure, looks at how SQL Server 2019 and Azure Storage work together to offer enterprise-ready, highly scalable, and flexible storage solutions at competitive prices.

Chapter 5, SQL Server 2019 on Linux, looks at how SQL Server 2019 is building on the Linux features in the 2017 release to offer even more functionality.

Chapter 6, SQL Server 2019 in Containers and Kubernetes, explains how virtualization features have evolved and how you can deploy SQL Server across Docker and Kubernetes.

Chapter 7, Data Virtualization, highlights SQL Server 2019's position as a modern enterprise data hub and how you can use features such as hybrid transactional and analytical processing to query across disparate systems.

Chapter 8, Machine Learning Services Extensibility Framework, explores machine learning, the components and architectures in SQL Server 2019 you can use to implement such services, and the process you follow for your solutions.

Chapter 9, SQL Server 2019 Big Data Clusters, builds on the concepts covered in the previous chapter to show how SQL Server 2019 can be leveraged to handle scaled-out datasets.

Chapter 10, Enhancing the Developer Experience, covers the tools to develop and manage SQL Server projects, including Visual Studio, SQL Server Management Studio, and—especially for cross-platform development—Visual Studio Code.

Chapter 11, Data Warehousing, highlights mission-critical security features such as Row-Level Security, Always Encrypted, and data masking.

Chapter 12, Analysis Services, looks at how SQL Server 2019 provides superior performance for decision support and business analytics workloads via multidimensional mode and tabular mode.

Chapter 13, Power BI Report Server, looks at new features that are included in the latest releases of Power BI Report Server, as well as key differences between Power BI Report Server and SSRS.

Chapter 14, Modernization to the Azure Cloud, finishes the book with a discussion of Azure's role regarding modernization and the data platform.

Conventions

Code words in text, database table names, folder names, filenames, file extensions, pathnames, dummy URLs, user input, and Twitter handles are shown as follows: "A non-durable table is declared with **DURABILITY=SCHEMA_Only**."

A block of code is set as follows:

```
USE master;
GO
BACKUP CERTIFICATE MyServerCert
TO FILE = 'C:\SQLSERVER\MyServerCert.cer'
WITH PRIVATE KEY
(FILE = 'C:\SQLSERVER\certificate_Cert.pvk',
ENCRYPTION BY PASSWORD = '!£$Strongpasswordherewelikesqlver#')
```

New terms and important words are shown like this: "Most Windows Server-based WSFCs (and SQL Server deployments) use **Active Directory Domain Services** (**AD DS**)."

Words that you see on the screen, for example, in menus or dialog boxes, appear in the text like this: "Go to **Actions** and select **Get Shared Access Signature** as shown."

System requirements

You will need the following hardware and software to complete the examples in this book:

- SQL Server 2019 Developer edition or higher with SQL Server Management Studio.
- A computer that has a 1.4 GHz or faster x64 processor (2 GHz recommended)
- 1 GB of memory (4 GB recommended)
- 6 GB of available hard-disk space
- Super VGA 800 x 600 or higher resolution display
- Internet connection to download software, as described in applicable chapters.
- For non-Windows platforms such as Linux or virtual machines, please refer to the release documentation.

Depending on your Windows configuration, you might require local administrator rights to install or configure SQL Server 2019 and related products.

Prerelease software

To help you become familiar with SQL Server 2019 as soon as possible after its release, we wrote this book by using examples that worked with SQL Server 2019 Release Candidate. Consequently, the final version might include new features, the user interface might change, or features that we discuss might change or disappear. Refer to *What's New in SQL Server* 2019 at https://docs.microsoft.com/en-us/sql/sql-server/what-s-new-in-sql-server-ver15?view=sqlallproducts-allversions for the most up-to-date list of changes to the product.

AdventureWorks Database

Some demonstrations make a reference to the `AdventureWorks` database. This is a sample database published by Microsoft and used to demonstrated SQL Server 2019's new features. The database, along with download and setup instructions, can be found at https://docs.microsoft.com/en-us/sql/samples/adventureworks-install-configure?view=sql-server-ver15.

1

Optimizing for performance, scalability and real-time insights

Companies are optimizing their computing resources to get more transactional performance out of the same hardware resources. At the same time, the demand and pace of business and customer focus is increasing; they need real-time insights on the transactional data.

In recent years, many companies have turned to No-SQL solutions that allow very high write performance of transactions while allowing eventual consistency, but that later require data mining and analysis.

Microsoft SQL Server has taken on this challenge and, with every release, continues to expand the workloads in many dimensions. This chapter will discuss many of the features that allow both high-performance transaction processing while simultaneously allowing real-time analytics on transactional data without the need for a separate set of ETL processes, a separate data warehouse, and the time to do that processing.

Microsoft SQL Server 2019 is built on a database engine that is number one for TPC-E (On-Line Transaction Processing Benchmark) and TCP-H (Decision Support Benchmark). See http://www.tpc.org for more information.

Changes in hardware architecture allow dramatic speed increases with Hybrid Buffer Pool, which utilizes persistent memory (PMEM), also known as **Storage Class Memory (SCM)**.

Microsoft SQL Server 2019 can be used in the most demanding computing environments required today. Using a variety of features and techniques, including in-memory database operations, can make dramatic increases in your transaction processing rate while still allowing near-real-time analysis without having to move your transaction data to another "data warehouse" for reporting and analysis.

Microsoft SQL Server 2019 has also expanded the number of opportunities to tune database operations automatically, along with tools and reports to allow monitoring and optimization of queries and workloads. Comprehensive diagnostic features including Query Store allow SQL Server 2019 to identify performance issues quickly.

By upgrading to SQL Server 2019, the customer will be able to boost query performance without manual tuning or management. **Intelligent Query Processing (IQP)** helps many workloads to run faster without making any changes to the application.

Hybrid transactional and analytical processing (HTAP)

Hybrid transactional and analytical processing (HTAP), is the application of tools and features to be able to analyze live data without affecting transactional operations.

In the past, data warehouses were used to support the reporting and analysis of transactional data. A data warehouse leads to many inefficiencies. First, the data has to be exported from the transactional database and imported into a data warehouse using ETL or custom tools and processes. Making a copy of data takes more space, takes time, may require specialized ETL tools, and requires additional processes to be designed, tested, and maintained. Second, access to analysis is delayed. Instead of immediate access, business decisions are made, meaning the analysis may be delayed by hours or even days. Enterprises can make business decisions faster when they can get real-time operational insights. In some cases, it may be possible to affect customer behavior as it is happening.

Microsoft SQL Server 2019 provides several features to enable HTAP, including memory-optimized tables, natively compiled stored procedures, and Clustered Columnstore Indexes.

This chapter covers many of these features and will give you an understanding of the technology and features available.

A more general discussion of HTAP is available here: https://en.wikipedia.org/wiki/Hybrid_transactional/analytical_processing_(HTAP).

Clustered Columnstore Indexes

Clustered Columnstore indexes can make a dramatic difference and are the technology used to optimize real-time analytics. They can achieve an order of magnitude performance gain over a normal row table, a dramatic compression of the data, and minimize interference with real-time transaction processing.

A columnstore has rows and columns, but the data is stored in a column format.

A rowgroup is a set of rows that are compressed into a columnstore format — a maximum of a million rows (1,048,576).

There are an optimum number of rows in a rowgroup that are stored column-wise, and this represents a trade-off between large overhead, if there are too few rows, and an inability to perform in-memory operations if the rows are too big.

Each row consists of column segments, each of which represents a column from the compressed row.

Columnstore is illustrated in *Figure 1.1*, showing how to load data into a non-clustered columnstore index:

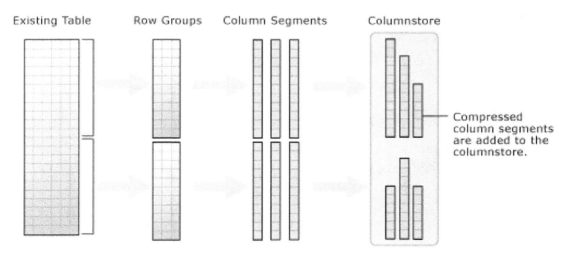

Figure 1.1: Loading data into a non-clustered columnstore index

A clustered columnstore index is how the columnstore table segments are stored in physical media. For performance reasons, and to avoid fragmenting the data, the columnstore index may store some data in a deltastore and a list of the IDs of deleted rows. All deltastore operations are handled by the system and not visible directly to the user. Deltastore and columnstore data is combined when queried.

A delta rowgroup is used to store columnstore indexes until there are enough to store in the columnstore. Once the maximum number of rows is reached, the delta rowgroup is closed, and a background process detects, compresses, and writes the delta rowgroup into the columnstore.

There may be more than one delta rowgroup. All delta rowgroups are described as the deltastore. While loading data, anything less than 102,400 rows will be kept in the deltastore until they group to the maximum size and are written to the columnstore.

Batch mode execution is used during a query to process multiple rows at once.

Loading a clustered columnstore index and the deltastore are shown in Figure 1.2.

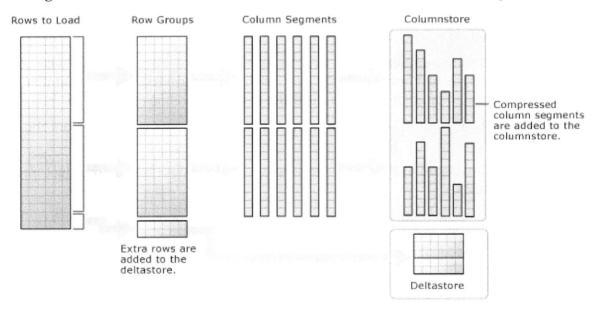

Figure 1.2: Loading a clustered columnstore index

Further information can be found here: https://docs.microsoft.com/en-us/sql/relational-databases/indexes/get-started-with-columnstore-for-real-time-operational-analytics?view=sql-server-2017.

Adding Clustered Columnstore Indexes to memory-optimized tables

When using a memory-optimized table, add a non-clustered columnstore index. A clustered columnstore index is especially useful for running analytics on a transactional table.

A clustered columnstore index can be added to an existing memory-optimized table, as shown in the following code snippet:

```
-- Add a clustered columnstore index to a memory-optimized table


ALTER TABLE MyMemOpttable
ADD INDEX MyMemOpt_ColIndex clustered columnstore
```

Disk-based tables versus memory-optimized tables

There are several differences between memory-optimized and disk-based tables.

One difference is the fact that, in a disk-based table, rows are stored in 8k pages and a page only stores rows from a single table. With memory-optimized tables, rows are stored individually, such that one data file can contain rows from multiple memory-optimized tables.

Indexes in a disk-based table are stored in pages just like data rows. Index changes are logged, as are data row changes. A memory-optimized table persists the definition of the index but is regenerated each time the memory-optimized table is loaded, such as restarting the database. No logging of index "pages" is required.

Data operations are much different. With a memory-optimized table, all operations are done in memory. Log records are created when an in-memory update is performed. Any log records created in-memory are persisted to disk through a separate thread. Disk-based table operations may perform in-place updates on non-key-columns, but key-columns require a delete and insert. Once the operation is complete, changes are flushed to disk.

With disk-based tables, pages may become fragmented. As changes are made, there may be partially filled pages and pages that are not consecutive. With memory-optimized tables, storing as rows removes fragmentation, but inserts, deletes, and updates will leave rows that can be compacted. Compaction of the rows is executed by means of a merge thread in the background.

Additional information can be found at this Microsoft docs link:

https://docs.microsoft.com/en-us/sql/relational-databases/in-memory-oltp/comparing-disk-based-table-storage-to-memory-optimized-table-storage?view=sql-server-2017.

In-memory OLTP

In-memory **on-line transaction processing** (**OLTP**) is available in Microsoft SQL Server for optimizing the performance of transaction processing. In-memory OLTP is also available for all premium Azure SQL databases. While dependent on your application, performance gains of 2-30x have been observed.

Most of the performance comes from removing lock and latch contention between concurrently executing transactions and is optimized for in-memory data. Although performed in-memory, changes are logged to disk so that once committed, the transaction is not lost even if the machine should fail.

To fully utilize in-memory OLTP, the following features are available:

- Memory-optimized tables are declared when you create the table.

- Non-durable tables, basically in-memory temporary tables for intermediate results, are not persisted so that they do not use any disk I/O. A non-durable table is declared with `DURABILITY=SCHEMA_ONLY`.

- Table values and table-valued parameters can be declared as in-memory types as well.

- Natively compiled stored procedures, triggers, and scalar user-defined functions are compiled when created and avoid having to compile them at execution time, thereby speeding up operations.

Additional information can be found at the following links:

- https://docs.microsoft.com/en-us/sql/relational-databases/in-memory-oltp/in-memory-oltp-in-memory-optimization?view=sql-server-2017

- https://docs.microsoft.com/en-us/sql/relational-databases/in-memory-oltp/survey-of-initial-areas-in-in-memory-oltp?view=sql-server-2017

Planning data migration to memory-optimized tables

Microsoft **SQL Server Management Studio** (**SSMS**) contains tools to help analyze and migrate tables to memory-optimized storage.

When you right-click on a database in SSMS and click on **Reports | Standard Reports | Transaction Performance Analysis Overview**, a four-quadrant report of all tables in the database will be made:

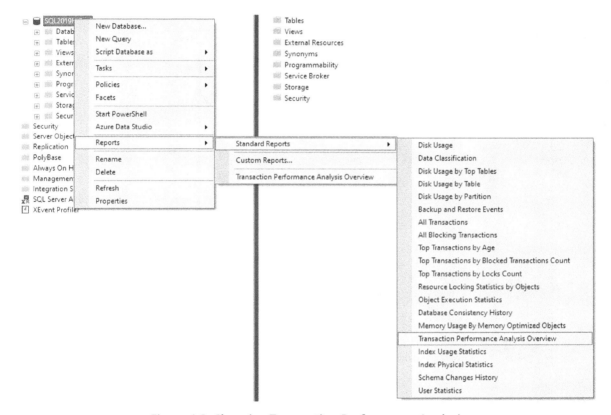

Figure 1.3: Choosing Transaction Performance Analysis

The report will look at each table and place it on the chart to show the ease of migration versus the expected gain by migrating the table to be memory-optimized:

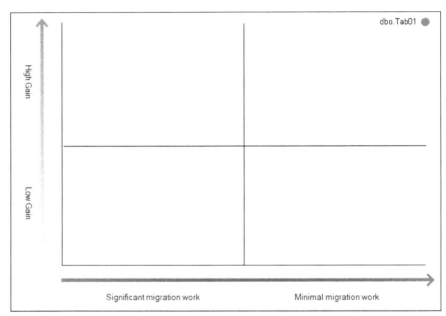

Figure 1.4: Recommended Tables Based on Usage

Once you have identified tables that might benefit, you can right-click on individual tables and run the Memory Optimization Advisor:

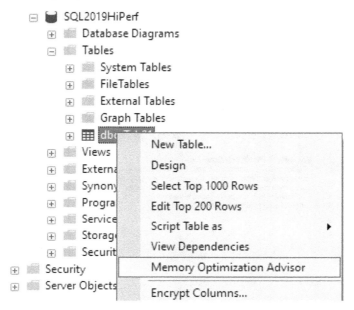

Figure 1.5: Selecting the Memory Optimization Advisor

The **Table Memory Optimization Advisor** is a "wizard" style of user interface that will step you through the configurations:

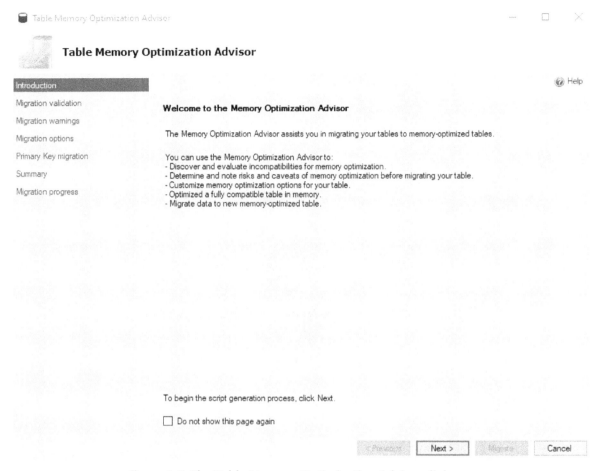

Figure 1.6: The Table Memory Optimization Advisor dialogue

The wizard will take you through a checklist with any failed issues:

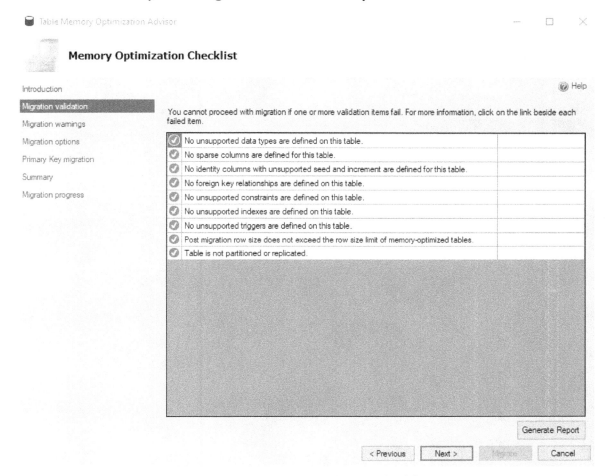

Figure 1.7: Memory Optimization Checklist

The warnings dialogue will flag up other important issues.

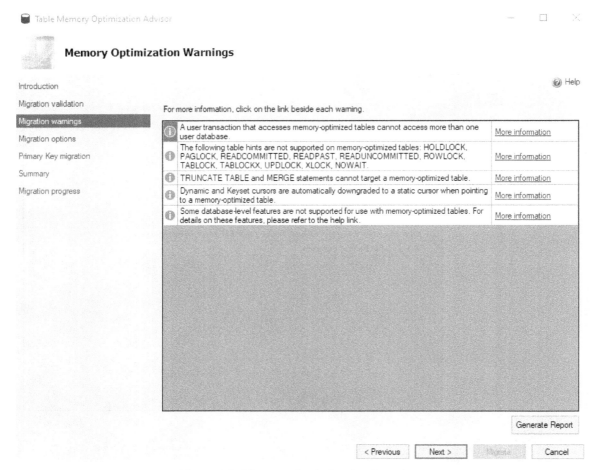

Figure 1.8: Memory Optimization Warnings

Next enter file names and check paths in the migration option dialogue.

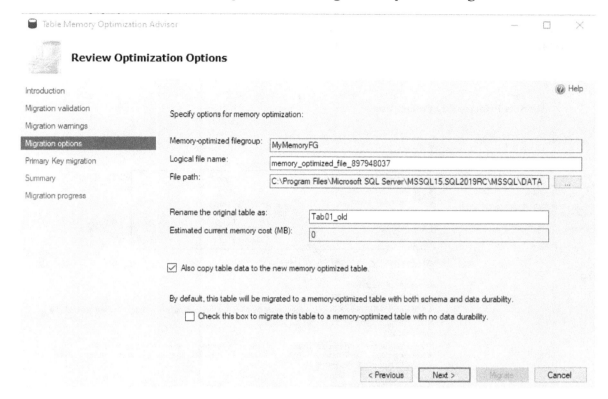

Figure 1.9: Review Optimization options

The wizard will detect the primary keys and populates the list of columns based on the primary key metadata. To migrate to a durable memory-optimized table, a primary key needs to be created. If there is no primary key and the table is being migrated to a non-durable table, the wizard will not show this screen.

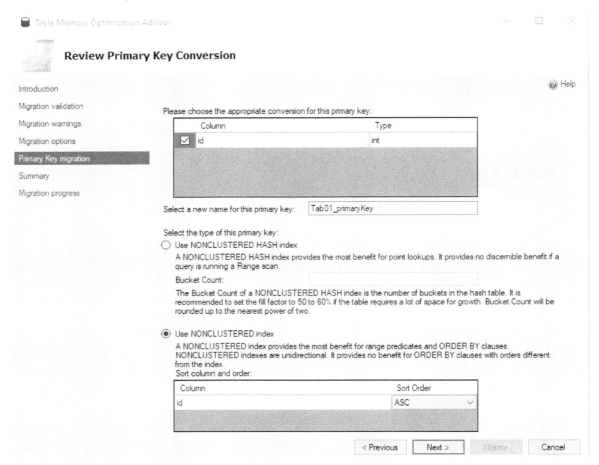

Figure 1.10: Review Primary Key Conversion

By clicking **Script** you can generate a Transact-SQL script in the summary screen.

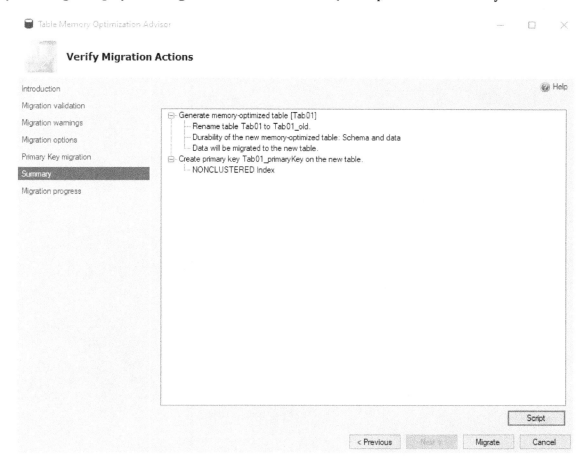

Figure 1.11: Verify Migration Actions Summary Screen

The wizard will the display a report as the table migrates.

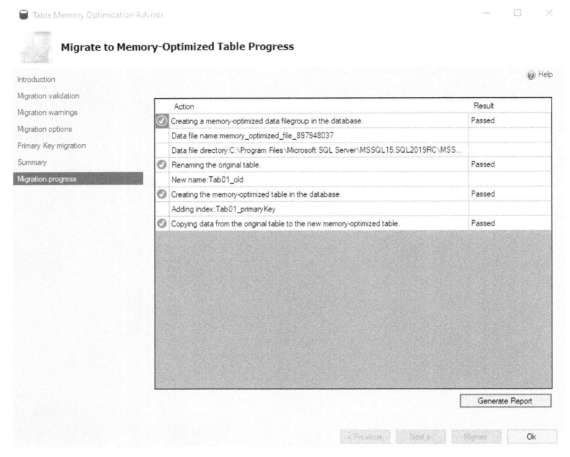

Figure 1.12: Migration progress report

Memory-optimized tables are a great feature, but you will need to plan carefully to make sure you get the performance and transactional reliability you require.

You can create a new database specifying memory-optimized, or alter an existing database to handle memory-optimized data. In either case, a filegroup for containing the memory-optimized data must be created.

In the following sample, we will create a memory-optimized database using SQL script:

```
-- Create Memory-Optimized Database
USE MASTER;

GO


CREATE DATABASE MemOptDB
   ON (Name = MemOptDB_Data, FileName = 'c:\sqldata\memoptdb_data.mdf',
size = 10 mb, maxsize = 20 mb, filegrowth = 5 mb)
   LOG ON (Name = MemOptDB_Log, FileName = 'c:\sqldata\memoptdb_log.
ldf', size = 2 mb, maxsize = 10 mb, filegrowth = 1 mb);

GO


-- Must declare a memory-optimized filegroup
ALTER DATABASE MemOptDB
   ADD FILEGROUP MemOptDB_FG contains MEMORY_OPTIMIZED_DATA;

ALTER DATABASE MemOptDB
   ADD FILE (Name = 'MemOptDB_MOFG', FileName = 'c:\sqldata\memoptdb_
mofg')
   TO FILEGROUP MemOptDB_FG;

ALTER DATABASE MemOptDB
   SET MEMORY_OPTIMIZED_ELEVATE_TO_SNAPSHOT = ON;

GO
```

You can also make a memory-optimized database by using SQL Server Management Studio and adding a memory-optimized filegroup:

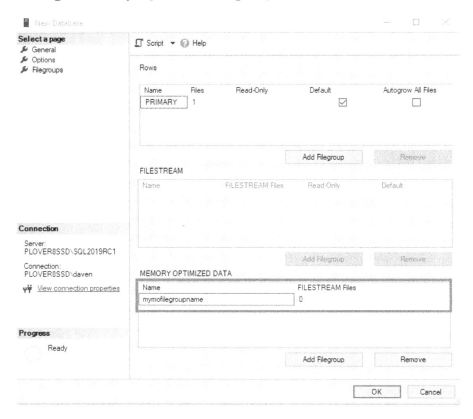

Figure 1.13: The new database dialogue window

Natively compiled stored procedures

Natively compiled stored procedures are compiled when created and bypass the query execution engine. The procedure is compiled when created, and also manually or when the database or server are restarted.

A few additional concepts are introduced here, including **SCHEMABINDING** and **BEGIN ATOMIC**, both of which are required for natively compiled stored procedures.

SCHEMABINDING locks the table definition to prevent alteration after the stored procedure is created. SCHEMABINDING allows the compiled stored procedure to be certain of the data types involved. The tables involved in the natively compiled stored procedure cannot be altered without dropping the SCHEMABINDING, making changes and then reapplying the SCHEMABINDING. SHEMABINDING also requires that explicit field names are used in the query; "`select *…`" will not work.

BEGIN ATOMIC is required in a natively compiled stored procedure and is only available for a natively compiled stored procedure. In interactive (non-natively compiled) procedures, you would use a BEGIN TRAN statement block. Using the ATOMIC block and transaction settings will be independent of the current connection/settings as the stored procedure may be used in different execution sessions.

If there is an existing active transaction, BEGIN ATOMIC will set a save point and roll back to that if it fails. Otherwise, a new transaction is created and completed or rolled back.

You indicated a natively compiled stored procedure in the create declaration of the stored procedure using the "NATIVE_COMPILATION" directive.

In the following sample, we will create a memory-optimized table and a natively stored procedure. Note that memory-optimized tables cannot have clustered indexes. Memory-optimized tables are stored as rows, not in pages, as with a disk-based table:

```
-- Create Memory-Optimized Table
USE MemOptDB;

GO

CREATE TABLE dbo.MyMemOptTable
(
   id int not null,
   dtCreated datetime not null,
```

```
    orderID nvarchar(10) not null

    CONSTRAINT pk_id PRIMARY KEY NONCLUSTERED (id)

    )

    WITH (MEMORY_OPTIMIZED = ON, DURABILITY = SCHEMA_AND_DATA)


GO


-- Create Natively Stored Procedure

CREATE PROCEDURE dbo.myNativeProcedure (@id int)

    WITH NATIVE_COMPILATION, SCHEMABINDING

    AS BEGIN ATOMIC WITH ( TRANSACTION ISOLATION LEVEL = SNAPSHOT,
LANGUAGE = N'us_english' )


    SELECT id, dtCreated, orderID

    FROM dbo.MyMemOptTable

    WHERE id = @id


    END


GO
```

The table schema is locked due to the reference to a natively compiled stored procedure. If you try to alter the table, an exception will be thrown, as shown here:

```
-- Try to alter the schema!

ALTER TABLE [dbo].[MyMemOpttable]

    ALTER COLUMN orderId nvarchar(20)

GO


Msg 5074, Level 16, State 1, Line 55

The object 'myNativeProcedure' is dependent on column 'orderId'.

Msg 4922, Level 16, State 9, Line 55

ALTER TABLE ALTER COLUMN orderId failed because one or more objects
access this column.
```

More information on natively compiled procedures can be found here:

https://docs.microsoft.com/en-us/sql/relational-databases/in-memory-oltp/creating-natively-compiled-stored-procedures?view=sql-server-2017.

TempDB enhancements

We have introduced another scalability enhancement with memory-optimized TempDB metadata. Historically, TempDB metadata contention has been a bottleneck to scalability for workloads running on SQL Server.

The system tables used for managing temp table metadata can be moved into latch-free non-durable memory-optimized tables.

Enabling memory-optimized TempDB metadata

Enabling this feature in SQL Server is a two-step process:

- First, alter the server configuration with T-SQL

- Restart the service

```
ALTER SERVER CONFIGURATION SET MEMORY_OPTIMIZED tempdb_METADATA = ON
```

The following T-SQL command can be used to verify whether **tempdb** is memory-optimized:

```
SELECT SERVERPROPERTY('IsTempdbMetadataMemoryOptimized')
```

Limitations of memory-optimized TempDB metadata

There are a few limitations associated with using this new feature.

- Toggling the feature on and off requires a service restart.

- A single transaction may not access memory-optimized tables in more than one database. This means that any transactions that involve a memory-optimized table in a user database will not be able to access TempDB System views in the same transaction. If you attempt to access TempDB system views in the same transaction as a memory-optimized table in a user database, you will receive the following error:

```
A user transaction that accesses memory-optimized tables or natively
compiled modules cannot access more than one user database or
databases model and msdb, and it cannot write to master.
```

- Queries against memory-optimized tables do not support locking and isolation hints, so queries against memory-optimized TempDB catalog views will not honor locking and isolation hints. As with other system catalog views in SQL Server, all transactions against system views will be in READ COMMITTED (or, in this case, READ COMMITTED SNAPSHOT) isolation.

- There may be some issues with columnstore indexes on temporary tables when memory-optimized TempDB metadata is enabled. It is best to avoid columnstore indexes on temporary tables when using memory-optimized TempDB metadata.

Intelligent Query Processing

Intelligent Query Processing (IQP) is a family of features that were introduced in Microsoft SQL Server 2017 as adaptive query processing and has been expanded with new features in Microsoft SQL Server 2019. By upgrading to SQL Server 2019 and with compatibility level 150, most workloads will see performance improvements due to added intelligence in the query optimizer.

Intelligent Query Processing features are automatically enabled based on the "COMPATIBLITY_LEVEL" of the database. To take advantage of the latest IQP features, set the database compatibility to 150.

Most of these are also available in Azure SQL, but it is best to check current documentation on exactly what is available there as this changes.

The following table summarizes some of the IQP features.

Feature Name	Available	Feature Description
Memory Grant Feedback - Batch Mode	SQL 2017	This feature will adjust the amount of memory granted in a query's execution plan and, after the first execution, will set a new minimum memory for the query plan that may be much less than the original estimate. This feature helps to conserve memory while providing an optimum amount for query execution.
Memory Grant Feedback - Row Mode	SQL 2019	Building on the batch mode memory grant feedback in SQL 2017, row mode will adjust the query plan for the next execution if the actual memory used is less than 50% of the granted memory.
Batch Mode on Rowstore	SQL 2019	Batch mode works in conjunction with columnstore indexes to process columnstore queries. The query processor now will consider batch mode when optimizing rowstore queries. Using batch mode is done dynamically, and the optimizer may decide not to use it.
Approximate Count distinct	SQL 2019	This new function is used to get an approximate on very large datasets where a quick response is more important than the exact number.
Scalar UDF Inlining	SQL 2019	Scalar user-defined function (UDF) is now transformed into a relational expression and optimized along with the execution query. This new processing allows another level of optimization and parallel execution that achieves much better performance.
Table Variable Deferred Compilation	SQL 2019	This change in SQL 2019 waits to compile a table variable used in a statement is executed. At that point, the actual number of rows involved (the cardinality) is known, resulting in better query optimization. Previously the compilation was based on a onerow guess.
Adaptive Joins – Batch Mode	SQL 2017	Dynamically selects nested or hashed joins after reading a specified number of rows. A nested join is appropriate for a small number of rows, but if the join contains a large number of rows, a hashed join is more efficient.

Table 1.14: Table summarizing IQP features

- These features can be disabled and monitored.

- For more information, refer to https://docs.microsoft.com/en-us/sql/relational-databases/performance/intelligent-query-processing?view=sql-server-2017.

Hybrid Buffer Pool

Microsoft SQL Server 2019 introduces Hybrid Buffer Pool. This feature allows access to **Persistent MEMory** (**PMEM**) devices. These persistent memory devices add a new layer to server memory hierarchy and filling the gap between high performance / high cost of DRAM (Dynamic Random Access Memory) and the lower cost lower performance of file storage drives using SSD.

This memory architecture has been implemented by Intel as Intel® Optane™ Technology; refer to https://www.intel.com/content/www/us/en/products/docs/storage/optane-technology-brief.html for more information:

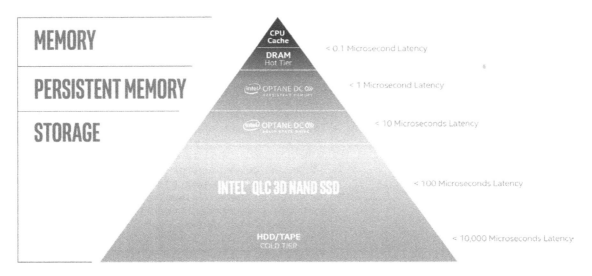

Intel® Optane™ technology fills memory and performance gaps in the data center

Figure 1.15: Intel memory architecture

Persistent memory is integrated at the memory controller level of the CPU chip and will retain data even when the server is powered off.

While many aspects of persistent memory devices can be realized without any software changes, features such as Hybrid Buffer Pool can take advantage of the new storage hierarchy and provide direct memory access to files.

For clean database pages, those that have not been modified, SQL server can directly access them as memory. When an update is made, and then marked as dirty, the page is copied to DRAM, changes persisted, and the page is then written back into the persistent memory area.

To enable Hybrid Buffer Pool, the feature must be enabled at the instance level of SQL Server. It is off by default. After enabling, the instance must be restarted:

```
ALTER SERVER CONFIGURATION

SET MEMORY_OPTIMIZED HYBRID_BUFFER_POOL = ON;
```

Furthermore, the Hybrid Buffer Pool will only operate on memory-optimized databases:

```
ALTER DATABASE <databaseName> SET MEMORY_OPTIMIZED = ON;
```

Or, in order to disable, execute the following command:

```
ALTER DATABASE <databaseName> SET MEMORY_OPTIMIZED = OFF;
```

To see the Hybrid Buffer Pool configurations and memory-optimized databases on an instance, you can run the following queries:

```
SELECT * FROM sys.configurations WHERE name = 'hybrid_buffer_pool';


SELECT name, is_memory_optimized_enabled FROM sys.databases;
```

There are many considerations when configuring a server with persistent memory, including the ratio of DRAM to PMEM. You can read more here:

- https://docs.microsoft.com/en-us/windows-server/storage/storage-spaces/deploy-pmem
- https://docs.microsoft.com/en-us/sql/database-engine/configure-windows/hybrid-buffer-pool?view=sql-server-2017

Query Store

The Query Store in SQL Server, first introduced in SQL Server 2016, streamlines the process of troubleshooting query execution plans. The Query Store, once enabled, automatically captures query execution plans and runtime statistics for your analysis. You can then use the `sys.dm_db_tuning_recommendations` view to discover where query execution plan regression has occurred and use the stored procedure, `sp_query_store_force_plan`, to force a specific plan that performs better.

In SQL Server 2019, we now have made some additional enhancements to the default Query Store features. In this section, we will discuss the following topics:

- Changes to default parameter values when enabling Query Store
- A new `QUERY_CAPTURE_MODE` custom
- Support for fast forward and static cursors

You can configure Query Store with SQL Server Management Studio (SSMS) or with T-SQL statements. SSMS configuration includes turning it on and off by setting the operation mode (off, read-only, or read/write), the Query Store size, and other settings. You can find Query Store parameters in the properties of a database by right-clicking on the database and selecting Query Store:

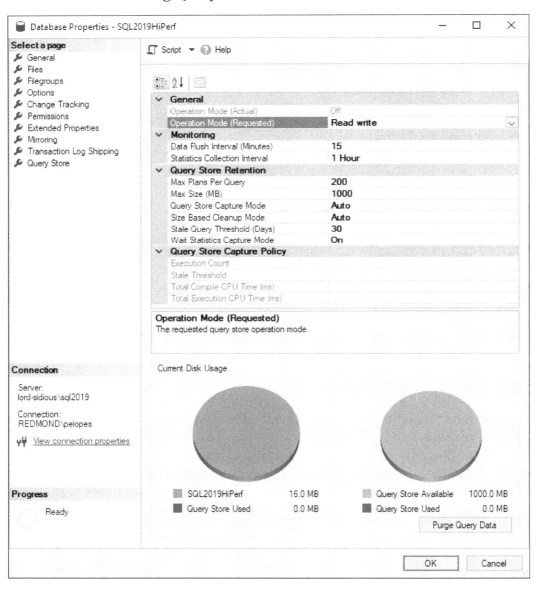

Figure 1.16: Database properties dialogue window

Changes to default parameter values

Two of the existing parameters have new default values compared to SQL Server 2017. These parameters are `MAX_STORAGE_SIZE_MB` and `QUERY_CAPTURE_MODE`. The new default values as of SQL Server 2019 are listed here:

- `MAX_STORAGE_SIZE_MB` has a default value of 1000 (MB)

- The `QUERY_CAPTURE_MODE` has a default value of AUTdO

QUERY_CAPTURE_MODE

In previous versions of SQL Server, the default value for the `QUERY_CAPTURE_MODE` was set to ALL, and therefore all query plans were captured and stored. As mentioned in the previous section, the default value has now been changed to `AUTO`.

Setting the `QUERY_CAPTURE_MODE` to `AUTO` means that no query plans or associated runtime statistics will be captured for the first 29 executions in a single day. Query plans and runtime statistics are not captured until the 30th execution of a plan. This default setting can be changed by using the new custom mode.

QUERY_CAPTURE_MODE: CUSTOM

Before 2019, there were three available values for the `query_capture_mode;` those values were `NONE`, `ALL`, and `AUTO`. We have now added a fourth option, which is `CUSTOM`.

The `CUSTOM` mode provides you with a mechanism for changing the default settings of the Query Store. For example, the following settings can be modified when working in CUSTOM mode:

- `EXECUTION_COUNT`

- `TOTAL_COMPILE_CPU_TIME_MS`

- `TOTAL_EXECUTION_CPU_TIME_MS`

- `STALE_CAPTURE_POLICY_THRESHOLD`

First, you can verify and validate the current Query Store settings by using the `sys.database_query_store_options` view:

```
SELECT actual_state_desc, stale_query_threshold_days, query_capture_
mode_desc,
  capture_policy_execution_count, capture_policy_total_compile_cpu_
time_ms,
  capture_policy_total_execution_cpu_time_ms
FROM sys.database_query_store_options
```

The output is as follows:

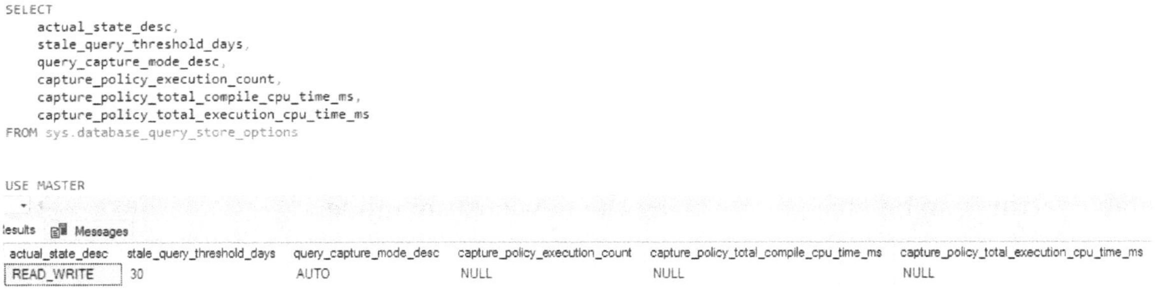

Figure 1.17: Verifying and validating the Query Store settings

To modify the default settings, you will first change the query capture mode to custom and then apply changes to the default values. Look at the following code by way of an example:

```
ALTER DATABASE AdventureWorks2017

SET QUERY_STORE = ON

(

  QUERY_CAPTURE_MODE = CUSTOM, QUERY_CAPTURE_POLICY =

  (

    EXECUTION_COUNT = 20,

    TOTAL_COMPILE_CPU_TIME_MS = 1000,

    TOTAL_EXECUTION_CPU_TIME_MS = 100,

    STALE_CAPTURE_POLICY_THRESHOLD = 7 DAYS

  )

);
```

The output is as follows:

```
ALTER DATABASE AdventureWorks2017
SET QUERY_STORE = ON
(
QUERY_CAPTURE_MODE = CUSTOM,
QUERY_CAPTURE_POLICY =
(
EXECUTION_COUNT = 20,
TOTAL_COMPILE_CPU_TIME_MS = 1000,
TOTAL_EXECUTION_CPU_TIME_MS = 100,
STALE_CAPTURE_POLICY_THRESHOLD = 7 DAYS
)
);
GO
```

actual_state_desc	stale_query_threshold_days	query_capture_mode_desc	capture_policy_execution_count	capture_policy_total_compile_cpu_time_ms	capture_policy_total_execution_cpu_time_ms
READ_WRITE	30	CUSTOM	20	1000	100

Figure 1.18: Modifying the default settings

Support for FAST_FORWARD and STATIC Cursors

We have added another exciting update to the Query Store. You can now force query execution plans for fast forward and static cursors. This functionality supports T-SQL and API cursors. Forcing execution plans for fast forward and static cursors is supported through SSMS or T-SQL using `sp_query_store_force_plan`.

Automatic tuning

Automatic tuning identifies potential query performance problems, recommends solutions, and automatically fixes problems identified.

By default, automatic tuning is disabled and must be enabled. There are two automatic tuning features available:

- Automatic plan correction
- Automatic index management

Automatic plan correction

To take advantage of automatic plan correction, the Query Store must be enabled on your database. Automatic plan correction is made possible by constantly monitoring data that is stored by the Query Store.

Automatic plan correction is the process of identifying regression in your query execution plans. Plan regression occurs when the SQL Server Query Optimizer uses a new execution plan that performs worse than the previous plan. To identify plan regression, the Query Store captures compile time and runtime statistics of statements being executed.

The database engine uses the data captured by the Query Store to identify when plan regression occurs. More specifically, to identify plan regression and take necessary action, the database engine uses the **sys.dm_db_tuning_recommendations** view. This is the same view you use when manually determining which plans have experienced regressions and which plans to force.

When plan regression is noticed, the database engine will force the last known good plan.

The great news is that the database engine doesn't stop there; the database engine will monitor the performance of the forced plan and verify that the performance is better than the regressed plan. If the performance is not better, then the database engine will unforce the plan and compile a new query execution plan.

Enabling automatic plan correction

Automatic plan correction is disabled by default. The following code can be used to verify the status of automatic plan correction on your database:

```
SELECT name, desired_state_desc, actual_state_desc
FROM sys.database_automatic_tuning_options
```

The output is as follows:

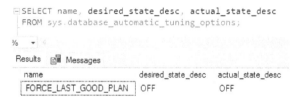

Figure 1.19: Automatic plan correction is turned off

You enable automatic plan correction by using the following code:

```
ALTER DATABASE current
SET AUTOMATIC_TUNING ( FORCE_LAST_GOOD_PLAN = ON )
```

If you have not turned the Query Store on, then you will receive the following error:

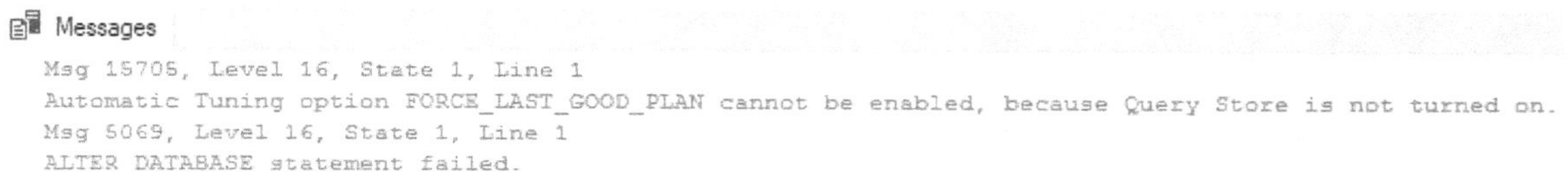

```
Messages
Msg 15705, Level 16, State 1, Line 1
Automatic Tuning option FORCE_LAST_GOOD_PLAN cannot be enabled, because Query Store is not turned on.
Msg 5069, Level 16, State 1, Line 1
ALTER DATABASE statement failed.
```

Figure: 1.20: Error report if the Query Store is off

Automatically forced plans

The database engine uses two criteria to force query execution plans:

- Where the estimated CPU gain is higher than 10 seconds

- The number of errors in the recommended plan is lower than the number of errors in the new plan

Forcing execution plans improves performance where query execution plan regression has occurred, but this is a temporary solution, and these forced plans should not remain indefinitely. Therefore, automatically forced plans are removed under the following two conditions.

- Plans that are automatically forced by the database engine are not persisted between SQL Server restarts.

- Forced plans are retained until a recompile occurs, for example, a statistics update or schema change.

The following code can be used to verify the status of automatic tuning on the database:

```
SELECT name, desired_state_desc, actual_state_desc
FROM sys.database_automatic_tuning_options;
```

```
SELECT name, desired_state_desc, actual_state_desc
FROM sys.database_automatic_tuning_options;
```

name	desired_state_desc	actual_state_desc
FORCE_LAST_GOOD_PLAN	DEFAULT	OFF

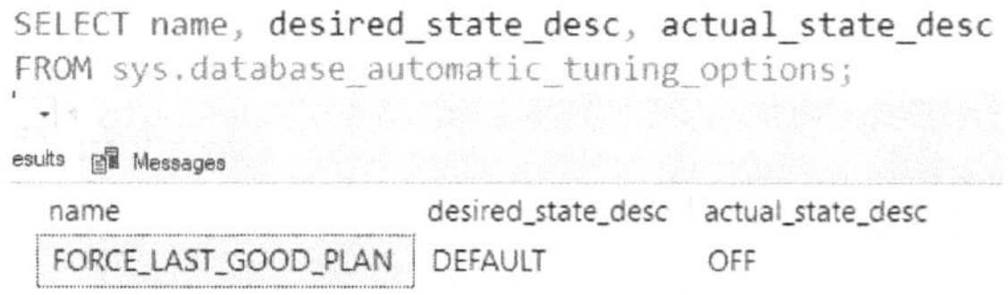

Figure 1.21: Verifying the status of automatic tuning on the database

Lightweight query profiling

Lightweight query profiling (**LWP**) provides DBAs with the capability to monitor queries in real time at a significantly reduced cost of the standard query profiling method. The expected overhead of LWP is at 2% CPU, as compared to an overhead of 75% CPU for the standard query profiling mechanism.

For a more detailed explanation on the query profiling infrastructure, refer to https://docs.microsoft.com/en-us/sql/relational-databases/performance/query-profiling-infrastructure?view=sqlallproducts-allversions.

New functionality in 2019

In SQL Server 2019, we have now improved LWP with new features and enhancements to the existing capabilities.

- In SQL Server 2016 and 2017, lightweight query profiling was deactivated by default and you could enable LWP at the instance level by using trace flag `7412`. In 2019, we have now turned this feature ON by default.

- You can also now manage this at the database level through Database Scoped Configurations. In 2019, you have a new database scoped configuration, `lightweight_query_profiling`, to enable or disable the `lightweight_query_profiling` infrastructure at the database level.

- We have also introduced a new extended event. The new `query_post_execution_plan_profile` extended event collects the equivalent of an actual execution plan based on lightweight profiling,unlike `query_post_execution_showplan`, which uses standard profiling.

- We also have a new DMF `sys.dm_exec_query_plan_stats;` this DMF returns the equivalent of the last known actual execution plan for most queries, based on lightweight profiling.

The syntax for **sys.dm_exec_query_plan_stats** is as follows:

```
sys.dm_exec_query_plan_stats(plan_handle)
```

For a more detailed analysis, refer to this online documentation: https://docs.microsoft.com/en-us/sql/relational-databases/system-dynamic-management-views/sys-dm-exec-query-plan-stats-transact-sql?view=sql-server-2017.

sys.database_scoped_configurations

If you are not certain of the current status of LWP, you can use the following code to check the status of your database scoped configurations. The value column is 1; therefore, using the sys.database_scoped_configurations view, you see that Query Plan Stats is currently enabled:

```
SELECT * FROM sys.database_scoped_configurations
WHERE name = 'LAST_QUERY_PLAN_STATS'
```

The output is as follows:

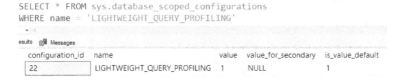

Figure 1.22: Check the status of the database scoped configurations

To enable or disable LWP, you will use the database scoped configuration lightweight_query_profiling. Refer to the following example:

```
ALTER DATABASE SCOPED CONFIGURATION
SET LIGHTWEIGHT_QUERY_PROFILING = OFF;
```

Activity monitor

With LWP enabled, you can now look at active expensive queries in the activity monitor. To launch the activity monitor, right-click on the instance name from SSMS and select Activity Monitor. Below Active Expensive Queries, you will see currently running queries, and if you right-click on an active query, you can now examine the Live Execution Plan!

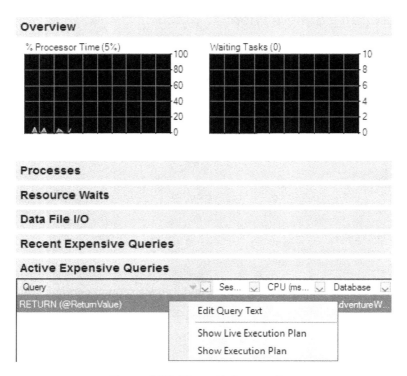

Figure 1.23: The activity monitor

Columnstore stats in DBCC CLONEDATABASE

DBCC CLONEDATABASE creates a clone of the database that contains a copy of the schema and statistics for troubleshooting and diagnostic purposes. More specifically, with DBCC CLONEDATABASE, you have a lightweight, minimally invasive way to investigate performance issues related to the query optimizer. In SQL Server 2019, we now extend the capabilities of DBCC CLONEDATABASE by adding support for columnstore statistics.

Columnstore statistics support

In SQL Server 2019, support has been added for columnstore statistics. Before SQL Server 2019, manual steps were required to capture these statistics (refer to the following link). We now automatically capture stats blobs, and therefore, these manual steps are no longer required:

https://techcommunity.microsoft.com/t5/SQL-Server/Considerations-when-tuning-your-queries-with-columnstore-indexes/ba-p/385294.

DBCC CLONEDATABASE validations

DBCC CLONEDATABASE performs the following validation checks. If any of these checks fail, the operation will fail, and a copy of the database will not be provided.

- The source database must be a user database.
- The source database must be online or readable.
- The clone database name must not already exist.
- The command must not be part of a user transaction.

Understanding DBCC CLONEDATABASE syntax

DBCC CLONEDATABASE syntax with optional parameters:

```
DBCC CLONEDATABASE
(
    source_database_name, target_database_name
)
    [ WITH { [ NO_STATISTICS ] [ , NO_QUERYSTORE ]
    [ , VERIFY_CLONEDB | SERVICEBROKER ] [ , BACKUP_CLONEDB ] } ]
```

The following T-SQL script will create a clone of the existing database. The statistics and Query Store data are included automatically.

```
DBCC CLONEDATABASE ('Source', 'Destination');
```

The following messages are provided upon completion:

🖼 Messages

```
Database cloning for 'Source' has started with target as 'Destination'.
Database cloning for 'Source' has finished. Cloned database is 'Destination'.
Database 'Destination' is a cloned database. This database should be used for diagnostic purp
DBCC execution completed. If DBCC printed error messages, contact your system administrator.
```

Figure 1.24: Cloned database output

To exclude statistics, you rewrite the code to include `WITH NO_STATISTICS`:

```
DBCC CLONEDATABASE ('Source', 'Destination_NoStats')
WITH NO_STATISTICS;
```

To exclude statistics and Query Store data, execute the following code:

```
DBCC CLONEDATABASE ('Source', 'Destination_NoStats_NoQueryStore')
  WITH NO_STATISTICS, NO_QUERYSTORE;
```

Making the clone database production-ready

Thus far, the database clones provisioned are purely for diagnostic purposes. The option `VERIFY_CLONEDB` is required if you want to use the cloned database for production use. `VERIFY_CLONEDB` will verify the consistency of the new database.

For example:

```
DBCC CLONEDATABASE ('Source', 'Destination_ProdReady')
  WITH VERIFY_CLONEDB;
```

The output is as follows:

🖼 Messages

```
NO_STATISTICS and NO_QUERYSTORE options turned ON as part of VERIFY_CLONE.
Database cloning for 'Source' has started with target as 'Destination_ProdReady'.
Database cloning for 'Source' has finished. Cloned database is 'Destination_ProdReady'.
Database 'Destination_ProdReady' is a cloned database.
Clone database verification has passed.
DBCC execution completed. If DBCC printed error messages, contact your system administrator.
```

Figure 1.25: Verifying the cloned database

Estimate compression for Columnstore Indexes

The stored procedure `sp_estimate_data_compression_savings` estimates the object size for the requested compression state. Furthermore, you can evaluate potential compression savings for whole tables or parts of tables; we will discuss the available options shortly. Prior to SQL Server 2019, you were unable to use `sp_estimate_data_compression_savings` for columnstore indexes and, thus, we were unable to estimate compression for columnstore or `columnstore_archive`.

We have extended the capability for `sp_estimate_data_compression_savings` to include support for COLUMNSTORE and COLUMNSTORE_ARCHIVE.

sp_estimate_data_compression_savings Syntax

Look at the following T-SQL syntax:

```
sp_estimate_data_compression_savings
      [ @schema_name = ] 'schema_name'
    , [ @object_name = ] 'object_name'
    , [@index_id = ] index_id
    , [@partition_number = ] partition_number
    , [@data_compression = ] 'data_compression'
  [;]
```

The following argument descriptions are provided by docs.microsoft.com: https://docs.microsoft.com/en-us/sql/relational-databases/system-stored-procedures/sp-estimate-data-compression-savings-transact-sql?view=sql-server-2017.

Arguments	Description
[@schema_name =]	This is the name of the database schema that contains the table or indexed view. *schema_ name* is **sysname**. If *schema_ name* is NULL , the default schema of the current user is used.
[@object_name =]	This is the name of the table or indexed view that the index is on. *object_ name* is **sysname**.
[@index_id =]	This is the ID of the index. *index_ id* is **int** and can be one of the following values: the iD number of an index, NULL, or 0 if _object__ *id* is heap. To return information for all indexes for a base table or view, specify NULL. If you specify NULL, you must also specify NULL for *partition_ number*.
[@partition_number =]	This is the partition number in the object. *partition_ number* is **int** and can be one of the following values: the partition number of an index or heap, NULL, or 1 for a non-partitioned index or heap.
[@data_compression =]	This is the type of compression to be evaluated. *data_ compression* can be one of the following values: NONE, ROW, PAGE, COLUMNSTORE, or COLUMNSTORE_ARCHIEVE.

Table 1.26: Description of the arguments

There are currently eight available outputs; you will primarily focus on the four outputs related to size.

Output:

```
object_name

schema_name

index_id

partition_number

size_with_current_compression_setting (KB)

size_with_requested_compression_setting (KB)

sample_size_with_current_compression_setting (KB)

sample_size_with_current_requested_setting (KB)
```

The following is an example of the procedure in action, followed by a comparison of the space savings for page and columnstore compression:

```
EXEC sp_estimate_data_compression_savings
    @schema_name = 'dbo',
    @object_name = 'MySourceTable',
    @index_id = NULL,
    @partition_number = NULL,
    @data_compression = 'PAGE'
```

Example with PAGE Compression:

size_with_current_compression_setting(KB)	size_with_requested_compression_setting(KB)	sample_size_with_current_compression_setting(KB)	sample_size_with_requested_compression_setting(KB)
20872	11568	20864	11568

Figure 1.27: PAGE Compression

```
EXEC sp_estimate_data_compression_savings
    @schema_name = 'dbo',
    @object_name = 'MySourceTable',
    @index_id = NULL,
    @partition_number = NULL,
    @data_compression = 'COLUMNSTORE'
```

Example with COLUMNSTORE compression:

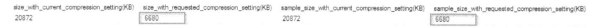

size_with_current_compression_setting(KB)	size_with_requested_compression_setting(KB)	sample_size_with_current_compression_setting(KB)	sample_size_with_requested_compression_setting(KB)
20872	6680	20872	6680

Figure 1.28: COLUMNSTORE compression

In this example, page compression has estimated space savings of roughly 45%, and columnstore compression has estimated space savings of 68%.

Troubleshooting page resource waits

A new and exciting feature in SQL Server 2019 is sys.dm_db_page_info. This new **dynamic management function** (**DMF**) retrieves useful page information, such as `page_id`, `file_id`, `index_id`, `object_id`, and `page_type`, that can be used for troubleshooting and debugging performance issues in SQL Server. Historically, troubleshooting has involved the use of DBCC Page and the undocumented DMF `sys.dm_db_page_allocations`.

Unlike DBCC Page, which provides the entire contents of a page, `sys.dm_db_page_info` only returns header information about pages. Fortunately, this will be sufficient for most troubleshooting and performance tuning scenarios.

This section will discuss the following topics:

- Database State permissions
- `sys.dm_db_page_info` parameters
- New column page_resource in (`sys.dm_exec_requests`, `sys.processes`)
- `sys.fn_PageResCracker`

sys.dm_db_page_info

First, to leverage this new DMF, we require the VIEW DATABASE STATE permission. The following code can be used to provide access:

```
GRANT VIEW DATABASE STATE TO [login]
```

There are four required parameters:

```
sys.dm_db_page_info ( DatabaseId, FileId, PageId, Mode )
```

The following argument descriptions are provided by docs.microsoft.com:

Arguments	Description
[DatabaseId]	This is the ID of the database. *DatabaseId* is **smallint**. Valid input is the ID number of a database. The default is NULL; however, sending a NULL value for this parameter will result in an error.
[FileId]	This is the ID of the file. *FileId* is **int**. Valid input is the ID number of a file in the database specified by a *DatabaseId*. The default is NULL; however, sending a NULL value for this parameter will result in an error.
[PageId]	This is the ID of the page. *PageId* is **int**. Valid input is the ID number of a page in the file specified by *FileId*. The default is the NULL, however, sending a NULL value for this parameter will result in an error.
[Mode]	This determines the level of detail in the output of the function. 'LIMITED' will return NULL values for all description columns, and 'DETAILED' will populate description columns. DEFAULT is 'LIMITED'.

Table 1.29: The description of the arguments

You can execute the function by itself if you have all the requisite parameters. The mode is set to `Limited` in this example, and this will return `NULL` values for all description columns:

```
SELECT OBJECT_NAME(object_id) as TableName,*
FROM SYS.dm_db_page_info(6, 1, 1368, 'Limited')
```

The output is as follows:

	TableName	database_id	file_id	page_id	page_header_version	page_type	page_type_desc
1	Person	6	1	1368	NULL	1	NULL

Figure 1.30: Output with LIMITED mode

Using the `Detailed` mode, you will get much more descriptive information than provided in the previous example. In this example, you can see that the `NULL` values have been replaced with descriptive information.

```
SELECT OBJECT_NAME(object_id) as TableName,*
FROM SYS.dm_db_page_info(6, 1, 1368, 'Detailed')
```

The output is as follows:

	TableName	database_id	file_id	page_id	page_header_version	page_type	page_type_desc
1	Person	6	1	1368	1	1	DATA_PAGE

Figure 1.31: Output with Detailed mode

To see a full list of all the columns returned, go to https://docs.microsoft.com/en-us/ sql/relational-databases/system-dynamic-management-views/sys-dm-db-page-info-transact-sql?view=sqlallproducts-allversions.

sys.fn_pagerescracker

In the previous example, you saw how to pass parameters to this new function manually. Fortunately, the parameters can be directly retrieved from **sys.dm_exec_requests** or **sys.processes**. To make this work, we added a new column called page_resource. The page_resource column returns the page ID, the file ID, and the database ID. It is also important to highlight that the new page_resource column in **sys.dm_exec_request** will be **NULL** when **WAIT_RESOURCE** does not have a valid value.

However, the page_resource column stores the data as an 8-byte hexadecimal value that needs to be converted. Therefore, we have added a new function called **sys.fn_pagerescracker**. This function returns the page ID, the file ID, and the database ID for the given page_resource value.

It is important to note that we require the user to **have VIEW SERVER STATE** permission on the server to run **sys.fn_PageResCracker**.

In this example, the page_resource column is being passed into the **sys.fn_PageResCracker** function, and then the database ID, file ID, and Page ID are passed to sys.dm_db_page_info:

```
SELECT OBJECT_NAME(page_info.object_id) AS TableName,page_info.*

FROM sys.dm_exec_requests AS d

CROSS APPLY sys.fn_PageResCracker (d.page_resource) AS r

CROSS APPLY sys.dm_db_page_info(r.db_id, r.file_id, r.page_id,

'Detailed') AS page_info
```

The output is as follows:

	TableName	database_id	file_id	page_id	page_header_version	page_type	page_type_desc
1	Person	6	1	1368	1	1	DATA_PAGE

Figure 1.32: Page resource column is being passed into a function

You can read more here: https://docs.microsoft.com/en-us/sql/relational-databases/system-functions/sys-fn-pagerescracker-transact-sql?view=sql-server-2017.

2
Enterprise Security

Securing sensitive data and staying compliant with industry regulations such as **PCI-DSS** (**Payment Card Industry Data Security Standard**) and **GDPR** (**General Data Protection Regulation**) is very important. A compromised database system can lead to a loss of revenue, regulatory fines, and a negative impact on the reputation of your business.

Tracking compliance and maintaining database security requires significant admin resources. SQL Server 2019 has tools such as Data Discovery and Classification, and SQL Vulnerability Assessment tools that allow DBAs to identify compliance issues and tag and classify specific datasets to ensure compliance.

SQL Server 2019 offers many security features that address these challenges, such as TDE (Transparent Data Encryption), Always Encrypted, Auditing, Dynamic Data Masking and Row-Level Security.

Combined with further enhancements to certificate management in SQL Server 2019, support for TLS 1.2, and confidential computing initiatives such as secure enclaves, you can be sure that you can build and deploy solutions to the highest security standards while becoming GDPR and PCI-DSS compliant. All these features are also available within Azure SQL Database.

SQL Data Discovery and Classification

The Data Discovery and Classification feature enables you to identify, classify, and label data held across your SQL Server estate. The sheer volume of data now held within databases makes this a challenging process, coupled with the fact that regulatory mandates such as GDPR, SOX, and PCI demand that businesses protect sensitive data. So you can see how this feature will help. Before you can develop a security strategy for your SQL Server databases, it makes logical sense to know what data you hold, and from this you can then classify and label the more sensitive data and implement the relevant security controls, therefore minimizing potential sensitive data leaks.

Key components for this feature include two metadata attributes, labels and information types. Labels are used to define the sensitivity of data. Information types are used to provide additional granularity into the types of data stored in a column. As you can see in *Figure 2.1*, email addresses and phone numbers have been classified as contact information under the GDPR label.

Figure 2.1: Classification confirmation

To start the classification process, you will need to right-click on the database and find the **Data Discovery and Classification** option (*Figure 2.2*).

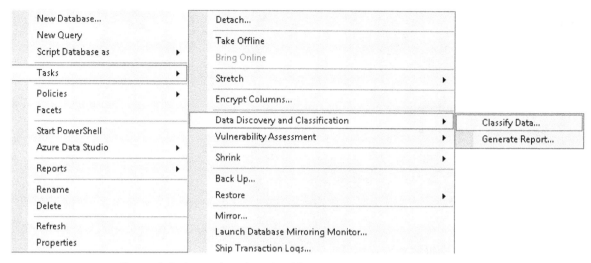

Figure 2.2: Accessing the Classify Data... option from the menu

While you are connected to the database via **SSMS** (**SQL Server Management Studio**), you can issue the following query to get a really good summary of the classification that has just taken place:

```
SELECT

    schema_name(O.schema_id) AS schema_name,

    O.NAME AS table_name,

    C.NAME AS column_name,

    information_type,

    sensitivity_label

FROM

    (

        SELECT

            IT.major_id,
```

```
            IT.minor_id,
            IT.information_type,
            L.sensitivity_label
    FROM
    (
        SELECT
            major_id,
            minor_id,
            value AS information_type
        FROM sys.extended_properties
        WHERE NAME = 'sys_information_type_name'
    ) IT
    FULL OUTER JOIN
    (
        SELECT
            major_id,
            minor_id,
            value AS sensitivity_label
        FROM sys.extended_properties
        WHERE NAME = 'sys_sensitivity_label_name'
    ) L
    ON IT.major_id = L.major_id AND IT.minor_id = L.minor_id
) EP
JOIN sys.objects O
ON  EP.major_id = O.object_id
JOIN sys.columns C
ON  EP.major_id = C.object_id AND EP.minor_id = C.column_id
```

	schema_name	table_name	column_name	information_type	sensitivity_label
1	SalesLT	Customer	EmailAddress	Contact Info	Confidential - GDPR
2	SalesLT	Customer	Phone	Contact Info	Confidential - GDPR

Figure 2.3: Successfully connected to the database

You can delegate this to SQL Server and let it carry out a review of the data and an automatic implementation of the classification process.

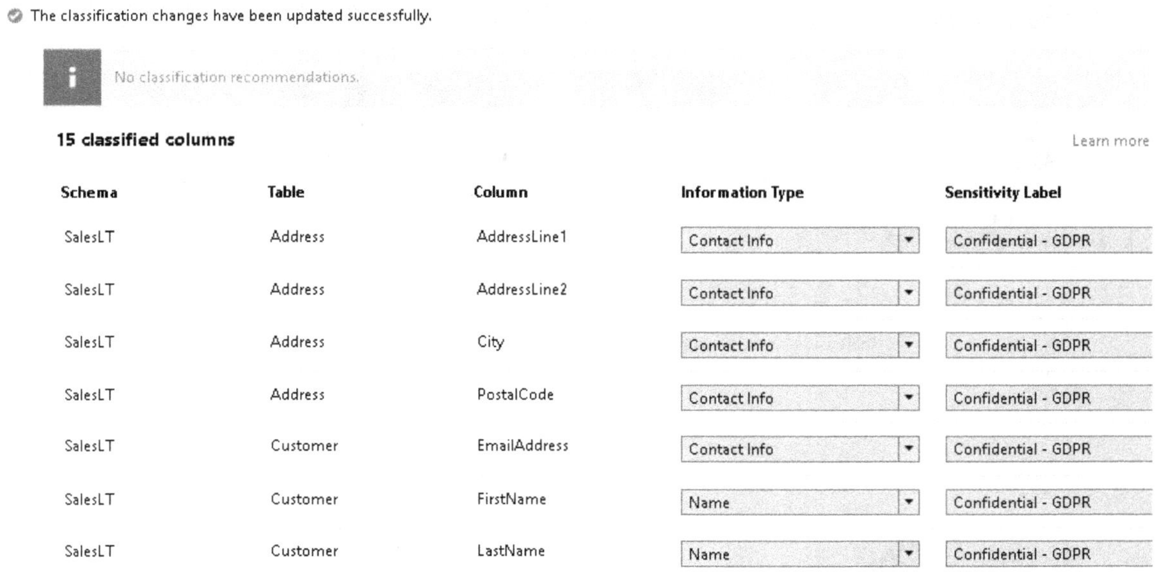

The classification changes have been updated successfully.

No classification recommendations.

15 classified columns   Learn more

Schema	Table	Column	Information Type	Sensitivity Label
SalesLT	Address	AddressLine1	Contact Info	Confidential - GDPR
SalesLT	Address	AddressLine2	Contact Info	Confidential - GDPR
SalesLT	Address	City	Contact Info	Confidential - GDPR
SalesLT	Address	PostalCode	Contact Info	Confidential - GDPR
SalesLT	Customer	EmailAddress	Contact Info	Confidential - GDPR
SalesLT	Customer	FirstName	Name	Confidential - GDPR
SalesLT	Customer	LastName	Name	Confidential - GDPR

Figure 2.4: Classification changes been implemeted

> **Note**
>
> With SQL Server 2019, is it not possible to use T-SQL to add metadata about the sensitivity classification, such as the following:
>
> ```
> ADD SENSITIVITY CLASSIFICATION TO
>
>     <object_name> [, ...n ]
>
>     WITH ( <sensitivity_label_option> [, ...n ]
> ```
>
> This is only possible with Azure SQL Database.

Another advantage of this feature is the visibility of the classification states in the form of a report, which you can then export to different formats as required. This will benefit you regarding compliance and auditing. The following screenshot shows a copy of a report in Excel format:

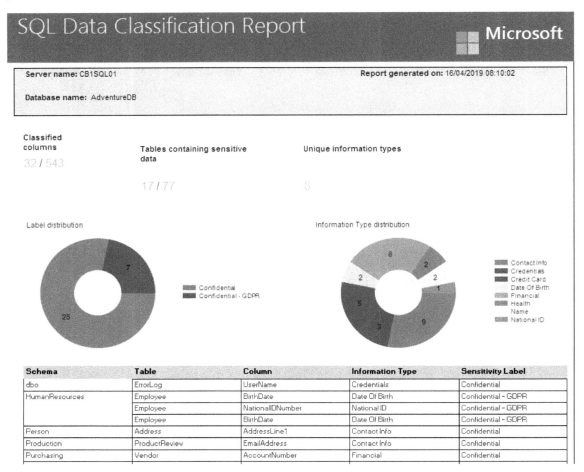

Figure 2.5: SQL Data Classification Report

Once you understand your data via the classification processes, you can then leverage different features from SQL Server 2019, such as Always Encrypted or Data Masking, to protect these sensitive columns.

SQL Vulnerability Assessment

While we're thinking about a sound security strategy for SQL Server, it is important to address current security issues that exist within your database estate. Where should you start? What technical work is required to address the issues found? SQL Vulnerability Assessment is the tool for this task. It will allow you to improve your internal processes and harden your security across a dynamic and ever-changing database environment.

> **Note**
>
> Vulnerability Assessment is supported for SQL Server 2012 and later and requires SSMS 17.4+.

This feature carries out a scan against the database(s) using a pre-built knowledge base of rules that will flag security concerns such as elevated accounts and security misconfigurations. To start this assessment, you will need to right-click on the database and click on **Vulnerability Assessment** (as shown in the following screenshot) and start a scan:

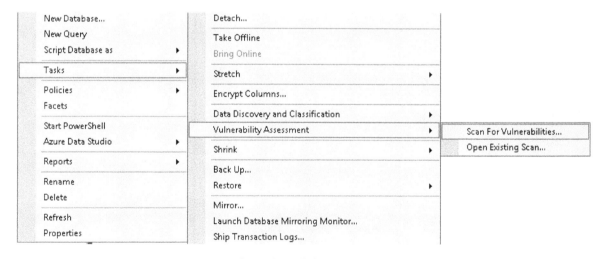

Figure 2.6: Accessing the vulnerabilities scan from the Tasks menu

There is a requirement to state a location to save the assessment to. This will be the location where you can open and view historical reports:

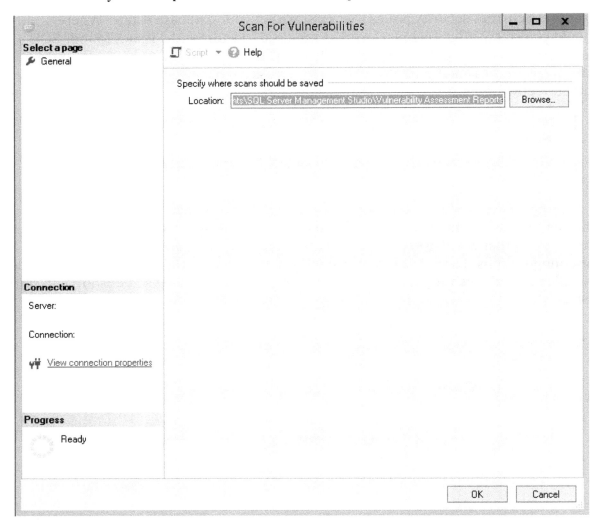

Figure 2.7: The scan dialog box

> **Note**
> The scan is lightweight and read-only. It will not cause performance degradation.

Vulnerability Assessment Results (read only)

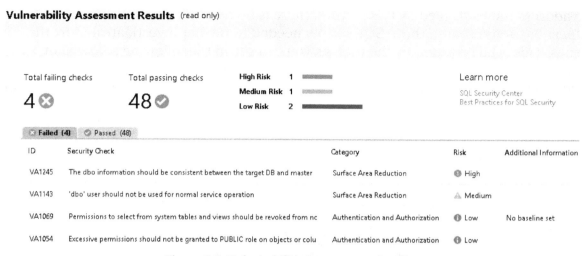

Figure 2.8: Vulnerability Assessment Results

As you can see, a wide range of different checks is carried out. The ones that fail will need special attention, especially if they are flagged as **High Risk**. You can think of this as your own personal security dashboard.

As you review your assessment results, you can mark specific results as being an acceptable baseline in your environment:

Figure 2.9: Assessment results

This is simply a way of approving a check so that it will be classed as a pass in future scans:

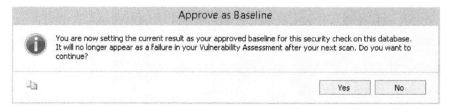

Figure 2.10: Baseline approval dialog box

To address issues flagged by this feature, there is no need for you to be a security expert or even research the T-SQL scripts needed to further investigate and fix the issues. This is all provided by the tool. As you can see in the following screenshot, the **VA2108** check, relating to the authentication and authorization of a specific account, failed. We purposely implemented this rogue account to see how the tool picks this up.

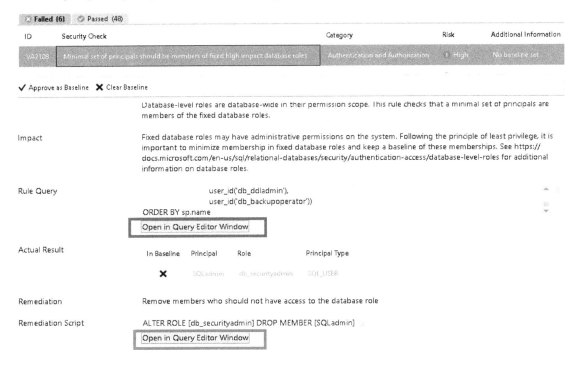

Figure 2.11: The VA2108 check

If you click the blue box in the preceding screenshot, it will show the code the scan used to deduce its conclusions:

```
SELECT user_name(sr.member_principal_id) as [Principal], user_name(sr.
role_principal_id) as [Role], type_desc as [Principal Type]

FROM sys.database_role_members sr, sys.database_principals sp

WHERE sp.principal_id = sr.member_principal_id

AND sr.role_principal_id IN (user_id('bulkadmin'),
```

```
                              user_id('db_accessadmin'),

                              user_id('db_securityadmin'),

                              user_id('db_ddladmin'),

                              user_id('db_backupoperator'))

ORDER BY sp.name
```

This gives the following result:

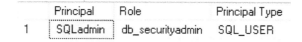

Figure 2.12: Assigned role is db_securityadmin

Clearly this is an issue. Having an SQL login granted the **db_securityadmin** role is bad practice. To resolve this, you then view the following remediation script, as shown in the red box in *Figure 2.11*:

```
ALTER ROLE [db_securityadmin] DROP MEMBER [SQLadmin]
```

Transparent Data Encryption

Transparent Data Encryption (**TDE**) is also known as "encryption at rest" and uses **Advanced Encryption Standard** (**AES**) encryption algorithms using keys sized at 128, 192, and 256 bits (AES_128, AES_192, and AES_256). This feature performs real-time I/O encryption and decryption of database files, and as a side effect, it also encrypts backups. The purpose of TDE is to prevent stolen copies of database files (or backups) from being attached/restored and queried. This feature is also important when running SQL Server in a hosted environment due to the risk that someone is trying to read the file system directly. This feature is available in both Standard and Enterprise edition of SQL Server 2019, and is on by default when using Azure SQL Database and Azure SQL Database Managed Instance.

A common approach to implementing TDE is the traditional encryption hierarchy shown in *Figure* 2.13:

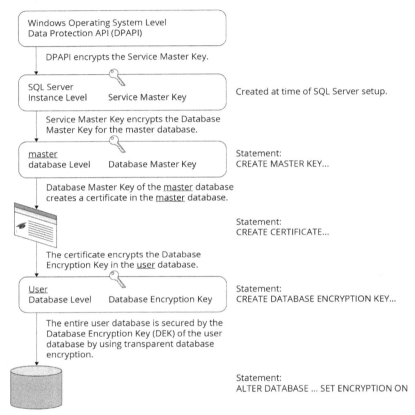

Figure 2.13: Transparent database encryption architecture

Setup

Following this hierarchy when setting up TDE in SQL Server 2019 is straightforward. This snippet shows the T-SQL code required to create the **MASTER KEY**, **CERTIFICATE**, and **DATABASE ENCRYPTION KEY**.

```
USE master;
GO
CREATE MASTER KEY ENCRYPTION BY PASSWORD = '<password>';
GO
CREATE CERTIFICATE MyServerCert WITH SUBJECT = 'My DEK Certificate';
GO


USE [MicrosoftDB];
GO
CREATE DATABASE ENCRYPTION KEY
WITH ALGORITHM = AES_256
ENCRYPTION BY SERVER CERTIFICATE MyServerCert;
GO
```

> **Note**
>
> The certificate used for encrypting the database encryption key has not been backed up. You should immediately back up the certificate and the private key associated with the certificate. If the certificate ever becomes unavailable or if you must restore or attach the database on another server, you must have backups of both the certificate and the private key or you will not be able to open the database.

A warning appears from SQL Server asking us to back up the **CERTIFICATE** and **PRIVATE KEY**, which is important to do for recovery purposes. Use this code to do so:

```
USE master;

GO

BACKUP CERTIFICATE MyServerCert

TO FILE = 'C:\SQLSERVER\MyServerCert.cer'

WITH PRIVATE KEY

(FILE = 'C:\SQLSERVER\certificate_Cert.pvk',

ENCRYPTION BY PASSWORD = '!£$Strongpasswordherewelikesqlver#')


ALTER DATABASE  [MicrosoftDB]

SET ENCRYPTION ON;

GO
```

Confirmation of successfully encrypting the database can be found by running the following query:

```
SELECT DB_NAME(database_id) AS DatabaseName, encryption_state,

encryption_state_desc =

CASE encryption_state

        WHEN '0' THEN 'No database encryption key present, no
encryption'

        WHEN '1' THEN 'Unencrypted'

        WHEN '2' THEN 'Encryption in progress'

        WHEN '3' THEN 'Encrypted'

  WHEN '4' THEN 'Key change in progress'

  WHEN '5' THEN 'Decryption in progress'

  WHEN '6' THEN 'Protection change in progress '

        ELSE 'No Status'

     END,

percent_complete, create_date, key_algorithm, key_length, encryptor_
type,encryption_scan_modify_date

  FROM sys.dm_database_encryption_keys
```

Figure 2.2 shows the encrypted state of both the user database and `tempdb`:

DatabaseName	encryption_st...	encryption_state_desc	percent_complete	create_date	encryption_scan_modify_date	key_algorithm	key_length	encryptor_type
tempdb	3	Encrypted	0	2019-04-02 07:18:19.907	2019-04-02 07:18:19.917	AES	256	ASYMMETRIC KEY
MicrosoftDB	3	Encrypted	0	2019-04-02 07:14:07.337	2019-04-02 07:18:20.243	AES	256	CERTIFICATE

Figure 2.14: Encrypting databases

New features – suspend and resume

When configuring TDE for a database, SQL Server must perform an initial encryption scan. This can sometimes be problematic with a large and highly transactional database. With SQL Server 2019, you can now suspend and resume this scan to fit your needs during specific maintenance windows. Prior to SQL Server 2019, the only way to stop the encryption scan was with Trace Flag 5004.

The T-SQL command that suspends the encryption scan is as follows:

```
ALTER DATABASE [AdventureDB] SET ENCRYPTION SUSPEND;
```

If you check the error log in *Figure* 2.15, you will see that the scan has been paused.

Message

Database encryption scan for database 'AdventureDB' was aborted. Reissue ALTER DB to resume the scan.

Beginning database encryption scan for database 'AdventureDB'.

Figure 2.15: Error log

To resume the scan, you then issue the **RESUME** command shown in the following snippet. Checking the state of encryption via the query from the previous section will show the percentage of completion which is the last point it resumed from.

```
ALTER DATABASE [AdventureDB] SET ENCRYPTION RESUME;
```

DatabaseName	encryption_state	encryption_state_desc	percent_complete	create_date	encryption_scan_modify_date
tempdb	3	Encrypted	0	2019-04-02 07:18:19.907	2019-04-02 07:18:19.917
MicrosoftDB	3	Encrypted	0	2019-04-02 07:14:07.337	2019-04-02 07:18:20.243
AdventureDB	2	Encryption in progress	39.44981	2019-04-02 12:46:56.523	2019-04-02 12:49:43.937

Figure 2.16: Completed scan percentage

The error log confirms that the scan is complete:

Message

Database encryption scan for database 'AdventureDB' is complete.

Beginning database encryption scan for database 'AdventureDB'.

Figure 2.17: Confirmation that scan is complete

You will also notice a new column within the table called `encryption_scan_modify_date`. This is stored within the `sys.dm_database_encryption_keys` dynamic management view. It holds the date and time of the last encryption scan state change, which is based on when the scan was last suspended or resumed. Suspending and resuming a scan also applies to the decryption process when encryption is turned off for TDE.

If you restart SQL Server while the encryption scan is in a suspended state, a message will be written to the error log to highlight this fact. It will also show you the `RESUME` command needed to complete the encryption scan:

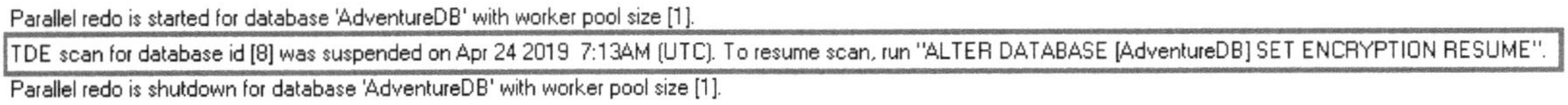

Parallel redo is started for database 'AdventureDB' with worker pool size [1].
TDE scan for database id [8] was suspended on Apr 24 2019 7:13AM (UTC). To resume scan, run "ALTER DATABASE [AdventureDB] SET ENCRYPTION RESUME".
Parallel redo is shutdown for database 'AdventureDB' with worker pool size [1].

Figure 2.18: Error log with the RESUME command

Extensible Key Management

When configuring TDE, you can follow the steps we've looked at so far to implement a traditional key hierarchy strategy. However, you can also use Azure Key Vault as an **Extensible Key Management** (**EKM**) provider, which uses an asymmetric key that is outside SQL Server, rather than a certificate within the master database. As you can imagine, this adds another layer of security, which is usually the preferred strategy for many organizations.

For further information on how to implement EKM using Azure Key Vault, please see the following guide: https://docs.microsoft.com/en-us/sql/relational-databases/security/encryption/setup-steps-for-extensible-key-management-using-the-azure-key-vault?view=sql-server-ver15.

Always Encrypted

SQL Server 2019 includes Always Encrypted, an encryption technology first introduced in SQL Server 2016 which allows clients to encrypt sensitive data inside client applications with the key benefit of never revealing the encryption keys to the database engine.

When using Always Encrypted, data never appears in plain text when querying it, and it is not even exposed in plain text in the memory of the SQL Server process. Only client applications that have access to the relevant keys can see the data. This feature is ideal for protecting data from even highly privileged users such as database administrators and system administrators. It does not prevent them from administrating the servers, but it does prevent them from viewing highly sensitive data such as bank account details.

Algorithm types

Always Encrypted uses the `AEAD_AES_256_CBC_HMAC_SHA_256` algorithm. There are two variations: **deterministic** and **randomized**. The deterministic encryption always generates the same encrypted value of a given input value. With this encryption type it is possible for your application to perform point lookups, equality joins, indexing and grouping on the encrypted column. The only potential issue of using this encryption type is if the encrypted column contains few values or if the statistics about plaintext data distribution is publicly known – in such cases, an attacker might be able to guess the underlaying plaintext values.

The randomized variation is far less predictable hence more secure but this means that it does not allow such operations mentioned earlier on potential encrypted columns. The different encryption types raise interesting choices for application developers. For example, if you know that your applications must issue group or join-based queries on encrypted columns, then you will have no choice but to use the deterministic algorithm. With the introduction of secure enclaves in SQL Server 2019 support for richer functionality on encrypted columns is now possible, which will be discussed later in the chapter.

Setup

Setting up Always Encrypted is straightforward. For a complete tutorial on how to do this please see the following link: https://docs.microsoft.com/en-us/sql/relational-databases/security/encryption/always-encrypted-wizard?view=sql-server-ver15.

Confidential computing with secure enclaves

As mentioned earlier, the main two challenges with Always Encrypted are the reduced query functionality and making it necessary to move data out of database for cryptographic operations, such as initial encryption or key rotation. To address this, Microsoft leverages cutting-edge secure enclave technology to allow rich computations and cryptographic operations to take place inside the database engine.

The enclave is a special, isolated, and protected region of memory. There is no way to view the data or the code inside the enclave from the outside, even with a debugger. You can think of it as a *black box*. This means that an enclave is the perfect place to process highly sensitive information and decrypt it, if necessary. While there are several enclave technologies available, SQL Server 2019 supports Virtualization Based Security (VBS) secure memory enclaves in Windows Server 2019. The Windows hypervisor ensures the isolation of VBS enclaves. The below screen shows what you would see if you try to access the memory of a VBS enclave with a debugger.

```
0:061> du 0x000001cc0e5a24f0
000001cc`0e5a24f0  "?????????????????????????????????"
000001cc`0e5a2530  "?????????????????????????????????"
000001cc`0e5a2570  "?????????????????????????????????"
000001cc`0e5a25b0  "?????????????????????????????????"
000001cc`0e5a25f0  "?????????????????????????????????"
000001cc`0e5a2630  "?????????????????????????????????"
000001cc`0e5a2670  "?????????????????????????????????"
000001cc`0e5a26b0  "?????????????????????????????????"
000001cc`0e5a26f0  "?????????????????????????????????"
000001cc`0e5a2730  "?????????????????????????????????"
```

Figure 2.19: When trying to access the memory of an enclave with a debugger

References:

- https://aka.ms/AlwaysEncryptedWithSecureEnclaves

- https://www.microsoft.com/security/blog/2018/06/05/virtualization-based-security-vbs-memory-enclaves-data-protection-through-isolation/

How does this benefit us from a database perspective? It now means that new types of computations, such as pattern matching (LIKE%) and comparisons (including range comparison operators, such as > and <), are now supported on encrypted database columns; this was not possible before. SQL Server delegates these computations to the enclave via the client driver over a secure channel. The data is then safely decrypted and processed in the enclave. Another advantage of this new feature is that it allows you to perform cryptographic operations, such as encrypting a column or re-encrypting it to change (rotate) a column encryption key, inside the enclave without moving the data outside of the database, thus boosting the performance of such tasks, especially for larger tables.

How is trust in the enclave established? There is an attestation service, which is used to verify that the enclave is trustworthy before the client attempts to use it:

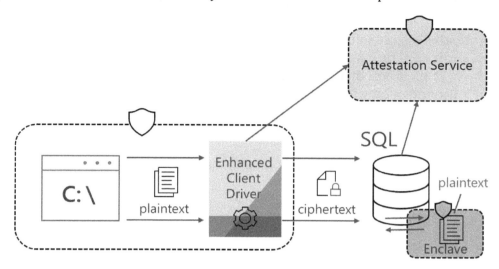

Figure 2.20: The architecture of Always Encrypted with secure enclaves

SQL Server 2019 supports attesting VBS enclaves using Host Guardian Service (HGS), which is a role in Windows Server 2019. HGS can be configured to use one of two attestation modes:

- Host key attestation authorizes a host by proving it possesses a known and trusted private key. Host key attestation does not allow a client application to verify the Windows hypervisor on the machine hosting SQL Server has not been compromised. Therefore, this attestation mode, which is easy to configure and supported in a broad range of environments, can be only recommended for testing and development.

- TPM attestation validates hardware measurements to make sure a host runs only the correct binaries and security policies. It provides a SQL client application with a proof that the code running inside the enclave is a genuine Microsoft SQL Server enclave library and that the Windows hypervisor on the machine hosting SQL Server has not been compromised. That is why the TPM attestation is recommended for production environments. TPM attestation requires SQL Server runs on a machine supporting TPM 2.0.

For a step-by-step tutorial on how to get started with Always Encrypted using enclaves, see: https://aka.ms/AlwaysEncryptedEnclavesTutorial.

Dynamic Data Masking

SQL Server 2019 provides **dynamic data masking** (**DDM**), which limits sensitive data exposure by masking it to non-privileged users. This is not really a form of encryption at disk but nevertheless is useful in certain scenarios, such as if you want to hide sections of a credit card number from support staff personnel. Traditionally, this logic would have been implemented at the application layer; however, this is not the case now because it is controlled within SQL Server.

> **Note**
> A masking rule cannot be applied on a column that is Always Encrypted.

Types

You can choose from four different masks where selection usually depends on your data types:

- **DEFAULT**: Full masking according to the data types of the designated fields
- **EMAIL**: A masking method that exposes the first letter of an email address, such as `aXXX@XXXX.com`
- **RANDOM**: A random masking function for use on any numeric type to mask the original value with a random value within a specified range
- **CUSTOM**: Exposes the first and last letters and adds a custom padding string in the middle

Implementing DDM

The following example creates a table with different masking rules applied to the columns. `FirstName` will only expose the first letter, `Phone` will use the default masking rule, and for `Email`, we will apply the email masking rule:

```
CREATE TABLE dbo.Users
  (UserID INT IDENTITY PRIMARY KEY,
   FirstName VARCHAR(150) MASKED WITH (FUNCTION =
'partial(1,"XXXXX",0)') NULL,
   LastName VARCHAR(150) NOT NULL,
```

```
Phone VARCHAR(20) MASKED WITH (FUNCTION = 'default()') NULL,

Email VARCHAR(150) MASKED WITH (FUNCTION = 'email()') NULL);



GO


INSERT dbo.Users

(FirstName, LastName, Phone, Email)

VALUES

('Arun', 'Sirpal', '777-232-232', 'Asirpal@company.com'),

('Tony', 'Mulsti', '111-778-555', 'TMulsti@company.com'),

('Pedro', 'Lee', '890-097-866', 'PLee@company.com') ,

('Bob', 'Lee', '787-097-866', 'Blee@company.com');

GO
```

	UserID	First Name	Last Name	Phone	Email
1	1	Arun	Sirpal	777-232-232	Asirpal@company.com
2	2	Tony	Mulsti	111-778-555	TMulsti@company.com
3	3	Pedro	Lee	890-097-866	PLee@company.com
4	4	Bob	Lee	787-097-866	Blee@company.com

Figure 2.21: Table with masking rules applied

To confirm your masking rules, the following query should be executed:

```
SELECT OBJECT_NAME(object_id) TableName,

    name ColumnName,

    masking_function MaskFunction

  FROM sys.masked_columns

  ORDER BY TableName, ColumnName;
```

TableName	ColumnName	MaskFunction
Users	Email	email()
Users	First Name	partial(1, "XXXXX", 0)
Users	Phone	default()

Figure 2.22: Table with query executed

If you connect to the database as a SQL login that has only read access (as indicated by the following code), you will see the masked data. In other words, the login does not have the right to see the true value of the data, as demonstrated in the following code.

```
EXECUTE AS USER = 'support'

SELECT SUSER_NAME(), USER_NAME();

SELECT * FROM  dbo.Users
```

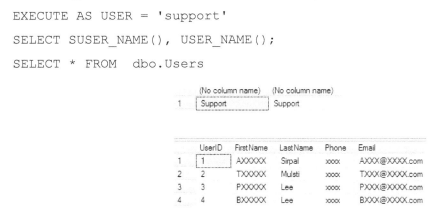

Figure 2.23: Table with data partially masked

If you decide to allow the user to see the data in its native form, you can issue the **GRANT UNMASK** command as shown here:

```
GRANT UNMASK TO support;

 GO


 EXECUTE AS USER = 'support'

SELECT SUSER_NAME(), USER_NAME();

SELECT * FROM  dbo.Users
```

	(No column name)	(No column name)
1	Support	Support

	UserID	First Name	Last Name	Phone	Email
1	1	Arun	Sirpal	777-232-232	Asirpal@company.com
2	2	Tony	Mulsti	111-778-555	TMulsti@company.com
3	3	Pedro	Lee	890-097-866	PLee@company.com
4	4	Bob	Lee	787-097-866	Blee@company.com

Figure 2.24: Table with data unmasked

Issue the **REVOKE** command to remove this capability:

```
REVOKE UNMASK TO support;


EXECUTE AS USER = 'support'
SELECT SUSER_NAME(), USER_NAME();
SELECT * FROM  dbo.Users
```

	(No column name)	(No column name)
1	Support	Support

	UserID	FirstName	LastName	Phone	Email
1	1	AXXXXX	Sirpal	xxxx	AXXX@XXXX.com
2	2	TXXXXX	Mulsti	xxxx	TXXX@XXXX.com
3	3	PXXXXX	Lee	xxxx	PXXX@XXXX.com
4	4	BXXXXX	Lee	xxxx	BXXX@XXXX.com

Figure 2.25: Table with unmask revoked

As you can see, implementing this feature requires no changes to application code and can be controlled via permissions within SQL Server by deducing who has and has not got the ability to view the data. Even though this is not a true form of encryption at disk level, this feature is only a small element of the wider security strategy for your SQL servers and is best used in conjunction with other features discussed so far to provide broader defense.

Row-Level Security

Row-level security (**RLS**) gives database administrators and developers the ability to allow fine-grained access control over rows within tables. Rows can be filtered based on the execution context of a query. Central to this feature is the concept of a security policy where, via an inline table-valued function, you would write your filtering logic to control access with complete transparency to the application. Real-world examples include situations in which you would like to prevent unauthorized access to certain rows for specific logins, for example, only giving access to a super-user to view all rows within a sensitive table and allowing other users to see rows that only the super-user should see. The following example shows how simple it is to implement RLS via T-SQL. At a high level, access to a specific table called `rls.All_Patient` is defined by a column called `GroupAccessLevel`, which is mapped to two SQL logins called `GlobalManager` and `General`. As you can imagine, the `General` login will not be able to view the data that `GlobalManager` is authorized to see.

The following code is the T-SQL required to create the table-value function and the security policy with the state set to ON:

```
CREATE FUNCTION rls.fn_securitypredicate(@GroupAccessLevel AS sysname)
    RETURNS TABLE
WITH SCHEMABINDING
AS
    RETURN SELECT 1 AS fn_securitypredicate_result
WHERE @GroupAccessLevel = USER_NAME() OR USER_NAME() =
'GlobalManager';
GO



CREATE SECURITY POLICY UserFilter
ADD FILTER PREDICATE RLS.fn_securitypredicate(GroupAccessLevel)
ON rls.All_Patient
WITH (STATE = ON);
GO



GRANT SELECT ON RLS.fn_securitypredicate TO GlobalManager;
GRANT SELECT ON RLS.fn_securitypredicate TO General
```

Running the code as the `GlobalManager` user will return all rows within the table, in contrast with the `General` user, who will only see the rows that they are entitled to see:

```
EXECUTE AS USER = 'GlobalManager';
  SELECT * FROM rls.All_Patient
  ORDER BY AreaID
REVERT;
```

The following screenshot confirms the data that the `General` user can only see:

	GroupAccessLevel	GroupPeopleID	AreaID	SurgeryID	Reg_Date	SpecialNote
1	General	9	5	47	2003-07-07 00:00:00.0000000	N/A
2	GlobalManager	23	22	49	1999-08-08 00:00:00.0000000	Sensitive data - read on
3	GlobalManager	98	52	77	2001-07-07 00:00:00.0000000	Last updated - see doc123
4	General	9	52	3	1999-07-07 00:00:00.0000000	Address updated
5	General	96	54	2	2000-07-07 00:00:00.0000000	N/A
6	GlobalManager	78	74	555	2013-07-07 00:00:00.0000000	Please see list45
7	General	87	86	65	2001-07-01 00:00:00.0000000	N/A
8	General	83	103	201	2003-01-01 00:00:00.0000000	N/A
9	GlobalManager	87	233	854	2001-01-01 00:00:00.0000000	Please see extract 12
10	GlobalManager	96	333	2174	2007-08-08 00:00:00.0000000	XRAY request sent
11	General	99	871	236	2009-01-01 00:00:00.0000000	Changed contact

Figure 2.26: A table with access set to GlobalManager

Executing the following code switches the execution context to the `General` user:

```
EXECUTE AS USER = 'General';
  SELECT * FROM rls.All_Patient
  ORDER BY AreaID
REVERT;
```

	GroupAccessLevel	GroupPeopleID	AreaID	SurgeryID	Reg_Date	SpecialNote
1	General	9	5	47	2003-07-07 00:00:00.0000000	N/A
2	General	9	52	3	1999-07-07 00:00:00.0000000	Address updated
3	General	96	54	2	2000-07-07 00:00:00.0000000	N/A
4	General	87	86	65	2001-07-01 00:00:00.0000000	N/A
5	General	83	103	201	2003-01-01 00:00:00.0000000	N/A
6	General	99	871	236	2009-01-01 00:00:00.0000000	Changed contact

Figure 2.27: The same table with access set to General

If you check the properties of the clustered index scan, you will see the predicate being evaluated:

Figure 2.28: Selecting properties of clustered index scan

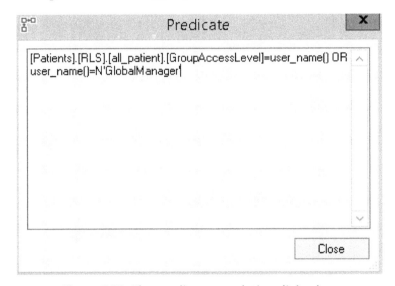

Figure 2.29: The predicate evaulation dialog box

This type of predicate is called a filter predicate, but you also can create a block predicate to explicitly block write operations (such as **AFTER INSERT**, **AFTER UPDATE**, **BEFORE UPDATE**, and **BEFORE DELETE**) that violate the predicate.

For administration purposes, you can query the following system tables to see the security policies and security predicates that have been defined:

```
SELECT * FROM sys.security_policies
```

	name	object_id	principal_id	schema_id	parent_object_id	type	type_desc	create_date	modify_date	is_ms_shipped	is_enabled
1	UserFilter	1093578934	NULL	1	0	SP	SECURITY_POLICY	2019-07-16 09:40:26.617	2019-07-16 09:40:26.617	0	1

Figure 2.30: Output of a security_policies query

```
SELECT * FROM sys.security_predicates
```

	object_id	security_predicate_id	target_object_id	predicate_definition	predicate_type	predicate_type_desc	operation	operation_desc
1	1093578934	1	981578535	([RLS].[fn_securitypredicate]([GroupAccessLevel]))	0	FILTER	NULL	NULL

Figure 2.31: Output of a security_predicates query

To maintain the best performance, it is best practice to not involve many table joins within the predicate function, to avoid type conversions, and to avoid recursion.

Auditing

If implementing an auditing strategy is paramount to your business to satisfy regulations such as the **Health Insurance Portability and Accountability Act** (**HIPAA**), the **Sarbanes-Oxley Act** (**SOX**), and the **Payment Card Industry Data Security Standard** (**PCI-DSS**), then leveraging SQL Server 2019 to achieve this is possible with SQL Server Audit. With this feature, you will be able to ensure accountability for actions made against your SQL servers and databases, and you can store this log information in local files or the event log for future analysis, all of which are common goals of an auditing strategy.

To implement SQL Server auditing, first the main audit should be created at the server level, which dictates where the files will be located for information to be logged to. From this main audit, you can then create a server-level audit specification. At this level, you will be able to audit actions such as server role changes and whether a database has been created or deleted. Alternatively, you can scope this feature to the database level via a database-level audit specification, where you can audit actions directly on the database schema and schema objects, such as tables, views, stored procedures, and functions (see https://docs.microsoft.com/en-us/sql/relational-databases/security/auditing/sql-server-audit-action-groups-and-actions?view=sql-server-ver15 for a full list of the capabilities for both server- and database-level auditing).

The following example shows the code required to audit a specific table, `[HumanResources].[EmployeePayHistory]`, for a DELETE activity using a database AUDIT specification:

```
USE [master]
GO


CREATE SERVER AUDIT [MainAudit]
TO FILE
(  FILEPATH = N'D:\AUDIT\'
  ,MAXSIZE = 1024 MB
  ,MAX_FILES = 10
```

```
      ,RESERVE_DISK_SPACE = OFF
  )
  WITH
  (  QUEUE_DELAY = 1000
     ,ON_FAILURE = CONTINUE
     ,AUDIT_GUID = 'A164444-d7c8-4258-a842-9f2111f2c755'
  )
  ALTER SERVER AUDIT [MainAudit] WITH (STATE = ON)
  GO


  USE [AdventureDB]
  GO


  CREATE DATABASE AUDIT SPECIFICATION [DeleteAuditHR]
  FOR SERVER AUDIT [MainAudit]
  ADD (DELETE ON OBJECT::[HumanResources].[EmployeePayHistory] BY [dbo])


  GO
  DECLARE @files VARCHAR(200) = 'D:\AUDIT\*.sqlaudit';
  SELECT * FROM sys.fn_get_audit_file (@files, default, default)
```

	database_name	schema_name	object_name	statement
1	AdventureDB	HumanResources	EmployeePayHistory	DELETE FROM [AdventureDB].[HumanResources].[EmployeePayHistory] WHERE BusinessEntityID = 12
2	AdventureDB		DeleteAuditHR	ALTER DATABASE AUDIT SPECIFICATION [DeleteAuditHR] WITH (STATE = ON)

Figure 2.32: The results statement dialog

As you can see, it is very simple to set up auditing, and you can do so with minimal performance overhead.

Securing connections

Service Socket Layer (**SSL**) and **Transport Layer Security** (**TLS**) are cryptographic protocols that provide encryption between two endpoints, such as a calling application and the SQL Server. This is a form of "encryption in transit." This is a very important concept for companies that process payments. They have to adhere to PCI-DSS. SSL is the predecessor to TLS and supports the need to address vulnerabilities found with SSL, thus providing more secure cipher suites and algorithms. Microsoft's recommendation is to use TLS 1.2 encryption, which supports all releases of SQL Server (assuming that the latest service packs are installed) up to and including SQL Server 2019. The ultimate goal of using TLS is to establish a secure connection. This is done by SQL Server sending its TLS certificate to the client. The client must then validate its copy of the **Certification Authority** (**CA**) certificate. The CA is a trusted third party that is trusted by both the owner of the certificate and the party relying upon the certificate.

Assuming that you have configured the **Microsoft Management Console** (**MMC**) snap-in, you will then need to use it to install the certificate on the server. It can then be used by SQL Server to encrypt connections.

Configuring the MMC snap-in

To open the MMC certificates snap-in, follow these steps:

1. To open the MMC console, click **Start**, and then click **Run**. In the **Run** dialog box, type the following:

   MMC

2. In the **Console** menu, click **Add/Remove Snap-in**.

3. Click **Add**, and then click **Certificates**. Click **Add** again.

4. You are prompted to open the snap-in for the current user account, the service account, or for the computer account. Select **Computer Account**.

5. Select **Local computer**, and then click **Finish**.

6. Click **Close** in the **Add Standalone Snap-in** dialog box.

7. Click **OK** in the **Add/Remove Snap-in** dialog box. Your installed certificates are located in the Certificates folder in the Personal container.

For the complete steps to install a certificate, please see the following link: https://support.microsoft.com/en-us/help/316898/how-to-enable-ssl-encryption-for-an-instance-of-sql-server-by-using-mi.

Enabling via SQL Server Configuration Manager

For SQL Server to use the certificate, you will need to select it within SQL Server Configuration Manager and then finally set **Force Encryption** to **Yes**:

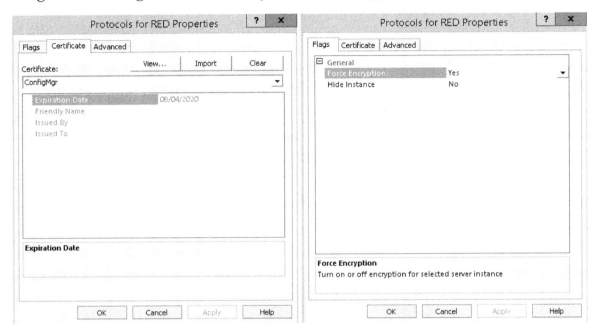

Figure 2.33: Protocols for RED Properties dialog box

In SQL Server 2019, improvements have been made to SQL Server Configuration Manager, such as optimizations for administration and setting up certificates. First, more information is presented to the administrator regarding expiration dates, a simple but useful addition. More importantly, from an availability group or failover cluster perspective, it is now possible to deploy certificates across multiple machines that form the failover cluster or availability group. This reduces the administration overhead of separately installing and managing certificates across multiple nodes, which can become time-consuming for complex architectures.

Azure SQL Database

Security is absolutely at the forefront of Microsoft's strategy, and this is no different when operating with their cloud services. If you want to run database workloads in Microsoft Azure, you can be assured that Azure SQL Database (the PaaS offering) has all the features mentioned in this chapter so far, and more. For the remainder of this chapter, Azure SQL Database's specific security features will be discussed.

SSL/TLS

SSL/TLS is enforced for all connections. This means that data between the database and client is encrypted in transit (as mentioned in the previous section). For your application connection string, you must ensure that `Encrypt=True` and `TrustServerCertificate=False` because doing this will help prevent man-in-the-middle attacks. No manual certificate configuration is needed; this is all done by Microsoft as the default standard.

A typical connection string should look like this:

```
Server=tcp:yourserver.database.windows.net,1433;Initial
Catalog=yourdatabase;

Persist Security Info=False;User ID={your_username};Password={your_
password};MultipleActiveResultSets=False;Encrypt=True;

TrustServerCertificate=False;Connection Timeout=30;
```

Firewalls

Microsoft implements a "deny all by default" policy for Azure SQL Database. That is, when you create a "logical" SQL server in Azure to host your database you as the administrator will need to make further configuration changes to allow for successful access. This is usually in the form of firewall rules (which can be scoped to the server level or the database level), where you would state which IP addresses are allowed access and **Virtual Network** (**VNet**) rules.

VNet rules should be implemented where possible. A VNet contains a subnet address; you can then create a VNet rule that is scoped to the server level, which will allow access to databases on that server for that specific subnet. This means that if you have virtual machines built within a specific subnet bound to the VNet rule, it will have access to Azure SQL Database (assuming that the Microsoft.sql endpoint is enabled). Both firewall rules and VNet rules can be used together if there is a need.

Azure Active Directory (AD) authentication

With Azure AD authentication, you can now centrally manage database users from one central location. This approach is not only much more secure than SQL Server authentication, but also allows for password rotation to occur in a single place. You can control permissions via groups, thus making security management easier. Configuring this feature will also allow you to connect to the database using **multi factor authentication** (**MFA**), which includes verification options such as text messages, phone calls, mobile app integration, and smart cards with PINs. This idea of MFA is also built into tools such as SSMS, thus providing an extra layer of security for users that require access to Azure SQL Database. It is a highly recommended approach.

The trust architecture is shown in *Figure 2.47* and the setup is simple:

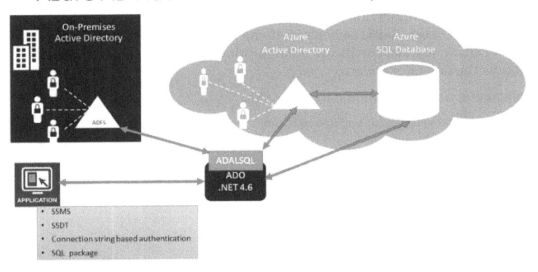

Figure 2.34: The trust architecture

Complete configuration steps can be found at https://docs.microsoft.com/en-us/azure/sql-database/sql-database-aad-authentication. Once configuration is complete, you will be able to issue the following code to create an Azure AD-based database user once you have connected to the "logical" SQL Server as the Azure AD Admin user:

```
CREATE USER [Anita.Holly@Adventureworks.com]

FROM EXTERNAL PROVIDER;


GRANT CONNECT TO [Anita.Holly@Adventureworks.com]



EXEC sp_addrolemember 'db_datareader', 'Anita.Holly@Adventureworks.
com';
```

Advanced data security

Advanced Data Security (**ADS**) is a suite of advanced features that you can enable for a small cost. The cost of this is based on Azure Security Center standard tier pricing (it's free for the first 30 days). The cost includes Data Discovery & Classification, Vulnerability Assessment (similar to what we discussed previously for on-premises SQL servers), and Advanced Threat Protection for the server:

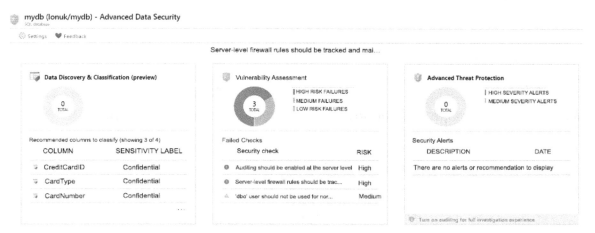

Figure 2.35: ADS suite dashboard

To enable this, you will need to navigate to the **Security** section of the database via the Azure portal:

Figure 2.36: Setting up a security alert on the Azure portal

Once you have selected the **Advanced Data Security** section, you will be prompted with the cost associated with the feature:

 Turn on Advanced Data Security for all databases on this server, at the cost of 11.179635 GBP/server/month. This includes Data Discovery & Classification, Vulnerability Assessment and Advanced Threat Protection for the server. We invite you to a trial period for the first 30 days, without charge.

Enable Advanced Data Security on the server

Figure 2.37: Cost prompt dialog

Finally, you will then have the option of enabling the setting as shown here:

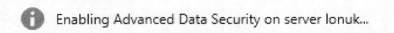

Figure 2.38: Advanced Data Security dialog

Advanced threat detection

Threat detection is the only feature from the previous section that is not available with on-premises SQL Server 2019, but it is available with Azure SQL Database. This service detects anomalous activities that indicate unusual and potentially harmful attempts to access or exploit databases such as SQL injection, brute force attacks, and unknown IP address analysis. Microsoft analyzes a vast amount of telemetry regarding cloud network activity and uses advanced machine learning algorithms for this proactive service. It is best practice to enable this setting. There is a cost associated with it, but the benefit outweighs this minimal cost. Cyber attacks are becoming more sophisticated, and this is where threat prevention and detection tools form an important piece of your defense strategy. This setting can be applied to the server or the database.

Figure 2.48 shows a real-time email alert being sent to administrators:

DETECTED BY	Microsoft
ACTION TAKEN	Detected
ENVIRONMENT	Azure
RESOURCE TYPE	SQL Server
SERVER	
DATABASE	
IP ADDRESS	
PRINCIPAL NAME	dev1
APPLICATION	.Net SqlClient Data Provider
VULNERABLE STATEMENT	SELECT * FROM sqli_users WHERE username = ''OR 1 = 1 - -' AND password = dfdfdfdfdf
THREAT ID	1

Figure 2.39: Real-time vulnerability alert

You can see the VULNERABLE STATEMENT that was used; a classic SQL injection-style attack was detected.

Hopefully, you can see the vast amount of effort that has gone into Azure SQL Database and SQL Server 2019 regarding security. All the tools and features discussed in this chapter, when put together, will help you create an enterprise-level data platform of trust.

3
High Availability and Disaster Recovery

It is important to safeguard your data not only from a security perspective but to ensure that it is available during an outage – planned or unplanned. This is known as providing business continuity. The ability to respond to local incidents and get back up and running is known as **High Availability (HA)**. For example, say the storage on a physical server fails and you need to switch production to another server quickly. That should be possible within the same data center with minimal impact.

A more catastrophic event, such as the loss of a data center, triggers what is commonly referred to as **Disaster Recovery (DR or D/R)**. D/R generally involves more than just ensuring that a database is ready for use elsewhere. For example, before bringing a database or instance online, ensuring that core aspects of the infrastructure are functioning is crucial.

Both HA and D/R matter and have one purpose: business continuity. Microsoft's SQL Server 2019 has built-in methods to increase availability, minimize downtime for maintenance, and assist when outages occur. This chapter will not only cover what those features are but also what's new in SQL Server as well as the improvements in Windows Server 2019 that impact SQL Server availability configurations.

SQL Server availability feature overview

This section will provide an overview of the availability features in SQL Server 2019. All of the features described in this section are supported using physical or virtualized servers (**virtual machines**, or **VMs**), whether those VMs are on-premises running under a traditional hypervisor or up in the public cloud as **Infrastructure as a Service** (**IaaS**). Other platform-based features, such as those provided by a hypervisor, are often part of an overall availability strategy for SQL Server but are outside the scope of this chapter.

Backup and restore

The cornerstone of any business continuity plan is a solid backup strategy with tested restores. In other words, the backup and restore feature is the most basic form of availability in any edition of SQL Server. No matter what else you implement, be it one of the built-in features of SQL Server or some third-party utility, ensure this key component of business continuity is implemented properly to meet your **Recovery Time Objectives** (**RTOs**), or how long you have to get up and running, and **Recovery Point Objectives** (**RPOs**), or how much data loss can be tolerated in a worst-case scenario.

SQL Server can generate three kinds of backups for databases: full, differential, and transaction log. A full backup is the entire database, a differential contains the changes since the last full backup, and a transaction log backup contains log records that were not backed up in a previous transaction log backup. Transaction log backups cannot be generated when a database is configured with the simple recovery model.

Backups can be created locally and stored on drives attached to the server, to a file share (copied or generated), or can even be backed up to a URL that uses Azure to store SQL Server backups. More information on backups to URLs can be found at https://docs.microsoft.com/en-us/sql/relational-databases/backup-restore/sql-server-backup-to-url?view=sql-server-2017. Backups should never be a single point of failure, and should always be copied somewhere else to be safe, even if some are kept locally to reduce the time it would take to restore if needed.

Third-party backup utilities can be used with SQL Server as long as they generate a proper SQL Server backup. If not done properly, SQL Server databases could suffer negative consequences. Check with your preferred backup vendor to see how they integrate with SQL Server.

Always On features

Always On is an umbrella term that covers two features, not just one: **Availability Groups (AGs)** and **Failover Cluster Instances (FCIs)**. This section will describe the two features. Links to more detailed documentation on how to plan and configure AGs and FCIs will be included at the end of the chapter.

Always On AGs

For configurations that are deployed for availability, an AG provides database-level protection and if using the Enterprise edition, additional instances known as secondary replicas can also be used as more than standby servers. The instance that contains the read/write database(s) for an AG is known as the primary replica. An instance can be a primary replica for one AG and a secondary replica for another. Replicas can be on-premises (physical or virtual) or up in the public cloud with IaaS VMs for a hybrid solution. Having a replica up in Azure or another cloud provider is one way to provide easier disaster recovery when you do not have your own additional data center.

AGs are supported by both Linux- and Windows Server-based configurations of SQL Server. As of SQL Server 2016, AGs are in both Standard and Enterprise edition. No matter which edition of SQL Server you use, the only limitation on the number of AGs is system resources.

For a secondary replica to be promoted and function as a primary, it needs to have everything required for applications and end users. Anything outside of the database, such as logins, linked servers, SQL Server Agent jobs, and more, must be synchronized manually.

Data synchronization can be done synchronously or asynchronously. The only difference between asynchronous and synchronous synchronization is that the primary replica waits for an acknowledgment from a secondary replica that the transaction has been hardened in its transaction log. For more information on the synchronization process, see https://docs.microsoft.com/en-us/sql/database-engine/availability-groups/windows/availability-modes-always-on-availability-groups?view=sql-server-2017.

By default, the AG feature is disabled in SQL Server. Enabling it is done via SQL Server Configuration Manager or PowerShell with Windows Server, or by using the `mssql-conf` utility or editing the `/var/opt/mssql/mssql.conf` file with Linux. Enabling AGs requires a restart of the SQL Server instance.

There are three main AG variants, which will be discussed in this section:

1. Traditional AGs

2. Distributed AGs

3. Read-scale AGs

Traditional Availability Groups

Traditional AGs were introduced in the SQL Server 2012 Enterprise edition and require an underlying cluster. In SQL Server 2016 and later, the AG feature in the Standard edition is called basic AGs. The Enterprise edition not only enables secondary replicas to be read-only and perform other tasks such as backups and **Database Consistency Checks** (**DBCCs**) if desired but allows more than one database to be in the same AG. The Standard edition is limited to a single database.

For Windows Server-based deployments, the underlying cluster is a **Windows Server Failover Cluster** (**WSFC**) and for all Linux-based deployments, it is **Pacemaker**.

> **Note**
>
> Different Linux distributions may call the feature something different. For example, Red Hat Enterprise Linux's (RHEL) feature is known as the High Availability Add-On.

Traditional AGs require all replicas in a single AG's configuration to be part of the same cluster, which means the same operating system version and type of cluster. Other types of AGs described later in this chapter may allow the mixing of OSes and cluster types.

To provide abstraction so that applications and end users do not need to know which instance is the primary instance, there is a component called the availability group listener, or just the listener. The listener can also be used to send traffic to secondary replicas configured to allow reading.

In a WSFC, the listener is the combination of two resources: a network name and an IP address. In Pacemaker, it is just an IP address resource. On the backend, if you are using Active Directory Domain Services with a WSFC-based AG, a computer object will need to be created for the listener as well as an entry in DNS. For Pacemaker-based AGs, only a DNS entry is required for the listener. For example, if you have **NodeA** and **NodeB** as the underlying servers and a WSFC with the name **MyWSFC**, the listener will have a completely different name, such as **AppLsnr**. All application connections, whether for reading or writing, would use **AppLsnr**, not the names of the nodes, instances (if named), or the WSFC.

AGs have no shared storage requirements but can be combined with FCIs (see the next section for more information) to increase resiliency. Because synchronous and asynchronous are set per replica, AGs allow you to have local availability and disaster recovery in the same feature since asynchronous is much more tolerant of the distance between data centers. Automatic failover can occur with synchronous data movement if the replicas are in a synchronized state.

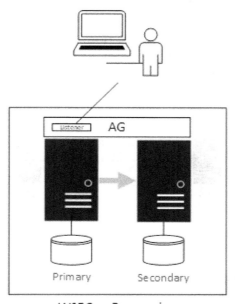

Figure 3.1: Always On Availability Group

For traditional AG deployments, the choice of OS will dictate the level of integration with the underlying cluster. A Windows Server-based AG (or FCI) has tight integration through a resource `.dll`, which makes SQL Server a cluster-aware application. Although Pacemaker ships with Linux distributions, it is not developed by them but can be customized. Microsoft provides an integration component (`mssql-server-ha`) for Pacemaker known as a resource agent, which must be downloaded (`mssql-server-ha`) and installed on the physical or virtual server. When creating an AG, you must select a cluster type. For Pacemaker, it is `EXTERNAL`.

> **Note**
>
> Whether you use Linux or Windows Server, the OS version and/or distribution must be the same for a Pacemaker cluster or WSFC. For example, you cannot mix Ubuntu and Red Hat Enterprise Linux in the same AG.

Most Windows Server-based WSFCs (and SQL Server deployments) use **Active Directory Domain Services** (**AD DS**). Windows Server 2016 enables the creation of a WSFC that does not use AD, called a Workgroup Cluster. You can also have servers participating in different domains, known as a Multi-Domain Cluster. Endpoint security uses certificates, not an AD DS account.

All of the servers, or nodes, of the cluster must be able to communicate with each other and see the domain name system. This allows SQL Server to be able to create AGs in non-domain-based environments. These are called domain-independent AGs. An example is shown in *Figure* 3.2 where the nodes in Data Center 1 could be domain-joined, while the ones in Data Center 2 are not. SQL Server calls this configuration a domain-independent AG and requires the use of certificates for the endpoints.

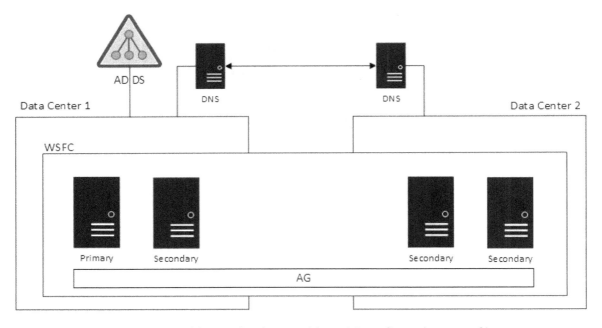

Figure 3.2: Multi-Domain Cluster with an AG configured on top of it

Full documentation on how to deploy AGs with Windows Server can be found at https://docs.microsoft.com/en-us/sql/database-engine/availability-groups/windows/overview-of-always-on-availability-groups-sql-server?view=sql-server-2017. For Linux, it can be found at https://docs.microsoft.com/en-us/sql/linux/sql-server-linux-availability-group-ha?view=sql-server-2017.

Distributed availability groups

In a typical configuration, where the underlying cluster is stretched across multiple sites for disaster recovery, the entire core infrastructure must usually exist in both places. This makes certain design elements, such as a witness for a WSFC, potentially more challenging. An example of an AG stretched across two data centers is shown in *Figure* 3.2.

Introduced in SQL Server 2016, distributed Availability Groups allow you to create an AG that spans more than one underlying AG. Each underlying AG is in its own cluster. That cluster could be on Linux, Windows Server, or even a read-scale Availability Group, which is described in an upcoming section. Using a distributed AG is one of the only ways to mix Windows Server and Linux, different OS versions such as Windows Server 2016 and Windows Server 2019, SQL Server versions, and AG types (Read-scale and "normal") in the same configuration. An example of a distributed AG that spans both a WSFC and Pacemaker is shown in *Figure* 3.3. For example, AG 1 could be SQL Server:

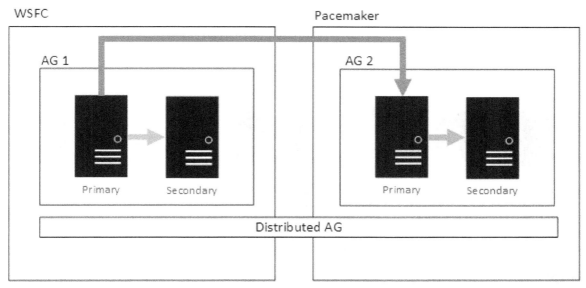

Figure 3.3: Distributed AG spanning two different clusters

For a distributed AG, instead of using the server names when configuring, the listener name (or IP address) is used. There is only one read/write copy of the data. In *Figure 3.4*, this is the database on the primary replica of AG 1. While the primary replica of AG 2 is technically a primary from an AG perspective, it is known as a **forwarder**. It is used to synchronize the secondary replica(s) in that AG. The data synchronization flow can be seen in *Figure 3.4*.

> **Note**
>
> A distributed AG is a SQL Server-only construct and does not appear in an underlying cluster. To administer, you need to use the DMVs. There is very little in SSMS as of version 18.

A single primary replica can feed two different AGs in a distributed AG, and a forwarder can also be used as the primary for another distributed AG, as shown in *Figure 3.4*. This configuration is good to scale out readable replicas. There is still only one read–write copy, and that is at AG1.

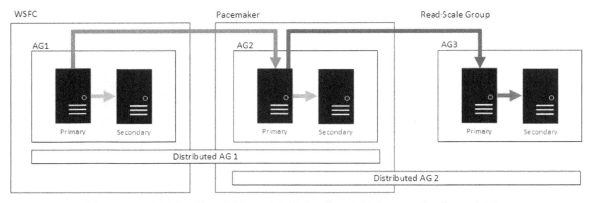

Figure 3.4: AG1 feeding AG2, and AG2 feeding AG3 in two distributed AGs

Another use of a distributed AG is for upgrades and migrations. For example, in *Figure 3.5*, a distributed AG is set up between the SQL Server 2016 and 2019 instances. Those instances are on different WSFCs with different OS versions. Once the cutover occurs, the distributed AG can be unconfigured and the older configuration can be retired.

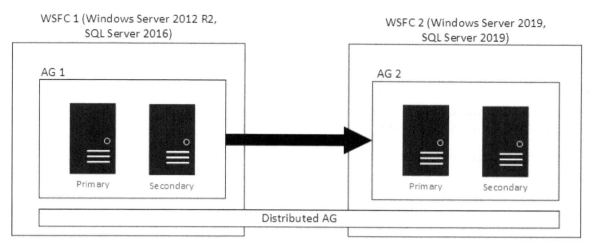

WSFC 1 (Windows Server 2012 R2, SQL Server 2016)

WSFC 2 (Windows Server 2019, SQL Server 2019)

Figure 3.5: Using a distributed AG to upgrade SQL Server and migrate to a different WSFC

> **Note**
>
> Distributed AGs do not work with versions of SQL Server older than 2016, so a 2012 or 2014 AG cannot participate in a distributed AG even for upgrades or migrations.

Read-scale Availability Groups

A read-scale AG is a specific variant in the Enterprise edition. A read-scale AG's purpose is to provide up to nine copies of data synchronized in near-real time if you need it for reading or reporting purposes. This type of AG is different than configuring read-only routing on a normal AG or using a distributed AG, both of which can be used to allow other replicas to access readable data.

A read-scale AG requires a cluster type of NONE, which means that it does not use a WSFC or Pacemaker, and is not considered an availability configuration because an underlying cluster provides things such as health checks and the ability to have automatic failover. Neither is possible with a cluster type of NONE. However, in certain circumstances, a read-scale AG can provide disaster recovery. An example would be if you deployed an FCI with Storage Spaces Direct, a traditional AG could not be configured, so a read-scale one would work for D/R.

In a read-scale AG, the primary replica is the listener and it allows Linux- and Windows Server-based SQL Server replicas to participate in the same AG. This is different than a traditional AG, which requires all replicas to be on the same OS/distribution or a distributed AG where Linux- and Windows Server-based AGs are in the same distributed AG, but in separate AGs.

Always On FCIs

An Always On FCI provides instance-level protection. Instance-level protection means that anything inside the instance, such as logins, SQL Server Agent jobs, and linked servers, exist after failover. FCIs require both an underlying cluster (WSFC or Pacemaker) as well as shared storage. Shared storage can be a challenge for some virtualized and public cloud-based implementations, and this is why AGs are often a better choice for non-physical SQL Server availability.

FCIs are not a scale-out feature; only one node of a cluster owns all the resources at any given time. For performance, the instance must be accounted for via scale-up methods. *Figure* 3.6 shows a high-level view of an FCI. The solid line indicates that that node owns the FCI and the connection to the storage, while the dashed line shows that the other node is connected and could own the resource, but currently does not.

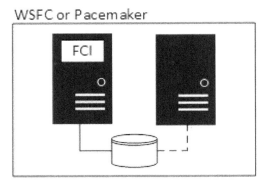

Figure 3.6: FCI example

When a failover occurs, the FCI stops on one node of a Pacemaker cluster or a WSFC and then starts on another. SQL Server goes through full recovery as it would if you started or rebooted a server. This means that there is no data loss in the sense that data will be consistent to the point of failover: if a transaction is incomplete, it will be rolled back and any data that needs to be rolled forward will be.

One major difference between a Pacemaker-based FCI and its WSFC counterpart is that the installation process is completely different. With a WSFC, FCIs are part of SQL Server setup, meaning they cannot be configured after SQL Server is installed. On Linux, SQL Server is fully installed locally on each node before the FCI portion is configured in Pacemaker.

Another difference between Linux-and Windows Server-based FCIs is that only one installation of SQL Server can be configured on Linux. That means every installation of SQL Server on Linux is a default instance; there is currently no concept of a named instance on Linux. Therefore, not more than one FCI can be configured per Pacemaker cluster. On a WSFC, up to 25 FCIs (resource dependent) are supported.

Log shipping

Log shipping is one of the oldest features in SQL Server for availability and is often used for disaster recovery, but also for upgrades and migrations. It is based on backup and restore. Like an AG, it provides database-level protection and any object outside the database must be accounted for separately. Log shipping uses SQL Server Agent jobs to back up the transaction log on the source, copy it to its destination, and restore it on the warm standby server. From the standpoint of RPO, you are only as good as the last transaction log that you have access to.

Because the unit of transaction is the transaction log backup, log shipping accounts for human error. If someone issues an UPDATE without a WHERE and that has not been applied to the standby, you could switch to the standby. All transactions are sent to a secondary replica in an AG immediately.

Log shipping can be combined with both AGs and FCIs, and allows Linux- and Windows Server-based instances to participate in the same solution. This is not possible with FCIs, and as described above, mixing SQL Server on different operating systems with AGs can only be done with certain configurations.

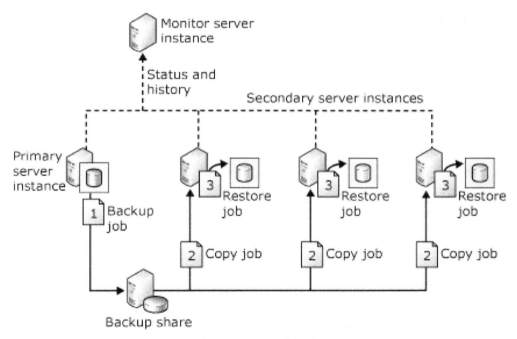

Figure 3.7: Log shipping

What About Database Mirroring and Replication?

Database Mirroring (**DBM**) was deprecated in SQL Server 2012. Its official replacement is AGs and they were documented as such when SQL Server 2016 introduced basic Availability Groups and the ability to use AGs with certificates. While DBM still ships as part of SQL Server 2019 for Windows Server (not Linux), it should not be used for new deployments. Microsoft often no longer removes deprecated features. Customers upgrading from previous versions of SQL Server, where DBM was the main business continuity strategy, should migrate to AGs.

Replication is not an official business continuity feature in the same way that AGs, FCIs, and log shipping are. However, it can be used to enhance the availability of data and many still use it in this capacity. Consider a scenario where executives need access to data. They may not need the whole database, but a subset. Replication enables this scenario – the schema can be different, have a different indexing strategy, and so on. If you want to use AGs or log shipping for reporting, you get all of the same data at the source and the same indexing strategy.

Availability improvements in SQL Server 2019

This section covers the new availability-related features and enhancements in SQL Server 2019.

Accelerated database recovery

Accelerated Database Recovery (**ADR**) is a feature that was introduced in Azure SQL Database but is now included in SQL Server 2019 for on-premises and IaaS deployments. ADR speeds up recovery when a database is brought online after a failover or an event where the database was not cleanly taken offline. Enabling ADR means databases will be online and ready for use by end users and applications faster, reducing downtime and unavailability.

Configuration-only replica

Although not new to SQL Server 2019, the concept of a configuration-only replica was introduced post-SQL Server 2017 in Cumulative Update 1. A configuration-only replica is required for a two-replica (primary and secondary) configuration when deploying AGs on Linux. To support the Standard edition and not impact licensing, a configuration-only replica can be configured on Express. The endpoint used must have a ROLE or WITNESS, as shown in the example code that follows:

```
CREATE ENDPOINT AGEP
STATE = STARTED
AS TCP (
```

```
    LISTENER_PORT = 5022,

    LISTENER_IP = ALL)

  FOR DATABASE_MIRRORING (

    AUTHENTICATION = CERTIFICATE JY_Cert,

    ROLE = WITNESS);

  GO
```

Figure 3.8 shows a Linux-based AG that has two replicas and a configuration-only replica.

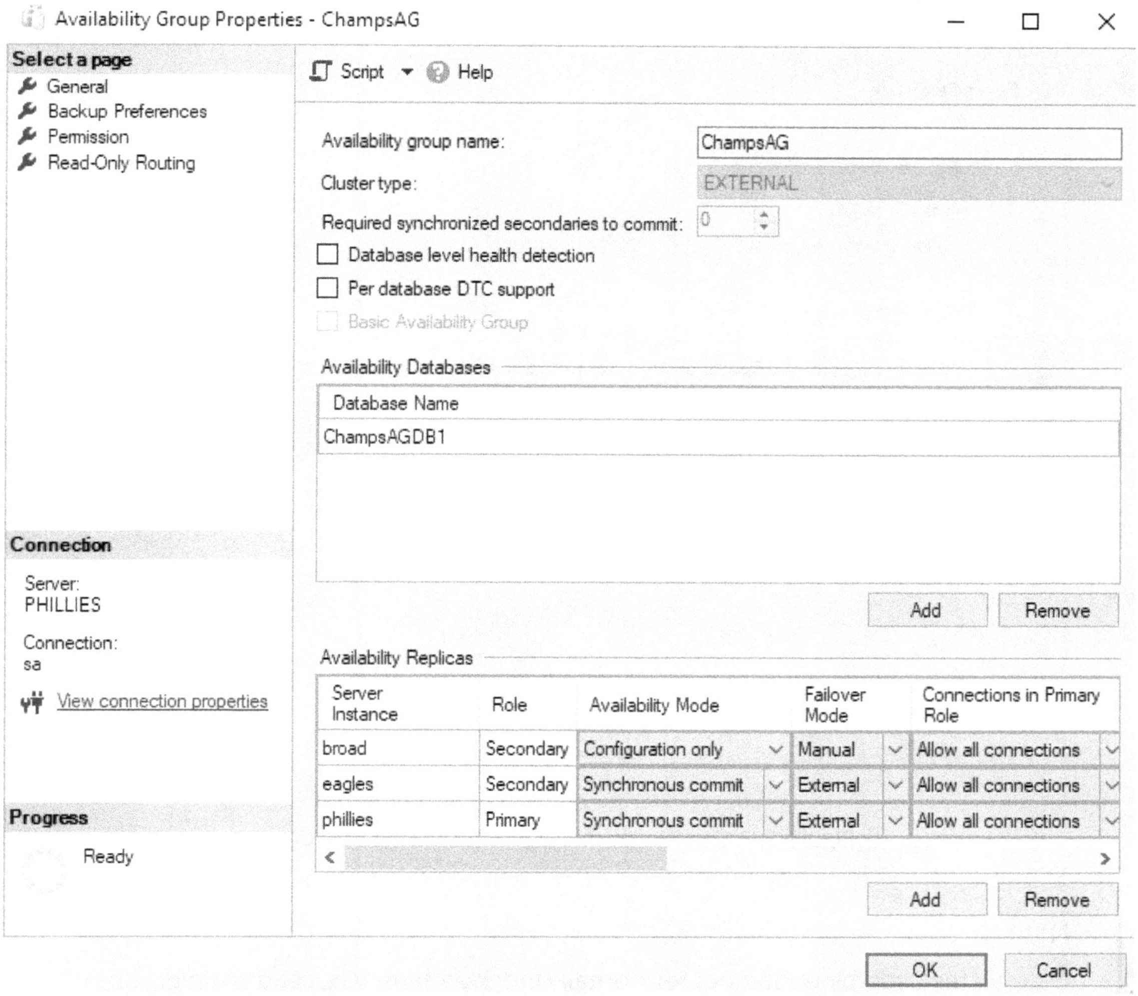

Figure 3.8: Example of an AG on Linux with a configuration-only replica

Certificate management in SQL Server Configuration Manager

Certificates are sometimes required for FCI or AG deployments. In this context, certificates are those associated with the names for the FCI or an AG's listener. Certificates for FCIs and listeners are network-level certificates. In the past, these certificates would need to be applied manually on each node of the cluster.

With SQL Server 2019, you can now apply a certificate across the nodes of a WSFC for FCIs and listeners using **SQL Server Configuration Manager** (**SSCM**). SSCM does not exist for Linux, so this enhancement is only for Windows Server-based AG and FCI configurations. Remember that a certificate's **Subject Alternate Name** (**SAN**) for AG nodes must include the listener(s) as well as the node name. *Figure* 3.9 shows an example of certificate management for an FCI:

Figure 3.9: Certificate management dialog for FCIs

> **Note**
>
> Certificates used by endpoints for domain-independent AGs, read scale groups, and distributed AGs are different; they are generated from within SQL Server and restored in SQL Server.

Clustered columnstore index online rebuild

Starting in SQL Server 2019, it is possible to build or rebuild a **Clustered Columnstore Index** (**CCI**) as an online operation. To do so, you would need to add the (ONLINE = ON) option to the CREATE or ALTER statement. Examples are shown below. The first example is the creation of a new CCI:

```
CREATE CLUSTERED COLUMNSTORE INDEX MyCCI
    ON MyTable
    WITH (ONLINE = ON);
```

This example shows how to rebuild a CCI online:

```
ALTER CLUSTERED COLUMNSTORE INDEX MyCCI
    ON MyTable
    REBUILD WITH (ONLINE = ON);
```

Database scoped default setting for online and resumable DDL operations

Through SQL Server 2017, all online maintenance operations must be specified as part of the Transact-SQL statement. The examples shown above use ONLINE = ON. In SQL Server 2019, you have the option of changing the default behavior for each database to ONLINE = ON so it does not need to be part of the Transact-SQL statement. The same is true of the new resumable index operation, where RESUMABLE = ON can be set.

To change the default behavior for a database, you modify the database scoped configuration. The two options are ELEVATE_ONLINE and ELEVATE_RESUMABLE. Example code follows. The options are OFF (the default behavior), WHEN_SUPPORTED, and FAIL_UNSUPPORTED:

```
ALTER DATABASE SCOPED CONFIGURATION
    SET ELEVATE_ONLINE = WHEN_SUPPORTED;
ALTER DATABASE SCOPED CONFIGURATION
    SET ELEVATE_RESUMABLE = WHEN_SUPPORTED;
```

Note

At the time of writing this chapter, this is a Transact SQL-only option and cannot be configured using SSMS.

Failover Cluster Instance Support for Machine Learning Services

Machine language functionality is now supported for installation as part of an FCI. However, it is not cluster-aware like SQL Server itself, SQL Server Agent, or an AG. The resource in the role, the SQL Server Launchpad, is just a generic service, meaning it has no health detection. The role will only fail over to another if the FCI itself does so since it is dependent upon the FCI resource itself. An example is shown in *Figure 3.10*:

Figure 3.10: FCI with the machine language resource

Increased number of synchronous replicas in the Enterprise edition

In the SQL Server 2019 Enterprise Edition, Microsoft increased the total number of synchronous replicas that can be configured to five (one primary and four synchronous secondary replicas), up from three in SQL Server 2016 and 2017 (one primary and up to two secondary replicas) and two in SQL Server 2012 and 2014 (only one primary and one secondary). Since synchronous data movement is required for automatic failover, this also means that up to five replicas can be configured for automatic failover. The number of replicas in SQL Server 2019 for basic AGs remains the same at a total of two replicas (one primary and one secondary).

More synchronous replicas enable different scenarios. For example, you can have:

- The read/write primary replica.

- A secondary replica dedicated to availability.

- Up to three more secondary replicas dedicated to just near-real time read-only access, spreading out load even further using the load balancing feature of read-only routing.

The trade-off of configuring more synchronous replicas is that your network must be robust and the IOPS must be optimized; otherwise, synchronization will lag behind. If you currently struggle with synchronization, adding replicas will not improve the situation.

Online builds or rebuilds for Clustered Columnstore Indexes

Columnstore indexes are an index type that improves query performance for workloads that use large amounts of data. An example would be a data warehouse. Instead of being stored in a traditional row-based format, columnstore indexes are stored in a column-based one and compress the data. Building or rebuilding a columnstore index prior to SQL Server 2019 was an offline operation, meaning no changes could occur while the index was being created or recreated.

With the SQL Server 2019 Enterprise edition, columnstore index maintenance can be done as an online operation. This means that any databases using columnstore indexes are more available for use.

An example Transact-SQL statement to build a new columnstore index as an online operation is shown here – the key is the **(ONLINE = ON)** portion:

```
CREATE CLUSTERED COLUMNSTORE INDEX MyCI

   ON MyTable

   WITH (ONLINE = ON);
```

An example Transact-SQL statement to rebuild an existing columnstore index to use the new online functionality is shown here:

```
ALTER INDEX MyCI

   ON MyTable

   REBUILD WITH (ONLINE = ON);
```

> **Note**
>
> This enhancement also applies to Azure SQL Database.

Read-only routing configuration in SQL Server Management Studio

The way to tell an AG that secondary replicas can be used for read access is to configure read-only routing. In older versions of **SQL Server Management Studio** (**SSMS**), this was not possible. Starting with SSMS 17.3, read-only routing can be configured in SSMS via the New Availability Group Wizard as well as in the properties of the AG itself. An example of using SSMS for read-only routing configuration is shown in *Figure 3.11*:

> **Note**
>
> If using SSMS, a listener must be configured before setting up read-only routing.

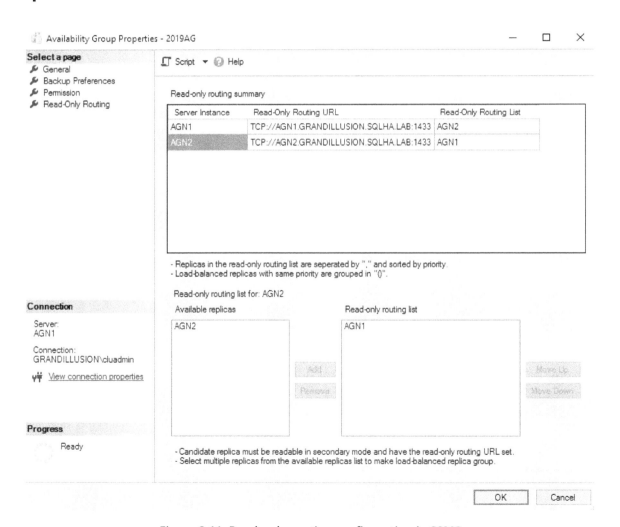

Figure 3.11: Read-only routing configuration in SSMS

Replication for Linux-based configurations

When SQL Server 2017 was released, one of the features missing for Linux was replication. In SQL Server 2019, replication is now an included feature for Linux-based SQL Server configurations. The following replication variants are supported:

- Snapshot replication
- Transactional replication
- Merge replication
- Peer-to-peer replication
- Replication with non-default ports
- Replication with Active Directory Domain Services authentication
- Immediate updates for transactional replication

At the time of writing this chapter, the following are not supported:

- Immediate update subscribers
- Oracle publishing

Unlike clustered configurations in SQL Server, replication does not care about the underlying operating systems so publishers, distributors, and subscribers can be running on your operating system of choice as long as the version restrictions are maintained for what can constitute a publisher, distributor, or subscriber.

Replication requires SQL Server Agent to be enabled. To do this on Linux, first check **/var/opt/mssql/mssql.conf** to see if Agent is enabled. If not, run the following commands. Enabling Agent requires a restart of SQL Server, meaning brief downtime:

```
sudo /opt/mssql/bin/mssql-conf set sqlagent.enabled true
sudo systemctl restart mssql-server
```

If the distributor will be running on a Linux-based SQL Server instance, create a **folder** for the snapshots used by SQL Server Agent. The **mssql** user must have access otherwise replication will not work. An example is shown here:

```
sudo mkdir /var/opt/mssql/data/Snapshots/
sudo chown mssql /var/opt/mssql/data/Snapshots/
sudo chgrp mssql /var/opt/mssql/data/Snapshots/
```

Secondary-to-primary read/write connection redirection

This new capability in SQL Server 2019 allows connections using a listener to ensure write-based commands always reach the primary replica even if it is pointed at a secondary replica. There are two aspects to consider in terms of the configuration:

- `READ_WRITE_ROUTING_URL` must be set, which is currently not exposed in SSMS at the time of writing this chapter.

- `ApplicationIntent` must be `ReadWrite`, not `ReadOnly`.

- `ALLOW CONNECTIONS` must be set to `ALL` for a secondary role.

The following is a sample Transact-SQL to change an existing AG to support this new functionality:

```
ALTER AVAILABILITY GROUP [2019AG]

MODIFY REPLICA ON N'AGN1'

WITH (PRIMARY_ROLE (ALLOW_CONNECTIONS = READ_WRITE));

GO


ALTER AVAILABILITY GROUP [2019AG]

MODIFY REPLICA ON N'AGN1'

WITH (PRIMARY_ROLE (READ_WRITE_ROUTING_URL = N'TCP://AGN1.CONTOSO.
COM'));

GO


ALTER AVAILABILITY GROUP [2019AG]

MODIFY REPLICA ON N'AGN1'

WITH (SECONDARY_ROLE (ALLOW_CONNECTIONS = ALL));

GO


ALTER AVAILABILITY GROUP [2019AG]

MODIFY REPLICA ON N'AGN2'

WITH (PRIMARY_ROLE (ALLOW_CONNECTIONS = READ_WRITE));

GO


ALTER AVAILABILITY GROUP [2019AG]
```

```
MODIFY REPLICA ON N'AGN2'

WITH (PRIMARY_ROLE (READ_WRITE_ROUTING_URL = N'TCP://AGN2.CONTOSO.
COM'));

GO


ALTER AVAILABILITY GROUP [2019AG]

MODIFY REPLICA ON N'AGN2'

WITH (SECONDARY_ROLE (ALLOW_CONNECTIONS = ALL));

GO
```

An example execution showing this new functionality working follows. `ApplicationIntent` is set to `ReadWrite`, as shown in *Figure 3.12*, for a connection made to `AGN2`. `AGN2` is currently the secondary replica:

Figure 3.12: Setting ApplicationIntent in the SSMS connection properties

After connecting to AGN2, note the output of the two queries in *Figure* 3.13. The first is asking SQL Server what replica the connection is using and if it thinks it is the primary replica, which in this case is **AGN1**. However, look at the highlighted box at the bottom – the connection is actually to **AGN2**:

Figure 3.13: Showing the new redirection capability of an AG

Windows Server 2019 availability enhancements

Windows Server 2019 also has a few new features or changes to existing ones that enhance the availability of Windows Server 2019-based SQL Server deployments even if they are not SQL Server 2019. Some new features, such as cluster sets, introduced in Windows Server 2019 currently do not apply to any version of SQL Server but may in the future.

> **Note**
>
> The versions of SQL Server supported on Windows Server 2019 are SQL Server 2016, 2017, and 2019.

Changing domains for a Windows Server Failover Cluster

Changing the AD DS status of a WSFC for all versions prior to Windows Server 2019 involved the complete destruction of the WSFC and anything running in it. That was very disruptive. Windows Server 2019 supports the ability to change the domain membership of a WSFC and its resources.

Cluster Shared Volumes support for Microsoft Distributed Transaction Coordinator

Cluster Shared Volumes (**CSV**) have been supported as storage for FCIs since SQL Server 2014. However, if you required a clustered **Microsoft Distributed Transaction Coordinator** (**MS DTC**, **MSDTC**, or just **DTC**), that needed to be placed on a disk with a drive letter. Windows Server 2019 enables DTC to be configured using CSV.

Figure 3.14 shows a clustered DTC. Note that the Value of the object matches the ID of the CSV:

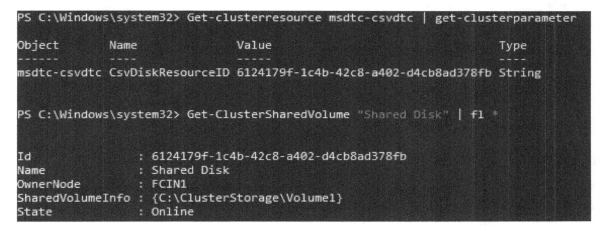

Figure 3.14: PowerShell output showing DTC created on a CSV

File share witness without a domain

Domain-independent AGs can utilize a WSFC that has nodes that are joined to Active Directory Domain Services. An important aspect of all WSFCs is configuring the right witness resource for the quorum. In Windows Server 2016, the only options that work for this configuration are cloud or disk witness. Cloud witness is Azure-based, which is not an option for some, especially those in a DMZ. Disk witness defeats the purpose of having a non-shared disk configuration and complicates certain types of deployments. A file share witness is the natural choice for a local WSFC where there is no shared storage, but a file share requires domain connectivity.

Windows Server 2019 allows the creation of a file share witness without a domain. All ACLs are set locally on the file share, and when the witness is created, the credentials are provided. An example of this is shown in *Figure* 3.15. A file share can even be something as simple as a USB stick plugged into a router:

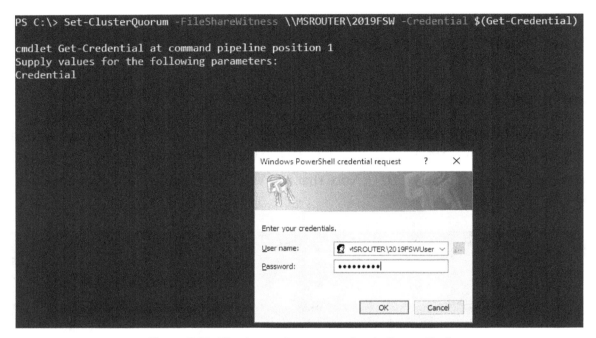

Figure 3.15: File share witness creation in PowerShell

Improved Windows Server Failover Cluster security

Pre-Windows Server 2019, WSFCs used NTLM for a lot of things, such as intra-node communication. In Windows Server 2019, Microsoft redesigned WSFC security and there are no more NTLM dependencies. Certificate-based SMB authentication is used between the WSFC nodes. Some applications may require NTLM, but the WSFC itself no longer requires it and, if desired, could be disabled on the server.

Storage Replica in the Standard edition

Storage Replica is a feature in Windows Server that enables you to have FCIs that span two locations for disaster recovery. This is achieved through disk-based replication. Storage Replica is not for AG configurations where the replicas are kept in sync via SQL Server.

Storage Replica handles the replication of disk volumes configured for use in a WSFC. The disk-based replication can be synchronous or asynchronous. Windows Server 2016 was the first version of Windows Server to feature Storage Replica, but it was only in the Datacenter edition. Windows Server 2019 enables Storage Replica in the Standard edition. There are two main limitations of the feature in the Standard edition:

- It only replicates a single volume.

- The volume size can be a maximum of 2 TB.

This means an FCI can have only a single disk configured with it.

Figures 3.16 and 3.17 show the output of a PowerShell script that shows the version and edition of Windows Server along with all of the features that have the word "**storage**" in them:

```
PS C:\backups> .\sr.ps1
Windows Server 2016 Standard

Display Name                                              Name                        Install State
------------                                              ----                        -------------
[X] File and Storage Services                             FileAndStorage-Services         Installed
    [X] Storage Services                                  Storage-Services                Installed
[ ] Enhanced Storage                                      EnhancedStorage                 Available
        [ ] Storage Replica Module for Windows Power...   RSAT-Storage-Replica            Available
[ ] Windows Standards-Based Storage Management            WindowsStorageManage...         Available
```

Figure 3.16: Windows Server 2016 features with storage in the name

```
PS C:\cert> .\sr.ps1
Windows Server 2019 Standard

Display Name                                              Name                        Install State
------------                                              ----                        -------------
[X] File and Storage Services                             FileAndStorage-Services         Installed
    [X] Storage Services                                  Storage-Services                Installed
[ ] Enhanced Storage                                      EnhancedStorage                 Available
        [ ] Storage Replica Module for Windows Power...   RSAT-Storage-Replica            Available
[ ] Storage Replica                                       Storage-Replica                 Available
[ ] Windows Standards-Based Storage Management            WindowsStorageManage...         Available
```

Figure 3.17: Windows Server 2019 features with storage in the name

> **Note**
>
> To use Storage Replica for an FCI, create all of the storage and the replication first, then select the disks during the FCI creation.

Storage Spaces Direct two-node configuration

In Windows Server 2016, **<u>Storage Spaces Direct</u>** (**<u>S2D</u>**) worked in a two-node configuration but was optimal with three or more. In Windows Server 2019, the two-node configuration works well and is robust. FCIs can be configured on S2D. S2D now has two different nested resiliency options in Windows Server 2019 to survive drive and node failure:

- Nested two-way mirror

- Nested mirror-accelerated parity

Figure 3.18 shows how a nested two-way mirror works. Windows Server contains four copies of the data across the two servers. There is only one read/write copy of the data, similar to a distributed AG:

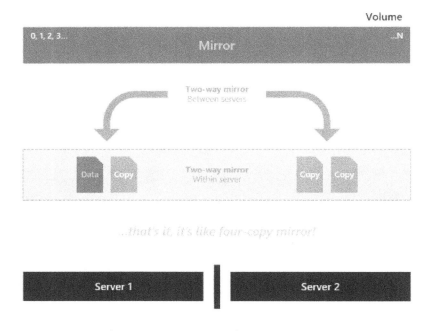

Figure 3.18: S2D nested two-way mirror

Nested mirror-accelerated parity combines the two-way mirror with nested parity. So, you get local parity for resiliency and mirroring between the servers. See *Figure 3.19* for what this looks like:

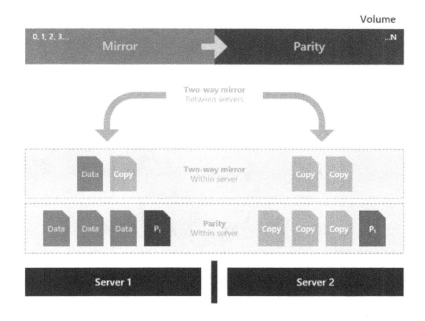

Figure 3.19: Nested mirror-accelerated parity

The trade-off of these architectures is capacity. The nested-two way mirror maintains four copies, so if your data size is 500 GB, you need 2 TB of physical storage. That means only 25% of your space is usable. Nested mirror-accelerated parity is better, but it depends on the number of capacity drives in each server as well as the mix of mirror and parity for the volume. Typically, you will see between 35 and 40% usable space.

For more information, see https://docs.microsoft.com/en-us/windows-server/storage/storage-spaces/nested-resiliency.

Windows Server Failover Cluster improvements in Azure

Currently, all clustered configurations of SQL Server in Azure require the use of an internal load balancer to handle the floating IP addresses for the listener, an FCI, or a WSFC. Windows Server 2019 is Azure-aware. The WSFC creation process will detect whether you are running on Azure and, if so, create a distributed network name. Normally, a network name requires its own IP address. A distributed network name uses the IP address of the underlying node.

This simplifies the configuration of an IaaS-based WSFC. The distributed network name does not work with SQL Server resources, so an ILB is still required for an AG's listener or the FCI's IP address(es). An example is shown in *Figure 3.20*:

Figure 3.20: Distributed network name for a WSFC

Another improvement in Windows Server 2019, when deployed in Azure, is that Windows Server now detects if there is maintenance occurring on the host for the IaaS VM and log events. This helps when troubleshooting. This is tracked in the Failover Clustering Operational log. The new event IDs are:

- 1136 – Node maintenance is imminent and about to occur.
- 1139 – Node maintenance has been detected.
- 1140 – Node maintenance has been rescheduled.

There is a new property in the WSFC called `DetectManagedEvents`. There are five values this can have:

- 0 – Do not log Azure scheduled events (default for on-premises).
- 1 – Log Azure scheduled events (default for Azure).
- 2 – Avoid placement (do not move roles to this node).
- 3 – Pause and drain roles when a scheduled event is detected.
- 4 – Pause, drain, and fail back roles when a scheduled event is detected.

Another new WSFC property is `DetectManagedEventsThreshold`. The default value is 60 seconds and is the amount of time before the event happens to move things off of the WSFC node.

4
Hybrid Features – SQL Server and Microsoft Azure

One of the unique capabilities of SQL Server is the ability to leverage the power of hybrid cloud infrastructure. There are several ways to leverage Azure to improve the high availability and disaster recover of an on-premises SQL Server deployment. Azure Storage is a core service offered by Microsoft Azure is Azure Storage. It offers enterprise-ready, highly scalable, flexible storage solutions at competitive prices. SQL Server 2019 and Azure Storage work together to benefit users. We can leverage Azure Blob storage to develop and deploy hybrid solutions, such as backing up on-premises SQL Server databases to the cloud (also called Backup to URL) and building SQL Server data files in Azure Storage to use file-snapshot backups.

It is also possible to enhance your disaster recovery strategy by leveraging Azure so that it ultimately becomes your secondary data center. There are many ways to benefit from this. A common approach is that you can extend your on-premises availability group by provisioning a secondary asynchronous replica to an Azure virtual machine with SQL Server installed. Another hybrid scenario used by enterprise customers is the configuration of transactional replication between on-premises SQL Server and Azure SQL Database to help with migration to Azure with minimal downtime.

Backup to URL

A great strategy for on-premises SQL Server databases is to back up to Azure Storage. There are many benefits to leveraging the massive scale of the cloud to hold backups.

Benefits

* You can think of using Azure Storage as a cost-effective off-site backup location that is an extension of your own local data center and is highly performant and highly available. With the help of Microsoft, you can quite easily scale your storage account to 5 PB.

* **Geo-Redundant Storage** (GRS) is designed to provide at least 99.99999999999999% durability over a given year by replicating your data to a secondary region that is hundreds of miles away from your primary region, that is, your paired region.

* There are no **Storage Array Networks** (SANs) or file shares for you to administer and support. Azure services will take care of this, thus reducing hardware administration costs.

* Using the latest version of **SQL Server Management Studio** (SSMS) makes setup quick and easy with native support for Backup to URL. Once you have understood the high-level requirements, using T-SQL is also a valid and simple alternative option.

Requirements

To successfully implement the backup to URL feature, you will need to configure and set up the following components:

* A private container within a storage account

* **Shared Access Signature** (SAS)

* A SQL Server credential that has a secret mapped to the SAS

The storage account

Typically, you would set up your storage account as shown in *Figure 4.1*:

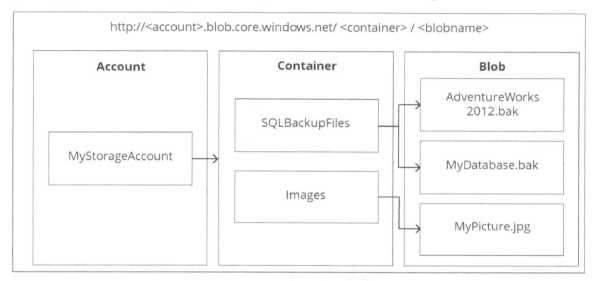

Figure 4.1: Setting up the storage account

You should create containers to organize the contents of your storage account. There are two types of blob storage that you could use, these being page and block blobs (technically, there is another blob type, called append blob, which will not be covered in this chapter). The type of blob you use is dictated by the security route that you take. If you decide to use a storage key within the SQL Server credential, then page blobs will be used; if you configure an SAS for the credential, then block blobs will be used. The best practice is to use block blobs for three main reasons. Firstly, using an SAS is a more secure way than using a storage key to authorize access to blob storage. It provides a more granular level of access without the need to expose the main storage account keys (primary or secondary). With block blobs as the target, you can leverage multiple blobs (striping) to improve the performance of backups and restores for larger databases. Finally, block blobs are the more cost-effective option when compared to page blobs.

Setup

1. Connect to the storage account via Azure Storage Explorer (https://azure.microsoft.com/en-gb/features/storage-explorer/) and get the SAS for the **sqlbackups** container, which is set to private, as shown in *Figure 4.2*:

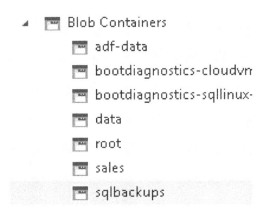

Figure 4.2: Blob Containers

2. Go to **Actions** and select **Get Shared Access Signature**, as shown in *Figure 4.3*:

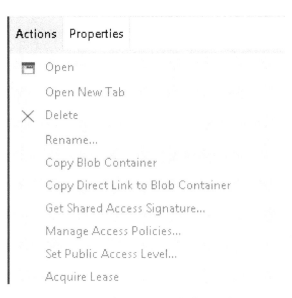

Figure 4.3: The actions dialogue box

3. Once you have completed the expiry times and permissions, you will need to click **Create and copy the query string**, as shown in *Figure 4.4*:

Figure 4.4: Setting the Share Access Signature

Let's break down an example SAS:

?st=2019-05-23T08%3A44%3A13Z&se=2019-05-24T08%3A44%3A13Z&sp=rwd&sv=2018-03-28&sr=c&sig=AXifSoEN Kdk403294xkd1SUE1DKDKFKvjkakla02302KSKSDK203D

Figure 14.5: Example SAS

- **st/se** defines the start time and expiry times defined for the SAS for the resource.
- **sp** shows the permissions defined—for this example, these are read, write, and delete (RWD).
- **sv** is the storage service version used.
- **sr** is the resource used for this example, which is a container (C).
- **sig** is the actual signature created using the SHA256 algorithm.

Now we have a grasp of the different components of the query string above. Ultimately, this will become the secret for the SQL Server credential in the Backup to URL process (obfuscated for security purposes):

```
CREATE CREDENTIAL [https://aksproddiag844.blob.core.windows.net/
sqlbackups]

WITH IDENTITY = 'SHARED ACCESS SIGNATURE',

SECRET = 'st=2020-04-05T07%ani&se=2019-04-
14T07%3A5aa6ryaesSQL&sv=2018-03-28&sr=c&sig=1LSEQkaJSCZ%anOayausca!;

GO
```

Once the credential has been created, it will allow the backup code to successfully execute:

```
BACKUP DATABASE

  [CodeDB] TO URL = N'https://aksproddiag844.blob.core.windows.net/
sqlbackups/CodeDB_Apr_5_2019_9_19AM.bak

  ' WITH COMPRESSION,  CHECKSUM, FORMAT, STATS = 10;

10 percent processed.

20 percent processed.

30 percent processed.

40 percent processed.

50 percent processed.

60 percent processed.

70 percent processed.

80 percent processed.

90 percent processed.

100 percent processed.

Processed 191264 pages for database 'CodeDB', file 'CodeDB_Data' on file
1.

Processed 1 pages for database 'CodeDB', file 'CodeDB_Log' on file 1.

BACKUP DATABASE successfully processed 191265 pages in 30.078 seconds
(49.679 MB/sec).
```

If you log back into the storage account via the Storage Explorer tool, you see the backup file:

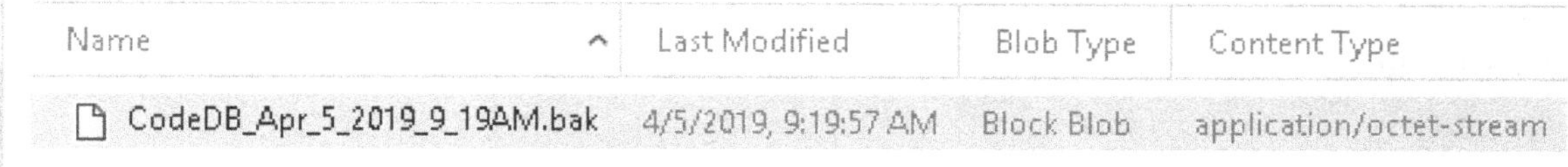

Name		Last Modified	Blob Type	Content Type
CodeDB_Apr_5_2019_9_19AM.bak	^	4/5/2019, 9:19:57 AM	Block Blob	application/octet-stream

Figure 4.6: Backup file

> **Note**
>
> Another benefit of this feature when utilizing block blobs is the fact that you can issue **WITH COMPRESSION**, **MAXTRANSIZE**, and **BLOCKSIZE** arguments for the backup commands to further enhance the performance of the backup and save space for those larger files.

Restoring from this backup is no different to what you would do with on-premises bound backup files. Simply state the **FROM URL** argument instead of **FROM DISK**:

```
USE [master]
RESTORE DATABASE [CodeDB2] FROM
 URL = N'https://aksproddiag844.blob.core.windows.net/sqlbackups/
CodeDB_Apr_5_2019_9_19AM.bak' WITH  FILE = 1,
  MOVE N'CodeDB_Data' TO N'D:\SQL\Codedb2.mdf',
    MOVE N'CodeDB_Log' TO N'D:\SQL\Codedb2_Log.ldf',
  NOUNLOAD,  STATS = 5
```

SQL Server data files in Azure

This feature enables users to create SQL Server 2019 databases on premises, but the underlying data files (MDF, NDF, and LDF) are bound to Azure Blob storage rather than local storage:

> **Note**
>
> This hybrid technique is only recommended and supported for user databases and not system databases.

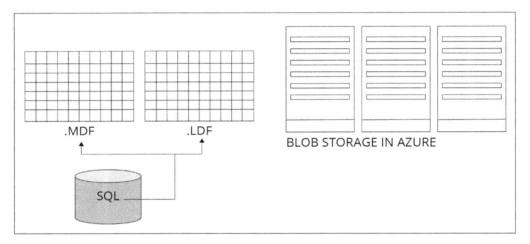

Figure 4.7: Saving database across platforms

The separation of the compute layer (`sqlservr.exe` being on premises) and storage layer (Azure Storage) makes the recovery benefits seem more obvious. For example, if you lose the on-premises SQL Server instance, you can set up a new one without any manual data movement. Quite simply, all that is needed is to re-attach the datafiles. Once successfully set up, you can then leverage file-snapshot backups for database files in Azure (see the next section). This feature provides near-instantaneous backups and quick restores, making it a compelling solution for bigger databases.

When using this separation technique, there is a small cost assigned to it for the actual storage and transactions that occur per database file in the form of blob lease renewals, which occur every 45-60 seconds.

> **Note**
>
> Please visit https://azure.microsoft.com/pricing/ to work out your monthly costs.

Setup and concepts

For set up, the concepts are very similar to those for Backup to URL. Best practices dictate that the container in Azure Storage should be private. This is where the data files will be located. An SAS will then need to be created against this container, where it will then become the secret within the SQL Server credential store.

This feature utilizes page blobs rather than block blobs, which is the more efficient blob type for random read-write patterns:

Generate the SAS via Storage Explorer. In *Figure 4.8* we have a new private container called **sqldatafiles**:

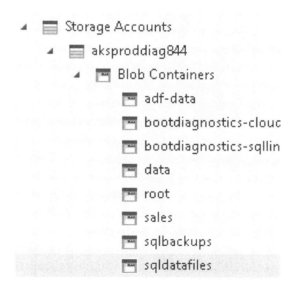

Figure 4.8: Storage explorer

4. Click **Actions** to build the secret:

Figure 4.9: Shared Access Signature dialogue box

5. Use the query string generated as the secret for a SQL Server credential, which is shown here and obfuscated for this chapter:

```
CREATE CREDENTIAL [https://aksproddiag844.blob.core.windows.net/
sqldatafiles]
WITH IDENTITY='SHARED ACCESS SIGNATURE',
SECRET = 'st=2020-04-05T09%d&se=2019-04-arj&!un=rwdl&sue=2018-03-
28ani&Asig=Ra0yanab1VJ2y5mTAnotherA000Rg3TeamrZfyhXs%Ar7unDddaa4rya
xxA'
```

6. Create the SQL Server database bound to Azure Storage:

```
CREATE DATABASE IOT_DB
ON
( NAME = IOT_DB,
    FILENAME = 'https://aksproddiag844.blob.core.windows.net/
sqldatafiles/IOT_DB.mdf' )
 LOG ON
( NAME = IOT_DB_log,
    FILENAME =  'https://aksproddiag844.blob.core.windows.net/
sqldatafiles/IOT_DBLog.ldf')
```

7. Confirm that the database files are now in Azure Storage:

Name	Last Modified	Blob Type	Content Type	Size	Status
IOT_DB.mdf	4/5/2019, 10:43:13 AM	Page Blob	application/octet-stream	8 MB	Active
IOT_DBLog.ldf	4/5/2019, 10:43:13 AM	Page Blob	application/octet-stream	8 MB	Active

Figure 4.10: A list of database files

8. Use an SSMS query to check the files are bound to Azure Storage:

```
SELECT * FROM sys.sysfiles
```

fileid	groupid	size	maxsize	growth	status	perf	name	filename
1	1	1024	-1	8192	2	0	IOT_DB	https://aksproddiag844.blob.core.windows.net/sqldatafiles/IOT_DB.mdf
2	0	1024	134217728	8192	66	0	IOT_DB_log	https://aksproddiag844.blob.core.windows.net/sqldatafiles/IOT_DBLog.ldf

Figure 4.11: System files

Considerations

There are a few important points to consider when discussing the merits of SQL Server data files. The storage account used to hold the data files should not use any form of storage-level geo-replication. More specifically, this means GRS accounts should not be used. This is because this option replicates data asynchronously across two geographic regions, and if failover occurs where the secondary location now serves as the primary one, then database corruption is possible because of the way asynchronous replication works.

As mentioned when we discussed Backup to URL, leases are used against Blob storage objects, with renewals occurring every 45-60 seconds. The impact of this is different for this feature because if SQL Server crashes and another instance is then configured to use the same blobs, the new instance could potentially have to wait up until 60 seconds for the lease to expire. You could overcome this by manually breaking the lease if you cannot wait for 60 seconds.

To break the lease, you would right-click on the object(s) within your container and click **Break Lease**:

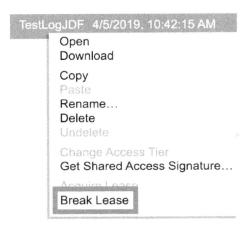

Figure 4.12: Breaking the lease

In this case, the lease would be broken against the transaction log. Alternatively, you could wait for it to expire for it to become available.

> **Note**
>
> In terms of SQL Server features, FILESTREAM and In-Memory online transaction processing (OLTP) are not supported. These will need local storage. AGs are supported as long as you do not add new database files to the primary database.

File-snapshot backups

One of the benefits of configuring SQL Server data files in Azure is the ability to leverage file-snapshot backups. This is summarized in *Figure 4.13*, where 1 shows the successful setup of the data files in Azure (a prerequisite covered earlier on) and 2 is the high-level design of how the data files and snapshot files interact with each other after a full backup takes place:

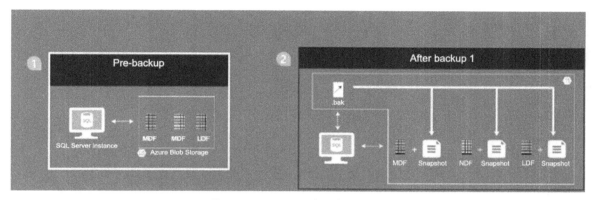

Figure 4.13: Snapshot backups

The full database backup using snapshot technology creates a snapshot of each data and log file that is part of the database and establishes the transaction log backup chain for point-in-time recovery. When consequent transaction log backups are taken, transaction log file-snapshot backups are generated, which contain file snapshots of all database files, too. These can then be used to perform a database restore or a log restore to a point in time. This approach means that you do not need additional full or differential backups after the initial first full backup. This simplifies your backup restore commands.

Setup

All the same components are needed as for previous features. The SQL Server credential with the relevant secret (based on the SAS) must be in place before doing this. For this example, we will be using the same private container as in the previous section. As you can see from the backup code, the key argument is **WITH FILE_ SNAPSHOT**:

```
USE master;

GO

ALTER DATABASE [IOT_DB]  SET RECOVERY FULL;
```

```
GO
```

```
BACKUP DATABASE  [IOT_DB]
TO URL = 'https://aksproddiag844.blob.core.windows.net/sqldatafiles/
IOTDB_FULL_SNAPSHOT.bak'
WITH FILE_SNAPSHOT;
GO
```

```
DECLARE @Log_Filename AS VARCHAR (300);
SET @Log_Filename = 'https://aksproddiag844.blob.core.windows.net/
sqldatafiles/IOTDB_Log_'+
REPLACE (REPLACE (REPLACE (CONVERT (VARCHAR (40), GETDATE (), 120),
'-','_'),':', '_'),' ', '_') + '.trn';
BACKUP LOG IOT_DB
 TO URL = @Log_Filename WITH FILE_SNAPSHOT;
GO
```

🗋 IOTDB_FULL_SNAPSHOT.bak	4/5/2019, 12:46:27 PM	Block Blob	application/octet-stream	512 KB	Active
🗋 IOTDB_Log_2019_04_05_12_47_02.trn	4/5/2019, 12:47:03 PM	Block Blob	application/octet-stream	512 KB	Active

Figure 4.14: New Entry added

To view the snapshot files, use this:

```
select * from sys.fn_db_backup_file_snapshots (null) ;
GO
```

file_id	snapshot_time	snapshot_url
1	2019-04-05T11:46:27.1321374Z	https://aksproddiag844.blob.core.windows.net/sqldatafiles/IOT_DB.mdf?snapshot=2019-04-05T11:46:27.1321374Z
1	2019-04-05T11:47:02.9222460Z	https://aksproddiag844.blob.core.windows.net/sqldatafiles/IOT_DB.mdf?snapshot=2019-04-05T11:47:02.9222460Z
2	2019-04-05T11:46:27.2352364Z	https://aksproddiag844.blob.core.windows.net/sqldatafiles/IOT_DBLog.ldf?snapshot=2019-04-05T11:46:27.2352364Z
2	2019-04-05T11:47:03.0523701Z	https://aksproddiag844.blob.core.windows.net/sqldatafiles/IOT_DBLog.ldf?snapshot=2019-04-05T11:47:03.0523701Z

Figure 4.15: Snapshot files listed

The restore speed is fast because the restore sequence is different to that of a traditional streaming backup setup, where you would need a full backup chain comprising a full backup (maybe a differential, too) along with the relevant log backups. With file-snapshot backups, looking at *Figure 4.16* where an issue occurred at **101.00** (red box), we would only need the last two log backups (red circles). This is because they also include a snapshot of all the data files (as mentioned earlier on) and the log file itself:

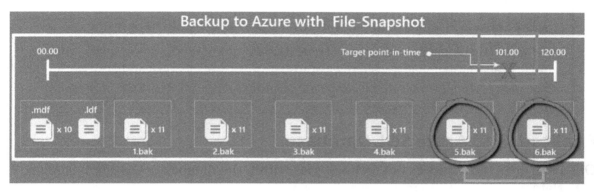

Figure 4.16: Backing up to Azure with file snapshots

Extending on-premises Availability Groups to Azure

With SQL Server 2019, you can extend your on-premises AG by building a secondary replica in a Microsoft Azure data center, thus producing a cost-effective hybrid disaster recovery solution. The replica(s) that you chose to build can be within a specific geographic region or across multiple regions that use multiple virtual networks. Not only is this approach a valid disaster recovery plan, but you could also leverage the replicas to offload your backup tasks and reporting requirements. Either way, you can be assured that your secondary data center is scalable, trusted, and extremely reliable.

One very important prerequisite for this hybrid technique is the need for a site-to-site VPN connection, which is required to connect your on-premises network to your Azure infrastructure.

> **Note**
>
> For more details on setup, please see the following documentation: https://docs. microsoft.com/en-us/azure/vpn-gateway/vpn-gateway-howto-site-to-site-classic-portal.

Via SSMS, you should leverage the Add Azure Replica wizard to guide you through the process where, ultimately, you are extending the AG to include a replica based in Azure (a virtual machine).

Once the AG has been created, you will then need to set up an internal listener. There are many steps to this process, such as creating an endpoint on each virtual machine in Azure that hosts a replica and creating client access point cluster resources.

> **Note**
>
> A full set of guidelines and scripts can be found at: https://docs.microsoft.com/en-us/azure/virtual-machines/windows/sqlclassic/virtual-machines-windows-classic-ps-sql-int-listener#create-load-balanced-vm-endpoints-with-direct-server-return.

Replication to Azure SQL Database

One of Azure's most successful technologies within the database ecosystem is Azure SQL Database. One of the main advantages of this technology is that it completely removes the physical administration that you are probably used to with on-premises SQL Server. We no longer need to manage the hardware, storage, backups, operating system, and the database software itself. Even tasks such as consistency checks (DBCC CHECKDB) are Microsoft's responsibility. This frees you up for other important tasks, such as query optimization and indexing strategies, where you can really focus on making your application faster. The other key driving factor for the move to Azure SQL Database is the built-in, fault-tolerant, highly available infrastructure that equates to a 99.99% uptime SLA guarantee.

You shouldn't be surprised to hear that Microsoft has a cloud-first strategy. With the fact that Azure SQL Database shares the same codebase as on-premises SQL Server Database Engine, all the newest features and capabilities are released to Azure first. This means you as the customer will gain from this by knowing that your database software is always patched and updated to the latest version available. Therefore, many customers choose this technology as their enterprise standard. When implementing transactional replication from on-premises SQL Server to Azure SQL Database, you will be able to migrate your data with minimal downtime.

> **Note**
>
> This section illustrates one-way transactional replication. For bidirectional replication, SQL Data Sync is required. This is out of scope for this chapter.

Classic approach

The most common method to migrate to Azure SQL Database is via the **Data Migration Assistant** (DMA) tool. As shown in figure 14.17, this involves many steps, from an actual assessment to any relevant changes and fixes, to the actual migration of data and the schema itself:

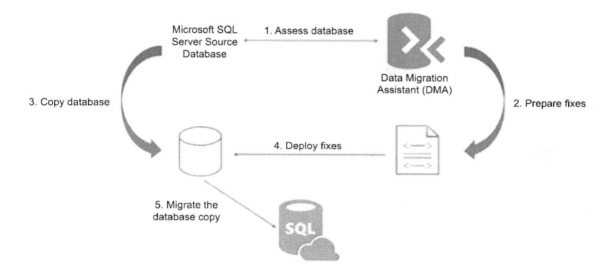

Figure 4.17: Migrating to Azure SQL Database via DMA

The disadvantage of this technique is that it leads to more downtime. So, if you cannot afford this downtime for production mission-critical databases, then transaction replication to Azure SQL Database should be seriously considered.

Transactional replication

Once you have completed setup and the final data changes have been applied to the subscriber (Azure SQL Database), all that is needed is application configuration redirection from your on-premises database to Azure. Please note that Azure SQL Database must be a push subscriber of a SQL Server publisher. Pull subscribers are not supported.

You could also use this technique to move a subset of tables to Azure, which would become a reporting database. Once set up, your users could then use tools such as **SQL Server Reporting Services** (**SSRS**) and Power BI to query the data. This is a great technique because not only are you splitting the OLTP workloads and read-based workloads from each other, but this secondary reporting database is benefiting from being in Azure. As such, all your high-availability and disaster recovery needs are being met with 99.99% SLA uptime:

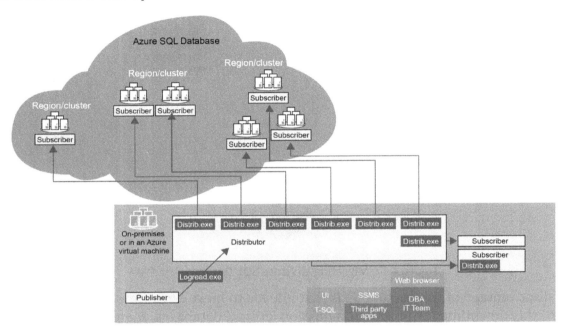

Figure 4.18: Transactional replication in Azure

Prerequisites

- The publisher and distributor must run the following SQL Server versions:

  SQL Server 2019 (15.x)

  SQL Server 2017 (14.x)

  SQL Server 2016 (13.x)

  SQL Server 2014 (12.x) SP1 CU3

  SQL Server 2014 (12.x) RTM CU10

  SQL Server 2012 (11.x) SP2 CU8 or SP3

- Install the latest version of SSMS (18.xx).

- Access to an Azure subscription.

- Access to an Azure SQL database (any region is allowed).

- Tables required for replication must have a primary key.

Setup

1. Under the replication node within SSMS, click **New Publication**:

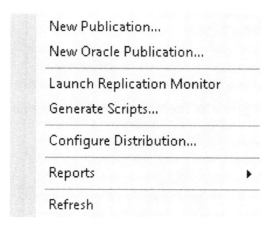

Figure 4.19: Setting up a new publication within SSMS

2. You will then be presented with the wizard:

Figure 4.20: The New Publication dialog box

3. Configure the distribution settings for your environment:

Figure 4.21: Distribution settings dialog box

4. State a UNC path where snapshots can be made accessible:

Figure 4.22: Snapshot dialog box

5. The on-premises SQL Server database will become the publisher:

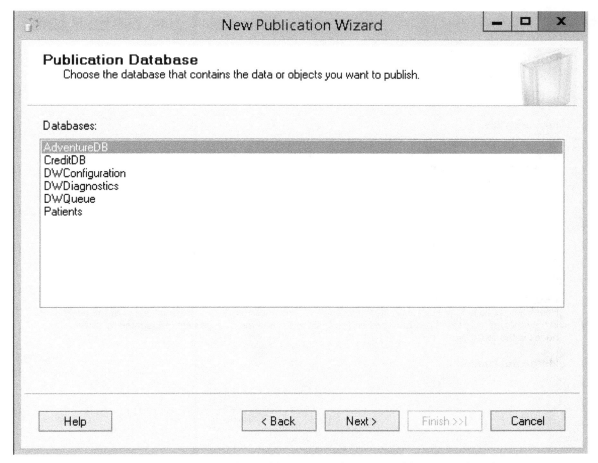

Figure 4.23: Choosing the publication in the New Publication Wizard

6. Only transactional replication is supported hence selected for this demo:

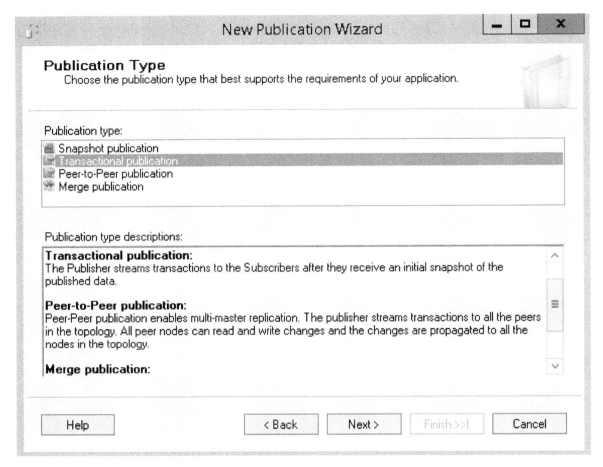

Figure 4.24: Publication type dialog box

7. Add all your tables or just select the tables you require:

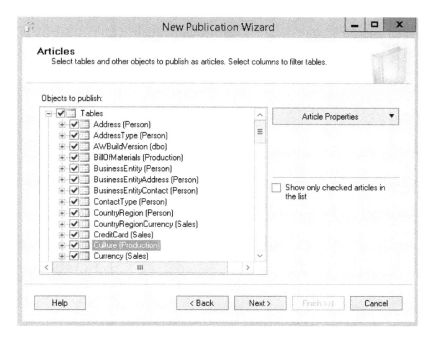

Figure 4.25: Choosing tables in the New Publication Wizard

8. Set up the **Snapshot Agent** as required:

Figure 4.26: Setting up the Snapshot Agent

9. From a security perspective, for production environments, dedicated accounts should be used:

Figure 4.27: Setting up agent security

10. Complete the publication setup:

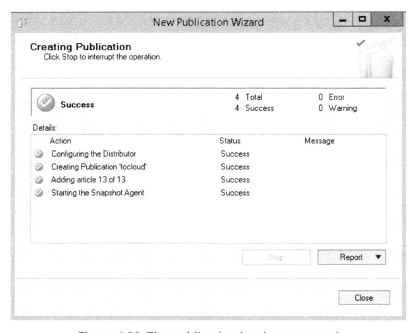

Figure 4.28: The publication has been created

11. Next, go to the subscription setup from the replication node:

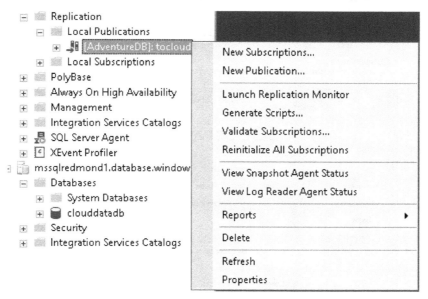

Figure 4.29: Subscription set up menu from the replication node

12. To complete the publication process, you will need to select the correct publisher. For this example, the publisher is called to the cloud:

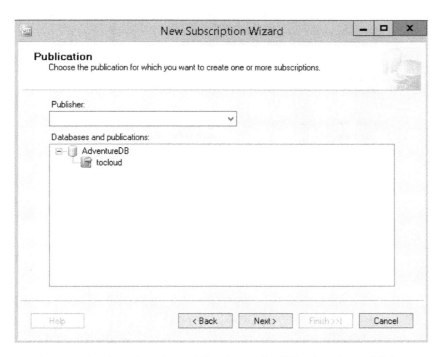

Figure 4.30: Choosing the publication to be linked to the publisher

13. The connection to the subscriber is required, this being Azure SQL Database. Again, dedicated accounts should be used:

Figure 4.31: Connecting to the server

14. Once connected, chose the correct database to become the subscriber:

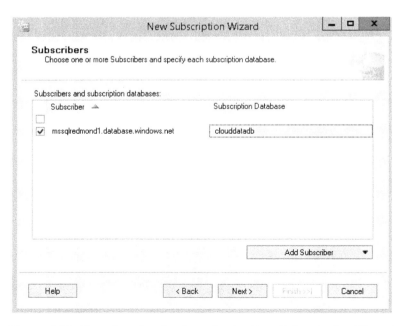

Figure 4.32: Choosing the database in the New Subscription Wizard

15. Next, chose when to initialize the subscription. **Immediately** is selected in the following screenshot:

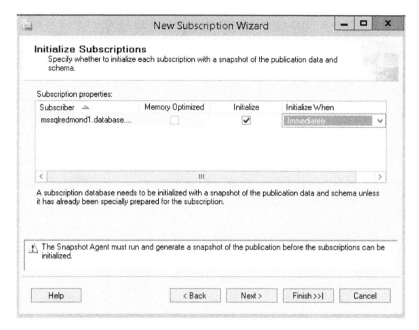

Figure 4.33: Setting up the initialization in the subscription wizard

16. The subscription has been created:

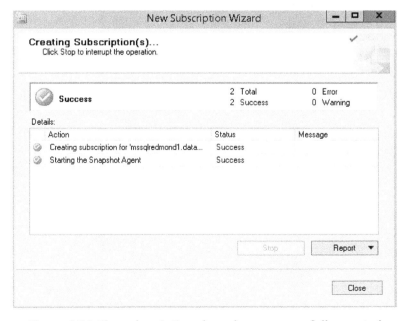

Figure 4.34: The subscriptions have been successfully created

Once complete, you will see, via replication monitor, the objects being created in Azure with the relevant transactions being sent across that hold the data:

Actions in the selected session:

Action Message	Action Time
4 transaction(s) with 217 command(s) were delivered.	21/08/2019 12:57:12
Delivered snapshot .	21/08/2019 12:57:11
Creating Primary Key index on table '[Production].[TransactionHistory]'	21/08/2019 12:57:11
Creating Primary Key index on table '[Person].[PersonPhone]'	21/08/2019 12:57:11
Creating Primary Key index on table '[Sales].[PersonCreditCard]'	21/08/2019 12:57:11
Creating Primary Key index on table '[Person].[Person]'	21/08/2019 12:57:11
Creating Primary Key index on table '[Person].[Address]'	21/08/2019 12:57:11
Bulk copied data into table 'Vendor' (104 rows)	21/08/2019 12:57:10
Bulk copying data into table 'Vendor'	21/08/2019 12:57:10
Bulk copied data into table 'TransactionHistory' (14560 rows)	21/08/2019 12:57:10
Bulk copying data into table 'TransactionHistory'	21/08/2019 12:57:09
Bulk copied data into table 'TransactionHistory' (14105 rows)	21/08/2019 12:57:09
Bulk conving data into table 'TransactionHistory'	21/08/2019 12:57:07

Figure 4.35: The actions displayed by the replication monitor

The replication monitor will display metrics such as performance, latency, and last synchronization:

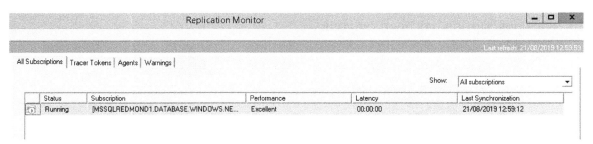

Figure 4.36: The replication monitor dialog

17. Connecting to Azure SQL Database, you will see that the schema and data now exist:

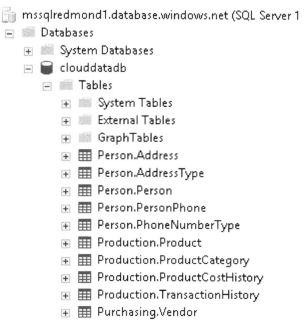

Figure 4.37: The newly created schema

If you decide to take this approach for your reporting strategy, then everything is now complete. However, as mentioned earlier, if this was done to migrate data, once you see that no more transactions need to be replicated, all that is now required is an application configuration change to point to this new cloud location.

The geographical locations of your Azure SQL Database and on-premises SQL Server instances dictates your latency figures. For this example, my data, based in the UK, is being replicated to West Europe with a total latency of 6 seconds, which is acceptable for my demo environment:

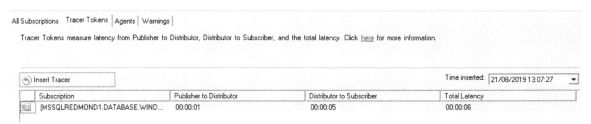

Figure 4.38: Using tokens to measure total latency

5

SQL Server 2019 on Linux

For those new to Linux, there is a rich and deep history of the platform, just as there is one for Windows. At one time, most **database administrators** (**DBA**s) avoided running databases on Linux due to the age of the **operating system** (**OS**) compared to more mature distributions of Unix. Linux was only introduced in 1991 by Linux Torvalds, and he was actively involved in much of its development after failed attempts with other distributions (including flavors of open-source Unix) such as **Hurd**.

As with other open-source Unix distributions, Linux development is done on the **GNU** or Intel C Compiler. Linus hoped to limit any commercial activity, but in the end, Linux has become the most widely used OS distribution used on enterprise servers. Numerous Linux distributions exist, including **Debian**, **Ubuntu**, **CentOS**, **RedHat**, and **Fedora**. Microsoft recently announced there are now more **virtual machines** (**VMs**) running Linux than Windows in the Azure cloud.

Recognizing the power of this shift, Microsoft has embraced the same enterprise OS for their enterprise database platform. This was accomplished with, amazingly, little change in the underlying SQL Server code. Microsoft first introduced Linux support with SQL Server 2017 and continued with the 2019 release of SQL Server 2019. There are incredible new features that offer data virtualization like PolyBase, allowing you to query any data source, including Hadoop clusters, NoSQL, Oracle and Teradata. The data scientist, for the first time ever, has access to Machine Learning Services as part of SQL Server 2019. Linux support has increased from a simple installation to advanced configurations, containers, and advanced multi-distribution support and, let's be honest, you're reading this chapter because you want to find out more about what's offered for Linux regarding SQL Server 2019.

2019 platform support

With SQL Server 2019, support is offered for a list of robust and well-known Linux distributions:

- Red Hat Enterprise Linux (versions 7.3-7.6)

- SUSE Enterprise Linux Server v12 SP2

- Ubuntu 16.04 Long-Term Support (LTS)

These distributions are supported on drive formats XFS or EXT4 and can be used in conjunction with Docker 1.8 on Windows, Mac, or Linux with your favorite platform of Linux container.

There is a wide array of Linux distributions available for installation, and you might be tempted to run SQL Server 2019 on a distribution that's not listed in the certification matrix. Outside of testing an installation, it's best to avoid non-certified Linux distributions for any production use of SQL Server 2019 in your environment. The certification matrix isn't a statement of the stability of any one Linux distribution platform over another, but you can guarantee the ones listed have been tested thoroughly by the SQL Server team to meet the demands of your enterprise database environment.

Many Linux distributions are descendants of a common code base and use similar installations and configurations. Understanding distribution similarities is important, and an example of this is the Linux Red Hat installation for SQL Server 2019. Very similar database software installation steps can be used on CentOS or Fedora, but this doesn't change the fact that of the three distributions listed, only Linux Red Hat is supported by Microsoft.

This results in the need for best practices in order for you to become comfortable with the supported Linux installations and to create policies to require the supported distributions for use with SQL Server 2019 to ensure you have support, along with certified updates that are required for any enterprise database environment.

Why move databases to SQL Server on Linux?

Our world is getting smaller, and all the while, technology is expanding to do more for more people. As with other data platforms, SQL Server has continued on its path to lead in Linux as it has in Windows for decades.

As agile development practices and DevOps become the norm, we are expected to move faster and with fewer environment silos. As teams begin to form across multiple technical areas, often including business stakeholders, SQL Server 2019 can also broaden to support all these areas.

The skills required to maintain a Windows server are very different than those required to support Linux. Although Linux is a "flavor" of Unix distribution, other direct Unix distributions, such as HP-UX and AIX, have mostly been abandoned for a unified Linux offering. Linux has become the preferred OS for this revolution.

Windows desktop installations still run the world, but research data has shown that Linux is the OS for enterprise endeavors. TOP 500 (https://top500.org) is a website that provides statistical information related to enterprise and supercomputers, including compute vendors, CPUs, and OSes. The data is based on the top 500 in any category and, as demonstrated by *Figure* 5.1, only Linux versions are in their top 500 of general-purpose systems used for high-end applications:

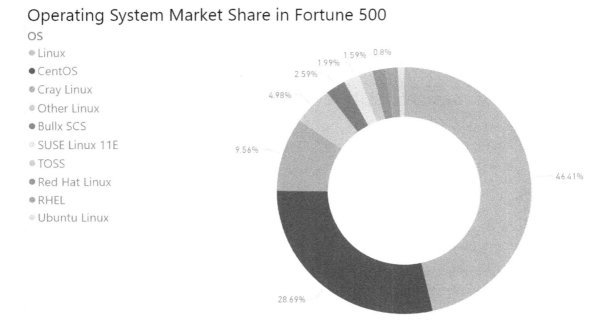

Figure 5.1: Linux rules the enterprise web server world. Source: https://top500.org

Armed with this type of valuable information, it is apparent why Microsoft has embraced Linux and chosen to make it part of the Azure cloud.

Installation and configuration

There are different installation utilities depending on the Linux distribution that you choose. The processes of installing SQL Server 2019 on the various distributions are very similar, no matter what distribution you are working on:

1. Download the package to the repository.

2. Install the package.

3. Configure the installation.

Using RedHat as an example (the commands may be different for other distributions), the first step is to update the repository with the SQL Server 2019 installation, which is currently in preview.

To find the correct installation in the repository, you can use a `list` command and grep (find) for the string you're searching, which in this case is mssql:

```
yum list installed
```

The distribution of Microsoft product containers is best retrieved from the official Microsoft Container Registry. This repository has a considerable variety of images beyond Microsoft, including other operating systems and applications. A `curl` command is used to access the repository, and the `-o` tells the **transfer** utility what file to transfer from the certified Microsoft repository, mcr.microsoft/mssql/server:vNext-CTP2.0.

To transfer the SQL Server 2019 installation from inside a Red Hat server, run the following command:

```
$ sudo curl -o <repository file> <repository location>
```

Or as an example, as follows:

```
sudo curl -o /etc/yum.repos.d/mssql-server.repo https://packages.
microsoft.com/config/rhel/7/mssql-server-preview.repo
```

Now that the installation has been added to the local repository, the next step is to install SQL Server using a `yum` command:

```
sudo yum install -y mssql-server
```

We must now configure and set up the password for the administrator:

```
sudo /opt/mssql/bin/mssql-conf setup
```

There are three main questions you will be asked during the configuration:

```
Choose an edition of SQL Server:
  1) Evaluation (free, no production use rights, 180-day limit)
  2) Developer (free, no production use rights)
  3) Express (free)
  4) Web (PAID)
  5) Standard (PAID)
  6) Enterprise (PAID) - CPU Core utilization restricted to 20 physical/40 hyperthreaded
  7) Enterprise Core (PAID) - CPU Core utilization up to Operating System Maximum
  8) I bought a license through a retail sales channel and have a product key to enter.

Details about editions can be found at
https://go.microsoft.com/fwlink/?LinkId=852748&clcid=0x409

Use of PAID editions of this software requires separate licensing through a
Microsoft Volume Licensing program.
By choosing a PAID edition, you are verifying that you have the appropriate
number of licenses in place to install and run this software.

Enter your edition(1-8): 2
```

Figure 5.2: Configuration of the SQL Server installation

In *Figure 5.2*, I chose to enter 2 for the Developer edition.

You will then be asked to confirm your agreement with the licensing terms and then to set the SQL Server administrator password, and then confirm it. If the entries don't match, you will be given another chance to enter the password and confirmation.

Once this is done, then the configuration script will complete the process. A symlink will be created and the SQL Server processes will be restarted to finish the installation.

Then we can verify that the service is running. As this is a Linux process, there are two ways to do this:

```
systemctl status mssql-server
```

The output is as follows:

```
[mssql@Redhat2019 ~]$ systemctl status mssql-server
● mssql-server.service - Microsoft SQL Server Database Engine
   Loaded: loaded (/usr/lib/systemd/system/mssql-server.service; enabled; vendor preset: disabled)
   Active: active (running) since Thu 2019-05-09 21:20:13 UTC; 6min ago
     Docs: https://docs.microsoft.com/en-us/sql/linux
 Main PID: 10172 (sqlservr)
   CGroup: /system.slice/mssql-server.service
           ├─10172 /opt/mssql/bin/sqlservr
           └─10196 /opt/mssql/bin/sqlservr
```

Figure 5.3: Status of the SQL Server service on Linux

The system control will return a validation of the service (if it's running) and identify what process IDs are part of the service. For SQL Server, there are two that fork from the service, shown in the preceding example as `10172` and `10196`.

You can also see this same information by using the following process utility command:

```
ps -ef | grep sqlservr
```

```
[mssql@Redhat2019 ~]$ ps -ef | grep sqlservr
mssql      10172       1  0 21:20 ?        00:00:00 /opt/mssql/bin/sqlservr
mssql      10196   10172  5 21:20 ?        00:00:29 /opt/mssql/bin/sqlservr
```

Figure 5.4: checking for running processes on Linux

As you can see in the example, the same two processes are displayed (`10172` and `10196`), along with the parent process IDs (`1`, `10172`), the start time (`21:20`), and the executable path (`/opt/mssql/bin/sqlservr`).

The last step is to ensure that the ports required for remote connections are open. If this step isn't performed, connections will time out:

```
sudo firewall-cmd --zone=public --add-port=1433/tcp –permanent
```

The **firewall** must be restarted to put the changes into effect:

```
sudo firewall-cmd --reload
```

Once you have installed SQL Server, there are multiple ways to interact with your instance. It's essential to have access from the host, and to do so requires the **sqlcmd utility**. To install it, first you must add it to the repository (if it's not already available). You must switch over to the root user to update the repository files:

```
$ sudo su
```

Once you're switched over, update the repository with a new entry:

```
$ curl https://packages.microsoft.com/config/rhel/7/prod.repo > /etc/
yum.repos.d/msprod.repo
$ exit
```

After you've exited as a super-user, run the installation. Answer yes to any questions confirming the installation:

```
$ sudo yum remove mssql-tools unixODBC-utf16-devel
$ sudo yum install mssql-tools unixODBC-devel
```

Once the installation is complete, you can log into your new SQL Server instance using the following command, and entering the password when prompted:

```
$ sqlcmd -S locahost,1433 -U <username>
```

Now that you have installed SQL Server, configured your installation, and have command-line tools in order to interact with the instance, it's time to find out more about interacting with Linux.

Improvements in SQL Server 2019

This book contains chapters that focus on different areas of the SQL Server 2019 release, but there are significant enhancements around the SQL Server 2019 release for Linux that deserve to be highlighted in their own chapters. It is worth taking the time to understand how these enhancements affect performance, features, and interaction with Linux. One of the most important enhancements is the interaction between SQL Server 2019 on Linux and services such as Azure Machine Learning and the Azure Kubernetes Service.

Machine Learning Services on Linux

Machine Learning is a service, but it's accessible from a SQL Server 2019 on a Linux virtual machine or on-premises Linux host. Data Scientists can connect to and create new data models in Azure Notebooks or the well-known Jupyter Notebooks, using Python and/or R to choose pipelines or run pipelines to perform machine learning.

Supported Linux distributions and installation formats include:

- Redhat Enterprise Server
- Ubuntu (apt)
- SUSE (zypper)
- Redhat, SUSE, and CentOS (RPM)

Following the installation and configuration of SQL Server 2019 on Linux, a subsequent installation of the `mssql-mlservices` package must be performed in the same repository as the existing SQL Server. The process of installing this is dependent upon the Linux distribution (`yum` for RedHat, `apt-get` for Ubuntu, and so on), but there are steps that need to be performed afterward in order to complete it successfully:

1. Add the MSSQL Linux user to the configuration account for the Machine Learning service.

2. Issue the command to accept the end-user license.

3. Configure the networking and port settings for Python.

4. Set the environment variables for R in the `.bashRC` file

5. Update the SQL Server configuration to make external scripts enabled.

6. Restart all services and the database to put the configuration changes into effect.

admin-cli is required to configure and manage the web and compute nodes that are part of operationalizing machine learning servers. This includes stopping and starting Linux resources that are part of the machine learning server configuration and running diagnostics when something is amiss.

The `az` command is used to perform the next steps to test and configure endpoints:

```
az login
```

The next step is to use the specific machine learning commands to configure servers that will be part of the Machine Learning service:

```
az ml -admin -endpoint <endpoint>
```

Once you've run the command to add any and all servers to the configuration, run a diagnostic to validate the additions:

```
az ml -admin diagnostic run
```

The command-line utility uses similar commands in Azure, utilizing the `az ml admin` command, and this includes the `help` option to return arguments and descriptions of each:

```
az ml admin -help
```

Data can then be stored inside SQL Server 2019 and pre-packaged stored procedures simplify machine learning and utilize resources from Azure Machine Learning to distribute the workload.

Predictions on continuous models (also known as regression modeling), forecasting, and classifications can be performed using `AutoMLTrain`. This will train, validate, black-and white-list, along with other machine learning data modeling training, and are then stored inside SQL Server tables. Metrics are then returned when the `AutoMLGetMetrics` stored procedure is executed, and new predictions are created from the originally trained values with the `AutoMlPredict` stored procedure.

This is an impressive update considering that only Python was available in SQL Server 2017, and we needed `sp_execute_external_script` to run Python inside the database.

The biggest takeaway for the data platform professional is to understand that machine learning is available to beginner and expert data scientists using SQL Server 2019 and Azure Machine Learning without extensive knowledge, allowing everyone to reap the benefits of machine learning. To read more about this scenario, go to: https://cloudblogs.microsoft.com/sqlserver/2019/04/16/automated-machine-learning-from-sql-server-with-azure-machine-learning/.

Kubernetes

Microsoft, to further embrace containers open-source paradigm, have added additional capabilities in SQL Server 2019 when running docker images in Kubernetes-based deployments. Just as with other deployment orchestration platforms, Kubernetes primary purpose is to run orchestrated container-based workloads within clusters of multiple nodes. For the SQL Server database administrator, Kubernetes is often used with the goal of either **high availability (HA)**, or **scalability**. SQL Server 2019 can take great advantage of this orchestration, allowing for faster recovery times due to interruption of service and failover orchestration deployments within multiple pods between clusters, which can also increase scalability opportunities.1

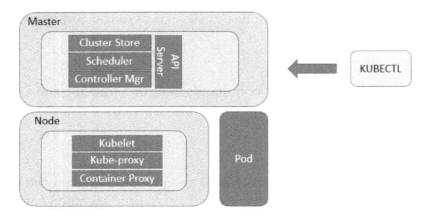

Figure 5.5: Diagram of Kubernetes cluster architecture

A pod, as demonstrated in *Figure* 5.5, can contain single or multiple containers. One of the benefits of pods is that they have all the benefits associated with containerization, including portability and highly optimized resource utilization. Along with the pods and containers, there are deployment controllers that execute

For SQL Server 2019 containers to run successfully inside Kubernetes, state persistence must be set up. It relies on storage resources, (that is, volumes) accessible by underlying cluster nodes.

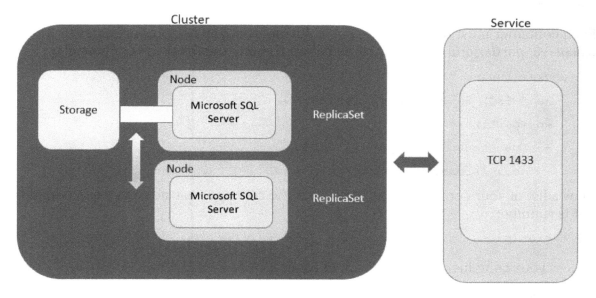

Figure 5.6: Diagram of high availability Kubernetes cluster with SQL Server 2019 and persistent storage for fast recovery scenario.

The generic volumes typically serve as persistent stores for containerized workloads. They can also serve as local disks attached directly to individual cluster nodes or shared storage mounted across multiple nodes if needed for specific configurations.

In case of failure for a SQL Server 2019 deployed to a Kubernetes cluster, quicker recovery due to clustering can be achieved thanks to the storage and clustering configuration.

For monitoring, standard Kubernetes tools are the best choice and SQL Server containers are available to monitor from standard database monitoring and management tools. With the increased recovery, flexibility and scalability options, Kubernetes is an attractive choice for SQL Server 2019 with Linux.

Working with Docker and Linux

To create a Docker container with an installation of SQL Server 2019 included, you'll require a local installation of Docker or Docker server access. Using an example for Windows, open Command Prompt (running Docker commands inside the PowerShell command line can lead to inconsistent results).

Check for existing Docker containers that are currently available and their status:

```
$ docker ps -a
```

Each container must have a unique name. Ensure that you use proper values for the **password**, port(s), and container name before running the following command:

```
$ docker run -e "ACCEPT_EULA=Y"

    -e "MSSQL_SA_PASSWORD=<password>"

    -p <port:port>

    --name <container name>

    -d mcr.microsoft.com/mssql/server:2019-CTP3.2 ubuntu
```

View a list of your containers and verify that the container has not only been created, but is running:

```
$ docker ps -a
```

Access your container, log in, and run in Bash:

```
$ docker exec -it <container name> "bash"
```

Docker should log you into the container, and the command prompt should be displayed. You are now interacting with Linux and not your workstation command prompt. Although these steps aren't very different to other Docker commands, knowing how easy it is to build a Docker image with Linux and SQL Server is important. If you have a Linux Docker image already in place, the instructions for installing SQL Server can be performed with minor changes to add SQL Server to it, then an image can be created in order to save time and management going forward.

Adding Kubernetes to this combination then pushes it farther by allowing pods to be built out of Docker containers that are part of a group: application, database, and web containers that all belong as part of one deployment, granting the DBA the ability to work with the rest of the IT system to serve the business better. By doing this all in Linux, the SQL Server DBA can be more collaborative, less siloed, and can do it all faster.

Change data capture

The **change data capture (CDC)** feature in SQL Server is a valuable way to ingest data from a source, transform it, and then publish it to new tables or a secondary database. This feature is now available in SQL Server 2019 for Linux.

As the code base is the same in SQL Server for Linux as it is for Windows, the same process is required to enable the feature:

```
EXEC sys.sp_cdc_enable_db
```

This will create the system objects, the CDC user, metadata, and the CDC schema as part of the procedure to set up CDC.

The same templates available from **SQL Server Management Studio (SSMS)** in the Template Explorer will work for CDC in Linux and can speed up the process of implementing a CDC solution.

Hybrid Buffer Pool and PMEM

Eliminating latency is the goal of optimization and persistent memory. **PMEM**, or storage class memory, is a new tool that helps by bypassing making a copy of data in the clean pages area of the buffer pool and instead stores these pages in PMEM so that they can be directly accessed in a new feature called Hybrid Buffer Pool.

PMEM stands for persistent memory, and it's an area of non-volatile storage that performs similarly to memory. As the term can also be used to describe hardware, there may be some confusion as to what it's called, the following should clarify this:

- PMEM or PM (**Persistent Memory**) ← This is the correct term for SQL Server 2019
- **Storage Class Memory** (SCM)
- **Non-Volatile Memory** (NVM)
- **Byte-Addressable Storage** (BAS)

For SQL Server 2019, PMEM is part of the memory bus and eliminates I/O latency. It does this by eliminating the extra need to copy pages to **DRAM** or the I/O penalty of going to disk. There's a performance gain from accessing persistent storage designed specifically for this purpose. To enhance this feature, Microsoft has added the ability for Hybrid Buffer Pool to run in enlightened mode, letting it use **memcpy** operations to access persistent storage directly.

Database files that can take advantage of PMEM include:

- Database files
- Transaction logs
- In-memory OLTP checkpoint files

To utilize PMEM, you need to enable enlightenment of the files you want SQL Server to take advantage of PMEM with. This will require a Linux utility used to manage non-volatile memory, named **ndctl**. If it isn't already on the Linux host you have installed SQL Server 2019 on, you will need to install it, most likely using **yum** or **apt-get**. Depending on the Linux distribution, the following steps may have to be performed to configure **NDCTL** after the installation:

```
$ sudo install ndctl

Installed:

  Ndctl.x86_64 0:62-1.el7

$which ndctl

/usr/bin/ndctl
```

Once configured, to enable PMEM on a file, you need to create a namespace, a location of isolated storage that will be used for PMEM:

```
$ndctl create-namespace -f -e namespace0.0 –mode=devdax –map=mem
```

In the example, I've created a PMEM namespace using cloud storage I created specifically for the Hybrid Buffer Pool. You can view what namespaces have been created using the following command:

```
$ ndctl list
```

The next step is to mount the namespace and set the extent size. For our example, we'll name the mount **pmem1** and make the extent size **2m**:

```
$ mkfs.xfs -f /dv1/pmem1 mount -o dv1,noatime /dv1/pmem1 /mnt/dv1

xfs_io -c "extsize 2m" /mnt/dv1
```

Once configured, then we can allocate files to use PMEM, but you must restart SQL Server before the changes can take effect:

```
$ sudo systemctl stop mssql-server

$ sudo systemctl start mssql-server
```

And once you've restarted SQL Server, check the status:

```
$ sudo systemctl status mssql-server
```

Now that you've verified that the restart has completed, you can create a new database to take advantage of PMEM or choose to move files from an existing SQL Server to the PMEM location. Moving datafiles to this new location is no different than moving files to another existing drive.

Log into the database using **sqlcmd** and move the files:

```
sqlcmd -U <login> -S "<localhost,port>"

ALTER DATABASE database_name SET OFFLINE;

GO

ALTER DATABASE database_name MODIFY FILE ( NAME = logical_name,
FILENAME = '/dv1/pmem1/<dbname>/data' );

GO
```

Once this is complete, bring the database online and available:

```
ALTER DATABASE database_name SET ONLINE;

GO
```

For data files that were moved to the new PMEM location, you can enable Hybrid Buffer Pool using:

```
ALTER SERVER CONFIGURATION SET MEMORY_OPTIMIZED HYBRID_BUFFER_POOL =
ON;
```

Or:

```
ALTER DATABASE <databaseName> SET MEMORY_OPTIMIZED = ON;
```

It's important to remember that only clean pages are directly referenced on a PMEM device. Dirty pages will be kept in DRAM and will eventually be written back to the PMEM device once they're clean.

Distributed Transaction Coordinator on Linux

With the introduction of the endpoint mapper functionality for SQL Server 2019 on Linux, the addition of **Microsoft Distributed Transaction Coordinator (MSDTC)** has become easy, too. MSDTC on a Linux host or VM will need port 135 open for the RPC endpoint mapper process to bind (**network.rpcport**). Best practice also dictates that you should definitely set the port MSDTC listens to (**distributedtransaction. servertcpport**); otherwise, a random port can be chosen upon restart, creating a loss in service when a firewall exception hasn't been prepared for the change in ports that are open to the outside.

To statically set the port for MSDTC to listen to, use the following command:

```
$ sudo /opt/mssql/bin/mssql-conf set network.rpcport 13500
```

SQL Server must be restarted for this change to take effect:

```
$ sudo systemctl restart mssql-server
```

After this configuration change, the firewall rules will need to be updated on the Linux host. Depending on the Linux distribution, the command could differ, but for Red Hat, it's as follows:

```
$ sudo firewall-cmd –zone=public –add-port=135/tcp
```

Do this for each port that must be open for MSDTC, then reload to put the changes into effect:

```
$ sudo firewall-cmd –reload
```

To complete the process, you must install the stored procedures for MSDTC into the database that will be taking advantage of the host configuration. Log into the database with **sqlcmd** and enter the following commands:

```
$ sqlcmd -U <login> -S "<dbserver>.database.windows.net" -d <database name>
    exec sp_sqljdbc_xa_install
```

After installing these valuable stored procedures, you'll be able to use the XA procedures in the database for MSDTC. For those who want MSDTC on all their databases, SQL Server 2019 now provides it on Linux as well.

Replication

A DBA's ability to provide access to the data for the business is an essential part of the role. Replication of data to secondary databases, either for reporting, data protection, or transformation, is an important feature. SQL Server 2019 on Linux now includes support for replication outside of VM replication with Site Recovery. The architecture support includes SQL Server 2019 on Linux in a container with the SQL Agent.

In any SQL Server replicated environment, there are three main identifiers:

- Publisher
- Subscriber
- Distributer

Due to the goal of replication being failover if a failure occurs, a SQL Server instance that is part of a replication scenario can be any one of the three options. Replication configuration can be performed from the command line with stored procedures, or from SSMS Publication types are decided by the subscriber's needs:

- **Transactional**: A per transaction replication from publisher to subscriber.

- **Snapshot**: A set of replicated transactions and updates on a regular interval are collected and applied to the subscriber.

- **Merge**: Changes are merged from the publisher to the subscriber environment.

A solid replication architecture design, including geo-replication, can offer disaster recovery, secondary reporting environments, and manual high availability. With this addition to SQL Server 2019 on Linux, this offers more options for the business regarding which OS to run SQL Server on.

SQL Server tools

The tools you use to interact with the database are incredibly important to how you work every day. With the introduction of Linux, the shift in how you manage the database doesn't have to change as much as you might expect.

Azure Data Studio

Azure Data Studio is the newest cross-platform tool available from Microsoft. While many database professionals still use SSMS, this required a Windows or Windows VM to run the product. Azure Data Studio provides support for not just Windows, but also macOS and Linux.

Azure Data Studio also keeps in step with application/development integration, including integration via Git/GitHub, and the output from the console can be saved in various formats, including CSV, text, and JSON.

There are monthly releases of the product, and these updates mean new features and consistent enhancements. Azure Data Studio is available for most common Linux distributions:

- Red Hat Enterprise Linux 7.4

- Red Hat Enterprise Linux 7.3

- SUSE Linux Enterprise Server v12 SP2

- Ubuntu 16.04

There are three different installation methods to support the various Linux distributions in the form of a Debian file, an RPM file, and a gzipped TAR file.

Depending on the Linux distribution, the installation will be slightly different. All the following commands assume that you are logging in with the user that will be copying the file to the host and that the installation will be performed in the user's home directory. For Debian, a simple Bash command will perform the installation. While logged into your host or VM, open a terminal after downloading the file and perform the following, depending on the installation.

DEB for Debian:

```
cd ~

sudo dpkg -i azuredatastudio-linux-<version>.deb
```

YUM for Redhat or CentOS:

```
cd ~

yum install ./azuredatastudio-linux-<version>.rpm
```

TAR for Ubuntu, SUSE, etc.

For the TAR file installation, again, log into the host or VM and then you must untar (extract) the file and add the environment path to the main path in order to run the command file (`.bashrc`):

```
cd ~

cp ~ /<directory the file was downloaded to/azuredatastudio-linux-
<version>.tar.gz ~

tar -xvf ~/azuredatastudio-linux-<version>.tar.gz

cat 'export PATH=$PATH:~/azuredatastudio-linux-x64"' >> ~/.bashrc
```

Once you have installed Azure Data Studio, you can launch it by typing the following at the terminal:

```
azuredatastudio
```

Once it's launched, click on **New Connection**. The following values are required to connect successfully:

- **Connection type**: Microsoft SQL Server, (Azure SQL, Azure Data Warehouse), Microsoft BDC

- **Server**: For Azure, this information is displayed in the server resource overview:

Figure 5.7: Azure host information in the Azure portal

- **Authentication type**: SQL Login or Windows Authentication or Azure Active Directory

- **Username**: Self-explanatory and depends on the choice in Authentication Type

- **Password**: Password for the user

- **Database**: Database to connect to once logged into the server

- **Server group**: Optional (set to default in the connection)

- **Name**: Optional

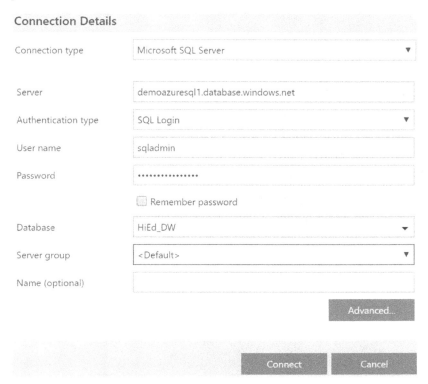

Figure 5.8: Configuring a connection in Azure Data Studio

If you haven't logged into the Azure resource previously, a prompt will take you through setting up a firewall rule to access the resource; otherwise, you'll be connected to the database and you'll be ready to manage resources.

There are numerous keyboard shortcuts pre-configured in Azure Data Studio, and you can personalize and add your own. Click on **File | Preferences | Keyboard Shortcuts**. The following window will pop up:

Figure 5.9: Keyboard shortcut configurations for Azure Data Studio

From the Ubuntu console, you can start a new notebook by typing *Ctrl* + N. The JSON configuration has been minimized as much as possible to make it easier for those who are more accustomed to using SQL, providing as much value as possible when using SQL to complete what is needed.

The benefit of Azure Data Studio is the ability to build out what is needed to make you most productive. There are extensive visualizations to monitor database performance and usage, which is a benefit for those who are new to managing databases on Linux hosts.

Command-line query tools for SQL in Linux

There are two primary command-line query tools that are available for SQL Server on Linux, one that is old and one that is brand new:

- sqlcmd

- mssql-cli

SQLCMD

For the SQL DBA, SQLCMD is a familiar command-line tool that is also available in Linux. This is part of the mssql-tools installation that will be available for most, if not all, SQL Servers on Linux, and can be used to run scripts, query databases, and system procedures.

Installation differs depending the Linux distribution, but for our example, the Ubuntu installation will be used to show how an installation would be performed to update the package to your Ubuntu update for the latest mssql-tools package and then installation:

```
sudo apt-get update
sudo apt-get install mssql-tools
```

Updates are regularly available for the SQLCMD utility. The newest additions are available for the following Linux distributions, and now include Azure Active Directory multi-factor authentication:

- Red Hat Linux, Enterprise

- Ubuntu

- SUSE Linux Enterprise Server

- Docker

- MacOS

The following is an example of using `sqlcmd` to log into a SQL Server database on Linux and run a query:

```
sqlcmd -U <username> -S "<vmname>. <zone>.cloudapp.azure.com" -P
"<password>" -d "<database>" -Q "<sqlstatement>; "


sqlcmd -U <username> -S "<vmname>. <zone>.cloudapp.azure.com" -P
"<password>" -d "<database>" -i "<filename>.sql"
```

One of the biggest additions to sqlcmd is an older feature that's been rediscovered and is beneficial to large table migrations in the cloud: **Bulk Copy Protocol** (**BCP**). Many databases have only a few very large tables as part of a migration that aren't fulfilled by traditional migration means. One of the ways to accomplish a successful data migration is to use a simple migration utility that removes all complex user interfaces and added features, such as BCP.

MSSQL-CLI

The newer command-line tool focused on the Linux server, MSSQL-CLI was added in SQL Server 2017 as a tool with the future in mind. The installation is maintained via GitHub, and a large set of Linux distributions are currently supported:

- Debian 8 and 9

- Ubuntu

- CentOS 7

- OpenSUSE 42.2

- Red Hat Enterprise Linux 7

- SUSE Enterprise Linux 12

- Fedora 25 and 26

Installation is a single simple command:

```
$ pip install mssql-cli
```

Once it's installed, you have access to another query tool to use in interaction with SQL Server databases on Linux, macOS, and Windows. Unlike sqlcmd, MSSQL-CLI includes T-SQL IntelliSense, so as you type in your query, potential options for columns, tables, and procedures will be provided to ease demands on the user, decrease the amount of manual entry, and decrease the potential for errors:

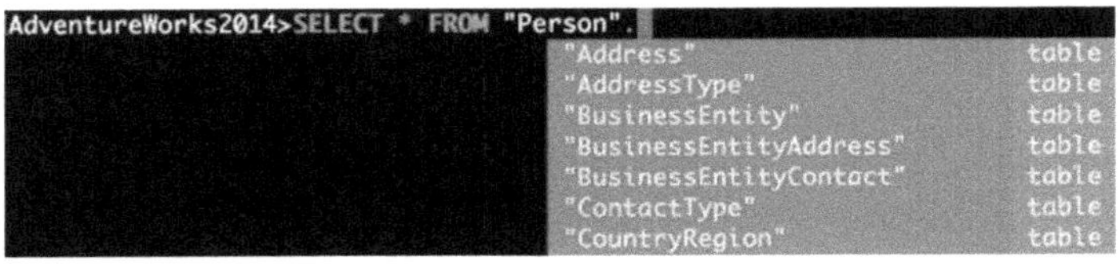

Figure 5.10: IntelliSense population for columns in MSSQL-CLI

Multi-line edit mode and syntax highlighting provides the ability to format statements for ease of readability and management. A configuration file can personalize settings to create a better end-user experience, too.

Enhanced focus on scripting

With the release of SQL Server 2019, a significant amount of enhancements and feature releases for the Linux release provide a more robust experience. Recognizing that the technology industry has embraced Linux as the enterprise OS platform of choice, Microsoft has invested heavily in making it easy for the SQL DBA to move current database workloads to Linux, with as little impact as possible on the business.

One of the biggest breakthroughs from the DBAs point of view was the addition of PowerShell on Linux. A DBA is often viewed as only as good as the suite of scripts they are using to ease the management, maintenance, and monitoring of the database environment. Having the ability to lift and shift these scripts and their workload reduces the demand for the DBA to recreate something they'd already invested considerable time in.

An important fact remains. No matter how essential PowerShell is to the SQL DBA, it still isn't at a point where it can compete with the history and maturity of Bash. In all areas of SQL Server 2019 tools, there will be an option to export templates in multiple scripted formats. The one that is listed as the **command-line interface (CLI)** is really **Bash** scripting.

It can be a bit intimidating for anyone who strongly identifies with PowerShell that another shell scripting language currently has the upper hand, but as PowerShell builds from its infancy on Linux, it faces an uphill struggle with Bash. As someone who was trained on the Korn shell, the situation resonates with me. Although my preferred scripting language is Korn, I recognize that Bash is the shell scripting language with the most seniority, and it's important to understand that knowing more than one scripting language makes you more of an asset in your technical career.

The SQL DBA in the Linux world

There are some vital differences between Linux and Windows. An essential difference is that in Linux, everything is configured as a file. Even directories and device drivers are identified as text files. The kernel views the directory structure as a series of files with a clear hierarchal layout that culminates in the root directory (also known as /). The concept of alphabetical identifiers as mount points is different on windows, which are more likely to be identified by user (u) or disk (d).

For all this identification, very little of it has any meaning for the Linux kernel. As it identifies everything as a file, it doesn't require an understanding of hierarchy and is programmed to identify everything in a horizontal structure. The kernel refers to everything via nodes. The unique identifiers that represent each file, directory, and permission among the nodes allows the kernel to search, locate, and identify all processing at immense speeds.

Users and groups

Along with root, there are users that are created to create clear and defined logins and access. These are the logins and owners of files on the OS, and each of these users is assigned to one or more groups that allow them a set of permissions for different file structures. For the Oracle DBA, it is common to log in as their username (for example, **dsmith**) and then switch user (with the su command) over to **Oracle** (the database and Oracle installation owner) to perform critical tasks.

Figure 5.11: Switching user with the su command

Belonging to a group allows you to perform the same tasks and have access to files in directories. Each user in an enterprise Linux server environment has a home directory that contains configuration files and aliases for the user. The names of these files are often prepended with a dot, and this is to ensure they aren't displayed by a simple list (1s) command unless specifically requested.

Azure Cloud Shell

If you are working on a VM with SQL 2019, you have the option to interact with the host via the command line in Azure Cloud Shell. This web interface offers simplified access to all cloud resources inside your Azure environment, and with the addition of Azure cloud storage, a static storage resource to house files and scripts. Azure Cloud Shell provides the option to set the session to Bash or PowerShell, but both types of scripts can be executed from either shell profile.

The benefit of Azure Cloud Shell is quicker access to resource information, the automation of mass deployments, and VM changes from the command line. The Azure portal allows those who are less comfortable with the CLI to manage most of these same things. Numerous extensions are also available specifically to facilitate management and deployment tasks, including Azure DevOps, GitHub, and Jenkins.

Windows Subsystem for Linux

The second option for many to consider is for those users on Windows 10. It's the new **Windows Subsystem for Linux version 2 (WSL2)**. Unlike an emulator, WSL2 is a full Linux kernel inside Windows, providing the ability to run any terminal commands as you would on a full Linux system. This means that an emulator is no longer required. WSL1 was released with Azure Sphere last year, but this is the first time a Linux kernel will ship with Windows, and WSL2 will take the Windows professional to the next step of true kernel-level performance and interaction.

Root, the super-user

Root is similar, but not equivalent to the Administrator on a Windows server. **Root** is referred to as the super-user and the owner of the top-level directory and the OS on a Linux server.

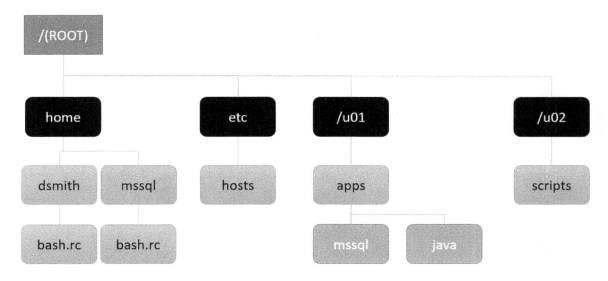

Figure 5.12: Example of files and directories in Linux

Root has power over everything inside the Linux OS. A DBA must remember this when granting root access to a Linux host. Best practice says that no one should log in as root unless a distinct requirement exists, and then it should be done with extreme caution.

Switch User Domain Owner (**SUDO**) privileges are granted to a user with the knowledge to perform deep-level actions, but all SUDO actions are logged and are easily audited in the server logs if no switch from their original login was performed. SUDO should also be used with caution and only when necessary due to the sheer capability of the root user. The login to the Linux box should be owned by a unique user, and then the user should switch user (`su - <super user>`) to perform the task that requires escalated privileges.

An increase in security breaches across the globe, along with the addition of the cloud, has emphasized the importance of server design, including users who have access to super-user and other privileges. Application user logins should only use SUDO, stick bit, iptables, **SUID**, **SGID**, and other proper group creation/allocation when required.

Most current installations of SQL Server on a Linux host I've encountered are installed as root, also known as the domain owner. This isn't a viable installation, and the vulnerability can be understood if we use an example of a Linux host with SQL Server that utilizes a traditional Excel data load process.

If an Excel spreadsheet with undetected malware is uploaded onto the Linux host, it will be owned by root, offering a hacker full access and privileges as root. If a proper configuration had been chosen, with the SQL Server installation and folders owned by an application user with limited privileges, this type of attack would be isolated and therefore would have less of an impact.

DBAs follow strict guidelines regarding granting database privileges, and Linux administrators will consistently request that a DBA or application developer justifies greater permissions to any directory or protected file on the Linux host.

By using `su` and `sudo` privileges, the Linux OS can audit who is performing tasks that require su privileges and clearly identify the original user. The need to switch over to a more privileged user may assist in deterring human mistakes. `su` and `sudo` have less data access than the owner of the files, providing data security.

The goal of this chapter was to introduce you to the impressive new features of SQL Server 2019 on Linux and the vast enhancements since the release of SQL Server 2017, including:

- Supported distributions of Linux

- Installation of SQL Server on Linux

- Machine learning services

- High availability and containers

- SQL Server tools for Linux

- Understanding Linux as a SQL Server DBA

This information should give you a strong foundation for the features and changes required to manage SQL Server 2019 on Linux to help you understand why so many have brought this OS platform into their own organization. Also consider spending the time to dig into chapters dedicated to features such as AGs, containers, and SQL tools to get the most out of this book.

6

SQL Server 2019 in Containers and Kubernetes

Most SQL Server deployments are achieved via traditional methods: on physical servers or virtual machines (on-premises or in the cloud). Cloud-based offerings such as Azure SQL Database or Azure SQL Database Managed Instance are considered **Platform as a Service** (**PaaS**) offerings and offer the ability to deploy databases and instances respectively without needing to worry about managing the underlying **operating system** (**OS**). There is now a newer option to consider for deploying SQL Server: containers.

SQL Server 2017 was the first version of SQL Server to support containers. While containers are part of SQL Server Big Data Clusters (see *Chapter 9, SQL Server 2019 Big Data Clusters*), there is more to them than just being a component of that story. This chapter will cover what containers are, why they are important, and how they have been improved in SQL Server 2019.

Why containers matter

Virtualization revolutionized server deployments. Instead of buying and installing a physical server for every SQL Server instance, one server, known as a hypervisor, could run multiple **virtual machines** (**VMs**) that virtualized the hardware and could have an OS installed inside of it. A VM is a software-defined representation of a physical server that provides agility for IT in a way that traditional hardware cannot.

A container is similar, yet different, and arguably the evolution of virtualization. Instead of virtualizing the host and managing it as you would a traditional physical server, such as installing software and patching the OS and applications, containers virtualize the OS, not the hardware. The abstraction is completely different and will be explained more in the *Container technical fundamentals* section.

While an OS is still required for a SQL Server container, the major difference is that the OS (specifically its kernel) is shared, or virtualized, across all containers running on the host running the same container image. Just like traditional virtualization, a host can run one or many containers, each of which has its own processor and memory resources, along with separate process IDs. A container is smaller, and therefore, more portable than a VM.

VMs provide a natural security boundary because the OS and what is running inside of the guest are isolated. VMs do not offer isolation for applications since a change to one can affect the other because they are running in the context of the same OS installation. Containers provide isolation for applications and all dependencies are within the container image so they can be updated independently. However, understand that multiple containers could be affected if something happens to the underlying shared kernel, so heeding security updates is important.

Because a container does not have a full OS installation, it provides abstraction for applications. You can bundle code and dependencies together, such as scripts and executables, inside a container in a way that is challenging to do with a VM. Need to deploy one or a hundred of the same application across the globe easily? Use a container. You have the ability to deliver new versions of software (SQL Server, an application, whatever you have) quickly and be able to roll them back (or forward with an update) easily. It is basically as simple as swapping the container; you do not run individual installers. Without having to patch an OS and SQL Server in a traditional way, things get more interesting.

Size, portability, ease of deployment, and isolation intersect with the DevOps and **continuous integration/continuous deployment** (**CI/CD**) movements. For application developers, the ability to ship changes as a whole unit and manage updates in a controlled fashion gives production environments the ability to deal with issues much quicker. Need to revert to a previous version? Swap out the container. Want to update the version? Swap out the container. All of this takes very little time compared to traditional deployment methods.

Figure 6.1 shows the difference between containers and VMs at a high level:

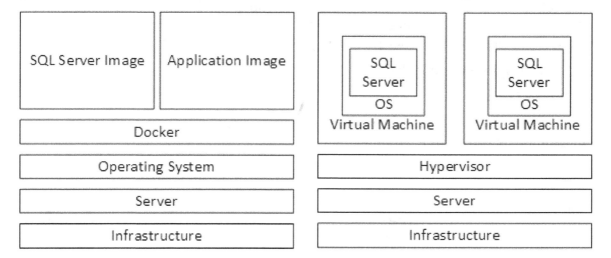

Figure 6.1: Containers versus VMs

Container technical fundamentals

Containers can currently be deployed in two ways: using Docker and through an orchestration method such as **Kubernetes** (**K8s**), both of which will be addressed in this chapter in a bit more detail. The fundamentals described in this section apply to both.

Think of an OS in two parts: the core functionality and APIs, and the presentation layer. A command-line interface or **graphical user interface** (**GUI**) is just an application/presentation layer that interacts with the core OS. It is the core OS that is virtualized across different containers.

A container image is the most fundamental component in the container ecosystem and is published to a registry. Microsoft provides SQL Server container images that are based on Docker. Docker is what allows you to build a container image, but it also allows you to run an image. Docker runs natively on many OSes, which makes it convenient for developers to write container-based applications.

By default, storage for container images is ephemeral or temporary. This means that if the container image is swapped out for a new one, anything stored would be lost. SQL Server requires storage that does not go away, which is possible with both Docker and K8s.

Deploying an SQL Server container using Docker

Docker is a good deployment method for non-production containers. Persistent storage is achieved on Docker using volumes (https://docs.docker.com/storage/volumes/), which tell the container what to use and where to map it. This section will cover how to deploy a SQL Server container using Windows 10, the built-in Hyper-V feature, and Docker. If you are using another platform, you can adapt the instructions accordingly:

1. Ensure **Hyper-V** is enabled.

2. Install Docker.

3. Configure Docker so that deployed containers can use at least **2** GB of memory. An example is shown in *Figure* 6.2:

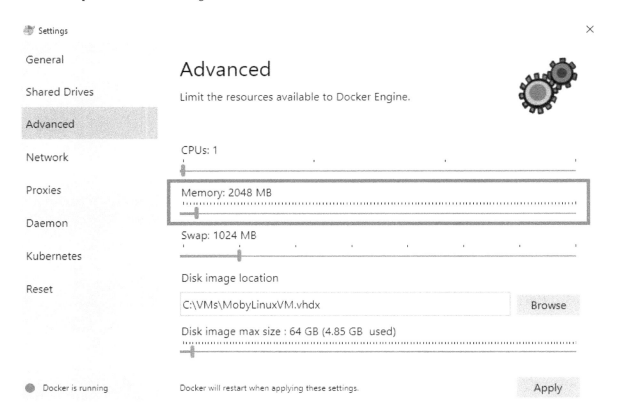

Figure 6.2: Setting the memory to 2 GB in Docker

The default is 1 GB. If you do not configure this setting, you will get the following error when trying to create a container:

```
sqlservr: This program requires a machine with at least 2000
megabytes of memory.
/opt/mssql/bin/sqlservr: This program requires a machine with at
least 2000 megabytes of memory.
```

4. Pull the SQL Server image from the repository. This example is for SQL Server 2019 CTP 3.0. You could have more than one image downloaded. An example pull can be seen in *Figure 9.3*:

```
docker pull imagename
```

Here, **imagename** is the proper name of the image in the online repository:

```
C:\>docker pull mcr.microsoft.com/mssql/server:2019-CTP3.0-ubuntu
2019-CTP3.0-ubuntu: Pulling from mssql/server
59ab41dd721a: Pull complete
57da90bec92c: Pull complete
06fe57530625: Pull complete
5a6315cba1ff: Pull complete
739f58768b3f: Pull complete
0d276c043d9d: Pull complete
c0f263646886: Pull complete
c9c5f85f2056: Pull complete
8c615d7dfaf2: Pull complete
Digest: sha256:e1e633563ca9fcfae49e430f0b5d2a9ad98afc8bea7ea5f4bf037444bdea1b3c
Status: Downloaded newer image for mcr.microsoft.com/mssql/server:2019-CTP3.0-ubuntu
```

Figure 6.3: Pulling the SQL Server 2019 container image

5. Create the container with the following command:

```
docker run -e ACCEPT_EULA=Y -e SA_PASSWORD=StrongPassword -d -p
host_port:sql_port --name containername imagename
```

Here, the following applies:

- **-d** means to run the container in the background.
- **host_port** is the endpoint port on the host.
- **sql_port** is the port where SQL Server is listening in the container.
- **containername** is the name of the container that is being created.

- **imagename** is the name of the container image that was pulled.

If successful, you should see something similar to *Figure 6.4*:

```
C:\>docker run -e ACCEPT_EULA=Y -e SA_PASSWORD=P@ssword1 -p 1402:1433 -d --name ch8contnr2 mcr.microsoft.com/mssql/serve
r:2019-CTP3.0-ubuntu
3d5ca3a8e41a46753d0dd5035d710b606d69ac542c558837e14eab7bedfb1239
```

Figure 6.4: Creating a Docker container

> **Note**
>
> On Docker for Windows, do not put anything after the -e in single quotes. The container will not start. Other platforms may require them.

Without -d, the container will start as shown in the example in *Figure 6.5*, and will be running in the context of that command window. You can hit **Ctrl + C** and the container will still be running, but that is not apparent until you run the command in the next step:

```
C:\>docker run -e ACCEPT_EULA=Y -e SA_PASSWORD=P@ssword1 -p 1401:1433 --name ch8contnr mcr.microsoft.com/mssql/server:20
19-CTP3.0-ubuntu
This is an evaluation version.  There are [155] days left in the evaluation period.
2019-06-15 20:45:41.28 Server      Setup step is copying system data file 'C:\templatedata\master.mdf' to '/var/opt/mssq
l/data/master.mdf'.
2019-06-15 20:45:41.36 Server      Did not find an existing master data file /var/opt/mssql/data/master.mdf, copying the
 missing default master and other system database files. If you have moved the database location, but not moved the data
base files, startup may fail. To repair: shutdown SQL Server, move the master database to configured location, and resta
rt.
2019-06-15 20:45:41.37 Server      Setup step is copying system data file 'C:\templatedata\mastlog.ldf' to '/var/opt/mss
ql/data/mastlog.ldf'.
2019-06-15 20:45:41.38 Server      Setup step is copying system data file 'C:\templatedata\model.mdf' to '/var/opt/mssql
/data/model.mdf'.
```

Figure 6.5: Running a container in the foreground

The previous examples create containers with ephemeral storage. That means every time the container is started, everything will be reset. To create a container with permanent database storage, first ensure that the drive containing the folder is shared, as shown in *Figure 6.6*:

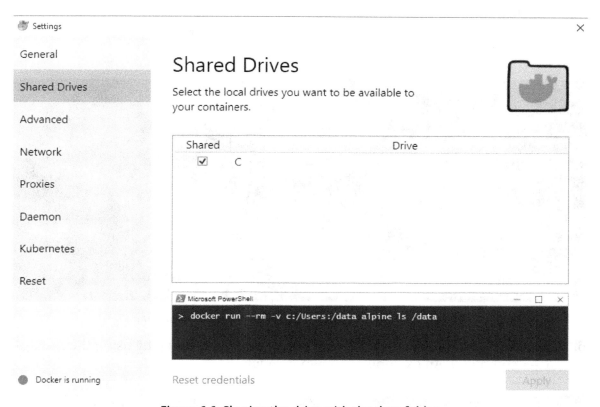

Figure 6.6: Sharing the drive with the data folder

Add the **-v** option, which bind mounts a volume in the container. If you want to use **C:\sqldata**, execute the following command, where **foldername** is the path to the mounted storage. An example showing a folder before and after container creation is shown in *Figure 6.7*:

```
docker run -e ACCEPT_EULA=Y -e SA_PASSWORD=StrongPassword -d
-p host_port:sql_port -vfoldername:/var/opt/mssql/data --name
contanername imagename
```

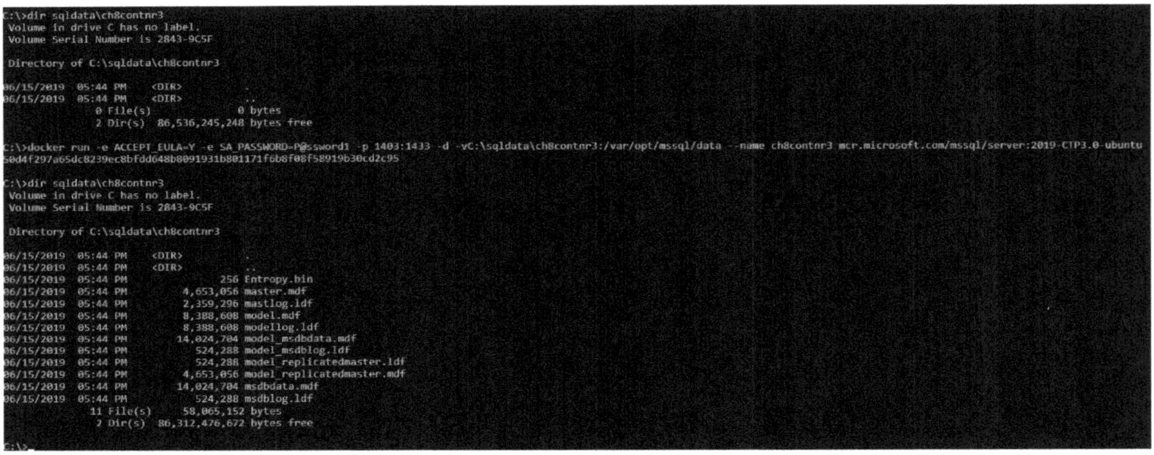

Figure 6.7: Folder before and after creating the container

6. Check that the SQL Server container just created is running by using the **docker ps -a** command. An example is shown in *Figure 6.8*:

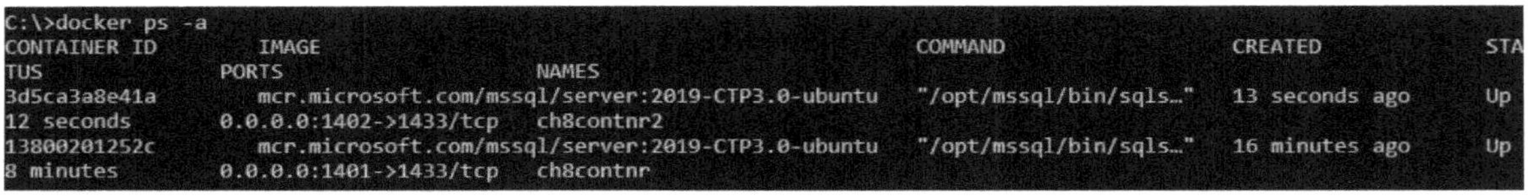

Figure 6.8: Verifying that the container is running

7. At this point, you can test connectivity to the container running SQL Server. There are two ways to approach this: connect directly using Docker and Bash, or via local SQL Server utilities on your workstation.

Using Docker and Bash

1. Run the `docker exec -it containername` command, where `containername` is the name of the container.

2. At the command prompt, run `/opt/mssql-tools/bin/sqlcmd -S localhost -Usa -PStrongPassword`. You should now connect to the instance running in the container and be able to execute commands. An example is shown in *Figure 6.9*:

```
C:\>docker exec -it ch8contnr4 "bash"
root@04e62d33da36:/# /opt/mssql-tools/bin/sqlcmd -S localhost -Usa -PP@ssword1
1> SELECT @@VERSION
2> GO

-----------------------------------------------------------------------------

-----------------------------------------------------------------------------
-----------------------------------------------------
Microsoft SQL Server 2019 (CTP3.0) - 15.0.1600.8 (X64)
        May 17 2019 00:56:19
        Copyright (C) 2019 Microsoft Corporation
        Developer Edition (64-bit) on Linux (Ubuntu 16.04.6 LTS) <X64>

(1 rows affected)
1> exit
root@04e62d33da36:/# 
```

Figure 6.9: Connecting to the container using sqlcmd

Using local SQL Server utilities

You can use `sqlcmd`, `bcp`, **SQL Server Management Studio** (**SSMS**), Azure Data Studio, or any other compatible tool to connect to the local Docker container. You need to specify the IP address of the local machine with the local port you specified when the container was created with the `sa` account and password. An example IP address with the port is `192.168.1.104,1403`. *Figure 6.10* shows SSMS on a workstation with that IP address connected to a Docker container running on it. Note that the value for `@@SERVERNAME` is the same as the `container ID`, not the friendly name:

Figure 6.10: Connected to a Docker container in SSMS

Customizing SQL Server containers

A base SQL Server container image has the Database Engine, SQL Server Agent, and **Customer Experience Improvement Program** (**CEIP**). That means Agent and CEIP can be enabled or disabled. By default, SQL Server Agent is disabled and CEIP is enabled. The easiest way to customize the container is when it is created with `docker run` (or in the `YAML` scripts for Kubernetes). The `-e` option specifies the runtime parameters when creating the container. The options follow what is listed in the *"Configure SQL Server settings with environment variables on Linux"* topic at https://docs.microsoft. com/en-us/sql/linux/sql-server-linux-configure-environment-variables?view=sql-server-2019. For example, to enable SQL Server Agent, add `-e MSSQL_AGENT_ENABLED=true`.

Unlike SQL Server on Linux deployed on a physical or virtual server, there is no `mssql-conf` utility to configure SQL Server using Bash, so any configuration of major items such as SQL Server Agent should be done at creation.

Outside of enabling or disabling those two components, the options for customizing a container image published by Microsoft for SQL Server are somewhat limited. For example, you can change collation and language.

If you want a fully customized container image, you would need to start with a base image (Ubuntu or Red Hat), install SQL Server and add all the supported components for customization that you need. This can be done via Docker file or (https://docs. docker.com/engine/reference/builder/#usage) by taking the image and modifying it such as creating a database that will be used by all deployments. You can then create the new image by committing the changes which will render it ready for deploying, and in some cases, building the image.

While Microsoft may provide more flexibility or more options in the future for customizing the provided SQL Server container images, as noted earlier, you just get core SQL Server functionality today in the provided container images. Some of the features, such as Always On **Availability Groups** (**AGs**), cannot be added by customizing the image.

Availability for SQL Server containers

For any production environment, ensuring availability is an important aspect of any architecture. Traditional availability solutions for SQL Server use an underlying cluster (**Windows Server Failover Cluster** (**WSFC**) or Pacemaker on Linux). For containers, load balancing, clustering, orchestration, and more are provided by K8s. Examples of K8s are **Azure Kubernetes Service** (**AKS**) and Red Hat's OpenShift.

Kubernetes clusters have nodes, which are the servers that the containers will run on. These nodes can be physical servers or VMs running on-premises or in the public cloud. A container is deployed in a K8s cluster into a pod, which is a wrapper that allows them to be deployed on a node. A pod can represent one or more containers in a logical group. Storage is presented using persistent volumes (https://kubernetes.io/docs/concepts/storage/persistent-volumes/), which are slightly different than volumes in Docker. There are two concepts: the disk, or persistent volume, and a claim, which is the actual request for disk I/O.

As of Kubernetes 1.14, along with Windows Server 2019, Windows Server and Linux servers can participate in the same Kubernetes cluster. Windows Server 2019 allows a Linux-based container to run under it. Kubernetes 1.9 introduced beta support for Windows Server containers, which opens the door to running Windows-based .NET applications and down the road, possibly SQL Server in Windows Server 2019-based containers. There were Windows-based containers from Microsoft for SQL Server 2017, but only SQL Server Express was supported.

With Windows Server 2019, a Kubernetes cluster can span both Windows Server and Linux nodes. A Windows Server node can run a Linux container, and a Linux node can run a Windows Server container if it is at 1.14. An example of what that may look like is shown in *Figure 6.11*:

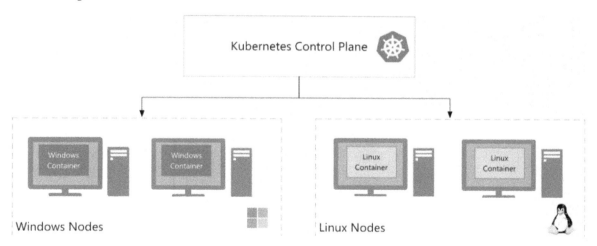

Figure 6.11: Kubernetes cluster spanning OSes

When they were first introduced in SQL Server 2017, containers could be deployed in a way similar to that of an Always On **Failover Cluster Instance** (**FCI**). In a traditional FCI, the instance of SQL Server can be hosted by the properly configured nodes of a WSFC or Pacemaker cluster.

Pods under Kubernetes can work in a similar fashion using storage that is persistent. As shown in *Figure 6.12*, a node of the Kubernetes cluster failed, and SQL Server was rehosted on another node in another pod:

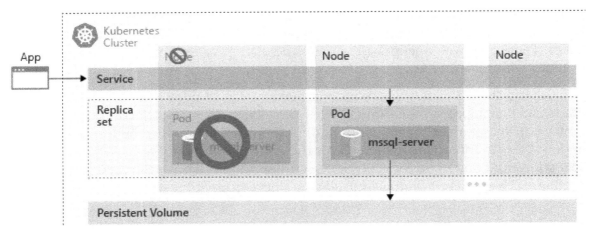

Figure 6.12: High availability for a single deployment with Kubernetes

> **Note**
>
> For more information and instructions on how to configure availability using this method, see https://docs.microsoft.com/en-us/sql/linux/tutorial-sql-server-containers-kubernetes?view=sql-server-2019.

7

Data Virtualization

Traditional analytical systems provide intelligence and insight for organizations by integrating disparate sources into a single system, moving and isolating the analytical workload from the operational workload. In this chapter, you are going to learn about a different approach to data integration–data virtualization. You will start by immersing yourself in the challenges faced when performing data integration projects so that you can differentiate data virtualization use cases from more established data movement patterns. Once you have understood the kinds of problems you can solve with this approach, you will then explore the underlying technology in SQL Server 2019 before being walked through a concrete, end-to-end solution in Azure.

Data integration challenges

The traditional approach taken with traditional analytical systems has typically leveraged data integration tools to build pipelines that extract source system data, transform it, cleanse it, and finally load it into a data mart or data warehouse.

This data integration approach, also known as "schema on write," can lead to long development lead times as the target data model has to be defined before the data movement pipeline can be completed. Meanwhile, the physical act of copying data both multiplies storage costs, courtesy of data duplication, and introduces the challenge of data latency to the data movement pipeline. Furthermore, data movement and duplication increase the data management burden when meeting security and compliance requirements as multiple versions of the same data now exist.

This "data movement" pattern is also intrinsic to modern big data architectures. While some data integration velocity challenges have been addressed via "schema-on-read" approaches, data management challenges remain. Data still ends up being duplicated from operational systems and can require further copies as the data is consolidated, transposed, and reformatted into analytical file formats such as Parquet. Data quality issues are also not magically solved by data lakes either. If the source data is poor or incomplete, then this will still need to be addressed. Furthermore, with the advent of self-service data wrangling you can easily end up with multiple versions of the same data all applying slightly different data quality measures. If left unchecked, self-service empowerment can lead to significant waste of resources, quickly reducing the data lake (a good thing) into a data swamp (a bad thing).

Data lake architectures also introduce new challenges to organizations. It can be tough for analysts to easily query file-based data using existing tools and technology. Big data tools, such as Apache Spark, can be used to issue SQL queries, but these compute engines lack the ability to efficiently process complex set-based queries featuring many joins, for example. This is compounded when we add requirements for granular security control and auditing, or scaling the system to address the concurrency needs of an organization. In these scenarios, relational database technology still outshines its big data counterparts.

So, what should you do?

Learn how data virtualization helps you address these challenges, of course!

Introducing data virtualization

Data virtualization is the name given to any approach that enables you to query across disparate systems from a single source without having to know where that data physically resides.

Queries can be executed against a wide variety of relational and non-relational datasets, some of which may have their own compute engines, while others may not. When a remote compute engine exists, data virtualization technology enables you to push down computation to that data source. Advanced data virtualization engines also provide additional transparent caching of data to reduce the impact on the source system. These capabilities achieve a number of important benefits, which are summarized here for you:

- Consolidate query processing at the source, **reducing spend on resources**.
- Manage a single, semantic, and logical view of your data, **avoiding duplication**.
- Address data issues at the source, **improving data quality**.
- Query disparate data in real time without building a data pipeline, **maximizing freshness**.
- Access data using the source system security model, **simplifying management**.
- Joins and filters can be pushed down to the source, **improving query performance**.
- Only query results travel securely over the network, **enhancing network efficiency**.
- Transparently cache data, **reducing the impact on source systems**.

By federating queries across disparate data from a single source, data virtualization empowers you to build a *modern enterprise data hub* for all of these systems without having to build complex pipelines:

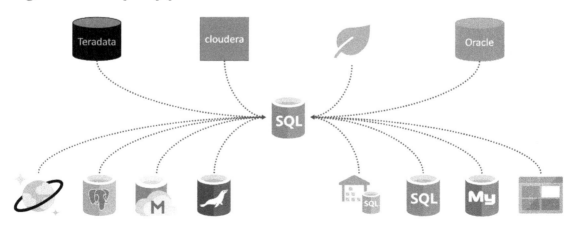

Figure 7.1: A modern enterprise data hub

Data virtualization use cases

In this section, you will review three specific scenarios where a modern enterprise data hub implemented using data virtualization technology adds significant value to your solution.

Data virtualization and hybrid transactional analytical processing

One approach that has gained popularity in recent times is operational analytics, also known as **hybrid transactional analytical processing** (**HTAP**). With this approach, you blend the operational workload and the analytical workload into a single system for that dataset. This has the advantage of consolidation and can limit data duplication. It also addresses data quality issues at the source, which leads to a reduction in the data management burden. However, there is a notable downside. Most enterprises have multiple-source systems, which would result in multiple HTAP systems. This introduces the challenge to users of querying across all their analytical data.

Enter your modern enterprise data hub. Data virtualization enables you to build a single semantic layer over these HTAP systems. You can take advantage of the enhanced data quality and analytical compute power in each source. This means you can query data in real time for maximum freshness and push down computation for resource efficiency.

Data virtualization and caching

Think about a popular dashboard in your organization. Every time it is accessed, the same requests are made of the data source. This pattern is very common in analytics. The same queries, and often the same data, is accessed over and over again—often producing the same result. Data virtualization technology can help offset this overhead by implementing various caching techniques.

> **Note**
>
> Refer to *Chapter 9, SQL Server 2019 Big Data Clusters* for more information on SQL Server 2019's new file caching technology—HDFS tiering.

Data virtualization and federated systems

Data warehouses and analytical platforms have often espoused the "single view of the truth" architecture. However, it is not always practical to achieve. Some organizations are spread all over the world, operating over multiple time zones and making data movement challenging. Others operate in a subsidiary model with many different business units contributing to the group's success. These business units may have grown organically but it's just as likely that the company has grown through acquisition.

It is not uncommon to see different technologies being used for analytics in these types of organizational models. As a result, these companies often choose a federated model for their analytics platform.

In a federated model, each unit of the business is empowered to build their own analytical solutions. In cases where the federation is geographic, the KPIs might be the same. However, that does not mean that the technology used is identical. When the federated model is split by business unit, the KPIs are likely different to reflect the needs of each business. However, that does not help the board get a single view of all KPIs. In both cases, the group organization still needs an easy way to understand the health of the company *across* the business units.

As data virtualization abstracts the technology away from the semantic view, your modern enterprise data hub provides a unified layer for analytical queries across all your data. Data virtualization provides a way for you to logically bring metrics and measures together in the modern enterprise data hub irrespective of the underlying technology.

Data virtualization and data lakes

Data lakes have gained significant traction in recent years for building analytical solutions. However, these systems are naturally file-based and files aren't always the easiest of things to query. **Optimized Row Columnar (ORC)** and Parquet, in particular, can't simply be opened, inspected, and queried, especially when those files have been compressed. Direct access to the files also introduces security questions. Should an analyst have access to all the rows and columns in this file? Possibly not.

Data virtualization technology enables you to put an abstraction layer between the files and the data analysts looking to query the data. This means that analysts are presented with a solution that they understand very well, namely SQL and tables. Security can also be managed on behalf of data analysts, ensuring that end users only see the data they should. Finally, advanced data virtualization technology providers take advantage of database engine query processing, which provides analysts with the ability to execute much more complex queries against underlying file-based data.

Contrasting data virtualization and data movement

While data virtualization is a great solution for several scenarios, there are some cases where a data movement pipeline is preferred. Data virtualization interrogates the data source at query time, so you see the latest, freshest state of the data. However, your queries are limited to data available at query time and you are dependent upon the source system for row versioning. What should you do when you need to perform historic analysis over time? When a data source doesn't support historic states of the data, you need to curate this data using a data movement approach.

Even when the data is available, data virtualization provides a more limited set of data transformation capabilities compared to a data movement strategy. While you can implement some rudimentary data quality rules in your query, if the data itself requires significant cleansing or transformation, then a data movement approach offers ultimate flexibility for data curation.

Analytical queries may also need to be able to determine the state of the data at *any* given point in time and not just provide the most recent status. You may have built a data warehouse in the past for this purpose. Data warehouses incorporate curated data and embrace a data movement strategy to build slowly changing dimensions and fact tables that version the data under management. You could, of course, change the source system to be able to provide this level of data and curation. However, this isn't always practical, and so a data movement strategy tends to be preferred in these cases.

Does a data movement strategy mean you cannot use data virtualization? The answer is no.

Data virtualization can be used by data warehouses to prototype a new pipeline or integrate with a central reference catalog. Alternatively, if you are building an enterprise data hub, you could move data inside the hub using your data virtualization platform and then curate that data to provide the insight you require. This approach enables you to build conformed dimensions, for example, in the data hub. This allows them to be easily re-used as part of the data virtualization solution without needing a separate system.

In short, data virtualization and data movement can be complementary technologies.

Data virtualization in SQL Server 2019

The technology SQL Server uses to deliver data virtualization capabilities in 2019 is PolyBase. PolyBase was first introduced into SQL Server in the 2016 release to help customers integrate their Hadoop clusters with relational data. SQL Server 2019 significantly extends PolyBase and enhances these capabilities to bring data virtualization capabilities to the platform.

In this chapter, you will focus on the latest innovations in PolyBase so you can create a modern enterprise data hub in your organization.

Secure data access

PolyBase uses the security model of the underlying data source to access data. As you will only be reading data, the permissions required on the data source are limited to `SELECT` or read-only access. However, the credentials used to read the data are stored inside your data hub so you will need to know how to create and secure them. In this section, you will learn how to do this.

The database master key

The master key is created inside the SQL Server database you are using to act as the data hub. It is then used to secure the private keys created by *database scoped credentials*. You can only have one master key in a database. An example of the syntax to create a database master key is shown here:

```
CREATE MASTER KEY ENCRYPTION BY PASSWORD = '@rsen@l@re@m@zing!'
;
```

If you are using the data hub for other purposes, it is quite possible that you have already created a master key as other product features can require one. If you have, that's great; you can re-use it for securing database scoped credentials for data virtualization. You can check to see whether your data hub has a master key by using the following query:

```
SELECT * from sys.symmetric_keys
;
```

Database scoped credentials

Database scoped credentials are user-created objects that exist inside the database you are using as the data hub. They contain the identity and the secret required to access an external data source. You only need to create one database scoped credential per external data source. However, you can create more than one if you want to access the external data source using a different credential. You will also need to create a second external data source object, however, to use the second database scoped credential.

Database scoped credentials provide the abstraction to the security model used to access the data source. SQL Server 2019 supports the following security models when using PolyBase for data virtualization:

- Proxy authentication (username and password)

- Kerberos integrated authentication (pass-through authentication)

- Storage access key (shared secret)

> **Note**
>
> A proxy account can be a basic login and password combination, such as SQL authentication for SQL Server, or a more complex configuration such as a Kerberos identity, which requires additional setup. The key point to note is that whichever proxy method is used, all access to the external data source is through this account.

Ultimately, it is the external data source that determines which security model can be used with each data source. Review the compatibility matrix in the *Supported data sources* section of this chapter for more information.

Here is an example of the syntax used to provide SQL Server with the security context for a connection to a PostgreSQL external data source:

```
CREATE DATABASE SCOPED CREDENTIAL pg_credential
WITH IDENTITY = 'jrj@jrjpg'
,     SECRET    = '!@rsen@l@re@m@zing!'
;
```

> **Note**
>
> The identity equates to the username of the external data source. For example, in the preceding case, the username is defined using the username@servername convention as this is how the username is defined in PostgreSQL. If you forget to specify the identity using the correct naming convention of the data source, you may find you get an error when you try to create an external table as the credentials will not be validated until that time.

You can validate which database scoped credentials exist in your data hub by querying the catalog view for database scoped credentials:

```
SELECT * FROM sys.database_scoped_credentials
;
```

Once you have your data access set up you can go ahead and create the external data source.

External data sources

External data sources are your path to virtualizing data from other systems. They collate the connectivity metadata into a single database object. Each external data source provides the location, port, credential, and connectivity options required to access the external source. Just like the other objects discussed, external data sources are database scoped, residing in the database chosen as the data hub.

Supported data sources

The number of external data sources has significantly increased in SQL Server 2019 and now supports many relational database management systems, key-value stores (non-relational), and big data file formats for querying data that's resident in Hadoop. The following table summarizes all the external data sources available in SQL Server 2019, highlighting the required security model for that source:

External Data Source	Windows	Linux	SQL 2019 Big Data Clusters	Versions Supported	Authentication Security Model
Cloudera	✓	✓	✓	CDH 5.x	Proxy
Hortonworks	✓	✓	✓	HDP 2.6, 3.0, 3.1	Proxy
SQL Server	✓	✓	✓	2008 and above	Basic only
Oracle	✓	✓	✓	?	Basic only
Teradata	✓	✓	✓	?	Basic only
MongoDB	✓	✓	✓	?	Basic only
Cosmos DB	✓	✓	✓	?	Basic only
Generic ODBC	✓	X	X	Any ODBC v3 compliant driver	Basic only
Azure Blob storage	✓	✓	X	wasb[s] interface	Storage Key SAS token
Data pool	X	✓	✓		Kerberos Integrated
Storage pool	X	✓	✓		Kerberos Integrated

Table 7.2: Table summarizing the external data sources

> **Note**
>
> In the preceding table, SQL Server includes the whole SQL Server family of databases: SQL Database, SQL managed instance, and SQL Data Warehouse.
>
> Azure Cosmos DB is accessed via the MongoDB API. The data pool and storage pool are features of SQL Server 2019 Big Data Clusters. For more information, refer to *Chapter 9, SQL Server 2019 Big Data Clusters*.

Extending your environment using an ODBC external data source

One of the most interesting external data sources in SQL Server 2019 is the **Open Database Connectivity (ODBC)** external data source. The ODBC standard provides an open extensibility model, which dramatically increases the number of external data sources you can connect to. For example, you can **bring your own driver** (**BYOD**) and connect directly to other Azure SQL Database engines, such as PostgreSQL, MySQL, and MariaDB. You can even connect to third-party systems such as Salesforce and SAP Hana.

The following example shows you all the arguments you need when creating an external data source for an Azure Database for PostgreSQL server.

Azure Database for PostgreSQL currently supports versions 10, 9.6, and 9.5. You need to know which version you are using as this impacts your driver choice. For PostgreSQL, you can download the ODBC driver from their website: https://www.postgresql.org/ftp/odbc/versions/msi/. Generally speaking, you should be using the latest driver for your version.

To configure the PostgresSQL driver for an Azure instance, you will need the following information:

Parameter	Default/Naming Convention	Example
Server_name	*.postgres.database.azure.com	jrjpg.postgres.database.azure.com
Port	5432	5432
Database	Postgres	postgres
Username	<username@instancename>	jrj@jrjpg
Password		!D3nn1sB3rgk@mp!
Sslmode	require	require

Table 7.3: Information required to configure the Postgres driver

Use this information to complete the configuration of the driver. Once complete, you can test and save the configuration. Here is an example of the configuration screen prior to saving:

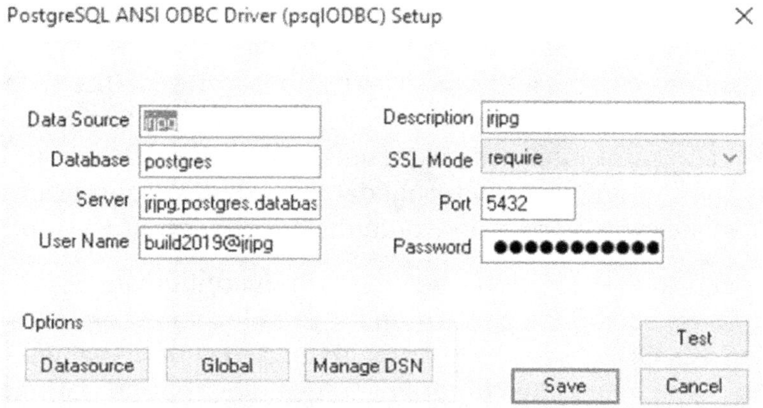

Figure 7.4: Setting up the ODBC driver for PostgreSQL

> **Note**
>
> Remember to leave the SSL Mode field set to **require** for connectivity with Azure. If you change this, your communication to the database may fail with the following error: **FATAL: SSL connection is required**. Please specify SSL options and retry.

You can now create the external data source using the following syntax below:

```
CREATE EXTERNAL DATA SOURCE pg_eds
WITH
( LOCATION            = 'odbc://jrjpg.postgres.database.azure.com:5432'
, CONNECTION_OPTIONS = 'Driver={PostgreSQL ODBC Driver(ANSI)};
sslmode=require'
, CREDENTIAL          = pg_credential
, PUSHDOWN            = ON
)
;
```

The LOCATION argument specifies the communication protocol as well as the server name and port for connectivity.

The CREDENTIAL argument maps in the database scoped credential you created earlier. Remember that all queries over this external data source will use this database scoped credential.

The PUSHDOWN argument can be set to ON or OFF and is optional (the default is ON). This argument is used to tell PolyBase whether it is permitted to optimize queries by "pushing down" computation to the external data source. JOINs and GROUP BYs of external tables that belong to an external data source are good examples of "push down." By setting PUSHDOWN to OFF, you would disable this optimization.

Finally, you may need to use additional settings when configuring an ODBC data source. You can use the CONNECTION_OPTIONS argument to tailor your connection to meet the driver's needs. For this ODBC scenario, you will need to set two values. The first is the Driver parameter, which states which driver to use. The second parameter is sslmode. This setting forces the connection over **Secure Sockets Layer** (**SSL**), which is a default requirement for communicating with Azure Database for PostgreSQL.

Once created, you can check the configuration of the external data source by querying the external data source catalog view:

```
SELECT * FROM sys.external_data_sources
;
```

You are now able to create an *external table*.

Accessing external data sources in Azure

In order for SQL Server to be able to access the external data source, you may need to allow inbound connections from your data hub to the Azure resource. This will largely depend on whether the external data source is inside or attached to the same virtual network as your SQL Server instance. The following screenshot shows the firewall configuration screen for Azure Database for PostgreSQL. If your external data source is not letting your SQL Server instance connect to the external data source, you should navigate to the connection security settings in the Azure Portal and add a rule to let traffic from SQL Server through. Have a look at this example:

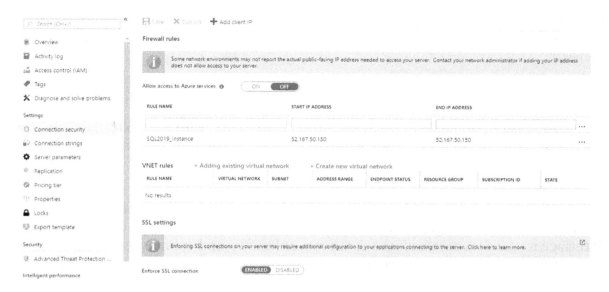

Figure 7.5: Azure Database for PostgreSQL firewall screen

> **Note**
>
> The preceding screenshot also highlights the default SSL settings for communication to PostgreSQL. As you saw earlier, this is important to remember when configuring the external data source. Communicating over SSL is the best practice.

External file formats

When you work with files such as CSVs, or even big data files such as ORC or Parquet, you need to create an external file format to tell SQL Server how to interpret the file. In the following example, the external file format is configured to interpret a CSV file using a caret as a field terminator. Other options exist for data compression, string termination, and file encodings:

```
CREATE EXTERNAL FILE FORMAT azure_adventureworks_eff
WITH
(FORMAT_TYPE = DELIMITEDTEXT
,FORMAT_OPTIONS( FIELD_TERMINATOR = '^')
);
```

Once created, you can reuse the external file format for all the external tables of that type. You can also check to see which ones you already have created using the catalog view:

```
SELECT * FROM sys.external_file_formats

;
```

Remember, external file formats are only required when creating an external table over a file. They are not needed for other relational or non-relational external data sources.

PolyBase external tables

External tables provide SQL Server with the schema to reason over data in the external data source. When you create an external table, you are establishing a strongly typed interface to the data that includes data type, nullability, and column-level collation. The columns can, and should, be strongly typed as this improves query performance and data quality.

> **Note**
>
> The data that you reference via an external table is not directly under SQL Server management. This means that the data could change or be removed and will not be included in operations such as backup or restore.

The columns in an external table are mapped by position and so you can choose whatever column names you like. You can, therefore, treat external tables as a useful abstraction for aliasing column names. In this sense, an external table operates as a view:

```
CREATE EXTERNAL TABLE [Sales].[SalesTerritory]
([TerritoryID]          INT              NOT NULL
,[Name]                 NVARCHAR(50)     NOT NULL
,[CountryRegionCode]    NVARCHAR(3)      NOT NULL
,[Group]                NVARCHAR(50)     NOT NULL
,[SalesYTD]             MONEY            NOT NULL
,[SalesLastYear]        MONEY            NOT NULL
,[CostYTD]              MONEY            NOT NULL
```

```
, [CostLastYear]        MONEY               NOT NULL
, [rowguid]             UNIQUEIDENTIFIER    NOT NULL
, [ModifiedDate]        DATETIME2(3)        NOT NULL
)
WITH
( DATA_SOURCE        = pg_eds
, LOCATION           = 'postgres.sales.salesterritory'
)
;
```

> **Note**
>
> The **LOCATION** value used for the external table is a three-part name:
> **<database>.<schema>.<table>**. The **DATA_SOURCE** parameter maps the external
> data source object to the table. Remember the external data source object
> includes the server name so that SQL Server can locate the instance.

You can validate your external tables by using the following command:

```
SELECT * FROM sys.external_tables
;
```

You now have the objects you need to execute a query against an external data source.
However, there is one final thing you can do to help the optimizer. You can create
statistics on the columns of the external table to provide the optimizer with additional
heuristics. Use standard **CREATE STATISTICS** syntax to do this.

Creating external tables with Azure Data Studio

Azure Data Studio is a cross-platform client tool for querying your data. It includes a helpful wizard that you can use for creating external tables in your data hub. To initiate the wizard, you first need to create a connection to Azure Data Studio. Leave the database defaulted to master so that you can see all the databases on the instance. Right-click on your data hub and choose the **Create External Table** option to initiate the wizard:

Figure 7.6: Initiate the wizard

The most important step in the create external table wizard is step 4–the table mapping screen, shown in the following screenshot. Here you can choose which external tables are generated in your data hub, decide which schema those tables will be created in, and either accept or adjust the names and type mapping of the source schema to SQL Server:

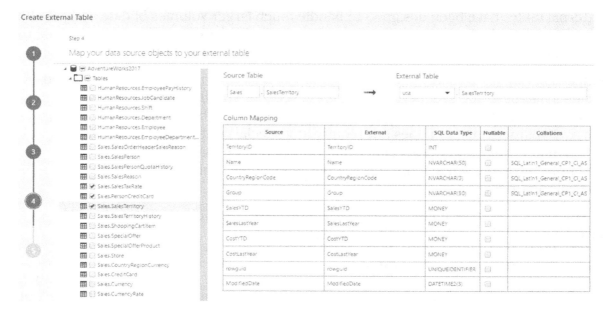

Figure 7.7: Azure Data Studio data virtualization wizard

Note

The primary benefit of using the External Table Wizard in Azure Data Studio is that you can generate many external tables at once.

The external table wizard is available for creating both SQL Server and Oracle external tables. You can also create external tables overviews as well as tables.

Contrasting linked servers and external tables

Linked servers have been available in SQL Server for a very long time. They provide users with the ability to connect disparate data sources together and provide a mechanism for executing queries across instances. At a superficial level, they can feel similar to PolyBase external tables. However, there are some significant differences that you should be aware of when choosing which technology to use.

External tables have been designed to handle much larger volumes of data and are able to scale out reads against large data sets. External tables are therefore better suited to analytics scenarios, such as data virtualization, where this pattern is more common.

Linked servers operate at the instance level, whereas external tables are contained inside a database and are therefore database scoped. This has some important benefits. It means that an external table will automatically be included in an Always On Availability Group and does not require any special configuration. Database containment is very handy for consolidation and release management as there are no additional artifacts leaking into the rest of the instance, which would otherwise require special treatment.

In summary, if you are building a modern enterprise data hub, then you should be leveraging PolyBase external tables in SQL Server 2019.

Installing PolyBase in SQL Server 2019

PolyBase is an optional component in SQL Server. You must either include it as part of the initial install or add it after install to be able to use it. You will also need to enable it once installed.

PolyBase can be installed in one of two modes: standalone mode or as a scale-out group. In standalone mode, SQL Server operates as both the "head" and a singular "compute" node. This is a good option when connecting to smaller, relational sources. When you set up PolyBase as a scale-out group, SQL Server operates as a cluster with a "head" and multiple "compute" nodes. This provides enhanced scalability and performance for the solution. Scale-out groups are particularly relevant when querying very large systems with partitioned tables or a big data system, which may contain billions of records.

In this section, you will learn about how you install PolyBase in either mode. The steps to perform this task are different depending on whether you are using Windows, Linux, or Docker, so each option is covered in the next section.

> **Note**
>
> If you are using a SQL Server 2019 virtual machine from the Azure gallery, then SQL Server is already installed. However, you will still need to update the installation to include PolyBase and then enable it.

General pre-installation guidance

When you install PolyBase on Windows, it is worth deciding whether you also want to connect to a Hadoop external data source. A Hadoop data source enables connectivity to distributions from Cloudera or Hortonworks but also includes cloud object stores such as Azure Blob storage. These external data sources require you to also install a **Java Runtime Environment** (**JRE**) for you to install PolyBase. Fortunately, SQL Server now ships with its own supported JRE, which will install as part of the installation process. If you would rather use your own JRE, you can use that instead:

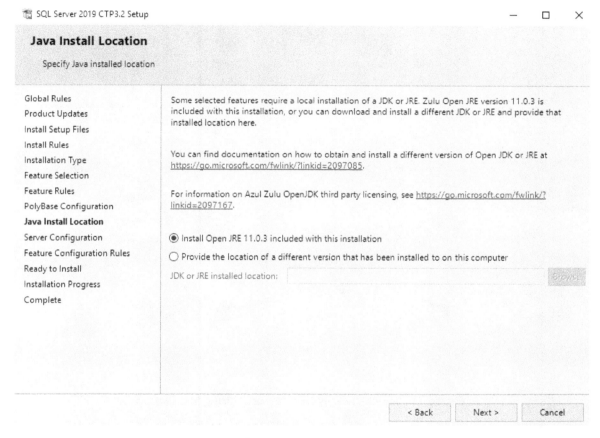

Figure 7.8: The Java Install Location window

> **Note**
>
> Installing a JRE is only required if you want to connect your SQL Server instance to use Azure Blob storage or a big data system such as Cloudera. You don't have to do this if you only plan to use relational external data sources. You can also add it later on if needed.

Installing PolyBase on Windows

The SQL Server Installation Center, also known as the installer, is the most straightforward way to install PolyBase on Windows. You can choose to install PolyBase as part of the initial install or update an existing deployment and add it on later.

The most critical screen in the installation process is as follows:

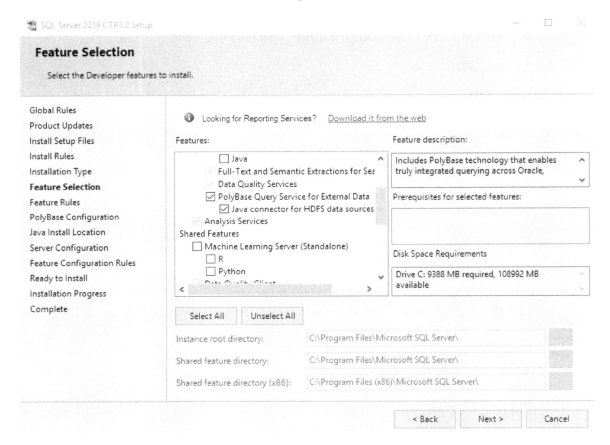

Figure 7.9: Select the PolyBase feature during installation

As you can see, the Java connector for **Hadoop Distributed File System (HDFS)** data sources is an additional option.

For more advanced deployments, you can install SQL Server from the command line and include the switches to also enable PolyBase. An example is provided here:

```
Setup.exe /Q /ACTION=INSTALL /IACCEPTSQLSERVERLICENSETERMS /
FEATURES=SQLEngine,PolyBase

/INSTANCENAME=MSSQLSERVER /SQLSYSADMINACCOUNTS="\<fabric-domain>\
Administrator"

/INSTANCEDIR="C:\Program Files\Microsoft SQL Server" /PBSCALEOUT=TRUE

/PBPORTRANGE=16450-16460 /SECURITYMODE=SQL /SAPWD="<StrongPassword>"

/PBENGSVCACCOUNT="<DomainName>\<UserName>" /
PBENGSVCPASSWORD="<StrongPassword>"

/PBDMSSVCACCOUNT="<DomainName>\<UserName>" /
PBDMSSVCPASSWORD="<StrongPassword>"
```

Once installed, you can move onto the post-installation steps.

Installing PolyBase on Linux

As of SQL Server 2017, you are able to operate SQL Server on Linux. Today, SQL Server supports the following distributions:

- **Red Hat Enterprise Linux** (**RHEL**)
- **SUSE Linux Enterprise Server** (**SLES**)
- Ubuntu

To install SQL Server on Linux, you should follow the guidance given in the product documentation, as covering the full installation process is out of scope for this chapter. This is covered in *Chapter 5, SQL Server 2019 on Linux*.

The following URLs will direct you on how to perform the initial setup for your preferred distribution:

- RHEL: https://docs.microsoft.com/sql/linux/quickstart-install-connect-red-hat
- SLES: https://docs.microsoft.com/en-us/sql/linux/quickstart-install-connect-suse
- Ubuntu: https://docs.microsoft.com/sql/linux/quickstart-install-connect-ubuntu

From your terminal, you can update your SQL Server installation using one of the following commands:

```
# RHEL
sudo yum install -y  mssql-server-polybase

# Ubuntu
sudo apt-get install mssql-server-polybase

# SLES
sudo zypper install  mssql-server-polybase
```

Once installed you will be prompted to restart your SQL Server installation. You can do so with the following command from your terminal window:

```
# RHEL, SLES and Ubuntu all use the same command for restart
sudo systemctl restart mssql-server
```

That's all there is to it. You can now move onto the post-installation steps.

Installing PolyBase on SQL Server running in Docker

SQL Server 2019 is available for download as a Docker image. However, the image does not contain optional components such as PolyBase. You will need to build a Docker image and include the PolyBase package. Fortunately, this is very easy to do using a Dockerfile.

Firstly, you need to create a Dockerfile to tell Docker what to build. Create a file called **dockerfile** in a directory and then navigate to that directory in your cmd window or terminal. Copy the following code into your Dockerfile:

```
# mssql-server-polybase

# Maintainers: Microsoft Corporation

# GitRepo: https://github.com/Microsoft/mssql-docker


# Base OS layer: Latest Ubuntu LTS
FROM ubuntu:16.04


# Install pre-requisites including repo config for SQL server and
PolyBase.
```

```
RUN export DEBIAN_FRONTEND=noninteractive && \
    apt-get update && \
    apt-get install -yq apt-transport-https curl && \
    # Get official Microsoft repository configuration
    curl https://packages.microsoft.com/keys/microsoft.asc | apt-key
add - && \
    curl https://packages.microsoft.com/config/ubuntu/16.04/mssql-
server-preview.list | tee /etc/apt/sources.list.d/mssql-server-
preview.list && \
    apt-get update && \
    # Install PolyBase will also install SQL Server via dependency
mechanism.
    apt-get install -y mssql-server-polybase && \
    # Cleanup the Dockerfile
    apt-get clean && \
    rm -rf /var/lib/apt/lists


# Run SQL Server process
CMD /opt/mssql/bin/sqlservr
```

You can access a copy of this Dockerfile at the following URL: https://github.com/microsoft/mssql-docker/tree/master/linux/preview/examples/mssql-polybase.

You are now able to build the image and give it a tag using the following command below:

```
docker build . -t mssql-polybase-2019
```

The build will download all of its dependencies and build a new image that includes SQL Server and the Docker image. Now all you need to do is create the container, which you can do with the following **docker run** command:

```
docker run -e 'ACCEPT_EULA=Y' -e 'SA_PASSWORD=@rsenal@re@mazing' -p
1433:1433 -d mssql-polybase-2019
```

In a matter of seconds, you have a Docker container up and running and you can move onto the post-installation steps.

When using SQL Server on Docker, you may find you need to increase the resources available to Docker to run the containers successfully. SQL Server typically needs at least 2 GB RAM, for example. When using PolyBase, you will probably want to increase that amount further as you are going to use memory when querying external data sources:

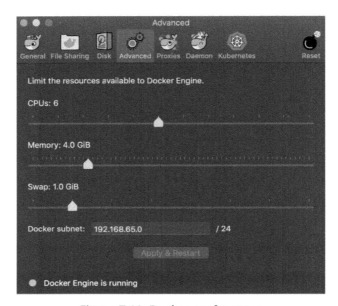

Figure 7.10: Docker preferences

Post-installation steps

You should first validate that PolyBase is installed by executing the following command:

```
SELECT SERVERPROPERTY ('IsPolyBaseInstalled') AS IsPolyBaseInstalled;
```

Now that you have validated the installation, you will need to enable PolyBase using the following command:

```
exec sp_configure @configname = 'polybase enabled', @configvalue = 1;
RECONFIGURE WITH OVERRIDE;
```

> **Note**
>
> Knowing that the instance has PolyBase installed and enabled is a great place to start when troubleshooting a deployment. It is easy to forget to enable PolyBase after installation, but the feature won't work unless you do so!

Installing PolyBase as a scale-out group

To enhance the performance and scalability of SQL Server 2019, you can deploy PolyBase as a scale-out group. In this mode, all instances in the group operate as one when querying external data sources. Scale-out groups are particularly useful when querying large partitioned tables or big files out in Hadoop or in Azure Blob storage. Scale-out groups sub-divide and parallelize query processing across the nodes of the scale-out group, which takes full advantage of the distributed architecture.

> **Note**
>
> Scale-out groups are supported on the Windows operating system only. If you want to build a scale-out data virtualization platform on Linux, then use SQL Server 2019 Big Data Clusters, which is optimized for this scenario using Kubernetes. For more information on SQL Server 2019 Big Data Clusters, refer to *Chapter 9, SQL Server 2019 Big Data Clusters*.

Setting up a scale-out group is relatively straightforward, provided you follow a methodical process. There are some important factors you need to take into consideration, so having a plan is important for a smooth deployment. The following diagram summarizes a functional topology you can use for your deployment. You should also review the additional guidance for implementing this topology to help ensure you are successful:

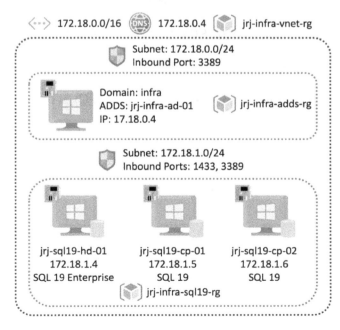

Figure 7.11: Azure virtual machine PolyBase scale-out group topology

Tip #1: Use different resource groups for each part of the architecture

Using different resource groups for each component in the architecture helps you manage the assets you create. This way, you can easily remove the scale-out group by deleting its resource group without destroying the domain controller for example.

Tip #2: Create the virtual network and secure subnets before building virtual machines

By creating the virtual network first, you can establish the networking and security topology *at the subnet level* before you deploy any virtual machines (VMs). You can also create network security groups (NSGs) and associate your subnet(s) to an NSG. When you deploy the VMs, you can simply associate each VM to the virtual network and subnet as you create the machine.

If you create the VMs first, then the networking provisioning blade will try to create the NSGs at the network interface level. Using NSGs at the network interface level makes your deployment much more complex as you will have introduced another barrier that you will need to deal with when trying to get machines to communicate with one another.

At this point, you can also go ahead and add any inbound rules to the NSG you might require so that you can configure the VMs. Remote desktop (3389) and SQL traffic (1433) are the most common ports to open. However, these should be carefully configured, limiting access from known source IP addresses only.

Tip #3: Place your scale-out group SQL Server instances inside one subnet

All the VMs in a scale-out group communicate over a number of ports. By default, the port range for PolyBase is 16450-16460. However, scale-out groups also utilize **Microsoft Distributed Transaction Coordinator** (**MSDTC**), which uses a dynamic port range, making network management more challenging.

By placing all the scale-out group VMs inside a single subnet, you simplify the topology. All the VMs can communicate on any port as the network is secured at the subnet level and you don't need to worry about fixing MSDTC onto a known port.

With this configuration, there is no need for you to create additional inbound rules in the NSG. The subnet acts as the security boundary for communication between machines in the scale-out group.

Tip #4: Complete this pre-installation checklist!

Deploying a scale-out group contains a few wrinkles that might catch you out. This checklist is designed to help smooth out your experience. Review it and make sure you have an answer for each question:

- Have you created DNS names for each of your VMs?

- Are all machines in the scale-out group joined to the same domain?

- Do you have an extra domain user account to run the PolyBase services?

- Is one of the machines licensed with SQL Server 2019 Enterprise Edition?

- Have you added client access inbound rules to the NSGs so you can remotely access the VMs from your machine?

- Does the account you are using to install PolyBase have access to SQL Server?

- Have you installed any ODBC drivers on all the nodes in your scale-out group?

The last question is particularly important. Scale-out groups need to have the ODBC driver installed on each node of the scale-out group. If you forget to do this, then you could get sporadic query failures when the node that does not have the driver installed is used by a query.

Scale-out group installation

The first and most important point is that *all* nodes in the scale-out group must have PolyBase installed using the second option, **Use this SQL Server as part of PolyBase scale-out group**. It does not matter whether the SQL Server instance you are installing is going to be the head node or a compute node—make sure you use this option:

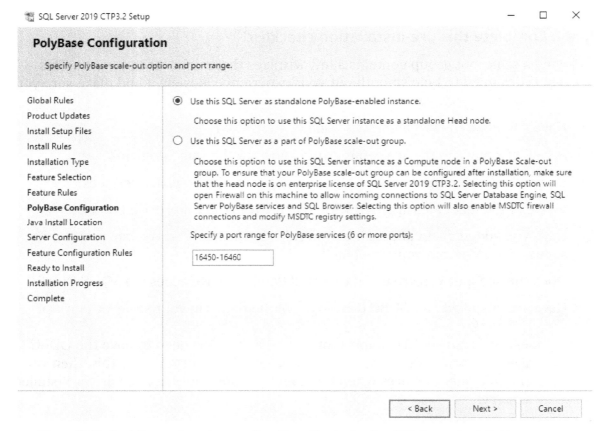

Figure 7.12: Enabling scale-out group functionality during the SQL Server installation process

If you do not choose the second option, MSDTC will not be configured correctly and the additional firewall rules to allow for the network traffic to pass through will not be enabled. Changing an installation from a standalone instance to a scale-out group requires you to uninstall the PolyBase feature and reinstall it, which is cumbersome. It is best to get it right the first time.

You may need to expand or change the default port range of 16450-16460, depending on your network administrator rules and guidance. Furthermore, any firewalls that exist between the machines in this domain will need to let traffic pass over these ports, otherwise PolyBase will not function correctly.

On the configuration page, you will need to provide the same domain user account for both PolyBase services. It is important to note that you must use the same domain user account for both services on all instances. Otherwise, you will not be able to proceed on this screen:

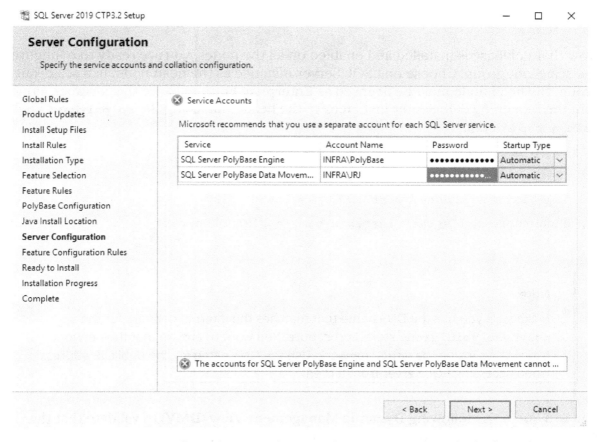

Figure 5.13: Server configuration—use the same domain user account for both services

Before we can move on to configure the scale-out group, you must first complete the post-installation steps discussed earlier to enable PolyBase. Log in, execute the following script, and restart all the nodes:

```
SELECT SERVERPROPERTY ('IsPolyBaseInstalled') AS IsPolyBaseInstalled
;

exec sp_configure @configname = 'polybase enabled', @configvalue = 1
;

RECONFIGURE WITH OVERRIDE
;
```

Now that PolyBase is installed and enabled on all the nodes, you are ready to configure the scale-out group. Choose one SQL Server instance as the head node. In a scale-out group, the head node must be licensed as Enterprise Edition. Leave this instance alone. Join the remaining SQL Server instances to the head node using the **sp_polybase_join_group** system:

```
EXEC sp_polybase_join_group
    @head_node_address                   = N'jrj-sql19-cp-01.infra.internal'
  , @dms_control_channel_port          = 16450
  , @head_node_sql_server_instance_name = N'MSSQLServer'
;
```

> **Note**
>
> Make sure you use the DNS name that matches the internal network for the **sp_polybase_join_group** stored procedure. You want to ensure that the network traffic stays inside the virtual network. Use the DNS name for the public IP address when accessing SQL Server from a client.

You can query the following **Dynamic Management View (DMV)** to validate that the machine has been incorporated into the scale-out group:

```
SELECT * FROM sys.dm_exec_compute_nodes
;
```

That's all there is to it. While there are a number of steps to go through, with a little planning and forethought you can easily build your own scale-out group. Now that you have understood all the concepts and installed your own modern enterprise data hub, you can move on and build your first solution using data virtualization.

Bringing it all together: your first data virtualization query

AdventureWorks is a globally distributed business. Each business has implemented their own HTAP system using the technology of their choice. The architects at AdventureWorks have done a good job of federating the model across the business units and so each subsidiary is able to provide the same KPIs. The board of directors has asked you to build a solution that provide group-level reporting across the business units:

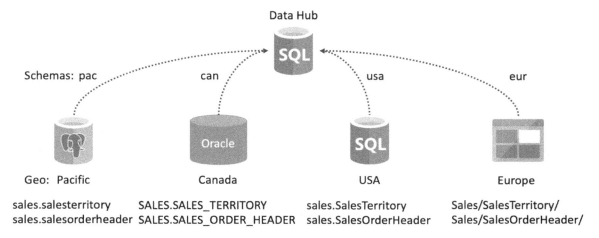

Figure 7.14: AdventureWorks—a modern enterprise data hub

To implement the preceding architecture, you will need to create the following objects in your data hub:

- Four schemas
- One database master key
- Four database scoped credentials
- One external file format (Europe)
- Four external data sources
- Eight external tables

Using the knowledge you've gained in this chapter, you can create all the objects you need in your data hub. All that's left to do is create and run the query. For this, you can use the latest feature in Azure Data Studio—a SQL notebook:

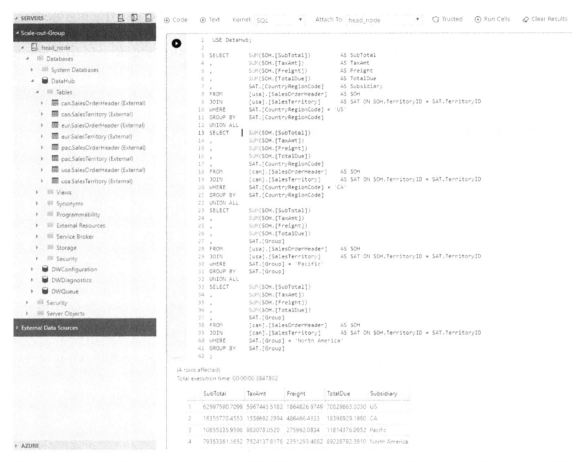

Figure 7.15: Group-level reporting using SQL 2019 data virtualization in an Azure Data Studio SQL notebook

Success! Notice how the end query is "just" SQL? Using familiar tools and technology, you have been able to query four external sources in real time and provide the latest state of sales to the board.

We have seen how SQL Server 2019 empowers you to create a modern enterprise data hub using data virtualization technology powered by PolyBase. You have seen how you can design your data hub to query across all of your source systems in real time. You have been through the installation process for Windows, Linux, and Docker, and have seen how to build a scale-out group in Azure. Finally, you brought everything together in a single query to provide group-level reporting in your data hub to the board of AdventureWorks using the latest innovation in Azure Data Studio—a SQL notebook.

8

Machine Learning Services Extensibility Framework

"Data science" is the broader term given to data analysis techniques done in a scientific manner: create a hypothesis, create a test of the hypothesis, and validate the results (most often with a peer review). It involves standard data analysis techniques, such as queries, reports, and data exploration using business intelligence, and goes further by setting up tests using statistical and algorithmic tools for machine learning.

In this chapter, you'll briefly explore machine learning, the components and architectures in SQL Server 2019 you can use to implement these services, and a process you can follow to include them in a solution. You'll learn the new features in SQL Server 2019 for machine learning platform.

You'll start with a quick overview of machine learning, and then move on to working with the tools to create predictive models and classification. You'll then move on to installing the feature, and then cover the architecture and components of the system, which you'll need to have in order to work with the languages you'll use for machine learning workloads. You'll end this chapter with a complete process to follow to combine the architecture, components, languages, and environments so as to create a complete solution.

Machine learning overview

In a moment, you'll cover the installation of SQL Server Machine Learning Services and get it up and running. You'll also gain an understanding of its components, configuration, and security, at which point you're ready to get started with your workloads. But just what is machine learning and where would you use it? Let's examine the basics.

Within data science, there are three primary branches for prediction and categorization:

1. **Machine learning**: Using patterns and inferences from data rather than explicit programming to perform a task

2. **Artificial intelligence**: Applying sensory inputs to learn from data (often using machine learning techniques)

3. **Deep learning**: Using layers of machine learning methods to create networks that mimic the human mind's processing of data

Machine learning is the "core" of most of the techniques used in all three branches, and SQL Server 2019 provides a Machine Learning Services feature so that you can implement machine learning, artificial intelligence, or even deep learning directly in the database engine over data stored in a database or combined with external data.

How machine learning works

Machine learning involves ingesting data into a system and applying an algorithm to the dataset to either predict an outcome or group the data in a meaningful way. There are two general types of machine learning algorithms:

1. **Supervised**: You have data (called features) that includes the answer you want to get (called labels)

2. **Unsupervised**: You have data (called features) that does not include the answer you want to get (unlabeled)

For instance, if you wish to predict a certain salary level of a random person, you would first gather lots of data about lots of people, including their salaries (the label). From the data, you would select features that highly correlate with the label you want to predict. You might find that education, experience, location, and so on (the features) are very useful in predicting how much someone makes in a year. You then take that data, feed it in through one or more algorithms, and the system "learns" how those features affect the value of the label. Once it produces a result, you can save that "trained" algorithm as a machine learning model. Then, using only the features from someone the model has never seen, the system produces the label you were looking for – this is called a prediction, or a score, since the prediction usually contains information about how "sure" the algorithm is of its prediction. This is an example of supervised learning, since you originally provided the labeled data.

In another example, you may want to group (cluster) people together – perhaps to find their common spending habits, but you are not sure what makes them similar. In this case, you provide many features, but no labels, since you're not sure what you're looking for. The algorithm in this case compares all the features, and tries to minimize the distance between the points of the datasets. The result is the groupings of data that show the most similarity between the people. This is an example of unsupervised learning, since no labels were provided.

> **Note**
>
> The most involved part of this process for either type of learning is gathering the right data (the most predictive – the features) and cleaning that data so that the algorithms can process it properly. These tasks make up the job of "data engineering," which is usually part of the data science team. The "data scientist" is most often someone who works with the algorithms to create the trained model.

Use cases for machine learning

In his excellent video introduction called *Data Science for Beginners*, *Brandon Rohrer* explains the five types of questions that data science can answer:

1. Is this A or B?

2. Is this weird?

3. How much or how many?

4. How is this organized?

5. What should I do next?

Taking the first question as an example, our salary prediction allows a bank to decide whether to market a retirement services offering to you, even if they don't know your salary (you might have more than one bank). In the case of *Is this weird?*, they can monitor your spending habits to see whether something is fraudulent in your account. The *How much or how many?* question can be used to see whether they should give you a loan based on how much your salary has increased over the years. *How is this organized?* allows the bank to group you with other customers for marketing. And the *What should I do next?* answer can automate the fraud response for the bank.

All of these questions have "families" of algorithms that provide answers. If you look around your organization, you can find your specific use cases within one of these questions. For instance, assume you do want to find out why some of your store locations are experiencing a higher level of returns than other stores. You could use a clustering algorithm (such as k-means) to show the groups of customers returning products, and what makes them similar.

To find the algorithms that can answer a given problem, visit https://aka.ms/mlalgorithms.

The general process for creating a machine learning prediction or classification works like this:

1. Select the problem area and the data that supports the answer.

2. Ingest and examine the data.

3. Select the most predictive columns (features).

4. "Train" with the data by passing it through one or more algorithms, using the features (in supervised learning) and the answers (labels) to create a model.

5. "Test" the model by running it against more data that you have the answer for.

6. Iterate on the last step by changing the algorithm or the variables the algorithm uses (called hyperparameters).

7. Save the desired model in a binary format so that it can be called to do predictions or classifications – called "scoring."

8. Use the model from software that calls it.

Languages and tools for machine learning

The datasets required to produce reliable predictions and calculations are too large and complex to calculate by hand. Various programming languages, most notably, R, Python, and Java are most often used for these calculations.

There are four methods you can use to work with these large datasets in machine learning using SQL Server 2019:

1. The Machine Learning Services extensibility framework: A combination of the SQL Server Launchpad service, a language server that runs the code, and a stored procedure that allows the service and the language runtime to interact securely.

2. The `PREDICT T-SQL` command: Runs a trained model you stored in binary format in the database using either R or Python. Uses the native C++ extensions in SQL Server.

3. The `rx_Predict` stored procedure: Runs a trained model stored in a binary format in the database that was created with the Microsoft modeling libraries (more on that in a bit) and implements the `CLR` extension – this is language-agnostic and executes with no dependencies on R or Python runtime engines.

4. Spark in SQL Server 2019 Big Data Clusters: Uses the `Spark` libraries to create, train, store, and score machine learning models using libraries such as `PySpark`, `SparkR`, or `SparkML` statements.

Microsoft SQL Server 2016 introduced "R Services for SQL Server" to embed the capability to send data from an SQL server query to a series of R statements and return the results. In SQL Server 2017, Microsoft added Python to the server, and renamed the feature "Machine Learning Services." In SQL Server 2019, Java is also available. In this chapter, you'll learn how to implement those languages for machine learning, and about the components within the platform that runs them. There are changes you'll discover from the previous configurations of R services (2016) and Machine Learning Services (2019). In this chapter, you'll also focus on the addition of Java, since R and Python existed in previous versions, but we'll briefly touch on those in case you are new to them.

Microsoft SQL Server 2019 Machine Learning Services are available for the R and Python languages in the following editions:

*   Enterprise (basic and enhanced functions)

*   Standard (basic and enhanced functions)

*   Web (basic functions)

*   Express with Advanced Services (basic functions)

The R language extension is available on the Microsoft Azure database platform for single databases and elastic pools using the vCore-based purchasing model in the general-purpose and business-critical service tiers.

SQL Server 2019 Machine Learning Services architecture and components

You can install Machine Learning Services using the SQL Server installer either with a new instance or by adding features to a currently installed instance. The installer then marks the base components for each instance to be able to run external language calls for installation:

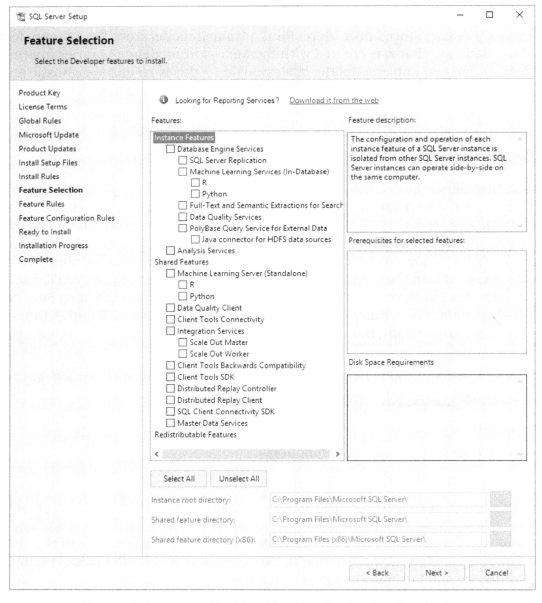

Figure 8.1: SQL Server 2019 Machine Learning Services installation

After you make the selection, you can pick the languages you want to work with, and the installer marks further components for that language to be installed. As in any installation of SQL Server, it's important to understand all of the ramifications and interactions, which you can find here: https://docs.microsoft.com/en-us/sql/advanced-analytics/install/sql-machine-learning-services-windows-install?view=sqlallproducts-allversions.

The Linux installation is different – you'll install a series of packages in a given order, and there are slight variations depending on your Linux distribution. It's best to consult the full installation instructions here: https://docs.microsoft.com/en-us/sql/linux/sql-server-linux-setup-machine-learning?view=sqlallproducts-allversions.

Note that while the Java language is now supported in SQL Server 2019, it is not included in Machine Learning Services. You will need to install **Oracle Java SE** or **Zulu OpenJDK Java** on your server. If it's not there and you select it (or call for it from the Linux installer), the prerequisites will fail and you'll exit the installer. Once you install your Java and set a `JRE-HOME` system setting (`SET` in Windows, `export` in Linux), then you can restart the installer and select it again.

In Linux, there's a different process to install Java support. Using your distribution's package manager (such as `apt` or `yum`), you'll install the `mssql-server-extensibility-java` package once your base installation of SQL Server 2019 and Java is complete, as described in the full documentation.

You can see a full explanation for the installation process for Java for both Windows and Linux here: https://docs.microsoft.com/en-us/sql/advanced-analytics/java/extension-java?view=sqlallproducts-allversions.

> **Note**
>
> SQL Server will only call languages that have been coded to work with this architecture, called a **trusted launcher**. In SQL Server 2019, these languages are R, Python, and Java.

Working together, several components allow the calls to work quickly and securely across the instance. Each component area gets a process space to protect the integrity of the databases and processing engines. Along with other components, this makes up the Machine Learning Services extensibility framework.

> **Note**
>
> The Java language extension runs differently than the chart of processes shown in the next figure. It uses the `LaunchPad` (in Windows) or `mssql-launchpad` (in Linux) service, but then invokes `commonlauncher.dll` (in Windows) or `commonlauncher.so` (in Linux). For more details on Java interaction, visit: https://docs.microsoft.com/en-us/sql/language-extensions/concepts/extensibility-framework?view=sqlallproducts-allversions.

Components

The following diagram illustrates the primary components in the Machine Learning Services extensibility framework, and shows the path of a call to the `sp_execute_external_script` stored procedure that starts the process:

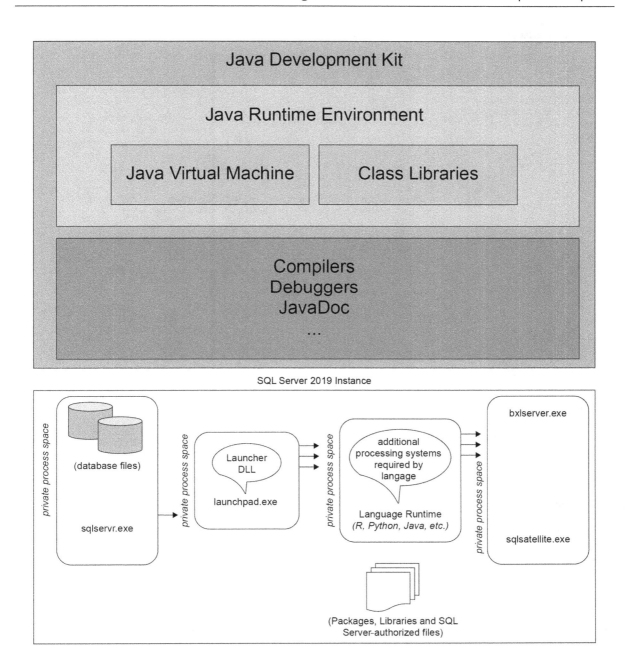

Figure 8.2: SQL Server 2019 Machine Learning Services extensibility framework

These are the primary components in the order they are used:

Component	Description	Observe/Control with
SQL Server Process (sqlsrver.dll)	SQL Server engine. Calls the Launchpad service.	Operating system and SQL Server tools
Launchpad (launchpad.exe in Windows, mssql-launchpadd in Linux)	Service/daemon that executes and manages the external script process. Calls a launcher DLL specific to the language.	Operating system and SQL Server tools (note: only use the configuration manager tool for setting the service account that runs this service)
Launcher DLL (RLauncher.dll for R, PythonLauncher.dll for Python)	Extension for each language. Calls the language executable.	N/A
R, Python, Java	The environments that run the languages for machine learning. The specific versions, editions, releases, and bit-levels are installed for you by the SQL Server installer, even if you have them installed already. Calls a BxLServer.	Language-specific tools and SQL Server tools
BxlServer (bxlserver.exe)	Manages communication between SQL Server and external languages using Windows job objects. Receives and makes calls from and to the SQL Satellite.	Operating system (you'll see more than one of these based on workload)
QL Satellite (sqlsatellite.exe)	Handles input and output variables and data exchange, including basic data type resolution and error handling. (Note: you should still explicitly control data type transformations in code.) Receives and makes calls to and from the SQL Server process.	Operating system and SQL Server Extended Events (you'll see more than one of these based on workload)

Figure 8.3: Table mentioning the primary components

As regards the calls to the server, standard SQL Server communications such as TCP/IP, the **Tabular Data Stream (TDS)**, and Encryption still apply.

> **Note**
>
> Failover clustering for Machine Learning Services is now enabled in SQL Server 2019 if the Launchpad service is up and running on all nodes.

Configuration

After Machine Learning Services and any languages you want to work with are installed, you can enable Machine Learning Services for the instance using Transact-SQL (**T-SQL**) with these commands:

```
EXEC sp_configure  'external scripts enabled', 1

GO

RECONFIGURE WITH OVERRIDE.

GO
```

You can test to see whether the implementation was successful with this script for R:

```
/* Test R */
EXEC sp_execute_external_script  @language =N'R',
@script=N'
OutputDataSet <- InputDataSet;
',
@input_data_1 =N'SELECT 1 AS [Is R Working]'
WITH RESULT SETS ((([Is R Working] int not null));
GO
```

And this one for Python:

```
/* Test Python */
EXEC sp_execute_external_script  @language =N'Python',
@script=N'
OutputDataSet = InputDataSet;
',
@input_data_1 =N'SELECT 1 AS [Is Python Working]'
WITH RESULT SETS ((([Is Python Working] int not null));
GO
```

If those return a value of 1, you're ready to use the Machine Learning Services extensibility framework for your machine learning workloads.

> **Note**
>
> If the system fails to run the scripts successfully, stop and start the instance again, and ensure that the SQL Server Launchpad service is running on your system.

Machine learning using the Machine Learning Services extensibility framework

The machine learning services extensibility framework is an architecture that allows a language processing environment (such as the R, Python, or Java runtimes) to run alongside the SQL Server engine. Using a service, the language runtime can then accept, process, and pass back data to and from SQL Server securely and quickly. We'll examine the complete Machine Learning Services extensibility framework architecture once you have learned more about working with the languages.

Python, R, and Java all use the Machine Learning Services extensibility framework to run machine learning code. The following sections will provide an overview of how that process works from the development process, starting with R.

> **Note**
>
> You can use two general methods to code machine learning systems in SQL Server: Writing the code in-database; or creating Python and R code locally and processing the calls on the database using functions in the Microsoft machine learning libraries in R or Python. This chapter focuses on the former. To learn more about the remote processing feature, refer to: https://docs.microsoft.com/en-us/sql/advanced-analytics/r/ref-r-sqlrutils?view=sql-server-ver15.

R for machine learning in SQL Server 2019

SQL Server 2019 uses the Microsoft R enhanced distribution of the R open source distribution. Microsoft improved the base R language by replacing certain lower-level libraries for processing data and calculations, adding in multiple functions and extended packages, and removing the in-memory limitation of R by enabling a file-read format for data structures, among a host of other improvements.

> **Note**
>
> Microsoft R was originally written by a company called *Revolution Analytics* (*Revo-R*), and you'll still notice vestiges of the product names in the libraries and function calls in Microsoft R that start with `rx_` and `revo`.

While R is a general-purpose data processing language, packages and libraries (more on those in a moment) make it a primary language for machine learning.

In SQL Server 2019, you run R code by:

1. Writing and testing your R code.

2. Using the `sp_execute_external_script` stored procedure, wrapping the R code with data you send in from SQL Server, and defining a structure for the data you receive from R.

The syntax to run R code takes the following basic format (refer to the official documentation for more parameters):

```
sp_execute_external_script
@language = N'R',
@input_data_1 = 'SQL_Code_Goes_Here'
@input_data_1_name = 'Name you'll use in R for the T-SQL data'
@script = N'R_Code_Goes_Here'
@output_data_1_name = N'output data name'
 WITH RESULT SETS ((column_name data_type));
```

Let's break this down a bit. Here are the parts of the statement:

*   `sp_execute_external_script`: The stored procedure that calls the processes that allow R (and other languages) to run. You'll learn more about the architecture of this process in a moment.

*   `@language = N'R'`: Sets the language that the external process uses, in this case, R.

*   `@input_data_1 = ' '`: Your T-SQL script for what you want to send to the R program goes here. You can span lines, but it needs to be within the tick marks.

*   `@input_data_1_name = ' '`: The name of the "variable" that R will use as the input data from SQL Server.

*   `@script = N' '`: Your R program text goes here. You can span lines, but it needs to be enclosed within the tick marks. It's passed as a `VARCHAR(MAX)` data type. Note that within the R script, you can use `input_data_1` as an R data frame, filled out by your T-SQL script.

- **@output_data_1_name = N'output data name'**: This is the name of the variable in the R script that is returned to T-SQL, which you can use to further process or simply display to the caller.

- **WITH RESULT SETS ((column_name data_type))**: When the results come from the R script back to SQL Server, there are no implied headers. It's best practice to declare the columns that are returned and the SQL Server data types you want.

> **Note**
>
> Of particular importance in the statistical functions used in machine learning are the differences between R data types and SQL Server data types. R supports about 9 basic data types, while SQL Server supports over 30. It's important to test each statement you run to ensure you declare explicit conversions appropriately.

Here's a quick example of this call. Using the **AdventureWorks** database, this calculates the sum of purchase orders:

```
USE AdventureWorks;
GO


EXEC sp_execute_external_script
@language = N'R'
, @input_data_1 = N'SELECT LineTotal FROM Purchasing.
PurchaseOrderDetail'
, @input_data_1_name = N'lineitems'
, @script = N'sumlineitems <- as.data.frame(sum(lineitems))'
, @output_data_1_name = N'sumlineitems'
  WITH RESULT SETS ((sumlineitems int));
GO
```

Python for machine learning in SQL Server 2019

The Python language and processing platform is open source software that is widely used for machine learning, artificial intelligence, and deep learning. It is a general-purpose, object-oriented language that is highly extensible, and is fast becoming a very popular language for machine learning. There are two primary versions of Python: 2.x and 3.x. Most modern implantations of Python are 3.x, and that's what SQL Server uses.

SQL Server 2019 Machine Learning Services installs the open source distribution of Python 3.x, and also allows you to use the **rx_** libraries to enhance the performance, parallelism, and scale of the language.

Using the Python language in SQL Server 2019 Machine Learning Services works the same as in R – you use the external stored procedure, provide the language name ("Python," in this case) and then send in the data from SQL Server, work with the data in Python, and return the result set. The syntax looks the same as the examples for R that you saw earlier – with one important distinction: Python is very sensitive to spacing. In the Python script you paste in, make sure the spacing is maintained from your original script.

The data types supported by Python are different than those in R (and SQL Server), so you should be aware of how it will be converted in the results. But the largest difference is that Python is highly sensitive to spacing and tabs – so, in the script declaration, you will need to be extremely careful in how the string is entered.

> **Note**
>
> You should always implicitly declare your data types as you work with various languages, especially since data science involves statistical formulas, and even a small difference in data types can completely throw off a calculation – and you don't always get a warning that the data is unreliable. Make sure you **CAST** or **CONVERT** the data into exactly what each language understands as you pass the data back and forth.

Java and machine learning in SQL Server

The Java language and processing platform is a cross-platform, sandboxed, general-use, object-oriented programming language. SQL Server 2019 introduces the Java environment to the external libraries you have available to your code.

Although Java isn't commonly associated with machine learning the way R and Python are, it is used in many big data processing systems and for general processing tasks. That isn't to say it's not used at all in machine learning; in fact, there are several libraries you can load for machine learning in Java. It is, however, well-suited for certain data processing tasks, such as extracting n-grams for natural language processing, calling out to a blockchain tag for inclusion in the machine learning process, and so on.

> **Note**
>
> The intention in SQL Server 2019 Machine Learning Services is that you have several processing languages to choose from based on the task you need to perform. You might process much of the data using T-SQL, further process the data in R, extract or transform data in Java, and pass the results to a deep learning library in Python, all while using SQL Server in a secure way.

For those not familiar with Java, some of the terms used in the Java environment can be confusing. To run Java programs, you need a **Java Virtual Machine** (**JVM**) – the abstraction layer that sandboxes the program from the rest of the operating system. Along with the JVM, you need the class libraries in your code. Those are combined into the **Java Runtime Environment** (**JRE**). Java developers also have compilers, debuggers, documentation tools, and more, and these are provided in a **Java Development Kit** (**JDK**):

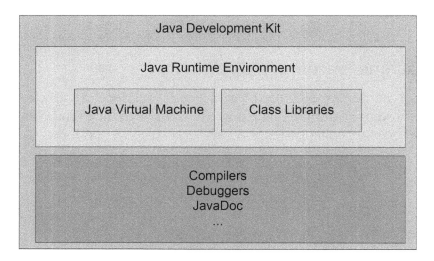

Figure 8.4: The Java programming environment

For SQL Server 2019 Machine Learning Services, you only need to install a JRE (version 8). If you do not already have a JRE installed on your system, you'll need to install it first – it isn't installed with the SQL Server installer the way R and Python are.

> **Note**
>
> While you do not need a full Java SDK to run Java code in SQL Server, you do need it in order to write, compile, and package Java code on your developer workstation. This section assumes that you are familiar with Java code development.

The Java code you write is compiled to bytecode and combined with other assets in an archive file (`.jar`) for use with JRE. That process means it works differently than R or Python in SQL Server 2019. In R and Python, you run code by simply wrapping it in a stored procedure. Since Java is compiled and run in JRE, the process has additional steps.

First, create a folder on the SQL Server system where you will store your compiled Java code as `.jar` files. This should be a secure location, since it allows code to run on your SQL Server.

The next step is slightly different for Linux and Windows, but, in general, you need to grant the Windows or Linux process that runs SQL Server 2019 extension permissions for the directory where your `.jar` files are stored.

While you can grant (in Windows, the `SQLRUsergroup` group, and, in Linux, the `mssql_satellite:mssql_satellite user`) permissions manually, it's better to install the Microsoft Java Extensibility SDK for Microsoft SQL Server, which downloads the `mssql-java-lang-extension.jar` file. (Search for this installer on the web, or check the SQL Server 2019 official documentation for the latest location.)

Place the `.jar` file it downloads in the directory you created a moment ago. This allows calls from your Java code back into the calling SQL Server program. It provides a handler class for the input and output data, dealing with certain data types, and handles the security setup for your `.jar` directory.

Next, you need to set an environment variable (`SET` with Windows, `export` with Linux) called `JRE_HOME` for the location of the JVM on your system. Make sure this is set permanently, either in the control panel in Windows or in the environment settings in your Linux distribution.

With these steps completed, the SQL Server instance is set up and you're ready to get started. Here's the complete process for using Java in SQL Server 2019:

1. Write your Java code as a `.class` file and save it in the folder where you granted SQL Server permissions. You'll need to include at least these lines:

    ```
    import com.microsoft.sqlserver.javalangextension.PrimitiveDataset;
    import com.microsoft.sqlserver.javalangextension.
    AbstractSqlServerExtensionExecutor;
    ```

    And if you are dealing with data coming in, you'll most probably require these lines as well:

    ```
    import java.util.LinkedHashMap;
    import java.util.LinkedList;
    import java.util.ListIterator;
    ```

    Now, you can use the SQL Server Java extensions like so:

    ```
    public class sumlines extends AbstractSqlServerExtensionExecutor {
    ```

    And then begin to create your classes. Your input dataset and any parameters take this form:

    ```
    public PrimitiveDataset execute(PrimitiveDataset input,
    LinkedHashMap<String, Object> params) {
            // Validate the input parameters and input column schema
            validateInput(input, params);
    ```

    > **Note**
    >
    > If this seems a bit complex, the documentation for the Java extensions in SQL Server 2019 has a lengthy example involving the use of **RegEx** (**Regular Expressions**) in Java that you can walk through. Java developers will be familiar with these code snippets – as a data professional, you will most often simply get the `.jar` file directly from the developer.

2. Compile the class into a `.jar` file (for example, `jar -cf sumlineitems.jar sumlineitems.class`).

3. Set a parameter for SQL Server to find the libraries. You have two options: you can use a system environment variable called **CLASSPATH** that has the location of your **.jar** files, or you may use the following code to set where the **.jar** files are located. The latter is the preferred method. Here's an example:

```
CREATE EXTERNAL LIBRARY sumlineitemsJar
FROM (CONTENT = 'c:\javajars\')
WITH (LANGUAGE = 'Java');
GO
```

4. Use the **sp_execute_external_script** stored procedure to send in data, run the class, and then receive the results. In this example, you have a **.jar** file you compiled, and that **Java** file has a class that sums the lines of the data sent to it, just the same as in the R and Python examples:

```
EXEC sp_execute_external_script
   @language = N'Java'
, @script = N'package.sumlines'
, @input_data_1 = N'SELECT CONVERT(LineTotal to INT) FROM
Purchasing.PurchaseOrderDetail'
, @params = N''
with result sets ((sumlines int));
```

As you can see, working with Java in SQL Server is a bit more complex than using the R and Python extensions, but the power and flexibility of the Java language provides benefits to the shop that has standardized on Java development. This allows the entire data processing system to exist within a single platform and security boundary.

Machine learning using the PREDICT T-SQL command

Once you have created a model (also called a "trained model"), you can save it in a binary format for "scoring" the results of a prediction. Both R and Python have methods to store the trained models as binary outputs. It's common to store these models in the database itself, which then allows you to process requests from clients in a T-SQL statement and return the results as a dataset. This process requires the runtime (R or Python) to process the request.

As an example, if you were to create the k-means clustering solution around the customer returns mentioned earlier, you could save that model as a binary object, perhaps even from another server that holds the customer data. You could then deploy that model to a server located at each store and run it using the PREDICT statement to alert the salespeople to the behavior that might lead to a return, thereby preventing customer dissatisfaction.

Functions from **RevoScaleR** (for R) and **revoscalepy** (for Python) have C++ implementations, and SQL Server 2019 can use models they create (using the **rxSerialize** for R, and **rx_serialize_model** for Python, functions) even without R or Python being present on the server. These C++ implementations have various prediction algorithms, including logistic regression and decision trees, and are optimized for fast processing.

> **Note**
>
> Using the PREDICT command is also called **Native Scoring**.

The process to use the PREDICT command is as follows:

1. Create a table with a binary column to store the trained model.

2. Create a prediction model using the algorithms supported by native scoring.

3. Serialize the trained model using either the **rxSerialize** for R, or **rx_serialize_model** for Python, functions.

4. Call the model using the SELECT ... FROM PREDICT(...) commands. Note that the models return data in various formats based on what you define, so you need to have the WITH RESULTS clause to specify the schema of the data returned from the prediction.

To see a complete example of this process, refer to: https://docs.microsoft.com/en-us/sql/t-sql/queries/predict-transact-sql?view=sql-server-2017.

A good reference for the algorithms you can use can be found here: https://docs.microsoft.com/en-us/sql/advanced-analytics/sql-native-scoring?view=sql-server-2.

Machine learning using the sp_rxPredict stored procedure

Another method you can use for scoring predictions in the database is to use the `sp_rxPredict` stored procedure. As you can see in the name, this process involves using the `RevoScaleR` or the `MicrosoftML` functions (a full list of the algorithms in those functions can be found in the following link).

> **Note**
>
> To use `sp_rxPredict`, you'll need to enable the **common language runtime** (**CLR**) in SQL Server, but you don't need to install R or Python. You'll also need to enable real-time scoring by following the instructions here: https://docs.microsoft. com/en-us/sql/advanced-analytics/real-time-scoring?view=sql-server-ver15#bkmk_ enableRtScoring.

With the prerequisites completed, you then have to follow this process to score the predictions in T-SQL:

1. Load a trained model into a binary variable.

2. Select the data you want to score.

3. Call the `sp_rxPredict` function.

4. Receive the results.

Here's a simple example that assumes you have a model stored in the database in a table called `my_models` and model name is `predict_purchase`:

```
DECLARE @modelname varbinary(max)

SELECT @modelname = [model_name] from [my_models]

WHERE model_name = 'predict_purchase'

AND model_version = 'v1''


EXEC sp_rxPredict

@model = @modelname,

@inputData = N'SELECT * FROM customer_features'
```

To see a complete example of this process and the functions you can use, visit: https:// docs.microsoft.com/en-us/sql/advanced-analytics/real-time-scoring?view=sql- server-ver15.

Libraries and packages for machine learning

In R, Python, and Java environments, the base language comes with multiple functions, statements, operators, and calls. But the real power in all of these languages is the ability to add additional constructs written to extend the language for other purposes – in this case, machine learning. These constructs are bundled together in packages and libraries.

These terms can be a bit confusing. In R, a package contains one or more functions, the help files, and sample data – all grouped as files. An R library is where packages are stored.

In Python, a package is a collection of modules, which contain functions and other code.

Since Java is an object-oriented language, libraries contain classes. Since Java is operating system-independent, it includes the **Java Class Library** (**JCL**), which provides low-level access to calls for things such as file and networking access. These are most often bundled into a Java archive (`.jar`) file for easy transport, and loaded with a `CLASSPATH` call as you saw in the discussion for using Java in SQL Server.

In all cases, package and library management is of paramount importance. Packages and libraries affect everything the system can do, from functionality to security. The version of the language environment and the version of the package or library also impact one another.

Because you are installing a language server alongside SQL Server, you have all of these concerns and more, since you are mixing a multi use environment with languages that are often intended for a single programmer to interact with.

A full course on package and library management is beyond the scope of this book, but you should know that it is one of the most important areas to understand for the developer, administrator, and data scientist.

In the R and Python languages, Microsoft includes several packages and libraries for machine learning. They are stored in the location you select during installation, which is different for Linux and Windows.

> **Note**
>
> You can find the path of your libraries and packages using standard R, Python, and Java code, using the `sp_execute_external_script` stored procedure. You can get a list of the packages and libraries that are currently installed the same way.

You can install new packages and libraries that you need on SQL Server with various methods, specific to each language, as an administrator from the command line on your server. However, the best method for R, Python, and Java with SQL Server 2019 is the enhanced T-SQL **CREATE EXTERNAL LIBRARY** command. You'll need to be part of the **db_owner** role, and then you simply download the packages or libraries to the appropriate folder for that language. After that, it's a standard call to the installation process in each language, since the package or library will be available in the secure location for that language.

Here's an example of loading an **R** package with this method:

```
CREATE EXTERNAL LIBRARY customPackage

FROM (CONTENT = 'C:\Program Files\Microsoft SQL Server\MSSQL15.
MSSQLSERVER\MyPackage.zip') WITH (LANGUAGE = 'R');

GO
```

Then, you can run the **R** code to use it:

```
EXEC sp_execute_external_script

@language =N'R',

@script=N'library(customPackage)'
```

It's a similar process for Python. You saw an example of the Java process call earlier – while Java is more involved, the package management associated with this statement is fairly trivial.

For more information on this command, refer to: https://docs.microsoft.com/en-us/sql/t-sql/statements/create-external-library-transact-sql?view=sql-server-ver15.

Management

Management of any system involves security, safety, monitoring and performance, and optimization. In the case of SQL Server Machine Learning Services, the safety portion (backups, availability, and the like) are part of the database environment. Performance tuning involves optimizing the T-SQL and language-specific code and calls. That leaves you with a specific set of processes and tools for security, as well as monitoring and performance.

Security

For the most part, the security for using Machine Learning Services follows the same model as other SQL Server securables. The person or SQL Server principal calling the Machine Learning Services extensibility framework functions needs to be a Windows or SQL Server database user, must have access to the tables or views they are passing in, the ability to write data out (if they do that with the returned data), and be able to create stored procedures if they are making new code to run the models.

There are differences in security for the languages themselves. If the user is going to include packages and libraries for R or Python, in their code, they will need the appropriate permissions to install these software additions. For a complete discussion of these changes, refer to: https://docs.microsoft.com/en-us/sql/advanced-analytics/security/user-permission?view=sql-server-ver15.

One interesting side effect of working with external processes is that the **Transparent Data Encryption** (**TDE**) feature in SQL Server is not supported for Machine Learning Services, since the processes described previously are isolated from the main SQL Server process where TDE is maintained.

Monitoring and Performance

After you have installed, configured, and secured your system, it's now time to set up the monitoring of the system. This section covers the tools and processes you should add to your current monitoring and tuning process for your SQL Server instances – sizing, setting up monitoring, logging and reporting, setting a baseline, and so on.

To monitor the processes that make up the Machine Learning Services extensibility framework, you can use standard Windows or Linux process monitoring tools. Look for components running as services or daemons shown in the architecture components diagram earlier in this section to include in your operating system's monitoring tools.

For the SQL Server engine-specific components, the first place to start is with a set of Microsoft SQL Server Reporting Services reports written in **Report Definition Language** (**RDL**) format specifically for Machine Learning Services. Download the reports here: https://github.com/Microsoft/sql-server-samples/tree/master/samples/features/machine-learning-services/ssms-custom-reports, and then follow the installation instructions for those components. You can find everything in these reports, from the extended events you can monitor, to a list of the packages and libraries installed for each language. Most of the reports also include a button for the T-SQL script used to get this information, so this is the best place to start.

After installing the standard reports for Machine Learning Services, you can move on to using the **Dynamic Management Views** (**DMV's**) in SQL Server 2019 included with Machine Learning Services. These views work similar to other DMVs in SQL Server, and expose everything from session information to resource usage, and also Machine Learning Services-specific objects, such as the installed packages and libraries, and much more. You can find a complete list of these DMVs here: https://docs.microsoft. com/en-us/sql/advanced-analytics/administration/monitor-sql-server-machine-learning-services-using-dynamic-management-views?view=sqlallproducts-allversions.

To find detailed information about all parts of Machine Learning Services running on your SQL Server 2019 instance, you can use SQL Server's Extended Events subsystem. The complete list of events that you can monitor is here: https://docs.microsoft.com/en-us/sql/advanced-analytics/r/extended-events-for-sql-server-r-services?view=sql-server-ver15.

Once you've enabled your monitoring, you can set limits on how Machine Learning Services in SQL Server 2019 use the CPU, memory, and some of the I/O components on your instance. You can read a complete discussion on this process here – note that this feature is available on the Enterprise Edition only: https://docs.microsoft.com/en-us/sql/advanced-analytics/administration/resource-governance?view=sql-server-ver15.

Tuning the system follows the same process as any other SQL Server production application. Using the monitoring data you have been collecting, you will size your server, refactor your code (both T-SQL and the language you are using), scale the systems out and up, and constantly tune the top waits on the system.

You can read a complete discussion on tuning for model performance and other tasks at https://docs.microsoft.com/en-us/sql/advanced-analytics/r/managing-and-monitoring-r-solutions?view=sql-server-ver15.

Now that you have Machine Learning Services installed, configured, and secured, you're ready to use the tools for monitoring and performance to set a zero-use baseline for your system. That baseline is used as a comparison to the measurements you record later to find deltas for the performance of each component.

With an understanding of machine learning, you now have a platform to implement various languages to work with it. Next, let's pair that with a process that combines Machine Learning Services with many other features of SQL Server 2019 for a complete machine learning platform.

Using the team data science process with Machine Learning Services

You've explored the basics of machine learning, and you understand the languages, tools, and SQL Server 2019 components you can use to implement it, and now you're ready to get started on some actual data science. A data science project is different from traditional software development projects because it involves a single solution at a time, it is highly dependent on improving the solution once it is deployed, and it involves more stakeholders in the design and implementation.

In business intelligence, you can build a single cube that can answer many questions. But in data science, you can't use a k-means algorithm on a prediction that requires linear regression, and the features and labels needed for each would be entirely different – each question you want to answer requires a new project. Some will be small, others will be more involved, but all of them require that you work as a team.

In the earliest days of data science, a data scientist would define a problem area, obtain and curate a dataset, clean the data, perform statistical modeling, select the appropriate model, deploy the model for the predictions or classification, and then compare the results to the "ground truth" of what actually occurred so that the model could be retrained and improved. Over time, the data scientist became overwhelmed with multiple projects, spending much of their time in data cleansing, programming, or other non-algorithmic tasks. The data scientist might not be aware of the location of certain sets of data, the enterprise security model, the networking infrastructure, or any of dozens of other project factors.

For these reasons, teams have developed around the data science practice, including data engineers, data scientists, developers, and business analysts. With this complex arrangement, you need a formal process to control the project with defined roles and tasks for each team member, and a way to communicate between each stage of the project.

Understanding the team data science process

The **Team Data Science Process** (**TDSP** – https://aka.ms/tdsp) is an open framework for managing and controlling data science projects. It provides guidance, assets, and documentation that you can use to implement your solution. The TDSP also defines the roles described previously, such as data engineers.

The TDSP is made up of five "phases," each with defined steps. Let's take a look at each of these and where they map to features and components in SQL Server 2019 with Machine Learning Services.

Phase 1: Business understanding

The most important part of a data science project, even more than the algorithm, languages, platform, and every other component, is to ensure you have a clearly defined problem you want to solve. SQL Server 2019 helps you in this area by ensuring that the organization has exhausted every other query, report, and business intelligence function to get the answer they are looking for. Many machine learning projects could be replaced with a well-designed report or cube.

Machine learning problems involve the "five questions" defined in this chapter. Your organization should be very clear about what it wants to know, and what it will do when it finds out. Keep in mind that one prediction equates to one project in data science, unlike a reporting project that can answer many questions in a single report.

Phase 2: Data acquisition and understanding

With the question defined, you'll need to identify the data sources (internal or external) that you need to create the features and (optionally) labels that you require to create the prediction or classification. SQL Server 2019 has components such as master data services, data quality services, SQL Server integration services, and the database engine itself to source, move, document, store, and process data sources from multiple locations. In SQL Server 2019, the Big Data Clusters feature (covered in the next chapter) allows you to source and store data at tremendous scale.

You can use T-SQL, Reporting Services, R, Python, and Java to explore the data for pattern analysis, cleansing, and more.

Phase 3: Modeling

Using the `PREDICT` statement, the `sp_rxPredict` stored procedure, Python, R, and Java, you can create, train, and test models, and then store them in the database engine or elsewhere.

Phase 4: Deployment

With the models stored in the database, you can call a stored procedure to do a single prediction or classification directly from T-SQL code sent from a client application. You can also run the stored procedure containing the call against a table of data, storing the predictions and other data in yet another table for use in reporting, queries, or automation.

In addition, you can export the models from the database in a binary stream to another location for another system to use in scoring.

Phase 5: Customer acceptance

SQL Server 2019's rich set of reporting and classification features, along with **Continuous Integration** and **Continuous Deployment** (**CI/CD**) capabilities, allow you to transition the solution to the maintenance team, and also allows you to store the "ground truth" of the predictions for model retraining. You can also use Reporting Services to create outputs of the effectiveness of the models and predictions.

SQL Server 2019 provides everything that you need to create an entire data science ecostructure for secure architectures (on-premises, cloud, or hybrid) for any project your organization needs, using multiple languages and libraries to future-proof your data science environment.

If you would like to work through an entire tutorial involving all of these processes and tools in a clustering example, refer to: https://aka.ms/sqlserverml.

SQL Server 2019 Big Data Clusters

In *Chapter 8, Machine Learning Services Extensibility Framework*, you learned about Machine Learning Services using SQL Server machine learning services. The training phase of model development requires a lot of data – more examples are better for the algorithms to "learn" from. However, machine learning isn't the only use case that requires lots of information: everything from business intelligence to data mining takes advantage of large sets of data. The SQL Server 2019 Big Data Clusters feature facilitates working with datasets far larger than a traditional **Relational Database Management System** (**RDBMS**) can usually handle, while incorporating other benefits and features as well.

Because of the depth of technical information in any scale-out system, this chapter will focus on the primary concepts of this new feature, while providing concrete examples of their use. References are provided in each section to assist you in learning more about each area.

Big data overview

The first magnetic storage devices were, large, bulky, and expensive, and required massive amounts of power and cooling. They also failed quite often. But, as time has progressed, the sizes of computing components – especially storage – have shrunk, and costs have decreased. However, the capabilities, reliability, and power of those components have increased. This allows us to store much more data, and since we've had those technologies longer, we've been able to store more data over time.

And what can we do with it all – why keep it? Given a system that processes and delivers the data quickly enough, there are actually quite a few examples of specific use cases for large sets of data. The most basic use of big data is to simply query it, using standard T-SQL or **<u>Multidimensional Expressions</u>** (**<u>MDX</u>**).

Applying scale-out architectures to SQL Server

With an understanding of the source of big data, the uses for big data, and the technology for processing big data, there are changes and enhancements that are required for SQL Server to work in a scale-out environment. While SQL Server has long provided a parallel mechanism to scale processing within an instance, it requires new technologies to work with massive distributed datasets.

To scale out your computing environment, you need multiple computers, or nodes. But, of course, adding and removing physical computers from the ecostructure is expensive and time-consuming, not to mention complicated.

"Virtual" computers are a better solution. A technology called a **hypervisor** uses software to represent the physical computer's CPU, I/O, memory, and networking components to an operating system's installer, running an entire computer within a computer. The operating system installs onto a file that acts as a hard drive, encapsulating the entire computer in a file.

This solution allows a greater degree of flexibility to create and remove computers, is much less expensive, and it is faster to move them around. For instance, you can use a single physical computer to host multiple virtual computers running Hadoop and quickly and easily turn them off and on.

However, even this level of abstraction has drawbacks. You can only carve up the physical computer's components so many times before performance suffers. But the biggest drawback is that you are reinstalling the operating system multiple times, with all its drivers, patches, libraries to show the screen and work with the mouse, and so on. You really only want to run Hadoop, or Python, or some other software program, but, in a virtual PC, you have to carry the cost of the entire operating system.

Containers

Containers offer a better solution. A container system does not represent the CPU, I/O, memory, and networking sub-systems in a PC so that you can install a full operating system. Instead, it uses a container runtime engine on the current operating system. "Layers" of binary files run in the container runtime engine, isolated from other containers and the host operating system.

The advantages of a container system are best illustrated with an example. Assume you want to run a Python program. To do that, you need a computer, an operating system, the Python program binary files, any code you want to run, and any assets (graphics files, database and text files, and so on) that you create and use in the program that is installed for every version of the application you want to run. In a virtual machine, the architecture looks like this:

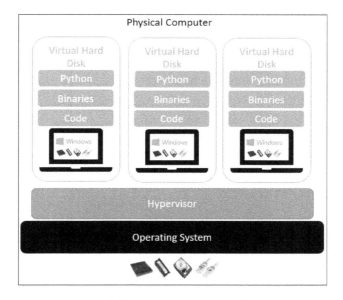

Figure 9.1: Virtual machine architecture

Using a container runtime engine, the architecture looks like this:

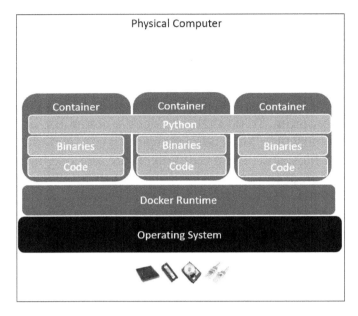

Figure 9.2: Container architecture (Docker shown)

The advantages of this architecture are that the system only carries the assets it needs to run the Python program, and that environment is completely encapsulated – its own version of Python, your application, and files. If the engine determines it's the same Python throughout, it only loads that version once. You could redeploy a copy of that program with a different version of Python or your application, and it would operate independently.

The other major advantage associated with this system is how a container is created and deployed. The general process is declarative:

1. You create a `text` file (in **Yet-Another-Markup-Language**, or **YAML**, format) that describes what binaries and files you want in your container.

2. You "compose" this file to an image, which is a binary file containing all of those assets. You can store this image in a public or private repository. You can then run a `pull` command to bring the binary image to your system.

3. Using a `run` command, the binary image is loaded into the container runtime engine (Docker, in our case) and starts up. This environment is now a container.

4. Depending on what your program needs to do, you can allow network access in and out of the container.

One of the most popular container platforms is called **Docker**, and it's the one that is used in SQL Server big data clusters. There's a complete course you can take online for Docker here: https://docs.docker.com/get-started/.

While container technology is revolutionary, it leads to a significant issue: how to manage multiple containers. You want a scale-out architecture for your big data processing system, and that means lots of containers running the processing – sometimes dozens, hundreds, or even thousands of containers. This can become overwhelming to deploy and manage.

Kubernetes

Kubernetes (*Greek for a ship's pilot*) is an orchestration system for containers. It also provides enhanced networking and storage systems that allow for a robust cluster environment. It's best understood by starting with definitions of its components. You already know the most basic component – the container. To manage the containers you wish to deploy, Kubernetes involves the following additional components:

Kubernetes component	Purpose
Pod	A logical boundary around one or more containers.
Node	Pods run on nodes, which are computers – virtual machines or full bare-metal systems. Each node will run at least the Docker runtime (to run containers), and the kubelet and kube-proxy processes, which handle node and pod operations and in-cluster networking.
Cluster	One or more nodes makes a cluster. There is always one special node, the Kubernetes Master, which controls the cluster.
Volume	A volume exists as a separate entity for storage. Since the pods and nodes can move around within the cluster, storage is accessed through a software claim. There are two types of volumes: persistent (which stays up even after the pods release it) and non-persistent, which does not.

Table 9.3: Kubernetes components

Here's a diagram of all those components together:

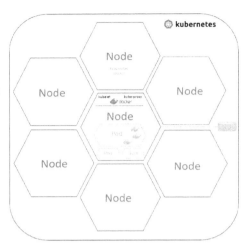

- Container(s) live in *Pods*
- Pod(s) are abstractions within *Nodes*
- Node(s) are PC's or VM's
- Cluster(s) are groups of *Nodes*
- Storage is by means of Volume(s) mounted through a *Claim*

Figure 9.4: Kubernetes components

A Kubernetes cluster is controlled with a set of `YAML` files that dictate the layout of the preceding components. The primary control program for deploying, configuring, and managing a Kubernetes cluster is called `kubectl`.

There is, of course, much more to know about Kubernetes – a good place to start is here: https://kubernetes.io/docs/tutorials/kubernetes-basics/.

SQL Server on Linux

Now that you understand what constitutes big data, the uses of big data, a way to scale out, compute, and process big data, the containers to hold that processing, and a clustering mechanism to control the containers, all that is left for SQL Server to scale this way is the ability to run on these components – most of which run on Linux.

SQL Server's origins are from Unix. The original code base for SQL Server was licensed from Sybase, but the entire product has been rewritten over time to have only Microsoft-developed, Microsoft Windows-based components. However, the architectures you'll learn about in this chapter are largely Linux-based.

You learned a lot about using SQL Server in Linux in an earlier chapter, but, as a review, to enable Linux-based customers to work with SQL Server, Microsoft implemented the **Platform Abstraction Layer** (**PAL**) to act as a "shim" between the lowest-level calls in SQL Server and the operating system it runs on. The PAL also allows SQL Server to run not just on bare-metal installations of Linux, but also on container technologies you learned about earlier. This also means that the entire system can be deployed using Kubernetes, as you saw previously.

> **Note**
>
> There are different distributions of Linux, and while the base commands work the same way in most, the primary difference you'll notice is the package management. A Linux package manager dictates how you install, upgrade, and remove software – it's usually a command rather than a graphical process. Check *Chapter 5, SQL Server 2019 on Linux*, for more information.

You can learn a lot more about Linux here: https://www.edx.org/course/introduction-to-linux.

PolyBase

You learned about PolyBase in *Chapter 5, Data Virtualization*, and the big data cluster feature takes advantage of this technology for much of its scale. SQL Server can store and process data in the petabyte range, given proper hardware and planning. A **RDBMS** has certain requirements on the consistency model that ensures the safety and reliability of the data that makes larger sizes more challenging. A **Massively Parallel Processing** (**MPP**) system breaks apart the data and processing in a similar way to the example discussed a moment ago, but this isn't the way an RDBMS works natively. However, there are ways to handle larger sets of data within an SQL Server environment, and SQL Server 2019's big data cluster features implement various components to work with those large sets of data.

Leveraging the scale-out features in PolyBase is the key to SQL Server 2019's big data cluster feature. As you learned in *Chapter 5, Data Virtualization*, PolyBase allows you to query multiple data sources, and while big data clusters allow those sources, it also allows you to query **Hadoop Distributed File System** (**HDFS**) data directly as you'll see in a moment. Adding to that ability, the Big Data Cluster's HDFS system can "mount" other storage (such as S3 and Azure sources), allowing yet another way to virtualize data. Let's now take a look at how all of this fits together.

SQL Server 2019 big data cluster components

With an understanding of big data, its processing, architecture, and technologies, and the ability for SQL Server to use these technologies, it's time to put it all together.

All of the components for SQL Server 2019 big data clusters run on a Kubernetes cluster, which you've already learned about. Various nodes on the cluster provide the capabilities you need to run your data workloads, from SQL Server itself, to control systems, storage, Spark, and HDFS. This increases the number of external data sources that you can query, scales out your query processing, provides push-down compute to `Parquet` and `CSV` files, and even allows you to mount other storage.

Once again, using a diagram to understand how each part fits together is useful:

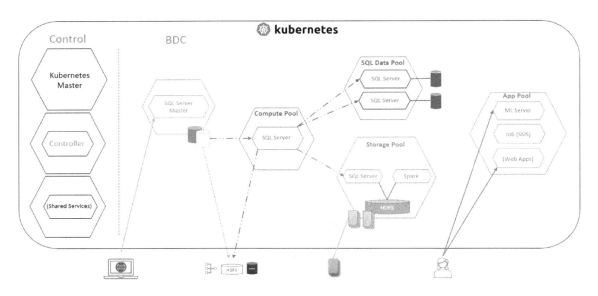

Figure 9.5: SQL Server 2019 big data cluster components

> **Note**
>
> You can specify the number of Kubernetes pods/nodes for many of these components, so the preceding diagram is simply an arbitrary arrangement to explain how it works. A big data cluster can use one or many nodes in various arrangements based on how you want to configure it.

There's a lot going on in this diagram, so here's a chart of what each component provides within the big data cluster system:

SQL Server 2019 big data cluster component	Purpose
Controller	Controls all of the big data cluster components in the system, including provisioning, management, and movement of the components.
Shared Services	Various services are required for management, monitoring, and security of the big data clusters. These include Grafana, Kibana, Active Directory, the HIVE metastore service and database, and more.
SQL Server Master Instance	An instance of SQL Server, running in a container, that accepts all standard SQL Server traffic. It acts as a single-point-of-query operation, and has the PolyBase engine and data movement service configured.
Compute Pool	One or more SQL Server instances with the PolyBase engine and data movement service installed to communicate with external and internal data sources at scale. It communicates with the SQL Server master instance for requests.
Data Pool	One or more SQL Server instances with the PolyBase engine and data movement service installed to store and process relational data at scale. It communicates with the SQL Server master instance.
Storage Pool	One or more pods with an instance of Spark and HDFS. It also contains an instance of SQL Server that has the ability to talk directly to HDFS files stored in CSV or Parquet format. It communicates with the SQL Server master instance.
Application Pool	One or more pods where you can deploy a containerized application such as Microsoft Machine Learning Server, Python web applications, SSIS packages, and other applications you wish to provide from within the security boundary of the big data clusters. These applications can talk to any part of the big data clusters through the SQL Server master instance. For more information on how to deploy applications on a SQL Server big data cluster, visit: https://docs.microsoft.com/en-us/sql/big-data-cluster/concept-application-deployment?view=sqlallproducts-allversions.
Spark Pool (not shown)	This is optional. One or more pods with Spark installed and configured for the cluster.

Table 9.6: Components in the big data cluster system

In a moment, you'll walk through common programming patterns for this architecture, so keep this section handy for reference as you work through the data paths.

Installation and configuration

Now that you understand the components within the big data cluster, you can plan your installation. For a comprehensive discussion of your choices, you can find a full reference for each of these options here: https://docs.microsoft.com/en-us/sql/big-data-cluster/deploy-get-started?view=sqlallproducts-allversions.

Let's now take a brief tour of the major options you have for deploying SQL Server 2019 big data clusters. You'll then examine the primary installation commands and learn about other options for deployment.

> **Note**
>
> A full description of the planning and installation process is quite lengthy, and you should take your time and review the installation documentation thoroughly before implementing the system in production. We'll cover the main installation and configuration concepts here so that you have an idea of the general process.

Platform options

You have a wide array of possible environments to deploy SQL Server 2019 big data clusters. These range from using a service from a cloud provider to setting up your own environment within a secure boundary you establish. Since SQL Server 2019 big data clusters use Kubernetes, you will need to have a cluster of appropriate size and storage to run the product, which you'll see for each environment in the following section. Once you've verified the resources for your cluster, you'll install and configure Kubernetes before you deploy an SQL Server 2019 big data cluster on it.

You have three primary targets to create a Kubernetes cluster (which includes *OpenShift*):

1. Using a Kubernetes service (such as the **Azure Kubernetes Service** (**AKS**)

2. Using an on-premises installation of Kubernetes

3. Using a local/laptop installation of Kubernetes

Let's get an overview of each of these.

Using a Kubernetes service

By far the easiest, quickest, and simplest way to install Kubernetes is not to install it at all. The Microsoft Azure cloud has a service called AKS that you can use for a Kubernetes cluster with just a few clicks. You can read more about AKS here: https://docs.microsoft.com/en-us/azure/aks/intro-kubernetes.

Deploying a Kubernetes cluster on AKS is quite simple, and it also provides logging, reporting, and more. The configuration that is the most important for SQL Server 2019 big data clusters is the size of the virtual machines, the networking configuration, and the number and type of disks for storage volumes.

You can read more about setting those up, along with the specifications for a "base" configuration, here: https://docs.microsoft.com/en-us/sql/big-data-cluster/deploy-on-aks?view=sqlallproducts-allversions.

Once the Kubernetes deployment to AKS is complete, you can move on to installing the big data clusters. More on that in a moment.

Using an on-premises Kubernetes installation

The next option you have for working with Kubernetes is to install it locally or in your own datacenter. The advantage to this deployment is that you completely control the environment, you can use physical hardware or virtual machine technology, and you can configure and control a completely private security boundary.

There are quite a few methods for deploying Kubernetes on-premises, but the primary process is to download the Kubernetes program and install it, and then use the `kubeadm` utility to configure the cluster, storage, and nodes you want. You can read more about how to do that here: https://kubernetes.io/docs/setup/.

Once again, the sizes of the nodes and the storage configuration is important to the function of the big data cluster. You can read more about the "base" configuration of a big data cluster deployed locally here: https://docs.microsoft.com/en-us/sql/big-data-cluster/deploy-with-kubeadm?view=sqlallproducts-allversions.

Once the Kubernetes on-premises deployment is complete, you can move on to installing the big data clusters. More on that in a moment.

Working with a Dev/Test environment

Another option for creating a Kubernetes cluster is to use `minikube`. This utility creates a single-node cluster, suitable only for development and testing. You should have at least 64 GB of RAM, fast storage, and ample processing power to use this environment for big data clusters.

The process for installing and configuring `minikube` is here: https://kubernetes.io/docs/tutorials/hello-minikube/, and the considerations regarding deployment size are here: https://docs.microsoft.com/en-us/sql/big-data-cluster/deploy-on-minikube?view=sqlallproducts-allversions.

> **Note**
>
> You can often deploy a Dev/Test environment faster and cheaper using AKS. The resources for a single-node deployment in `minikube` can be costly to implement on your own system.

Once the Kubernetes deployment on `minikube` is complete, you can move on to installing the big data clusters. More on that in a moment.

Deploying the big data clusters on a Kubernetes cluster

Before you complete the configuration for Kubernetes in preparation for deploying big data clusters, you should understand the storage impacts of working with a database in a Kubernetes cluster. Reliable, durable storage is essential for a database system, and Kubernetes implements durable storage as persistent volumes. These are often implemented as Storage Classes by the deployment target, and AKS, `kubeadm`, and `minikube` all have slightly different ways of ensuring the proper storage configuration. You can read more about those here: https://docs.microsoft.com/en-us/sql/big-data-cluster/concept-data-persistence?view=sqlallproducts-allversions.

With your Kubernetes cluster deployed and your persistent volumes configured, you're ready to create your SQL Server 2019 big data cluster.

Deploying the big data clusters is done using a Notebook in the Azure Data Studio tool, or a Python tool called `azdata`. Let's focus on the `azdata` utility. After downloading and installing it (more on that here: https://docs.microsoft.com/en-us/sql/big-data-cluster/deploy-install-azdata?view=sqlallproducts-allversions. you'll run `azdata`, targeting your Kubernetes cluster. The `azdata` utility uses several `YAML` files embedded within the tool, which specifies the configuration for all of the pods, nodes, and services you learned about earlier. You can override those settings with a switch when you call the command, or, with another switch, you can point the utility to a separate `YAML` file. For a complete description of the switches you can use and how to read the deployment `YAML`, visit: https://docs.microsoft.com/en-us/sql/big-data-cluster/reference-deployment-config?view=sqlallproducts-allversions. This describes the complete deployment using the utility and how you can alter those options using `YAML` files.

> **Note**
>
> The Azure Data Studio tool has a series of steps you can use to deploy big data clusters on your Kubernetes, and, after you enter various parameters, it runs the `azdata` utility for you.

Microsoft created a Python script that will set up a complete SQL Server 2019 big data cluster for you in AKS. You'll need a Microsoft Azure subscription with rights to create appropriate resources and the installation tools (such as Python, **kubectl**, and **azdata**) installed and configured. With all of that in place, it's a simple command to deploy a big data cluster:

```
python deploy-sql-big-data-aks.py
```

You can read more about how to install the tools and other preparations for the deployment here: https://docs.microsoft.com/en-us/sql/big-data-cluster/quickstart-big-data-cluster-deploy?view=sqlallproducts-allversions.

Once the system is installed, you can view the pods, nodes, and services it provides with the **kubectl** commands. This one, for instance, gets the service names and the internal and external IP addresses of the controller service:

```
kubectl get svc controller-svc-external -n <your-big-data-cluster-name>
```

Once you have that external IP address, you can use it to list all of the cluster components with the **azdata** tool. First, you log into the cluster using the information from the previous command, and the name and password you set during installation:

```
azdata login --controller-endpoint https://<ip-address-of-controller-svc-external>:30080 --controller-username <user-name>
```

And then you can list the endpoints you'll use to connect to the component you want:

```
azdata cluster endpoint list
```

> **Note**
>
> Endpoints are also shown in the Big Data Cluster's panel in the Azure Data Studio tool.

We'll go into more detail on the **kubectl** commands as they interact with the SQL Server 2019 big data clusters in a moment. There's a great reference on all available **kubectl** commands here: https://kubernetes.io/docs/reference/kubectl/cheatsheet/.

Programming SQL Server 2019 big data clusters

After you install your SQL Server 2019 big data cluster, it's time to put it to use. While the options for applications using big data clusters range from almost anything you can do with SQL Server to working with Spark, there are four general areas for using the system, with all ranges of data sizes: Online Transactional Processing (OLTP)/standard queries, data virtualization, as a data mart, and as a data lake with Spark processing capabilities.

> **Note**
>
> It's helpful to refer back to the complete architecture diagram to understand the flow of each of the following operations.

With all of these features in a single location, you can query across multiple systems, in multiple databases and formats, using Transact-SQL. It makes SQL Server your organization's data hub.

Let's start with an examination of the Azure Data Studio tool that you can use to work with big data clusters.

Azure Data Studio

You can use any tool that works with SQL Server, including SQL Server Management Studio, to run queries on the master instance of the big data cluster.

Microsoft Azure Data Studio is an enhanced source code editor based on Microsoft Visual Studio Code – and it can be installed on Windows, Linux, or a Mac. It has been modified to have a special set of operations for connections to various data sources and accepts many of the extensions in the Visual Studio Code Marketplace.

One of those extensions is called "SQL Server 2019." It provides several interesting innovations, including running Jupyter Notebooks inside the tool and even has an SQL kernel to run T-SQL commands. Those notebooks can also run a `PySpark` or other Spark-related kernel against the big data clusters' Spark instance, which you'll see in a moment. It also has built-in connectors for the big data cluster features, as well as being able to connect to any SQL Server instance.

While a complete tutorial for the product is beyond the scope of the book, the basics are that once you have installed the SQL Server 2019 extension, you can register your big data cluster server for access. Click the server icon in the left most panel, and you'll see three smaller icons to the right side of the Server's bar.

Clicking the first icon adds a new server registration. Simply type in the IP address, 31433 (or the DNS name, 31433, if you registered your master instance with a DNS server), of the master instance in the big data clusters and the SQL Server authentication name and password you set when you deployed the big data cluster:

Figure 9.7: Azure Data Studio server registration

From there, you can double-click the master instance and you'll get a management panel, and the ability to run queries and notebooks. You'll use this tool throughout this chapter.

Once you've logged in, you're presented with the main panel for the SQL Server 2019 big data clusters master instance:

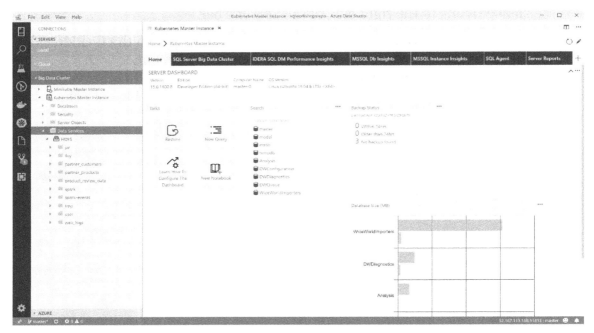

Figure 9.8: Azure Data Studio connection

If you double-click the instance name on the left side, you'll get a panel that allows you to perform various management tasks. Right-click the instance name and select **New query** from the menu that displays and you're ready to write your Transact-SQL code.

If you'd like a complete tutorial for the Azure Data Studio tool, along with how to install and configure it, refer to: https://docs.microsoft.com/en-us/sql/azure-data-studio/tutorial-sql-editor?view=sql-server-2017.

Relational operations

At its heart, the big data cluster is used for SQL Server data storage and processing. You can connect to the system using standard SQL Server tools (such as SQL Server Management Studio or Azure Data Studio) in the same manner as any SQL Server instance, although the TCP/IP port is port 31433 by default, as you saw in the last `kubectl` command. You can also connect to it from any application that you can connect to SQL Server with, for instance, using a .NET, Python, or other application. The general idea is that "it's just SQL Server."

Note that since the master instance of SQL Server in the big data cluster is running on a Linux container, you have access to most of the same features and configurations available in SQL Server on Linux. It's also important to note that SQL Server Machine Learning Services are installed but must be enabled. The same commands and configurations you learned in the last chapter apply to the SQL Server master instance in big data clusters.

Queries you write for the master instance can work not only with SQL Server relational data, but also with other sources of data inside and outside the cluster, in a hybrid fashion. Your developers write T-SQL code and can take advantage of data in other systems. Here's a standard query you can run:

```
/* Instance Version */
SELECT @@VERSION;
GO


/* General Configuration */
USE master;
GO
EXEC sp_configure;
GO


/* Databases on this Instance */
SELECT db.name AS 'Database Name'
, Physical_Name AS 'Location on Disk'
, Cast(Cast(Round(cast(mf.size as decimal) * 8.0/1024000.0,2) as
decimal(18,2)) as nvarchar) 'Size (GB)'
FROM sys.master_files mf
INNER JOIN
    sys.databases db ON db.database_id = mf.database_id
WHERE mf.type_desc = 'ROWS';
GO


SELECT * from sys.master_files
```

And further evidence of "it's just SQL Server" is that you can simply copy a backup file to the master instance pod's filesystem using the `kubectl cp` command:

```
kubectl cp WWI.bak master-0:/var/opt/mssql/data -c mssql-server -n
sqlbigdata
```

And then restore that backup, even if it was taken on an earlier version of SQL Server or on Microsoft Windows, with the same commands you use on any other instance:

```
/* Add the Customer Databases for Wide World Importers */
USE [master]
RESTORE DATABASE [WideWorldImporters]
FROM  DISK = N'/var/opt/mssql/data/WWI.bak'
WITH  FILE = 1
,   REPLACE
,   MOVE N'WWI_Primary' TO N'/var/opt/mssql/data/WideWorldImporters.
mdf'
,   MOVE N'WWI_UserData' TO N'/var/opt/mssql/data/WideWorldImporters_
UserData.ndf'
,   MOVE N'WWI_Log' TO N'/var/opt/mssql/data/WideWorldImporters.ldf'
,   MOVE N'WWI_InMemory_Data_1' TO N'/var/opt/mssql/data/
WideWorldImporters_InMemory_Data_1'
,   NOUNLOAD,  STATS = 5;
GO
```

Note the `WITH MOVE` clause, just as you would use on a Microsoft Windows-based SQL Server instance, but with the paths modified for a Linux filesystem. That's all there is to it – no other changes are necessary to work with the same database backup from Windows in the big data cluster.

Creating scale-out tables

There are many situations where you would want to keep a large amount of relational data for query operations. For instance, you might want to perform business intelligence over the top of multiple terabytes of relational data, or you might want to query to join multiple data sources and retain the results for later use.

You learned about the PolyBase feature in *Chapter 5, Data Virtualization*. The SQL Server 2019 big data cluster feature makes use of this technology throughout the cluster.

The master instance has the PDW engine and other PolyBase features installed and configured. The process to create an external table is in three parts:

1. Create an external data source.

2. This is optional if the source is text-based. Create a **format** file for the data elements in the external data source.

3. Create an external table.

From there, it's a simple matter of querying the data. Let's look at an example of creating and querying an external data source.

You'll notice in the architecture diagram that there is an HDFS system in the storage pool. SQL Server 2019 has been architected to read and write Parquet and **Comma Separated Values** (**CSV**) files, and those can be stored in HDFS in the storage pool. Using PolyBase, you can create an external data source, a format specification, and an external table. All of these point to the HDFS endpoint, and then you can load that directory in HDFS with text files. In this example, the code creates all of the assets to do precisely that:

```
/* Create External File Format */


USE WideWorldImporters;

GO


IF NOT EXISTS(SELECT * FROM sys.external_file_formats WHERE name =
'csv_file')

BEGIN

    CREATE EXTERNAL FILE FORMAT csv_file

    WITH (

        FORMAT_TYPE = DELIMITEDTEXT,

        FORMAT_OPTIONS(

            FIELD_TERMINATOR = ',',

            STRING_DELIMITER = '0x22',

            FIRST_ROW = 2,

            USE_TYPE_DEFAULT = TRUE)

    );

END
```

```
/* Create External Data Source to the Storage Pool */


 IF NOT EXISTS(SELECT * FROM sys.external_data_sources WHERE name =
'SqlStoragePool')
      CREATE EXTERNAL DATA SOURCE SqlStoragePool
      WITH (LOCATION = 'sqlhdfs://controller-svc:8080/default');
/* Create an External Table that can read from the Storage Pool File
Location */ IF NOT EXISTS(SELECT * FROM sys.external_tables WHERE name
= 'partner_customers_hdfs') BEGIN CREATE EXTERNAL TABLE [partner_
customers_hdfs] ("CustomerSource" VARCHAR(250) , "CustomerName"
VARCHAR(250) , "EmailAddress" VARCHAR(250)) WITH ( DATA_SOURCE =
SqlStoragePool, LOCATION = '/partner_customers', FILE_FORMAT = csv_file
); END
```

Now, you can query that data as if it were a standard SQL Server table object:

```
/* Read Data from HDFS using only T-SQL */


SELECT TOP 10 CustomerSource
, CustomerName
, EMailAddress
    FROM [partner_customers_hdfs] hdfs
WHERE EmailAddress LIKE '%wingtip%'
ORDER BY CustomerSource, CustomerName;
GO
```

There is also a wizard process inside Azure Data Studio that can guide you through the process of setting up external tables, and this is often the best place to start. You can see a guided tutorial of that process here: https://docs.microsoft.com/en-us/sql/big-data-cluster/tutorial-query-hdfs-storage-pool?view=sqlallproducts-allversions.

Creating a data lake

In some cases, the data that you need isn't in relational format. You'd like to bring in data from almost any source, and that's where two more components in the big data clusters come into play: the **HDFS** service and the **Spark** service.

Referring back to *Figure 9.5*, you'll notice in the storage pool that there is an SQL Server instance, a Spark deployment, and an HDFS deployment. Using standard Spark calls, you can import, manipulate and combine, and perform other operations on massive amounts of data.

You can load data directly to the HDFS service using `kubectl cp` commands, by calling the API associated with it, or by using an application to load from a source to storage directly.

You can see an example of using these methods here: https://docs.microsoft.com/en-us/sql/big-data-cluster/tutorial-data-pool-ingest-spark?view=sqlallproducts-allversions.

Note that in the Azure Data Studio tool, you can also see the HDFS node's data directories just below the database list in the **Object Browser** panel. You can right-click this menu entry to view a file, create a directory, or even upload a new file into a directory on the HDFS node.

In addition, you can mount a storage point in the HDFS of the storage pool that points to Amazon's S3 storage or Microsoft Azure's data lake storage (generation 2) so that you extend the reach of the data lake even further. Once you configure that setup, the remote storage is a directory within your HDFS system, and you can access it just as in the previous example for creating an HDFS data source.

You can read more about the process to do that and the restrictions on its use at https://docs.microsoft.com/en-us/sql/big-data-cluster/hdfs-tiering?view=sqlallproducts-allversions.

Working with Spark

You learned about Spark at the beginning of this chapter. You submit Spark jobs (in the form of `.jar` or `.py` files) to a Spark API, either by running a Spark job in Azure Data Studio, using a new Jupyter Notebook in Azure Data Studio with the kernel pointed to PySpark or SparkR, or by using IntelliJ. Let's take a brief look at each.

> **Note**
>
> If you're new to Spark job processing, here's a brief overview of the terms used in this section: https://spark.apache.org/docs/latest/cluster-overview.html.

Submitting a job from Azure Data Studio

Azure Data Studio provides two options for loading a Spark job: using a Juypter Notebook and using a **Submit Job** action. In the Jupyter Notebook, you'll connect to the cluster through the SQL Server master instance, and then set the kernel to PySpark, Scala, or SparkR, depending on which language you plan to use. Double-click the master instance node in the server browser of Azure Data Studio, and you'll be brought to the main management panel. Open the Big Data Clusters panel and you're presented with the ability to open a new Jupyter Notebook:

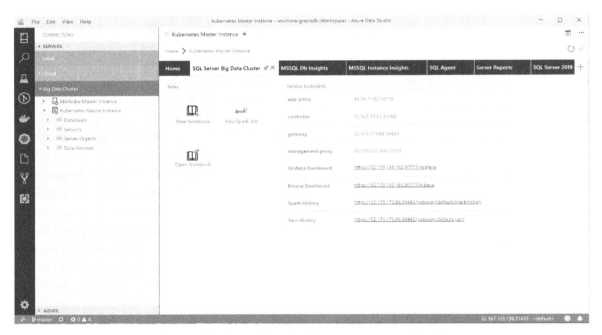

Figure 9.9: Azure Data Studio connection to Spark

Still connected to the master instance, change the kernel to the one you want to work with. Now, you're able to create code cells to run on Spark:

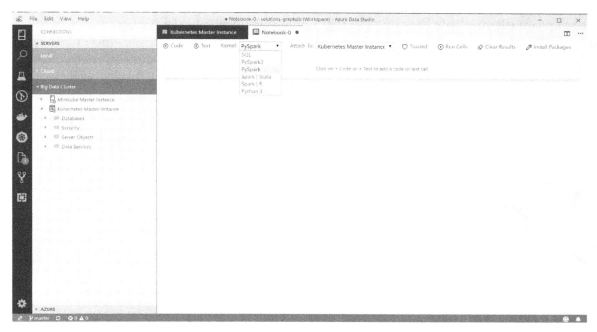

Figure 9.10: Azure Data Studio Spark Notebook

It is most often the case that you will want to write code containing many steps, designed to be scaled to multiple nodes. These are usually done in Java or Python.

In Java, as you learned in *Chapter 8, Machine Learning Services Extensibility Framework*, you can bundle multiple files in .`jar` format, and then submit that code to Spark for distribution from the driver program to the executors. You can do the same with .`py` files. To submit a job this way, from the Big Data Clusters panel, select the Submit Spark Job icon, and then fill out the location of the files you want to run:

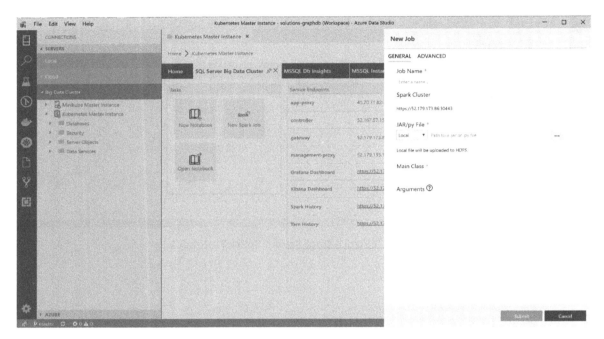

Figure 9.11: Azure Data Studio submits a job to Spark

Submitting a Spark job from IntelliJ

The IntelliJ system allows you to create, edit, and deploy Spark jobs. In SQL Server 2019 Big Data Clusters, this involves installing a **Software Development Kit** (**SDK**), the **Integrated Development Environment** (**IDE**), and a toolkit to connect IntelliJ to Microsoft Azure (and the big data cluster).

With all of the prerequisites set up (more on that later), you will either download and install the proper certificate to talk to the cluster or use a self-signed certificate. From there, you write your code, connect to the SQL Server big data cluster endpoint hosting the security routing for Spark (more on that in a moment), and submit the jobs, all from the IntelliJ environment.

Spark job files and data locations

Spark can work directly with data in the storage pool HDFS node or make a call out to the SQL Server using various libraries in a set of code. The Java, Python, R, or SparkML code can also make calls out to other data sources, and be used for streaming. The HDFS system in the SQL Server storage pool of the cluster can also house the `.jar` and `.py` files for your Spark jobs. You'll learn more about securing these files in the sections that follow.

There is, of course, much more to learn about working with Spark and, for more details, refer to: https://docs.microsoft.com/en-us/sql/big-data-cluster/spark-submit-job?view=sqlallproducts-allversions.

Management and monitoring

Although you can use and program the SQL Server 2019 big data clusters with standard T-SQL commands, there are quite a few components in addition to a single database server in the system. You'll need to employ some new tools to monitor the system, as well as to manage it.

In general, you'll use your regular SQL Server monitoring tools for database-specific operations, Kubernetes commands for the infrastructure, and visualization and logging tools for a complete overview of the system.

SQL Server components and operations

Since you are dealing with SQL Server in big data clusters, from the master instance to the computer pool, storage pool, and data pool, you can use the full range of tools for monitoring and management that work with any (Linux-based) SQL Server instance. You'll use the standard **Dynamic Management Views** (**DMVs**), T-SQL management and monitoring statements, graphical tools in SQL Server Management Studio and Azure Data Studio, and any third-party tools you can connect to SQL Server. You'll create users, objects, and more using the same tools you've been using for SQL Server monitoring and management.

Kubernetes operations

The primary tool for managing and monitoring a Kubernetes cluster is `kubectl`. Typing `kubectl` and pressing *Enter* will get you a reference to the complete documentation, and a list of the categories of commands you can work with.

To get specific help on a command, simply add `--help` to the end of that command:

```
kubectl get pods --help
```

Here are some basic commands for working with your cluster:

kubectl get pods --all-namespaces	Show the status of the pods in the cluster for either all namespaces or you can specify the big data cluster namespace.
kubectl describe pod -n	Shows detailed information for a pod – returns a JSON format file.
kubectl get svc -n	Shows the details for the big data cluster services.
kubectl describe pod -n	Shows information for a service.
kubectl exec -it -c -n -- /bin/bash	Logs in to a container's operating system layer.
kubectl cp pod_name:source_file_path -c container_name -n namespace_name target_local_file_path	Copies files from the container to your local system. If you reverse the source and destination, you copy to the container. Useful for testing, and for getting logs and other files.
kubectl delete pods -n --grace-period=0 --force	Deletes a pod – use this to simulate a pod failure during HADR testing.
kubectl get pods -o yaml -n	grep hostIP	Shows the IP address of the node a pod is on.

Table 9.12: Showing kubectl commands

SQL Server 2019 big data cluster operations

The SQL Server 2019 big data cluster is deployed and managed using a Python-based utility called `azdata`. This tool works similar to the `kubectl` command, but works specifically with the SQL Server 2019 big data cluster.

You've already used this tool to deploy your cluster, log in, and retrieve your service endpoints earlier in this chapter. Following that, there are a few other interesting commands to keep in mind:

azdata login --cluster-name ClusterName --controller-user username@whatever.com --controller-endpoint https://<ip>:30080 --accept-eula yes	Log in with the cluster name, controller username, controller endpoint, and EULA acceptance set as arguments. The environment variable, CONTROLLER_ PASSWORD, must be set.
azdata cluster create --accept-eula yes --config-file test.json	Create a cluster on AKS (AKS must exist already) with a configuration file called test.json.
azdata cluster status show	Show the status of the cluster you are logged into.
azdata cluster debug copy-logs --namespace -n	Copies the logs from the cluster to your current directory.

Table 9.13: Showing azdata commands

For a full list of these commands and more information on how they are used, type:

```
azdata --help
```

For more detailed information on working with the **azdata** tool, refer to: https://docs.microsoft.com/en-us/sql/big-data-cluster/reference-azdata?view=sqlallproducts-allversions.

Monitoring performance and operations with Grafana

Because the SQL Server 2019 Big Data Cluster feature involves multiple components, you require a cross-platform central tool to perform two primary monitoring functions: visualizations and log queries. Grafana is an open source technology that has very rich, customizable visualizations that display in a web page. SQL Server 2019 Big Data Cluster include Grafana as one of the "Support Services" shown in the overall architecture diagram. You can reach the visualization at the IP address shown with port **30777** in your **kubectl get service** query, and with the directory of **/grafana** selected:

https://serviceipaddress:30777/grafana

There's a general Host Node Metrics dashboard included in SQL Server 2019 Big Data Cluster, and also a specific set of SQL Server metrics included that you can see here:

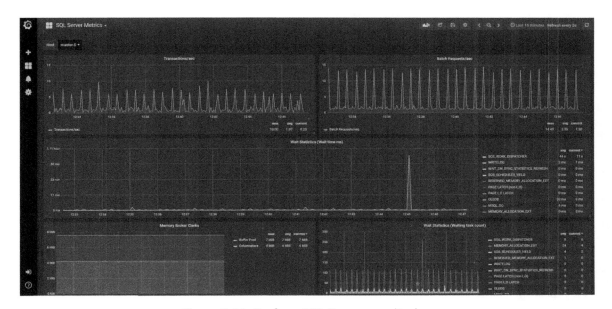

Figure 9.14: Grafana SQL Server monitoring

You can also add your own dashboards or customize the included visualizations, export the metrics, or share the dashboard with others. For more detailed information on working with Granfana, refer to: https://grafana.com/docs/.

Monitoring logs with Kibana

Visualizing the performance counters and other metrics within your cluster's components is very important, but you'll also need to examine the various logs in the system – and that's where another open source technology called Kibana comes in. This is another of the shared services located in the architecture diagram.

Kibana is a graphical log query and display tool, but it includes two additional features that make it more powerful than just a text-in-a-grid display: **Timelion** and **visualizations**. Timelion is a query and visualize system that plugs into Kibana, and it is a powerful tool for querying and manipulating time series data, which logs often are. In addition, you have the ability to visualization data in the logs to show clusters of incidents, and to group and view charts of other elements as well:

Figure 9.15: Log management with Kibana

For more detailed information on working with Kibana, visit: https://www.elastic.co/products/kibana.

Spark operations

Apache Spark is included in both the SQL Server storage pool and (optionally) an additional Spark pool. Apache Spark jobs run across various processing nodes that access a data sub system and are shown in a graph. To examine information on all of these processes, Spark uses multiple log files, such as:

- Master log files

- Worker log files

- Driver log files (client and cluster)

- Executor log files

You can log into the Spark cluster with the `spark-shell` command from the Spark node and then use Scala programming to read and search the files, or even use various calls (such as the Apache log file parser) in other code to read the logs. You can read more about that here: https://jaceklaskowski.gitbooks.io/mastering-apache-spark/content/spark-shell.html.

While you can read Spark logs with commands and programming, it is often easier to use the graphical interface that Spark provides: the history server. This server shows currently running jobs, the graph outline of where they are at the moment, and also allows you to get to the logs for each node, job, and most components within the system. The Spark History Server is shown as a panel in the Azure Data Studio tool, so you can work from one location for Spark.

For more detailed information on working with the Spark History Server, refer to: https://docs.microsoft.com/en-us/sql/big-data-cluster/spark-history-server?view=sqlallproducts-allversions.

Security

Security for SQL Server has always had a "defense-in-depth" strategy. This means that you start with the outermost layer of the system and ensure that you have two areas identified and mitigated for each layer: **Access** and **Authentication**. Access has to do with what a user or process (called a **Principal**) can see and work with (called **Securables**), and authentication is about verifying the Principal's credentials.

SQL Server has a very secure security environment, allowing you to control and monitor very fine-grained access to the platform, the databases, and the database objects. It supports working with Active Directory accounts, certificates, and also SQL Server-defined and -controlled user accounts. You can also audit and monitor all security activities, and the security profiles can reach the highest government levels of security.

In an SQL Server 2019 big data cluster, it gets a bit more complex, since you're dealing not only with SQL Server, but Spark, HDFS, and any applications you deploy.

A complete discussion of the security components and processes is beyond what we have time for in this chapter, but let's take a look at the general concepts you need to be aware of as regards security.

Access

Before you learn about the authorization a user will need in order to make calls to SQL Server and Spark, you need to understand the cluster endpoints (offered as TCP/IP addresses and ports) that each service provides. It's best understood by examining the tools that call to them:

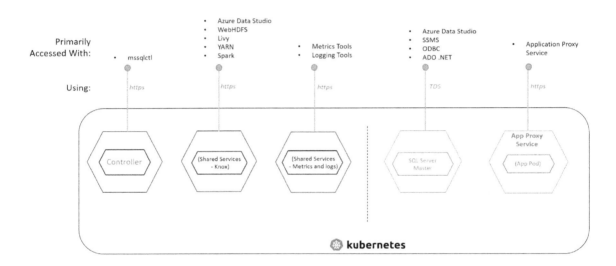

Figure 9.16: SQL Server 2019 big data cluster endpoints

As you can see, the primary communication method for SQL Server remains the same – the **Tabular Data Stream (TDS)**, or TDS. For everything else, you connect using the HTTPS protocol.

Security setup and configuration

You saw the initial setup for SQL Server 2019 big data clusters earlier in this chapter, but let's revisit that process with a bit more detail and focus on security. Instead of having to install Windows, join a domain, and then install SQL Server as you would normally do, the deployment process for SQL Server 2019 big data clusters asks you for a series of security parameters at the outset that it will use to handle creating the security environment for you.

You'll start by deciding what **Active Directory** (**AD**) the cluster will use. From there, you will create some AD groups: an AD group for the cluster admin for Hadoop and for the controller group, and another used for the sysadmin role in SQL Server in the cluster. Note the details you use for those groups – you'll need them next.

Next, you'll create a non-admin AD principal for users of the Spark jobs and for logins to the SQL Server master instance. Once again, note these details so that you can set them in your environment for installation and deployment of the big data cluster. Note that the non-administrator users will not have any permissions in SQL Server or in the HDFS; they will have to be granted explicitly later.

Next, during the deployment of SQL Server 2019 big data clusters, you will set various parameters, some of which tie back to the AD principals you created. These are part of the JSON installation of JSON explained earlier. Here is a snippet of the kind of variables you will set:

```
"security":

{

"distinguishedName": {distinguished name of domain including OU path}

  "big data clustersAdminPrincipals": {list of AD principals in the AD
which will be granted BIG DATA CLUSTERS admin rights}

  "big data clustersUserPrincipals": {list of AD principals in the AD
which will be granted BIG DATA CLUSTERS user (non-admin) rights}

  "appOwnerPrincipals": {list of AD principals in the AD which will be
admin rights on all apps} Optional

  "appReaderPrincipals": {list of AD principals in the AD which will
have read rights on all apps} Optional

"upstreamIpAddresses":{There can be multiple DNS servers for high
availability each with its own IP address.}

"domainControllerFullyQualifiedDns":{The fully qualified DNS name of
domain}

"realm":{domain realm}

 "}
```

Because SQL Server 2019 big data clusters use containers, it is at the process level, not at the server-joined level, as you would be if you joined a computer to an AD forest. This means that the system uses Kerberos-based constructs to route all the security calls through the system – a kind of impersonation so that you can log in once in AD and have that trusted identity flow through the system.

Each endpoint will use this "Active Directory to Kerberos" process. A **keytab** file will be distributed to each pod that requires authorization. The call back to the AD controller using SPNs is the key. The cluster controller registers each service to the AD controller using an SPN, and each service will then reach out to the domain controller as an SPN call.

> **Note**
>
> If you are not the security expert or domain administrator for your organization, it's important to work with the security team, carefully reading through the security documentation for SQL Server 2019 so that everyone understands how the security works. A thorough understanding is essential to maintaining a secure environment.

Authentication and authorization

Now that you have the AD and the Kerberos environment of the big data cluster established, you can combine that with what you know about the endpoints of the system to find out what happens when a user queries the system.

For SQL Server, you simply create users as you always have in the master instance. It has a Kerberos mechanism underneath to impersonate the users based on your initial setup. All of the Kerberos steps happen automatically for you.

As you will recall, you have not only an SQL Server engine working for you in the big data cluster, but also one or more Spark instances. As you saw in the initial setup for the cluster, putting the user in the proper AD group allows the user to submit Spark jobs, but what about the data? You will recall that Spark works with HDFS, so the key to permissions in this environment is using **Access Control Lists(ACLs)** (pronounced *Ackles*). Using the **azdata** tool, you can create a directory in the HDFS node for the Spark environment, and then change the ACLs to allow them to read and write to that directory. Here's an example that lets Buck read and write a directory in HDFS:

```
azdata hdfs acl set --path '/bucksdata' --aclspec 'user:buck:rw-'
```

You also have the standard POSIX-compliant calls of sticky bits, masking, and more.

Although a small command from `azdata` is all you need, there's actually quite a bit going on to make all that happen. There is, of course, much more to learn about the security in SQL Server big data clusters, and the official documentation will have the latest information and the greatest depth. Of all of the topics in this chapter, security is the one you should spend the most time on before you implement the system in production. SQL Server has long had one of the most secure platforms in the industry, and understanding the environment is the first step in keeping your system's security world-class.

We've only briefly explored the concepts of installation and configuration, use and programming, and monitoring and management of the SQL Server 2019 Big Data Cluster feature. There is much more to learn and explore. If you would like to work through an entire tutorial involving all of these concepts and tools in a big data cluster example, check out this resource: https://github.com/Microsoft/sqlworkshops/tree/master/sqlserver2019bigdataclusters.

10
Enhancing the Developer Experience

SQL Server 2019 opens new possibilities for developers while building and expanding on previously introduced features. This chapter will focus on a few of these features. While it's not covered in this chapter, SQL Server 2019 can be run in Docker containers and accommodate modern DevOps workflows. SQL Server 2019 can be used in almost any development environment, using native drivers and ODBC interfaces. The list is long and includes the following:

- All .NET languages using ADO.Net, ODBC, Entity Framework, and other object-relational mapping systems

- Java

- PHP

- R

- Python

- Ruby

There are a number of tools that you can use to develop and manage SQL Server projects. These include Visual Studio, SQL Server Management Studio, Azure Data Studio and, especially for cross-platform development, Visual Studio Code. Visual Studio Code is a modern, extensible tool that runs on Mac, Linux, and Windows, supporting dozens of programming languages.

Figure 10.1: Visual Studio Code Program

For more information and a free download of Visual Studio Code, visit https://code. visualstudio.com/.

For more information about what is new in SQL Server 2019, visit https:// docs.microsoft.com/en-us/sql/sql-server/what-s-new-in-sql-server-ver15?view=sqlallproducts-allversions.

SQL Graph Database

SQL Graph Database has powerful features for analyzing complex data. In a graph database, relationships are a built-in feature that can be easily and dynamically changed.

Compare this to a relational database, where relationships are created at design time. While relationships can be modified, it is not efficient to do this dynamically. When using a relational database, there is a performance penalty for both reads and writes that gets worse as the relationships become more complex.

With traditional relational databases, relationships can be made between entities (tables), but they are somewhat fixed, cumbersome, and difficult to maintain and change.

A graph database organizes data into nodes and edges. A node might represent a person, product, sale, address, or any other information that you would store in a relational table.

Relationships are stored in edges, which can be dynamically updated and express relationships as one-way or two-way. There is no practical limit on the number of edges or the relationships stored in them. Special operators allow you to filter data based on edge information.

Each edge can also store additional data about the relationship. For example, between customers and orders, the edge table might contain the number of orders.

SQL Graph Database, or SQL Graph, is a set of features that organize data into nodes and edges. In SQL Graph, node tables contain data and edge tables contain relationships. The edge tables make even complex queries very efficient to execute.

Azure Data Studio is another powerful tool for Data Engineers and Data Scientists. It has support for data exploration with both traditional SQL commands and also with Jupyter style notebooks.

More information about Azure Data Studio can be found at: https://docs.microsoft. com/en-us/sql/azure-data-studio/what-is?view=sql-server-2017:

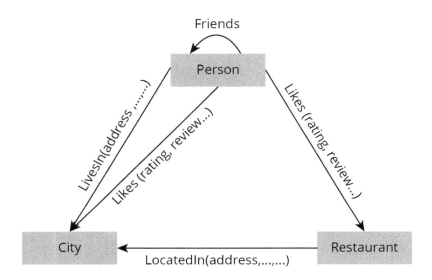

Figure 10.2: SSMS showing the management studio structure

SQL Server 2017 featured SQL Graph support for the first time. SQL Server 2019 extends this support in the following areas:

- Edge constraints

- Data integrity

- Match support in the MERGE statement

- Use of derived tables or view aliases in graph match queries

More information on SQL Graph can be found here:

https://docs.microsoft.com/en-us/sql/relational-databases/graphs/sql-graph-architecture?view=sql-server-2017

Why use SQL Graph?

SQL Graph can be especially useful for many-to-many relationships. While normal SQL Server can handle these, they can become hard to use and understand if they are too complex. Some use cases are as follows:

- A hierarchical structure such as a tree can be implemented and new relationships added by inserting nodes in a table. More importantly, a query can use the built-in graph operators.

- When there is a complex set of many-to-many relationships.

- High-performance data analysis on complex data.

Edge constraints

An edge or edge table creates relationships between nodes. An edge table has a format that includes a "from" node and a "to" node, thus creating a relationship between two nodes.

In SQL Server 2017, the edge table relationships were always many-to-many. With the new constraint feature in SQL Server 2019, you can restrict the edge to only one direction. This feature allows one-to-many relationships.

In the following example, we create two node tables and an edge table. Relationships in both directions can be inserted. Then we add a constraint that restricts the relationships to one-way. This is a very simple example intended to convey the concepts.

Create a new **database** called **SQLGraphDB** on SQL Server 2019:

```
create database SQLGraphDB

go

use SQLGraphDB

go
```

Create `Node` tables called `Person` and `City` with some data:

```
create table Person (PersonID int primary key, PersonName varchar(10))
as Node;

create table City (CityID int primary key, CityName varchar(10)) as
Node;


insert into Person values (1, 'Sam')
insert into Person values (2, 'Dave')


insert into City values (1, 'Miami')
insert into City values (2, 'Atlanta')
```

Create an `Edge` table that will relate data between `Person` and `City`. In this case, we will also add a column called `NodeCount` to use in later examples. It is optional and not required:

```
create table PersonCity (NodeCount int) as Edge;
```

You can insert into the `PersonCity` edge table in either direction, from `Person` to `City` or `City` to `Person`:

```
-- From Person into City
insert into PersonCity ($from_id, $to_id)
values (
   (select $node_id from Person where PersonID = 1),
   (select $node_id from City where CityID = 1))
-- From City into Person
insert into PersonCity ($from_id, $to_id)
values (
   (select $node_id from City where CityID = 2),
   (select $node_id from Person where PersonID = 2))


select * from PersonCity
```

Next, we will drop the `PersonCity` edge table and recreate it with a constraint that only allows the `Person` to `City` direction. This statement will not work on SQL Server 2017. The error `Incorrect syntax near 'connection'` is generated:

```
drop table if exists PersonCity
go


create table PersonCity
(
  NodeCount int,
  constraint EdgeConstraint_PersonCity connection (Person to City)
)
as Edge
```

Inserting edge data from `Person` to `City` still works, but attempting to insert data from `City` to `Person` does not:

```
-- Person to City still succeeds
insert into PersonCity ($from_id, $to_id)
values (
  (select $node_id from Person where PersonID = 1),
  (select $node_id from City where CityID = 1))


--  City to Person fails
insert into PersonCity ($from_id, $to_id)
values (
  (select $node_id from City where CityID = 2),
  (select $node_id from Person where PersonID = 2))
```

Attempting to insert data from `City` to `Person` fails and generates the following error:

```
Msg 547, Level 16, State 0, Line 51

The INSERT statement conflicted with the EDGE constraint
"EdgeConstraint_PersonCity". The conflict occurred in database
"SQLGraphDB", table "dbo.PersonCity".

The statement has been terminated.
```

You can also `alter` an existing table to add a constraint. If the constraint exists, you must drop it first. If there are multiple constraints, then all constraints must be met when inserting data:

```
alter table PersonCity add constraint EdgeConstraint_PersonCity
connection (Person to City);
```

For more information on edge constraints, go to https://docs.microsoft.com/en-us/sql/relational-databases/tables/graph-edge-constraints?view=sqlallproducts-allversions.

For more information on SQL Graph in SQL Server 2019, visit https://blogs.msdn.microsoft.com/sqlserverstorageengine/2018/09/28/public-preview-of-graph-edge-constraints-on-sql-server-2019/.

SQL Graph data integrity enhancements

With SQL Server 2017, there were no restrictions on deleting records when using graph tables with nodes and edges. For example, if you had an edge table that referenced a node record, you could successfully delete the node record, leaving an orphan edge record.

In SQL Server 2019, the referential integrity will be maintained and you will get an error if you try to delete a node record contained in an edge table.

Using the example `Person`, `City`, and `PersonCity` tables from earlier, try to delete an entry from the `Person` table contained in the `PersonCity` edge table. Attempting to do the deletion will cause an error:

```
delete from Person where PersonID = 1
```

The previous code will result in this error:

```
Msg 547, Level 16, State 0, Line 80

The DELETE statement conflicted with the EDGE REFERENCE constraint
"EdgeConstraint_PersonCity". The conflict occurred in database
"SQLGraphDB", table "dbo.PersonCity".

The statement has been terminated
```

SQL Graph MATCH support in MERGE

The `MERGE` statement is used to simplify inserting and updating data in a table. It can do this in one statement instead of using separate `INSERT`, `UPDATE`, and `DELETE` statements.

SQL Server 2019 now supports using SQL Graph MATCH clauses in a MERGE statement.

The MERGE statement is supported in both node and edge tables. In the case of node tables, MERGE is the same as with any SQL table.

The following sample of the MATCH statement references a row in a node table that already exists and will update the row with new data:

```
select PersonID, PersonName from Person

--

Declare @PersonID int = 1
Declare @PersonName varchar(10) = 'Bobbi'


MERGE Person
    USING (SELECT @PersonID, @PersonName)
    AS tmp (PersonID, PersonName)
    ON (Person.PersonID = tmp.PersonID)
WHEN MATCHED THEN
    UPDATE SET PersonName = tmp.PersonName
WHEN NOT MATCHED THEN
    INSERT (PersonID, PersonName)
    VALUES (tmp.PersonID, tmp.PersonName) ;
```

See if the update to the existing node table row succeeded:

```
Select PersonID, PersonName from Person
```

Now, to test the insertion, specify an ID that is not in the table:

```
Declare @PersonID int = 3
Declare @PersonName varchar(10) = 'Marc'


MERGE Person
```

```
        USING (SELECT @PersonID, @PersonName)

        AS tmp (PersonID, PersonName)

        ON (Person.PersonID = tmp.PersonID)

WHEN MATCHED THEN

        UPDATE SET PersonName = tmp.PersonName

WHEN NOT MATCHED THEN

        INSERT (PersonID, PersonName)

        VALUES (tmp.PersonID, tmp.PersonName) ;
```

See that a new row with **PersonName** Marc has been inserted into the node table by selecting data from the **person** table:

```
Select PersonID, PersonName from Person
```

In the case of an edge table, the SQL Graph relationship can now be used as part of the **MATCH** clause in the **MERGE** statement. The **MATCH** graph search syntax in SQL Server 2019 is defined as follows:

```
<graph_search_pattern>::=

    {<node_alias> {

                    { <-( <edge_alias> )- }

                    | { -( <edge_alias> )-> }

                <node_alias>

                }

    }

    [ { AND } { ( <graph_search_pattern> ) } ]

    [ ,...n ]


 <node_alias> ::=

    node_table_name | node_alias


<edge_alias> ::=

    edge_table_name | edge_alias
```

The **MATCH** condition in the **MERGE** statement can now contain a graph search pattern. In our **Person**, **City**, and **PersonCity** case, this pattern could be as follows:

```
.. on MATCH (Person-(PersonAndCity)->City)
```

It could also be this:

```
.. on MATCH (Person<-(PersonAndCity)-City)
```

For this example, we use the **NodeCount** field of the **PersonAndCity** edge table. To start, clean out the edge table:

```
delete from PersonCity
```

The following SQL will insert or update rows in the edge table. Because the edge table is empty, it will insert a row:

```
declare @PersonID int = 1
declare @CityID int = 1


-- From Person into City
Merge PersonCity
   using ((select @PersonID, @CityID) as tmp (PersonID, CityID)
      join Person on tmp.PersonID = Person.PersonID
      join City on tmp.CityID = City.CityID)
   on MATCH (Person-(PersonCity)->City)
when MATCHED then
   update set NodeCount = isnull(NodeCount, 0) + 1
when NOT MATCHED THEN
   insert ($from_id, $to_id, NodeCount)
   values (Person.$node_id, City.$node_id, 1);


select * from PersonCity
```

The result is one row with a **NodeCount** of **1** that will look something like the following:

$edge_id_B18C5187FDCE4C88BEE4EFF142482BD3	$from_id_CE8A14A5E80143B599C4982BDA684512	$to_id_D38AB4B60AC24B24A82EBFABCB7093D2	NodeCount
{"type":"edge","schema":"dbo","table":"PersonCity","id":0}	{"type":"node","schema":"dbo","table":"Person","id":0}	{"type":"node","schema":"dbo","table":"City","id":0}	1

Figure 10.3: Output of inserting/updating rows in the edge table

If you execute the MERGE statement again, there will still be only one row, but the NodeCount will equal 2.

For more information about SQL Graph MATCH support in the MERGE statement, see https://blogs.msdn.microsoft.com/sqlserverstorageengine/2018/07/16/match-support-in-merge-dml-for-graph-tables/.

Using a derived table or view in a graph MATCH query

In SQL Server 2019, you can utilize views or derived tables in a MATCH query. As an example, if you have two node tables that contain data, and a third table related to the first two by an edge table, you can combine the two node tables with a UNION ALL command into a view that can be used with an edge table in a MATCH statement. Using a table variable will also work but is not covered here.

We will drop and recreate some of the example tables and will make a view that combines Person and Company data related by the IsInCity MATCH clause in the union statement.

```
drop table if exists PersonCity


drop table if exists IsInCity
drop view if exists PersonCompany


drop table if exists Person
drop table if exists Company
drop table if exists City


create table Person (PersonID int, PersonName varchar(20), CityName
varchar(20)) as Node
create table Company (CompanyID int, CompanyName varchar(20), CityName
varchar(20)) as Node
create table City (CityID int, CityName varchar(20)) as Node


create table IsInCity as Edge


go


insert into Person values(1,'Amy', 'Atlanta')
```

```
insert into Person values(2,'Bob', 'Boston')


insert into Company values(1,'Acme', 'Atlanta')
insert into Company values(2,'Beta', 'Boston')


insert into City values(1,'Atlanta')
insert into City values(2,'Boston')


select * from  Person, Company, City


insert into IsInCity ($from_id, $to_id)
values (
   (select $node_id from Person where CityName = 'Atlanta'),
   (select $node_id from City where CityName = 'Atlanta'))


insert into IsInCity ($from_id, $to_id)
values (
   (select $node_id from Company where CityName = 'Boston'),
   (select $node_id from City where CityName = 'Boston'))


select * from IsInCity



create View PersonCompany as
select PersonID as id, PersonName as [PCName], CityName from Person
union all
```

```
select CompanyID as id, CompanyName, CityName from Company


select * from PersonCompany


select pc.id, pc.PCName, pc.CityName
from PersonCompany PC,
City,
IsInCity
where Match(PC-(IsInCity)->City)
and City.CityName = 'Atlanta'
```

Using views and table variables adds flexibility and options when working with graph search terms.

Java language extensions

SQL Server 2016 introduced an extensibility framework for running external scripts such as R and Python.

This extensibility framework is exposed using the `sp_execute_external_script` system stored procedure. SQL Server 2019 supports Java on both Windows and Linux.

The windows installation will is covered in this book and here: https://docs.microsoft.com/en-us/sql/language-extensions/install/install-sql-server-language-extensions-on-windows?view=sqlallproducts-allversions#java-jre-jdk

Linux installation instructions can be found at https://docs.microsoft.com/en-us/sql/linux/sql-server-linux-setup-language-extensions?view=sqlallproducts-allversions

Why language extensions?

Language extensions allow you to extend SQL Server to use external code as part of SQL operations. Writing complex procedures in high-level languages such as Java, Python, and R can be much easier and more straightforward to test.

Starting with SQL Server 2005, there was **Common Language Runtime** (**CLR**) Integration. This feature was not widely used, somewhat cumbersome, and not recommended in most cases.

The extensibility framework provides a solid base for allowing extensions in R, Python, and now Java. An example use case would be address correction. An address can be validated or corrected by way of a SQL stored procedure that calls custom Java code that can run arbitrary code and take advantage of existing code libraries.

You can add code that allows almost infinite extension of SQL Server's functionality.

Installation

You must have SQL Server 2019 installed and have added the Machine Learning Services and Language Extensions or select this option when you install the instance.

To get the Java extensions, you have to install SQL Server Language Extensions. You can install these on either Windows or Linux. The following screenshot shows the SQL Server feature installation screen on Windows. Java is now a built in feature of Machine Learning Services:

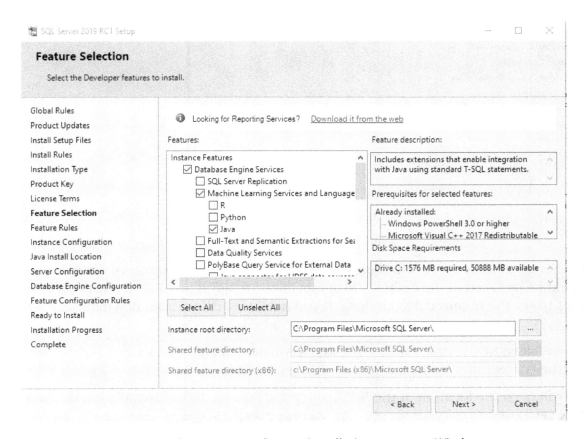

Figure 10.4: The SQL Server feature installation screen on Windows

This will install the default Java runtime, Zulu Open JRE (Java Runtime Environment) version 11.0.3. If you need the full JDK (Java Development Kit) for compilers and other dev tools or want to install your own distribution you are free to do that.

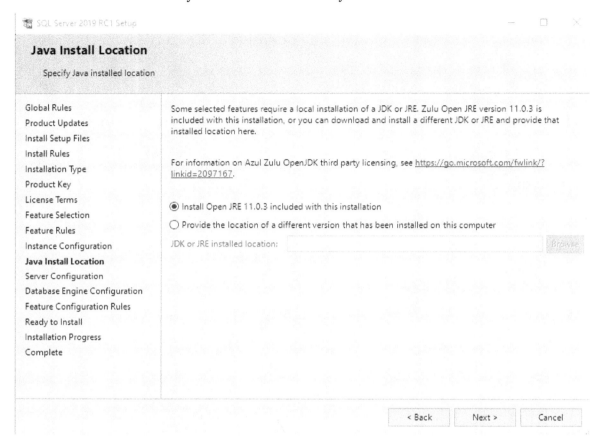

Figure 10.5: The Java Install dialogue

SQL Server 2019 support Java 11 on Windows. If you do install your own distribution, it should be installed in the default /Program Files/ folder if possible to avoid separate steps to set the required permissions. If you need the JDK you can download it from https://www.azul.com/downloads/zulu-community/.

You will need to add **JRE_HOME** as a system environment variable so that SQL Server can find the correct Java runtime.

You will need the location of the JRE home path. For the default installation this will be at: `C:\Program Files\Microsoft SQL Server\MSSQL15.<your instance name>\AZUL-OpenJDK-JRE`

There is more than one way to add/edit environment variables. On Windows 10, you can use File Explorer and browse to `Control Panel\System and Security\ System`. Click on **Advanced system settings**. In the dialog box that pops up, click on **Environment Variables**. `JRE_HOME` must be added as a system variable and should point to the `JRE` directory in your `JRE` or `JDK` installation, as shown here:

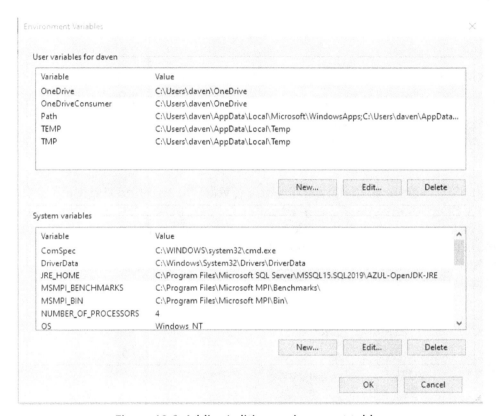

Figure 10.6: Adding/editing environment tables

If you did not install the `JDK` or `JRE` in the default location under **Program Files**, you need to give read and execute permission to SQL.

Next, enable external scripts with the `sp_configure` command. You can also execute the command with no arguments to see current settings. `RECONFIGURE` will set the run-time value of the configuration setting:

```
exec sp_configure 'external scripts enabled', 1
RECONFIGURE WITH OVERRIDE
```

Verify that the running version is enabled by executing the `sp_configure` command to see a list of the configuration items and both their configured and runtime status.

Now you need to create an external language. `javaextension.dll` is in the `BINN` directory in the `install` directory of SQL server after installing the extensions. Take this file, put it in a `ZIP` file, and refer to it. I put the `ZIP` file in my development directory. More information is available in the Microsoft docs: https://docs.microsoft.com/en-us/sql/t-sql/statements/create-external-language-transact-sql?view=sqlallproducts-allversions.

The following SQL script will create an external language from the code we have built:

```
CREATE EXTERNAL LANGUAGE Java
FROM (CONTENT = N'c:\Projects\SQL2019Java\javaextension.zip', FILE_
NAME = 'javaextension.dll');
GO
```

In that same SQL Server installation directory, you will also find the Microsoft Extensibility SDK: `mssql-java-lang-extension.jar`. I copied this to my development directory for later use when I compile my custom Java program. You also have to specify it as an external library for our Java language that we just created. On my system where I have multiple SQL instances, including a **Customer Technical Preview** (**CTP**) version the command looks like this:

```
-- Create external libraries
CREATE EXTERNAL LIBRARY SDK
FROM (CONTENT = 'C:\Program Files\Microsoft SQL Server\MSSQL15.
SQL20191600\MSSQL\Binn\mssql-java-lang-extension.jar')
WITH (LANGUAGE = 'Java');
GO
```

Sample program

Using the Java command-line compiler, we will create an extension and compile and load the library into SQL Server.

This program performs string splits on a text field and outputs two fields if the split was successful. It has one parameter: the split delimiter.

Create a database and table for testing:

```
CREATE DATABASE SQL2019Java
GO
```

```
USE SQL2019Java
GO
CREATE TABLE TestJava (
    id int NOT NULL,
    FullName nvarchar(100) NOT NULL
)
GO
```

Insert some data:

```
INSERT INTO TestJava (id, FullName) VALUES (1, 'Dave Noderer')
INSERT INTO TestJava (id, FullName) VALUES (2, 'John Smith')
INSERT INTO TestJava (id, FullName) VALUES (3, 'NoLastName')
GO
```

Copy the following code into a file called **NameSplit.java**:

```
package pkg;

import com.microsoft.sqlserver.javalangextension.PrimitiveDataset;
import com.microsoft.sqlserver.javalangextension.
AbstractSqlServerExtensionExecutor;
import java.util.LinkedHashMap;
import java.util.LinkedList;
import java.util.ListIterator;
import java.util.regex.*;

public class NameSplit extends AbstractSqlServerExtensionExecutor {
    private Pattern expr;

    public NameSplit() {
        // Setup the expected extension version, and class to use for
input and output dataset
        executorExtensionVersion = SQLSERVER_JAVA_LANG_EXTENSION_V1;
        executorInputDatasetClassName = PrimitiveDataset.class.
getName();
```

```
        executorOutputDatasetClassName = PrimitiveDataset.class.
getName();
    }


    public PrimitiveDataset execute(PrimitiveDataset input,
LinkedHashMap<String, Object> params) {
        // Validate the input parameters and input column schema
        validateInput(input, params);


        int[] inIds = input.getIntColumn(0);
        String[] inValues = input.getStringColumn(1);
        int rowCount = inValues.length;


        String delimchar = (String)params.get("delimchar");
       // expr = Pattern.compile(regexExpr);


        System.out.println("delimiter: " + delimchar);


        // Lists to store the output data
        LinkedList<Integer> outIds = new LinkedList<Integer>();
        LinkedList<String> outVal1 = new LinkedList<String>();
        LinkedList<String> outVal2 = new LinkedList<String>();


        // Evaluate each row
        for(int i = 0; i < rowCount; i++) {
            outIds.add(inIds[i]);
            if(inValues[i].contains(delimchar)) {
                String[] vals = inValues[i].split(Pattern.
quote(delimchar));
                outVal1.add(vals[0]);
                outVal2.add(vals[1]);
            }
            else {
```

```
                    outVal1.add(inValues[i]); // just output the input
string in val1

        outVal2.add("");

            }


    }


    int outputRowCount = outIds.size();


    int[] idOutputCol = new int[outputRowCount];
    String[] val1OutputCol = new String[outputRowCount];
    String[] val2OutputCol = new String[outputRowCount];


    // Convert the list of output columns to arrays
    outVal1.toArray(val1OutputCol);
    outVal2.toArray(val2OutputCol);


    ListIterator<Integer> it = outIds.listIterator(0);
    int rowId = 0;


    System.out.println("Output data:");


    while (it.hasNext()) {
        idOutputCol[rowId] = it.next().intValue();


        System.out.println("ID: " + idOutputCol[rowId] + " Val1: "
+ val1OutputCol[rowId] + " Val2: " + val2OutputCol[rowId]);

        rowId++;
    }


    // Construct the output dataset
    PrimitiveDataset output = new PrimitiveDataset();
```

```java
        output.addColumnMetadata(0, "ID", java.sql.Types.INTEGER, 0,
0);
        output.addColumnMetadata(1, "P1", java.sql.Types.NVARCHAR, 0,
0);
        output.addColumnMetadata(2, "P2", java.sql.Types.NVARCHAR, 0,
0);


        output.addIntColumn(0, idOutputCol, null);
        output.addStringColumn(1, val1OutputCol);
        output.addStringColumn(2, val2OutputCol);


        return output;
    }


    private void validateInput(PrimitiveDataset input,
LinkedHashMap<String, Object> params) {
        // Check for the regex expression input parameter
        if (params.get("delimchar") == null) {
            throw new IllegalArgumentException("Input parameter
'delimchar' is not found");
        }
        else if (params.get("delimchar").toString().length() != 1)
        {
            throw new IllegalArgumentException("Input parameter
'delimchar' must be a single character");
        }


        // The expected input schema should be at least 2 columns,
(INTEGER, STRING)
        if (input.getColumnCount() < 2) {
            throw new IllegalArgumentException("Unexpected input
schema, schema should be an (INTEGER, NVARCHAR or VARCHAR)");
        }
```

```
        // Check that the input column types are expected
        if (input.getColumnType(0) != java.sql.Types.INTEGER &&
                (input.getColumnType(1) != java.sql.Types.VARCHAR &&
input.getColumnType(1) == java.sql.Types.NVARCHAR )) {
            throw new IllegalArgumentException("Unexpected input
schema, schema should be an (INTEGER, NVARCHAR or VARCHAR)");
        }
    }


    private boolean check(String text) {
        Matcher m = expr.matcher(text);


        return m.find();
    }
}
```

You can compile this using the **javac** command with the **SDK JAR** file as follows:

```
javac -cp mssql-java-lang-extension.jar NameSplit.java
```

Make a directory named **pkg** and copy the compiled **NameSplit.class** file there.

The **jar** command will package the class that will be loaded into SQL Server. The resulting file is **NameSplit.jar**:

```
jar -cf NameSplit.jar pkg\NameSplit.class
```

Now create an **EXTERNAL** library from your program:

```
CREATE EXTERNAL LIBRARY namesplit
FROM (CONTENT = 'C:\Projects\SQL2019Java\namesplit.jar')
WITH (LANGUAGE = 'Java');
GO
```

If the library already exists, you can drop it with **DROP EXTERNAL LIBRARY namesplit**.

We will access the library through a stored procedure:

```
CREATE OR ALTER PROCEDURE [dbo].[java_namesplit]
@delim nvarchar(1),
@query nvarchar(400)
```

```
AS

BEGIN

--The method invoked in Java the "execute" method

EXEC sp_execute_external_script

    @language = N'Java'

  , @script = N'pkg.NameSplit

  , @input_data_1 = @query

  , @params = N'@delimchar nvarchar(1)'

  , @regexExpr = @expr

with result sets ((ID int, P1 nvarchar(100) , P2 nvarchar(100)));

END

GO
```

Execute the procedure with two parameters (the **delimiter** and a **query**) to get data from our test table:

```
EXECUTE [dbo].[java_namesplit] N' ', N'SELECT id, FullName FROM
TestJava'

GO
```

You should get this:

ID	P1	P2
1	Dave	Noderer
2	John	Smith
3	NoLastName	

Figure 10.7: Data from our test table

That's a quick run-through of creating a `Java` extension. Another example can be found at https://docs.microsoft.com/en-us/sql/language-extensions/tutorials/search-for-string-using-regular-expressions-in-java?view=sqlallproducts-allversions.

JSON

JSON support was first added to SQL Server 2016. Two functions support JSON, `OPENJSON` for parsing incoming data and `FOR JSON` for outputting JSON formatted data.

Why use JSON?

JavaScript Object Notation (**JSON**), is a text representation that's used to store and share data. JSON is standard in web applications of all kinds. It is the native format of JavaScript objects and is purely text. Using native JSON within SQL Server can make interfaces easier to use and make the handling of NoSQL, changing schemas, and RESTful data from the web much easier.

For example, an order from an e-commerce site or an **Internet of Things** (**IoT**) device might arrive on the server as a JSON-formatted string. You can write this "blob" of data into a database field and delay parsing it until later.

Another benefit for an order system would be to preserve the original order as is, as compared to a relational form where related data might change over time.

JSON consists of simple name/value pairs with some formatting characters. For example, if you wanted to provide a list of cities, that list might be formatted as follows in JSON:

```
[{
    { "city" : "Miami"},
    { "city" : "Ft Lauderdale" },
    { "city" : "Deerfield Beach" }
}]
```

With SQL Server, you can create or consume a JSON object using T-SQL. This capability can simplify your applications and prevent the necessity of relying on another tier of your development stack to encode/decode JSON objects.

JSON example

In the following example, we will create some JSON data, parse it into fields, insert the data into a SQL table, then pull it back out as formatted JSON.

First, create some JSON data that might have come from an IoT device:

```
Declare @DeviceJson nvarchar(max)


set @DeviceJson =
'[
  { "deviceid" : 1, "devicedata": { "sensor1": 1234}, "eventdate":
"2019-05-25T20:19:04"},
  { "deviceid" : 2, "devicedata": { "sensor2": 4321}, "eventdate":
"2019-05-25T20:21:11"}
]'
```

The following SQL script will parse the data in **@DeviceJson** and display it as a table and rows:

```
--
select *
from OpenJson(@DeviceJson)
  with (deviceid int '$.deviceid',
    sensor1 int '$.devicedata.sensor1',
    sensor2 int '$.devicedata.sensor2',
    eventdate datetime '$.eventdate'
)
```

Now, **create** a SQL table and insert the parsed JSON data into the table:

```
create table IOTData (deviceid int, sensor1 int, sensor2 int,
eventdate datetime)


insert into IOTData
select *
from OpenJson(@DeviceJson)
```

```
with (deviceid int '$.deviceid',

    sensor1 int '$.devicedata.sensor1',

    sensor2 int '$.devicedata.sensor2',

    eventdate datetime '$.eventdate'

)
```

Finally, read the SQL data and convert it into JSON using the **FOR JSON** function:

```
select deviceid, sensor1 as "devicedata.sensor1", sensor2 as
"devicedata.sensor2", eventdate

from IOTData

FOR JSON PATH
```

If you reformat the result a bit, it is identical to the original data:

```
[

{"deviceid":1,"devicedata":{"sensor1":1234},"eventdate":"2019-05-
25T20:19:04"},

{"deviceid":2,"devicedata":{"sensor2":4321},"eventdate":"2019-05-
25T20:21:11"}

]
```

For more information on JSON data in SQL Server, visit https://docs.microsoft.com/en-us/sql/relational-databases/json/json-data-sql-server?view=sqlallproducts-allversions.

UTF-8 support

Starting with SQL Server 2012, Unicode UTF-16 is supported with the **nchar**, **nvarchar**, and **ntext** data types. Starting with SQL Server 2019, UTF-8 encoding is enabled, through the use of a collation using a _UTF8 suffix and the non-Unicode data types of char and varchar become Unicode-capable data types, encoded in UTF-8.

Collations that support supplementary characters, either through the use of the _SC flag or because they are version 140 collations, can be used with the new _UTF8 flag.

Why UTF-8?

UTF-8, UTF-16, and UTF-32 can all found on the web. In recent years, UTF-8 has become the standard. It can represent any character, and in some cases uses less storage (at least with western languages which mostly use of ASCII characters) than UTF-16 and the fixed format of UTF-32. UTF-8 is also backward-compatible with 7-bit ASCII, which may or may not be important to you.

If you have issues with endianness, the way the processor you are using determines which bit or byte is most significant/least significate, UTF-8 may help in that it does not depend on endianness. For the most part, widespread use of the Intel x86 processor has prevented some of these problems. For more information endianness, take a look at this wiki: https://en.wikipedia.org/wiki/Endianness.

In the context of SQL Server, the collation will affect the way strings are searched and ordered.

For example, **CREATE** a **TABLE** with a **varchar** field:

```
CREATE TABLE [dbo].[TestUTF8](
  [id] [int] IDENTITY(1,1) NOT NULL,
  [utfdata] [varchar](50) NULL
) ON [PRIMARY]
GO
```

The **varchar** field is created with a **<database default>** collation. **SQL_Latin1_General_CP1_CI_AS** is the default database collation if this is not changed.

Now you can alter a column and set its collation to UTF-8 with an **alter** statement like this:

```
ALTER TABLE TestUTF8 ALTER COLUMN utfdata varchar(50) COLLATE Latin1_General_100_CI_AS_SC_UTF8
```

You can also enable a **_UTF8** collation at the database level. If creating a new database, all new columns will be encoded with UTF8 by default. For existing databases, only new columns will be encoded with UTF8. For existing columns, use the **alter** command above to convert to UTF8.

More information can be found here: https://docs.microsoft.com/en-us/sql/relational-databases/collations/collation-and-unicode-support?view=sqlallproducts-allversions.

Temporal tables

Temporal tables store data and all changes so that data from a previous point in time can be retrieved. SQL Server 2016 added support for temporal tables. Temporal tables are also known as system-versioned temporal tables.

Each temporal table is paired with a history table so that normal queries pull data from the table as normal, but historical queries can be constructed that pull data from the history table. The following diagram illustrates this:

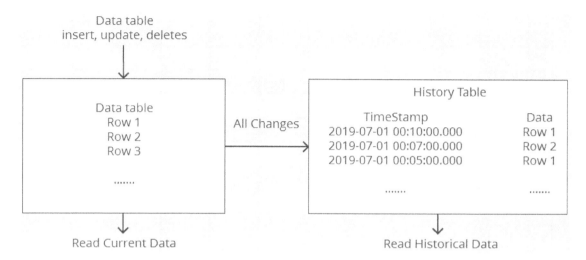

Figure 10.8: Temporal table structure

Why temporal tables?

Some use cases of temporal tables are as follows:

- Audit trail – Keep a full log of what changed in the table.
- Accidental changes – Easily restore data that was mistakenly changed or deleted.
- Historical reports – Be able to report on how data changes over time.
- Detect changes – Compare current and previous data more easily.

Temporal table example

When creating temporal tables, you are required to have a primary key and two `datetime2` columns that are used for the `SYSTEM_TIME` period.

Along with the main table, a history table is created to keep timestamped table row entries.

As an example, the following script creates **myTemporalTable**:

```
CREATE TABLE myTemporalTable
(
    id int not null,
    myText varchar(50) null,

    SysStartTime datetime2(7) GENERATED ALWAYS AS ROW START NOT NULL,
    SysEndTime datetime2(7) GENERATED ALWAYS AS ROW END NOT NULL ,
    PERIOD FOR SYSTEM_TIME(SysStartTime,SysEndTime),

    CONSTRAINT  PK_myTemporalTable PRIMARY KEY (id)
)
WITH
(
    SYSTEM_VERSIONING = ON
    (
        HISTORY_TABLE = dbo.my_history,
        DATA_CONSISTENCY_CHECK = ON
    )
)
GO
```

The **SYSTEM_TIME** definition will track when this row is valid. A primary key, while always a good idea, is required for temporal tables.

SYSTEM_VERSIONING = ON is what enables the temporal history table, which is created as part of the main table.

HISTORY_TABLE is the new or existing table that will hold historical data

DATA_CONSISTENCY_CHECK = ON performs several checks to make sure the data and structure of the history table are correct and consistent both at creation and runtime. More information can be found at https://docs.microsoft.com/en-us/sql/relational-databases/tables/temporal-table-system-consistency-checks?view=sql-server-2017.

Now, if you insert some data, wait for a while and then update the value.

When you do a query, you get back what you expect, that is, the current and updated data:

```
insert into myTemporalTable (id, myText) values(1, 'data at:' +
cast(GetDate() as varchar(50)))


select * from myTemporalTable

--

-- Wait some time

--

update myTemporalTable set myText = 'data at:' + cast(GetDate() as
varchar(50))

where id = 1


select * from myTemporalTable
```

To retrieve historical data, the query on your temporal table needs to use for **system_time** and one of the following sub-clauses:

- **AS OF <date_time>**
- **FROM <start_date_time> TO <end_date_time>**
- **BETWEEN <start_date_time> AND <end_date_time>**
- **CONTAINED IN (<start_date_time> , <end_date_time>)**
- **ALL**

For example, to retrieve all historical data, use this statement:

```
select * from myTemporalTable for system_time all
```

To retrieve data from some specific time, you can use a query such as this:

```
select * from myTemporalTable for system_time as of '2019-05-17 23:35'
```

If you look in the main table, there is only one row, but if you expand the temporal table, you will see a `my_history (History)` table, which will have old versions of the data:

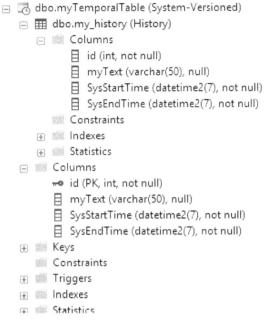

Figure 10.9: The temporal table expanded

You can also convert an existing table to a temporal table by adding the required columns and a history table.

One more reminder is that you may want to take steps to truncate or archive data in the history table, depending on how you use it!

For more information, go to https://docs.microsoft.com/en-us/sql/relational-databases/tables/temporal-tables?view=sqlallproducts-allversions.

Spatial data types

Spatial data types are used to work with mapping systems. There are two broad categories, geometry and geography. This discussion is focused on geography. You may need more general and flexible geometry options, especially if you are not specifically looking for a physical mapping capability.

Two new **spatial reference identifiers** (**SRIDs**) are available in SQL Server 2019. These Australian GDA2020 identifiers provide more accurate data for the Australian continent and are closely aligned with the latest **GPS satellites** (**GNSS**). For more information on these particular identifiers, go to http://www.ga.gov.au/scientific-topics/positioning-navigation/geodesy/datums-projections/gda2020.

Why spacial data types?

For any spacial or geometry calculations on spheres, such as the Earth, spacial data types allow easy calculation of distances and other calculations in a T-SQL query.

Which spatial identifier you use will depend on your location and your needs. Each identifier specifies the shape of the spatial coordinate system.

For a full list of identifiers on your system, use this query:

```
select * from sys.spatial_reference_systems
```

The special identifier we will use, **4326**, has this definition:

```
GEOGCS["WGS 84", DATUM["World Geodetic System 1984", ELLIPSOID["WGS
84", 6378137, 298.257223563]], PRIMEM["Greenwich", 0], UNIT["Degree",
0.0174532925199433]]
```

Dealer locator example

I have used spatial data for many years in dealer locator applications. In these applications, a list of dealers and their locations is available. When a user wants to find a dealer near them, they specify their location using latitude and longitude, at which point a spatial query can be made and sorts the dealers by distance.

Note that there are several ways to get a dealer's latitude and longitude. Two examples are a postal code database or a web map service using the dealer's address.

Create a **Dealers** table and fill in the latitude and longitude. Note that the **DealerGeo** field is of the **geography** type:

```
create table Dealers (DealerName nvarchar(50),latitude float, longitude
float, DealerGeo geography)
```

Insert some data. I've picked two points that are far from each other to illustrate the process:

```
insert into Dealers  (DealerName, latitude, longitude)
values
('Dealer in Deerfield Beach FL', 26.3109,-80.1005),
('Dealer in Watertown, MA', 42.3702,-71.1777)
```

Next, we update the `DealerGeo` field based on the `latitude` and `longitude`. This stores a `geography` "point" in the `DealerGeo` `GEOGRAPHY` field:

```
update Dealers set DealerGeo =  geography::STGeomFromText('POINT(' +
CAST(longitude AS VARCHAR(20)) + ' ' + CAST(latitude AS VARCHAR(20)) +
')', 4326)

where longitude is not null and latitude is not null and dealergeo is
null
```

If you take a look at the `Dealers` table, you can see the format of the geography point:

```
select * from Dealers
```

Now we collect data from a user, perhaps from the GPS on their phone to get latitude and longitude. We use this to create a point for the user and then make a query to calculate the distance from the dealers:

```
-- Define a potential customer in Connecticut

Declare @customerPoint geography

set @customerPoint = geography::STGeomFromText('POINT(-72.6791
41.8596)', 4326)
```

The query uses the spatial `STDistance` function and converts from meters to miles. The result is a list of dealers with their distances from the user:

```
select top 10  round(@customerPoint.STDistance(dealergeo)/1609.344,1)
as DistanceInMiles, DealerName

from Dealers

order by @customerPoint.STDistance(dealergeo)/1609.344
```

The `select` SQL query above will result in the following output:

DistanceInMiles	DealerName
84.8	Dealer in Watertown, MA
1151.9	Dealer in Deerfield Beach FL

Figure 10.10: Output of the select SQL query

For more information on spatial data in SQL Server, go to https://docs.microsoft.com/en-us/sql/relational-databases/spatial/spatial-data-sql-server?view=sql-server-ver15.

11
Data Warehousing

SQL Server has been delivering industry-leading capabilities for the modern data warehouse workload for many years. Mission-critical security features built into each edition of SQL Server such as row-level security, Always Encrypted, data masking, and others ensure that your data is secure at all times. Built-in advanced analytics using R and Python allows you to operationalize your data science models in a secure and performant way. SQL Server also offers industry-leading performance based on the TPC-E and TPC-H benchmarks for 3 TB and 10 TB data warehouse workloads (https://cloudblogs.microsoft.com/sqlserver/2019/05/16/sql-server-2017-achieves-top-tpc-benchmarks-for-oltp-and-dw-on-linux-and-windows/). Because of all this, SQL Server is a clear leader and trusted platform by organizations around the globe for data warehouse workloads both on-premises and in the cloud.

Many organizations use data warehouses to process and aggregate large volumes of data from many different systems for the purpose of enabling deeper analysis. A traditional data warehouse workload consists of loading data from operational systems, such as financial data, sales data, or inventory data, to enable long-term historical analysis of business facts and slowly changing dimensions. A data warehouse workload also supports complex analytical queries run by business analysts or other users who want to understand data to support data-driven decision making. In this chapter, we'll discuss some of the latest features and capabilities in SQL Server 2019 and how those capabilities can be used to improve and optimize your data warehouse workloads. We'll also discuss how investments being made in the intelligent cloud are enabling organizations to modernize their analytics ecosystems to unlock more value and insights for their data.

Extract-transform-load solutions with SQL Server Integration Services

SQL Server Integration Services (**SSIS**) is a platform for building enterprise-scale data integration, data transformation, and data loading (**extract-transform-load, ETL**) solutions. Since the release of SQL Server 2005, organizations around the world have been using SSIS to solve complex business problems by copying or downloading files, cleansing and mining data, managing SQL Server objects and data, and loading data warehouses. Even in the world of distributed systems and extract-load-transform (ELT) patterns, ETL design patterns using SSIS have a place in many organizations that struggle with sourcing data from multiple disparate data sources to cleanse data and implement business logic.

SSIS includes a rich set of built-in tasks and transformations, graphical tools for building packages, and the Integration Services Catalog database, where you store, run, and manage packages. Packages are collections of tasks and transformations used to perform activities such as integrating, transforming, and loading data into a variety of systems. SSIS can be used to extract and transform data from a wide variety of sources such as XML data files, flat files, and relational data sources that may be hosted on-premises or in Azure and then loaded into one or many different data sources.

SSIS offers significant flexibility and capability for connecting to data sources, transforming data, and loading data. SSIS is also very extensible. The developer and partner ecosystems are quite robust, featuring custom, developed tasks and transforms and a wide variety of training and consulting options. These facts make SSIS ideal for a wide variety of ETL scenarios including loading your enterprise data warehouse.

Best practices for loading your data warehouse with SSIS

SSIS is a trusted ETL platform for integrating and transforming data. When using SSIS to load your data warehouse, consider the following best practices.

- **Dynamically filter source data to only query changed records**: A key step for building scalable and well-performing data warehouse load processes is to query only the changed records from the source. This will reduce load on the source systems and ensure that ETL processes finish in as little time as possible. To accomplish this, record the maximum time stamp or key column value in a control table as a watermark during each data load. Then, in subsequent data loads, query the watermark value from the control table and store the value in a variable in the SSIS package. In the **Data Flow Task** used to load the table in the data warehouse, use the variable in a `WHERE` clause appended in the Data Flow Task source `SELECT` statement to filter the data and ensure that you load only new data into the data warehouse.

- **Add retry logic**: Using a Data Flow Task inside of a **For Loop container** is a great way to build retry logic into your data warehouse loading. Create one variable to use within the loop as the counter for the current try and a second variable that contains a constant value for the maximum number of retries. Add a Script task that performs a brief wait after the Data Flow Task and connect the Script task to the Data Flow Task with a failure precedence constraint. Also, add an expression task after the Data Flow Task using a success precedence constraint to update the current counter variable in order to break the For Each loop after the successful execution of the Data Flow Task.

- **Use the smallest data type possible in your Data Flow Tasks**: SSIS package Data Flow Task transformations occur in memory on the SSIS server. This means that Data Flow Task memory usage is managed within the Data Flow Task settings. To use memory as efficiently as possible, utilize the smallest data types possible. This will ensure that a maximum number of records will fit into each data buffer during execution of the Data Flow Task. To view and modify the data types of the columns being queried from a data source, right-click the source component and select Show Advanced Editor. Navigate to the Input and Output Properties tab and expand the Source Output section. Data types for a source component output are set under the Output Columns section.

- **Use the OLE DB destination table or view fast-load option**: When using the Data Flow Task OLE DB destination to load data to your data warehouse, be sure to use the fast-load data access mode. The fast-load option will ensure that SQL Server uses a bulk load when writing data into the destination table. This is ideal because a bulk load operation will be minimally logged and will generally improve data loading performance.

- **Avoid using the OLE DB Command transformation for loading dimensions**: The OLE DB Command transform is commonly used in data warehouse loading scenarios to handle slowly changing dimensions. It is recommended, however, to avoid using the OLE DB Command transform as the OLE DB Command transform executes a SQL statement for each row in the buffer. This means that if your Data Flow Task is updating 100,000 rows in a dimension table, your OLE DB Command transform will execute the embedded SQL statement 100,000 times, which can drastically degrade package performance and negatively impact the transaction log of the data source. A better pattern is to use the Data Flow Task to load the data to a staging table and then use an Execute SQL task to perform the updating of the dimension table.

Clustered Columnstore Indexes

SQL Server 2019 features **in-memory columnstore indexes**. Columnstore indexes store and manage data by using columnar data storage and columnar query processing. Data warehouse workloads that primarily perform bulk loads and read-only queries will very likely benefit from columnstore indexes. Use the columnstore index to achieve up to 10x query performance gains over traditional row-oriented storage and up to 7x data compresson over the uncompressed data size.

SQL Server supports both clustered and nonclustered columnstore indexes. Both use the same in-memory columnstore technology, but they do have differences in purpose and in features they support.

For example, a clustered columnstore index is the physical storage for the table and is the only index for the table. The clustered index is updatable so you can perform insert, delete, and update operations on the index.

Conversely, a nonclustered columnstore index is a read-only index created on an existing clustered index or heap table. The nonclustered columnstore index contains a copy of a subset of columns, up to and including all of the columns in the table. The table is read-only while it contains a nonclustered columnstore index.

The clustered columnstore index is considered the standard for storing large data warehousing fact tables and is intended to be used in most SQL Server data warehouse workloads. Columnstore indexes give substantial performance gains for queries that use full table scans. Columnstore index benefits include the following:

- Columns often have similar data, which results in high compression rates.

- High compression rates often improve query performance by using a smaller in-memory footprint. Query performance can improve because SQL Server can perform more query and data operations in-memory.

- Queries often select only a few columns from a table, which reduces total I/O from the physical media.

- A new query execution mechanism called batch mode execution has been added to SQL Server that reduces CPU usage by a large amount. Batch mode execution is closely integrated with, and optimized around, the columnstore storage format.

Review the following example to understand how to create a clustered columnstore index. This example creates a table as a heap and then converts the table to a clustered columnstore index. This changes the storage for the entire table from rowstore to columnstore:

```
CREATE TABLE T1 (

    ProductKey [int] NOT NULL,

    OrderDateKey [int] NOT NULL,

    DueDateKey [int] NOT NULL,

    ShipDateKey [int] NOT NULL);

GO

CREATE CLUSTERED COLUMNSTORE INDEX cci_T1 ON T1;

GO
```

> **Note**
>
> Review the following documentation to learn more about using clustered columnstore indexes: https://docs.microsoft.com/en-us/sql/database-engine/using-clustered-columnstore-indexes?view=sql-server-2014&viewFallbackFrom=sql-server-ver15.
>
> For a deeper understanding of columnstore indexes, read the following article: https://docs.microsoft.com/en-us/sql/relational-databases/indexes/clustered-and-nonclustered-indexes-described?view=sql-server-ver15.

Partitioning

Beginning with the release of SQL Server 2005, SQL Server has supported table and index partitioning, which allows the data of partitioned tables and indexes to be spread across multiple filegroups in a database. The data is partitioned horizontally so that groups of rows are mapped into partitions using a partition function that defines the range of values in a partition. Partitions can also be stored on separate filegroups to further increase the scalability of a workload, improve performance, and ease maintenance operations:

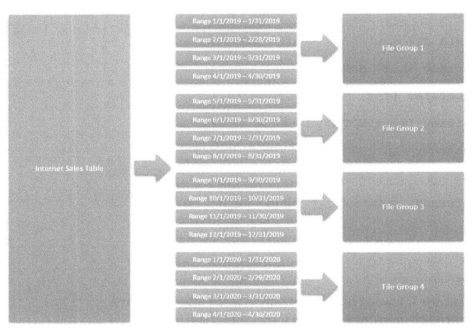

Figure 11.1: A well-designed partition strategy can improve data loading and querying performance while also simplifying the maintenance of large volumes of data

Partitioning large tables or indexes can provide benefits that can improve manageability and increase performance, especially in the case of data warehouse workloads that often deal with large volumes of data.

Transferring or accessing subsets of data quickly and efficiently is enabled while maintaining the integrity of a data collection. For example, an operation such as loading data into a large fact table in a data warehouse may take only seconds compared to minutes or hours if the data was not partitioned. Also, archiving or deleting old data as new data is loaded into a large fact table becomes a straightforward operation without affecting the performance or availability of the greater data collection.

You can perform maintenance operations on one or more partitions quickly. For example, you may choose to rebuild a single partition of a clustered columnstore index to improve compression rather than rebuilding the clustered columnstore index for the entire table.

You can improve query performance based on the types of queries you frequently run. Partitioning a table on a column commonly used in equi-joins and in WHERE clauses can increase query performance in a couple of different ways. First, the query optimizer may be able to eliminate certain partitions from being queried when the WHERE clause is used to filter the data using the partitioning column of the table. Also, the query optimizer can process equi-join queries between two or more partitioned tables faster when the partitioning columns are the same as the columns on which the tables are joined.

> **Note**
>
> It is important to validate that your partitioning strategy is effective and improves performance and manageability. Too many partitions can hurt performance and too few partitions may not provide a significant benefit, for example.
>
> Read the following article for an overview of partitioning, the components and concepts, and performance guidelines: https://docs.microsoft.com/en-us/sql/relational-databases/partitions/partitioned-tables-and-indexes?view=sql-server-ver15.
>
> See the following article to learn how to create partition functions and partition schemes and then apply them to a table and index: https://docs.microsoft.com/en-us/sql/relational-databases/partitions/create-partitioned-tables-and-indexes?view=sql-server-ver15.

Online index management

SQL Server 2019 introduces resumable online index creation in addition to rebuilding. The online option supports concurrent user access to the underlying table or index data during online index operations. Online index operations are recommended for business environments that require concurrent user activity during index operations for workloads that are online 24 hours a day and 7 days a week.

The `ONLINE` option is available in the following T-SQL statements:

- `CREATE INDEX`
- `ALTER INDEX`
- `DROP INDEX`
- `ALTER TABLE` (to add or drop `UNIQUE` or `PRIMARY KEY` constraints with the `CLUSTERED` index option)

When creating or rebuilding an index and the ONLINE option is set to ON, the underlying objects are available for querying and data modification. It is also possible to rebuild part of an index on a single partition.

Enabling online DML processing

To perform online index operations, the user requires `ALTER` permission on the table or view.

Online DML operations for indexes can be enabled using SQL Server Management Studio, Azure Data Studio, or T-SQL.

Using SQL Server Management Studio, complete the following steps to enable online DML operations for a given index:

1. Open **Object Explorer** and navigate to the table that contains the index for which you need to enable online index operations.

2. Expand the **Indexes** folder beneath the table on which you need to enable online index operations.

3. Expand the **Indexes** folder and right-click the desired index. Click **Properties**.

4. Under Select a page, select **Options**.

5. Select **Allow** online DML processing and then select **True**.

6. Click **OK**:

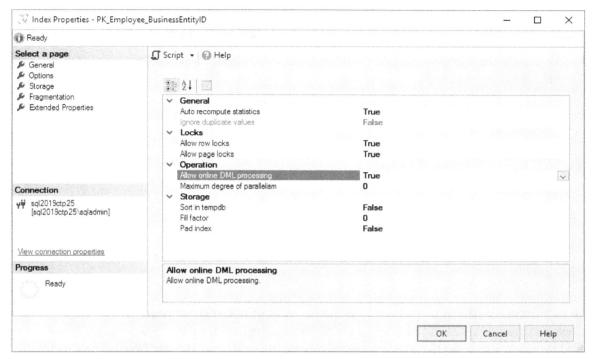

Figure 11.2: Enabling online DML processing with SQL Server Management Studio

To enable online DML processing for a given index using T-SQL, specify the `ONLINE = ON` argument as shown in the following example of rebuilding a clustered columnstore index:

```
USE [AdventureWorksDW2017]
GO
ALTER INDEX [cci_FactResellerSales] ON [dbo].[FactResellerSales]
REBUILD PARTITION = ALL WITH (ONLINE = ON)
```

Resuming online index create or rebuild

SQL Server 2019 adds pausing and resuming an index create or rebuild operation while online. Resumable online index create allows you to create an index, pause, and then resume later where the operation was paused or failed, instead of restarting the operation from the beginning.

Being able to pause and resume an index create or rebuild at a later date or time could be very useful in the following scenarios:

- An unexpected, high-priority task surfaces that requires more resources.

- The data warehouse maintenance window closes before the index create or rebuild completes.

- A failover occurs for the data warehouse database.

- A database runs out of disk space.

- There is a need to reduce long-running transactions to improve log space management.

> **Note**
>
> Clustered columnstore indexes can be created or rebuilt online but do not support pausing and resuming create and rebuild operations.

The **RESUMABLE** argument is specified in the DDL of the index create or rebuild statement rather than in the metadata of the desired index, as shown in the following example. To specify a DDL operation as resumable, the **ONLINE** argument must also be set to **ON**:

```
USE [AdventureWorks2017]

GO

CREATE UNIQUE NONCLUSTERED INDEX [AK_Employee_LoginID] ON
[HumanResources].[Employee]

(

   [LoginID] ASC

)WITH (ONLINE = ON, RESUMABLE = ON) ON [PRIMARY]

GO
```

To pause an index create or rebuild operation, either stop the ongoing command, kill the session using the **KILL <session_id>** command, or execute the **ALTER INDEX PAUSE** command as shown in the following example:

```
USE [AdventureWorks2017]

GO

ALTER INDEX [AK_Employee_LoginID]

ON [HumanResources].[Employee] PAUSE
```

Re-executing the original **CREATE** or **REBUILD** statement automatically resumes a paused index create operation.

To abort the index operation, use the **ABORT** command.

Build and rebuild online clustered columnstore indexes

Clustered columnstore indexes are the standard in SQL Server for storing and querying large data warehouse fact tables. In previous versions of SQL Server, creating clustered columnstore indexes was an offline process. SQL Server 2019 now supports creating and rebuilding a clustered columnstore index while online. This new feature means that workloads will not be blocked, and all modifications made to data are transparently added to the target columnstore table. This is ideal for business workloads that require near-100% availability.

Review the following examples to create and rebuild a clustered columnstore index online:

```
USE [AdventureWorksDW2017]

GO

CREATE CLUSTERED COLUMNSTORE INDEX cci_FactResellerSales

ON [dbo].[FactResellerSales]

WITH (ONLINE = ON);


USE [AdventureWorksDW2017]

GO

ALTER INDEX cci_FactResellerSales

ON [dbo].[FactResellerSales]

REBUILD WITH (ONLINE = ON);
```

Using ALTER DATABASE SCOPE CONFIGURATION

ALTER DATABASE SCOPE CONFIGURATION enables several database configuration settings at the individual database level. **ALTER DATABASE SCOPE CONFIGURATION** was introduced in SQL Server 2016 but now also supports the **ONLINE** and **RESUMABLE** arguments. This feature supports defining the default behavior at the database level rather than for each individual statement.

Use **ALTER DATABASE SCOPE CONFIGURATION** to set the default behavior for online and resumable operations to either **OFF**, **FAIL_UNSUPPORTED**, or **WHEN_SUPPORTED**.

OFF

This value is the default behavior. This value means that online and resumable operations will not be online or resumable unless specified in the statement.

FAIL_UNSUPPORTED

This value elevates all supported DDL operations to `ONLINE` or `RESUMABLE`. Operations that do not support online or resumable execution will fail and throw a warning.

WHEN_SUPPORTED

This value elevates all DDL operations to `ONLINE` or `RESUMABLE`. Operations that do not support online or resumable execution will be run offline.

View the following example to understand how to set the default behavior for configuring the database engine to automatically elevate supported operations to `ONLINE`:

```
USE [AdventureWorks2017]

GO

ALTER DATABASE SCOPED CONFIGURATION SET ELEVATE_ONLINE = WHEN_SUPPORTED
```

View the following example to understand how to set the default behavior for configuring the Database Engine to automatically elevate supported operations to `RESUMABLE`:

```
USE [AdventureWorks2017]

GO

ALTER DATABASE SCOPED CONFIGURATION SET ELEVATE_RESUMABLE = FAIL_
UNSUPPORTED
```

> **Note**
>
> For more information, review the following documentation on guidelines for online index operations: https://docs.microsoft.com/en-us/sql/relational-databases/indexes/guidelines-for-online-index-operations?view=sql-server-ver15.

Creating and maintaining statistics

SQL Server's Query Optimizer uses statistics to create query plans that improve query performance. Statistics contain statistical information regarding the distribution of values in one or more columns of a table or indexed view. The Query Optimizer uses statistical information to determine the number of rows in a query result, which enables the Query Optimizer to determine an optimal query plan. As such, up-to-date statistics are crucial for generating an optimal query plan and to ensure excellent performance.

Automatically managing statistics

The SQL Server Query Optimizer will automatically create statistics in two different ways:

- When an index is created, the Query Optimizer will create statistics on the key column(s) of the index.

- The Query Optimizer will create statistics in query predicates when the `AUTO_CREATE_STATISTICS` option is set to `ON`.

But there are three options that can be set to determine when statistics are created and updated.

The AUTO_CREATE_STATISTICS option

When the `AUTO_CREATE_STATISTICS` option is set to `ON`, the query optimizer creates statistics for individual columns in query predicates to improve query plans and query performance. This happens when the Query Optimizer compiles a query.

The AUTO_UPDATE_STATISTICS option

When the `AUTO_UPDATE_STATICS` option is set to `ON`, the Query Optimizer updates statistics when they are used by a query or when they could be out of date. Statistics become out of date when database operations alter the distribution of data in a table or indexed view. This could happen after an insert, update, or delete operation. The Query Optimizer determines whether statistics are out of date by counting the number of data modifications since the last statistics update.

The AUTO_UPDATE_STATISTICS_ASYNC option

The `AUTO_UPDATE_STATISTICS_ASYNC` option determines whether the Query Optimizer uses synchronous or asynchronous statistics updates. This option applies to statistics objects created for indexes, single columns in query predicates, and statistics created with the `CREATE STATISTICS` statement. The default value for the `AUTO_UPDATE_STATISTICS_ASYNC` option is `OFF`, which means that the Query Optimizer updates statistics asynchronously.

> **Note**
>
> To set `AUTO_UPDATE_STASTICS_ASYNC` to `ON`, both the `AUTO_CREATE_STATISTICS` and `AUTO_UPDATE_STATISTICS` options should be set to `ON`.

Statistics for columnstore indexes

Because the characteristics of a data warehouse workload are typically very different from those of a transaction workload, the methodology you follow for the maintenance of statistics will depend on the characteristics of your data. As you develop your plan, consider the following guidelines:

- For columns that contain static values, such as certain dimension tables, reduce the frequency of updates to the statistics.

- An ascending key column for which new values are added frequently, such as a transaction date or an order number, likely requires more frequent updates to the statistics. Consider updating the related statistics more often.

- Consider using asynchronous statistics for workloads, such as data warehouses, that frequently execute the same query or similar queries. Query response times could be more predictable because the Query Optimizer can execute queries without waiting for up-to-date statistics.

- Consider using synchronous statistics if your data warehouse ETL process includes truncating tables or bulk updates to a large percentage of rows. This will ensure that statistics are up to date before executing queries.

Modern data warehouse patterns in Azure

In today's world, modern enterprises have recognized that all data represents hidden value waiting to be unlocked by their organization. Data exists in all shapes, sizes, and formats, and often the differentiating factor between the most efficient and successful companies and less successful companies is how well those companies use data to drive intelligent decisions. More companies are recognizing that data and intelligence have little value if we can't properly manage it.

Today organizations need to be able to ingest large volumes of data into big data stores from a variety of data sources. Once in big data stores, Hadoop, Spark, and machine learning pipelines prepare and train the data. Once the data is ready for complex analysis, the data is loaded into the data warehouse to be accessed by business intelligence tools, such as Power BI or Excel. Azure provides the framework and ecosystem for designing and building cutting-edge big data and advanced analytics platforms. In this section, we're going to discuss technologies such as Azure SQL Data Warehouse, Azure Data Factory, Azure Databricks, Azure Data Lake, and Power BI and how these cloud technologies fit into modern data warehouse design patterns, offering limitless scale and flexibility.

Introduction to Azure SQL Data Warehouse

Azure SQL Data Warehouse democratizes **massively parallel processing (MPP)** capabilities and enables organizations of all sizes to take advantage of petabyte-scale data warehouse processing on demand. SQL Data Warehouse is a cloud-based enterprise data warehouse specifically built and optimized for data warehouse workloads for systems with small to very large amounts of data. Because SQL Data Warehouse leverages distributed compute and storage resources, SQL Data Warehouse allows queries to scale out and take advantage of parallel processing for large, complex, analytical queries.

Azure SQL Data Warehouse includes four components that make up the architecture, as shown in *Figure 11.3*:

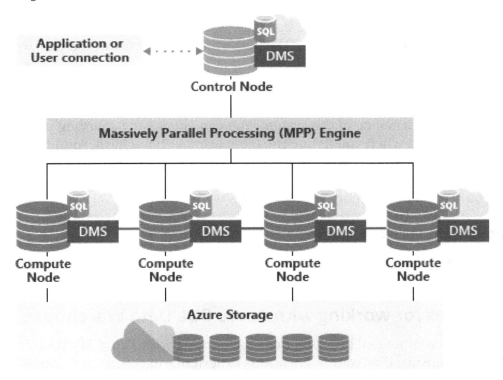

Figure 11.3: SQL Data Warehouse includes four main components

Control node

The control node is an Azure SQL database that coordinates data movement and computational workloads in a data warehouse. The control node receives the T-SQL queries and breaks them into units of work, which are parallelized across the compute nodes. No data is stored on the compute node. The compute node consists of metadata and statistics of the data warehouse.

Compute nodes

The compute nodes are separate Azure SQL databases that provide the computing horsepower for Azure SQL Data Warehouse. While the control node distributes data across compute nodes when loading new data into the data warehouse, the compute nodes return partial query results to the control node for final assembly of the query results. The number of compute nodes ranges from 1 to 60 and is determined by the **service level objective (SLO)** selected for the data warehouse.

The SLO is a scalability setting that determines the cost and performance level of your Azure SQL Data Warehouse instance. Azure SQL Data Warehouse Gen 1 service levels are measured in **data warehouse units** (**DWU**s) and SQL Data Warehouse Gen 2 service levels are measured in **compute data warehouse units** (**cDWU**s). DWUs and cDWUs represent an abstract and normalized way to measure CPU, I/O, and memory. Changing the SLO of your SQL Data Warehouse instance represents a change to the DWU or cDWU of the data warehouse, altering the performance and cost of the data warehouse.

Storage

The data is stored and managed by Azure Storage. The data is sharded into distributions to optimize the performance of the system. You can choose the sharding pattern to use to distribute the data when you define the table using either a hash, round-robin, or replication sharding pattern. Because the storage is decoupled from the compute, all data is persisted in storage regardless of how you scale or pause compute resources, allowing you to only pay for compute resources when in use.

Data movement services (DMSes)

DMSes coordinate data movement between nodes as required to respond to queries. DMSes work transparently as background services.

Best practices for working with Azure SQL Data Warehouse

Following the recommended best practices for working with Azure SQL Data Warehouse will ensure that your applications experience excellent performance and that your users will have a positive experience.

Reduce costs by scaling up and down

Because Azure SQL Data Warehouse separates storage from compute resources, scaling compute to meet performance and availability demands independently from data storage allows you to optimize your data warehouse workloads for maximum cost savings. If you don't need to use your data warehouse during a specific time frame, you can save compute costs by pausing compute resources.

> **Note**
>
> To learn more about scale-out steps, view the following documentation on managing compute: https://docs.microsoft.com/en-us/azure/sql-data-warehouse/sql-data-warehouse-manage-compute-overview.

Use PolyBase to load data quickly

SQL Data Warehouse supports loading and exporting data using a variety of tools including Azure Data Factory, SSIS, PolyBase, and BCP. But when loading or exporting large amounts of data or fast performance is required, PolyBase is the best choice. Because PolyBase is specifically designed to leverage the MPP architecture of SQL Data Warehouse, exporting and loading data will be much faster than any other tool.

> **Note**
>
> To learn more about the best practices for loading data in Azure SQL Data Warehouse, view the following documentation: https://docs.microsoft.com/en-us/azure/sql-data-warehouse/guidance-for-loading-data.

Manage the distributions of data

A distribution is the basic unit of storage and processing for parallel queries that run on distributed data. When SQL Data Warehouse runs a query, the work is divided into 60 smaller queries that run in parallel to access the data, which is distributed using one of three methods:

- **Hash distribution**: To shard data into a hash-distributed table, SQL Data Warehouse uses a hash function to assign each row to one distribution. The column to be used as the distribution column is determined in the table definition. A hash distribution can deliver higher query performance for joins and aggregations on large tables. For example, hash distributing two large fact tables on the same key values that are commonly used in joins will eliminate the need for data movement between compute nodes.

- **Round-robin distribution**: By default, tables use round-robin distribution. This makes it easy for users to get started creating tables without having to decide how their tables should be distributed. Round-robin tables may perform sufficiently for some workloads, but in most cases hash distributing a table based on a column that is commonly used in large joins or aggregation will provide optimal performance.

- **Replicated tables**: A replicated table provides the fastest query performance for small tables. A table that is replicated creates a full copy of the table on each compute node. Replicating small tables commonly used in lookups, such as a date table, can eliminate the need for data movement. Be aware that extra storage is required for replicating a table and there is additional overhead incurred when writing data to a replicated table. Replicating large tables is not ideal.

> **Note**
>
> Read the following documentation for guidance on designing distributed tables in Azure SQL Data Warehouse: https://docs.microsoft.com/en-us/azure/sql-data-warehouse/sql-data-warehouse-tables-distribute.

Do not over-partition data

Because of the distributed nature of Azure SQL Data Warehouse, data is partitioned into 60 databases. This means that if you create a table with 100 partitions, this results in 6,000 partitions. A high-granularity partitioning strategy that worked well on SQL Server may not work well with SQL Data Warehouse and may, in fact, hurt query performance.

Also, keep in mind that too many partitions can hurt the performance of a clustered columnstore index. Remember that rows in a table with a clustered columnstore index generally will not push data into a compressed columnstore segment until there are more than 1 million rows per table per partition. Having too many partitions may prevent your workload from benefiting from a clustered columnstore index.

> **Note**
>
> Read the following documentation to learn more about partitioning tables in Azure SQL Data Warehouse: https://docs.microsoft.com/en-us/azure/sql-data-warehouse/sql-data-warehouse-tables-partition.
>
> View the following article to understand the possible causes of poor columnstore index quality: https://docs.microsoft.com/en-us/azure/sql-data-warehouse/sql-data-warehouse-tables-index#causes-of-poor-columnstore-index-quality.
>
> Learn more about best practices for Azure SQL Data Warehouse by reading the following article: https://docs.microsoft.com/en-us/azure/sql-data-warehouse/sql-data-warehouse-best-practices.

Using Azure Data Factory

Azure Data Factory (**ADF**) is a highly available, fault-tolerant, cloud-based data integration service that automates the movement and transformation of data assets between your on-premises network and Azure data services based on a defined schedule or trigger. ADF supports the ingestion of a large variety of data sources, including structured or unstructured data sources, which makes ADF ideal for modern data warehouse implementations in Azure. Because ADF is natively integrated with other Azure Data Services, such as Azure SQL Data Warehouse, Azure Databricks, and Azure Storage, using ADF to automate data movement and transformation across a modern data ecosystem built in Azure becomes very easy. Azure Data Factory is the go-to data movement tool for automating the load of Azure SQL Data Warehouse.

New capabilities in ADF

The latest enhancements to ADF (ADF v2) were made generally available in June 2018. ADF v2 introduced a host of new capabilities.

Control flow

ADF includes control flow data pipeline constructs such as branching, looping, conditional execution, and parameterization to allow you to orchestrate complex data integration jobs that are flexible and reusable.

Code-free designing

ADF now supports designing, managing, maintaining, and monitoring your pipelines right in your browser. Native integration with Git repos in Visual Studio Team Services allows your development teams to collaborate on data pipelines as well as build and release management and automation.

Iterative pipeline development

The ADF design environment also includes the ability to iteratively develop pipelines and debug your pipelines interactively with iterative debugging built in.

Flexible scheduling

Schedule pipelines on a wall-clock scheduler or event-based triggers, or with tumbling window schedules.

Lift and shift SSIS packages into ADF

ADF provides integration runtime support that allows you to lift and shift your existing on-premises SSIS packages into the cloud by using ADF. There, you can then execute, schedule, and monitor your SSIS package executions in the cloud.

HDInsight Spark on demand and Azure Databricks

ADF now supports building ETL pipelines in the cloud to transform data at scale with Spark using HDInsight on-demand clusters or Azure Databricks notebooks.

SDK support

SDK support has been added and updated for Python, .NET, REST, and PowerShell to build custom applications with ADF.

Understanding ADF

ADF is composed of several key components, which serve as the platform on which you can build data-driven workflows with steps to move and transform data.

Pipeline

A pipeline is a logical grouping of activities that performs a unit of work. The activities in a pipeline perform a task, such as copying data from an on-premises SQL Server environment, transforming the data with a Mapping Data Flow activity, and then loading the data into an Azure SQL Data Warehouse instance.

Activity

An activity represents a step in a pipeline. ADF supports data movement activities, data transformation activities, and control activities. For example, Copy Activity can be used to copy data from one data store to another data store.

Datasets

A dataset represents data structures within data stores, which simply point to or reference the data you want to use in your activities as inputs or outputs. For example, a dataset can be tables that exist in a database or files in Azure Blob storage.

Linked services

A linked service functions as a connection string and defines the connection information required by ADF for connecting to an external resource. Linked services are used for two purposes in ADF:

- To represent a data store, such as an on-premises SQL Server database, Oracle database, file share, or Azure Blob storage account

- To represent a compute resource that can host the execution of an activity, such as a Hive query on an HDInsight Hadoop cluster or a stored procedure on a SQL Server database

The following diagram illustrates the relationships between a pipeline, activity, dataset, and linked service in ADF:

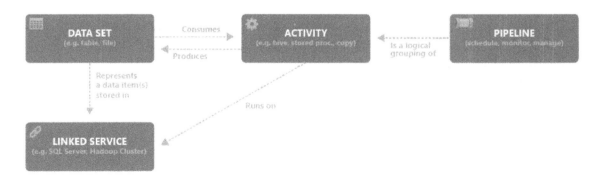

Figure 11.4: A pipeline is a logical grouping of activities that produces or consumes a dataset and is run on a linked service

Copying data to Azure SQL Data Warehouse

To copy data from on-premises to Azure data stores, we can use Copy Activity. Copy Activity supports a wide variety of data sources including SQL Server, Oracle, MySQL, Salesforce, and files.

> **Note**
>
> To find a complete list of supported data sources and destinations for Copy Activity, refer to the following documentation: https://docs.microsoft.com/en-us/azure/data-factory/v1/data-factory-data-movement-activities.

For example, you could copy data from an on-premises SQL Server instance to Azure SQL Data Warehouse using the following steps:

1. First, open the Azure portal (https://portal.azure.com). Then, click Create a resource in the top left. In the search bar, type "Data Factory" and press Enter. Select the Data Factory resource and then click Create. Complete the form to create a new Data Factory instance. Enter a globally unique name and select the subscription. Select whether you'd like to create a new resource group or use an existing resource group. Ensure the version is set to V2 and select the geographic location for the Data Factory instance. Finally, click Create.

2. When the new Data Factory instance has finished provisioning, open the Data Factory blade by selecting the newly created Data Factory. Click the Author & Monitor button on the Data Factory Overview blade.

3. ADF features many templates for creating pipelines that can perform a variety of tasks including copying data from Google BigQuery to Azure Data Lake Store, performing ETL with Azure Databricks, loading a type 2 slowly changing dimension, and more. For this example, we will use a predefined template to copy data from an on-premises SQL Server to Azure SQL Data Warehouse. Click the Create pipeline from template button:

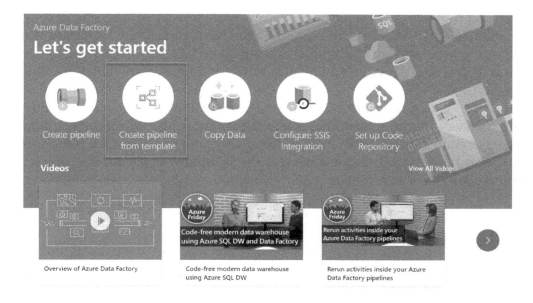

Figure 11.5: Create a Data Factory pipeline from a template

4. Once the Data Factory Editor window opens, search SQL Data Warehouse in the Filter text box. Click the template to Copy data from on-premise SQL Server to SQL Data Warehouse. The template requires you to complete the user input for creating the pipeline template. You must define the DataSourceConnection and DataDestinationConnection inputs.

5. In the DataSourceConnection input, select an existing linked service to use or define a new linked service by clicking + New. If you're creating a new linked service, enter a name and description for the linked service. In the drop-down box under Connect via integration runtime, click + New. In order to allow ADF to query an on-premises SQL Server, we must configure a self-hosted integration runtime in your on-premises network to facilitate the connection. Click the tile labeled Self-Hosted. Enter a name for the self-hosted integration runtime and click **Next**. You can use Option 1: Express setup to configure the self-hosted integration runtime on your current computer or you can use Option 2: Manual setup to download and install the integration runtime on a separate computer. When you have successfully configured the self-hosted integration runtime, click **Finish**.

6. With the self-hosted integration runtime configured, you can now finish creating the new linked service. Enter the server name, database name, authentication type, username, and password. Click **Finish**.

7. Next, you must define the Azure SQL Data Warehouse instance you wish to use in the DataDestinationConnection input. If you have an existing SQL Data Warehouse instance you've already configured as a linked service and would like to use, select it now. If you need to create a linked service for a new Azure SQL Data Warehouse instance, click + New. Enter the name and description for the new linked service. In the drop-down box under Connect via integration runtime, ensure you select AutoResolveIntegrationRuntime. Select the Azure subscription, server name, database name, authentication type, username, and password for the Azure SQL Data Warehouse instance you selected. Click **Finish**. Finally, on the template screen click Use this template:

> **Note**
>
> To allow ADF to connect to Azure SQL Data Warehouse, you must enable Allow access to Azure services in the SQL Server firewall settings for your Azure SQL Data Warehouse instance.

8. With the template now created, we simply need to update Datasets, Datasource1, and DataDestination1, which can be found in the Factory Resources blade under **Datasets**. Click **DataSource1** to select the dataset. Go to the **Connection** tab in DataSource1 and use the drop-down list next to Table and select the table you wish to copy to Azure SQL Data Warehouse. Then go to the **Schema** tab and click Import schema to populate the columns and data types found in the table.

9. To populate the schema for DataDestination1, complete the same steps previously mentioned. Once you've populated the schemas for both the DataSource1 and DataDestination1 datasets, navigate to the pipeline under Factory Resources and click on Copy Activity in the design canvas. First, navigate to the **Sink** tab for Copy Activity and disable the Allow Polybase option. Then, go to the **Mapping** tab and ensure that your source columns are correctly mapped to the destination columns. On the **Settings** tab, disable Enable staging. Click the **Publish All** button in the top left. To test your pipeline, click the **Debug** button in the Pipeline editor window.

10. If you need to schedule the pipeline to automatically execute on a recurring basis, click the Triggers button at the bottom of the Factory Resources blade. You have the option to define three different types of triggers.

    Schedule: A trigger that invokes a pipeline on a wall-clock schedule. For example, use this trigger when you need a pipeline to execute every day at 3 PM.

Tumbling Window: A trigger that operates on a periodic interval, while also retaining state. For example, use a Tumbling Window trigger when you wish to execute a pipeline once every 15 minutes.

Event: A trigger that responds to an event. For example, use an event-based trigger when you need to execute a pipeline when a file arrives or is deleted in Azure Blob storage.

> **Note**
>
> For more information on executing ADF pipelines with a Trigger, view the following article: https://docs.microsoft.com/en-us/azure/data-factory/concepts-pipeline-execution-triggers.

Hosting SSIS packages in ADF

ADF supports hosting SSIS packages on dedicated compute resources, which means you can now lift and shift existing SSIS workloads to Azure.

To support the execution of SSIS packages in Azure, you must first provision an Azure-SSIS **Integration Runtime** (**IR**) to natively execute SSIS packages. The Azure-SSIS IR is a fully managed cluster of Azure **virtual machines** (**VM**s) dedicated to running your SSIS packages. Your Azure-SSIS IR can be scaled up by specifying the node size and can be scaled out by specifying the number of nodes in the cluster. You can also manage the cost of running the Azure-SSIS IR by stopping and starting the Azure-SSIS IR based on your workload demands.

Optionally, you can use Azure SQL Database server with a virtual network service endpoint or an Azure SQL Database managed instance to host the SSIS catalog database. A prerequisite for using ADF-hosted SSIS packages to query data sources within your on-premises network is to attach the Azure-SSIS IR to an Azure virtual network and configure virtual network permissions/settings as necessary.

SSIS packages hosted in ADF can be executed by creating an ADF pipeline featuring an Execute SSIS Package activity. This will allow you to integrate your SSIS packages hosted in ADF within your ADF pipelines.

Alternatively, SSIS packages hosted in ADF can also be executed by using a stored procedure activity within an ADF pipeline.

The SSIS Feature Pack for Azure is an extension that provides a variety of components for building SSIS packages to connect to Azure services, transfering data between Azure and on-premises data sources, and processing data stored in Azure. Download the SSIS Feature Pack for Azure here: https://docs.microsoft.com/en-us/sql/integration-services/azure-feature-pack-for-integration-services-ssis?view=sql-server-2017.

For more information about hosting and running SSIS package in ADF, see the following articles:

- How to deploy SSIS packages to Azure, https://docs.microsoft.com/en-us/azure/data-factory/tutorial-create-azure-ssis-runtime-portal: This article provides step-by-step instructions to create an Azure-SSIS IR and uses an Azure SQL database to host the SSIS catalog.

- How to create an Azure-SSIS integration runtime, https://docs.microsoft.com/en-us/azure/data-factory/create-azure-ssis-integration-runtime: This article expands on the tutorial and provides instructions on using Azure SQL Database managed instance and joining the IR to a virtual network.

- How to monitor an Azure-SSIS IR, https://docs.microsoft.com/en-us/azure/data-factory/monitor-integration-runtime#azure-ssis-integration-runtime: This article shows you how to retrieve information about an Azure-SSIS IR and descriptions of statuses in the returned information.

- How to manage an Azure-SSIS IR, https://docs.microsoft.com/en-us/azure/data-factory/manage-azure-ssis-integration-runtime: This article shows you how to stop, start, or remove an Azure-SSIS IR.

- How to join an Azure-SSIS IR to a virtual network, https://docs.microsoft.com/en-us/azure/data-factory/join-azure-ssis-integration-runtime-virtual-network: This article provides conceptual information about joining an Azure-SSIS IR to an Azure virtual network.

Azure Data Lake Storage

Today, organizations are recognizing the value of all types of data and being able to effectively leverage their data assets. Many organizations are seeking to understand and analyze all data assets regardless of the size, shape, or perceived value of the data. Because of this, many organizations are adopting data lake architectures where data of all types is stored for future analysis. Azure Data Lake Storage is the foundation for building data lake architectures to store data of any shape, any volume, and any velocity in the cloud while defining the data schema at the time of read.

Azure Data Lake Storage and Azure SQL Data Warehouse are designed to work together to enable organizations to easily build and integrate their data lake and data warehouse environments seamlessly. Datasets stored in Azure Data Lake Storage can be easily queried for loading or analysis using Azure SQL Data Warehouse's PolyBase technology, as mentioned earlier in the chapter.

> **Note**
>
> Using Azure Data Lake Storage and PolyBase is the recommended best practice for loading and/or exporting large volumes of data in Azure SQL Data Warehouse.

Key features of Azure Data Lake Storage Gen2

Azure Data Lake Storage Gen2 (**ADLS Gen2**), the latest release of Azure Data Lake Storage, offers several new enhancements and capabilities over the previous version of Azure Data Lake Storage.

Hadoop-compatible access

ADLS Gen2 supports management and accessing data as you would with the Hadoop Distributed File System. The **Azure Blob Filesystem** (**ABFS**) driver is available for use within Apache Hadoop environments, including Azure SQL Data Warehouse and Azure Databricks, to access data stored in ADLS Gen2.

A superset of POSIX permissions

ADLS Gen2 features an access control model that supports both Azure **role-based access control (RBAC)** and POSIX-like **access control lists** (**ACL**s). In addition, these settings can be configured through Azure Storage Explorer or through frameworks such as Hive and Spark.

Cost-effective

ADLS Gen2 offers low-cost storage capacity and transactions. As data transitions through its complete life cycle, billing rates change, keeping costs to a minimum via built-in features such as the Azure Blob storage life cycle. Azure Blob storage life cycle management offers a rule-based policy that allows you to transition from blob to cooler storage to optimize for performance and cost, delete blobs at the end of their life cycle, define rules to be once per day at the storage account level, and apply rules to containers or a subset of blobs.

Optimized driver

The ABFS driver is optimized specifically for big data analytics, making Azure Data Lake Storage the go-to storage platform for advanced analytics in Azure.

> **Note**
>
> View the following tutorials to learn how to get started using Azure Data Lake Storage:
>
> How to extract, transform, and load data by using Azure Databricks, https://docs.microsoft.com/en-us/azure/azure-databricks/databricks-extract-load-sql-data-warehouse
>
> How to access Data Lake Storage with Databricks using Spark, https://docs.microsoft.com/en-us/azure/storage/blobs/data-lake-storage-use-databricks-spark
>
> How to extract, transform, and load data with Apache Hive on Azure HDInsight, https://docs.microsoft.com/en-us/azure/storage/blobs/data-lake-storage-tutorial-extract-transform-load-hive

Azure Databricks

Azure Databricks is a fast, easy, and collaborative Apache Spark-based analytics service optimized for Azure. Databricks was designed with the founders of Apache Spark and is tightly integrated with Azure to provide on-click setup, streamlined workflows, and an interactive workspace that enables collaboration between data scientists, engineers, and analysts.

Azure Databricks is tightly integrated with Azure data services such as SQL Data Warehouse, Data Lake Storage, Cosmos DB, SQL Database, Event Hubs, and Power BI. Databricks is ideal for working with structured or unstructured data, real-time data processing and analysis for analytical and interactive applications, machine learning and predictive analytics, graph computation, performing ETL operations, and other types of data engineering. Through a collaborative and integrated workspace experience, Azure Databricks eases the process of exploring data, visualizing data with interactive dashboards in just a few clicks, and documenting your progress in notebooks in R, Python, Scala, or SQL.

> **Note**
>
> With the serverless option, Azure Databricks abstracts the infrastructure complexity and the need for specialized expertise to set up and configure your data infrastructure.

Azure Databricks is a very flexible analytics platform but is especially useful in the following scenarios related to data warehouse applications leveraging Azure SQL Data Warehouse:

- Performing ETL operations for the purpose of cleansing and loading the data warehouse
- Integrating machine learning pipelines into your ETL process
- Ad hoc data exploration and analysis of the data warehouse
- Real-time data analysis in a real-time data warehousing workload

> **Note**
>
> Learning more about Azure Databricks by reviewing the following resources and tutorials:
>
> Extracting, transforming, and loading data into Azure SQL Data Warehouse by using Azure Databricks, https://docs.microsoft.com/en-us/azure/azure-databricks/databricks-extract-load-sql-data-warehouse
>
> Analyze near real-time streaming data with Azure Databricks, https://docs.microsoft.com/en-us/azure/azure-databricks/databricks-stream-from-eventhubs

Working with streaming data in Azure Stream Analytics

Azure Stream Analytics is an event-processing engine that allows you to analyze large volumes on streaming data in flight. Patterns and relationships can be identified in information extracted from a variety of input sources including devices, sensors, websites, social media feeds, and applications. The insights discovered can be used to trigger other actions as part of a workflow including creating alerts, feeding information to a reporting tool, or storing transformed data for later use.

Stream Analytics is ideal in scenarios related to real-time data warehousing. When used with event processing services such as Azure Event Hubs or Azure IoT Hub, Stream Analytics can be used to perform data cleansing, data reduction, and data store and forward needs. Stream Analytics can load data directly to Azure SQL Data Warehouse using the SQL output adapter, but throughput can be improved some increased latency by using PolyBase to read the streaming data from Azure Blob storage, as illustrated in *Figure 11.6*:

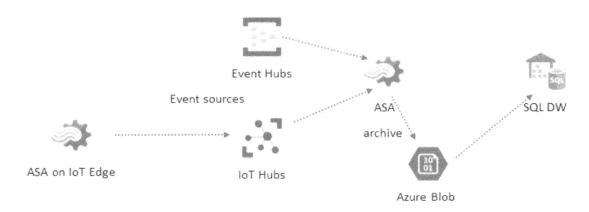

Figure 11.6: Using Azure Stream Analytics for real-time data warehousing scenarios

In *Figure 11.7* pattern, Azure Stream Analytics is used as a near real-time ETL engine. Newly arriving events are continuously transformed and stored in an Azure Blob storage container portioned by a date and time. The data stored in Azure Blob storage can then be loaded directly into Azure SQL Data Warehouse using PolyBase.

> **Note**
>
> Creating a Stream Analytics job by using the Azure portal, https://docs.microsoft. com/en-us/azure/stream-analytics/stream-analytics-quick-create-portal
>
> Azure Stream Analytics and custom blob output partitioning, https://docs. microsoft.com/en-us/azure/stream-analytics/stream-analytics-custom-path-patterns-blob-storage-output
>
> Analyzing phone call data with Stream Analytics and visualizing results in Power BI, https://docs.microsoft.com/en-us/azure/stream-analytics/stream-analytics-manage-job

Analyzing data by using Power BI – and introduction to Power BI

Power BI is a cloud-based analytics service that allows you to quickly and easily connect to your data wherever it exists. Once connected to your data, you can use Power BI to define rules and logic to transform and clean your data on an automated basis. Power BI allows you to build powerful data models to centralize relationships, hierarchies, key performance indicators, calculations, security roles, and partitions. Then your users and developers can build powerful, flexible, and dynamic dashboards to facilitate deep analysis with amazing capabilities such as natural language queries, machine learning, and custom visualizations.

Understanding the Power BI ecosystem

Power BI Desktop

Power BI Desktop is a free application that is installed on your local computer that lets you connect to, transform, and visualize your data. Power BI Desktop allows you to connect to multiple data sources and combine them into a data model for the purpose of assembling a collection of visuals called a report. This report can be shared with other people through the Power BI service or Power BI Report Server. Power BI Desktop is one of the main ways that BI developers and power users may create Power BI data models and reports.

> **Note**
>
> Download Power BI Desktop here to start creating data models and reports: https://powerbi.microsoft.com/en-us/desktop/.

Power BI service

The Power BI service, sometimes called Power BI online or app.powerbi.com, is where you publish and securely share content that you've created using Power BI Desktop. In the Power BI service, you can create dashboards for navigating across many reports and many data sources, dashboards for transforming data flows, dashboards for integrating and enriching big data, and reports based on shared data models. The Power BI service is the best way to distribute data and gain deeper insights across your organization.

Power BI Premium

Power BI Premium is an add-on to Power BI and provides dedicated and enhanced resources to run the Power BI service for your organization. Power BI Premium provides dedicated infrastructure for your Power BI workloads, which provides greater scale and performance, flexible capacity-based licensing, support for data residency by geography, unification of self-service and enterprise BI, and on-premises BI with Power BI Report Server.

> **Note**
>
> View the following documentation to learn more about Power BI Premium: https://docs.microsoft.com/en-us/power-bi/service-premium-what-is.

Power BI gateway

A Power BI gateway is software that is installed within your on-premises network to facilitate access to data within the network. The Power BI gateway may be referred to as a data gateway or an enterprise data gateway. The data gateway acts as the bridge between the Power BI service and your data sources within your network to support the refreshing of data flows, the direct querying of data sources, and data models.

> **Note**
>
> View the following how-to guide to understand how to install and configure a Power BI gateway: https://docs.microsoft.com/en-us/power-bi/service-gateway-install.
>
> View the following article to learn more about managing data sources used by Power BI: https://docs.microsoft.com/en-us/power-bi/service-gateway-manage.

Power BI mobile apps

Power BI offers a collection of mobile apps for iOS, Android, and Windows 10 mobile devices, which allow you to access your Power BI content in the Power BI service and Power BI Report Server. With the Power BI mobile apps, you can stay connected to your data, reports, and dashboards from any device and any location.

> **Note**
>
> Read the following article to learn more about optimizing reports for Power BI mobile apps: https://docs.microsoft.com/en-us/power-bi/desktop-create-phone-report.

Power BI Report Server

Power BI Report Server is an on-premises report server with a web portal that displays and manages reports and key performance indicators. This also includes the tools for creating Power BI reports, paginated reports, mobile reports, and key performance indicators. Power BI Report Server includes a superset of the features of SQL Server Reporting Services and is covered in detail in *Chapter 13, Power BI Report Server*.

> **Note**
>
> Read the following documentation to understand the differences between Power BI Report Server and the Power BI service: https://docs.microsoft.com/en-us/power-bi/report-server/compare-report-server-service.

Connecting Power BI to Azure SQL Data Warehouse

Power BI can quickly and easily connect to Azure SQL Data Warehouse with Power BI Desktop using the following steps.

1. First, open your local installation of Power BI Desktop and click Get Data. In the Get Data dialog window, search for SQL Data Warehouse, click **Azure SQL Data Warehouse**, and click **Connect**:

Figure 11.7: Search for SQL Data Warehouse to connect to your Azure SQL Data Warehouse instance with Power BI

2. Next, enter the server name for the Azure SQL Data Warehouse instance you want to connect to. Select the data connectivity mode you want to use and click **OK**. Select the type of credentials you wish to use to connect and enter the credentials or sign in. Azure SQL Data Warehouse supports authentication using database credentials or a Microsoft account. Click **OK**.

3. In the Navigator window, navigate to the database tables you would like to use and select the tables that contain the data you wish to visualize in Power BI. Click the checkboxes to select the tables and click Load when you're done. Now you're ready to start enhancing the data model and visualizing data.

> **Note**
>
> Use the Power BI Guided Learning path to get started with building data models and reports and sharing content with Power BI: https://docs.microsoft.com/en-us/power-bi/guided-learning/.

12

Analysis Services

Analysis Services provides superior performance for decision support and business analytics workloads via multidimensional mode and tabular mode. Multidimensional models, sometimes referred to as cubes, were introduced with the release of SQL Server 2000, while tabular mode was introduced with SQL Server 2012. Both multidimensional and tabular mode provide the ability to create analytical data models designed to support ad hoc data exploration capabilities by centralizing and standardizing entity relationships, key performance indicators, hierarchies, calculations, and security. The data models can then be integrated with client applications such as Power BI, Excel, Power BI Report Server, and many other third-party data visualization tools to support data exploration and self-service analysis. In SQL Server 2019, Microsoft is continuing to invest in Analysis Services with improvements designed to improve performance and the user experience.

Introduction to tabular models

SQL Server Analysis Services tabular models are very different compared to multidimensional models because, with tabular semantic models, data can be stored in a highly compressed, in-memory, columnar database designed to support business analytics over small to large volumes of data, in addition to supporting DirectQuery against supported data sources. Tabular models also use tabular modeling structures to store and analyze data:

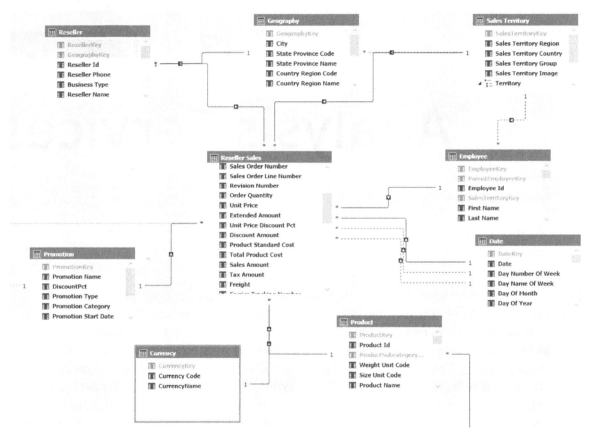

Figure 12.1: Tabular models use tabular modeling structures, including tables and relationships, to store and analyze data

A common development workflow for developing and deploying a tabular model is to use **SQL Server Data Tools** (**SSDT**) for Visual Studio or Visual Studio with Analysis Services extensions to design the model, deploy the model as a database to SQL Server Analysis Services or **Azure Analysis Services** (**AAS**), schedule the automatic reprocessing of the data model, and assign user membership to security roles to facilitate user access via business intelligence tools.

Another popular development for business users and power users developing and deploying tabular models is the ability to use Power Pivot and Power Query in Excel to connect to data sources, cleanse and transform data, and model data using a familiar interface. Data can be visualized using Excel's powerful visualization capabilities. Once the model is ready, the Excel file can be given to a business intelligence developer who can convert the Power Pivot data model to an Analysis Services data model using Visual Studio or by importing into **SQL Server Management Studio** (**SSMS**) with minimal work required.

Once deployed, the management of tabular model databases is typically performed using SSMS. SSMS can be used to initiate data refresh processes, modify security roles and role membership, complete backup and restore operations, issue data analysis expressions or multidimensional expression queries, and script new objects using the **Tabular Model Scripting Language** (**TMSL**).

Users will typically query the tabular model using popular client tools such as Power BI, Excel, Power BI Report Server, SQL Server Reporting Services, or other third-party tools. To query the tabular model, users will require read access to the model.

Introduction to multidimensional models

SQL Server Analysis Services multidimensional models use cube structures to analyze and explore data across dimensions. Multidimensional mode is the default server mode for SQL Server Analysis Services and includes a query and calculation engine for **online analytical processing** (**OLAP**) data with multiple storage modes to balance performance with data scalability requirements:

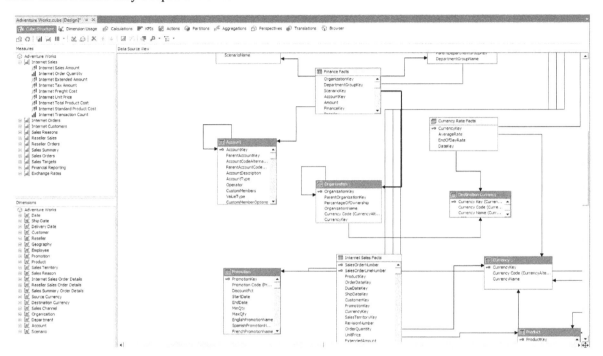

Figure 12.2: Multidimensional models feature cube modeling constructs, including measure groups, dimensions, and relationships

Like when developing a tabular model, the common workflow for developing and deploying a multidimensional model is to use SSDT for Visual Studio or Visual Studio with Analysis Services extensions to design the model, deploy the model as a database to a SQL Server Analysis Services server, configure in multidimensional mode, schedule the automatic reprocessing of the data model using SQL Server Integration Services and SQL Server Agent Jobs, and assign user membership to security roles to facilitate user access.

The management of a multidimensional model is also performed using SSMS. As with tabular models, SSMS can be used to initiate data refresh processes, modify security roles and role membership, complete backup and restore operations, issue **Data Analysis Expressions** (**DAX**) or **Multidimensional Expressions** (**MDX**) queries, and script new objects using the **Analysis Services Scripting Language** (**ASSL**).

Users will typically query a multidimensional model using popular client tools such as Power BI, Excel, Power BI Report Server, SQL Server Reporting Services, or other third-party tools. To query the tabular model, users will require read access to the model.

> **Note**
>
> Review the following article to understand the differences between tabular and multidimensional models and the considerations for deciding when to use tabular and multidimensional models: https://docs.microsoft.com/en-us/sql/analysis-services/comparing-tabular-and-multidimensional-solutions-ssas?view=sql-server-ver15.

Enhancements in tabular mode

SQL Server 2019 Analysis Services and AAS includes new features and capabilities to better support enterprise requirements. In this section, we will review the following enhancements and capabilities included in the latest release of Analysis Services to help you build better analytics solutions:

- Memory settings for resource governance
- Calculation groups
- Dynamic format strings
- DirectQuery
- Bidirectional cross-filtering
- Many-to-many relationships
- Query interleaving with short query bias
- Governance settings for Power BI cache refreshes
- Online attach

Query interleaving with short query bias

Query interleaving with short query bias allows concurrent queries to share CPU resources so that faster queries are not blocked behind slower queries. Short query bias means fast queries can be allocated a higher proportion of resources than long running queries.

Query interleaving is intended to have little to no performance impact on queries that run in isolation. A single query can still consume as much CPU as possible.

> **Note**
>
> To learn more about query interleaving with short query bias and how to enable this setting, read the following documentation: https://docs.microsoft.com/en-us/analysis-services/tabular-models/query-interleaving.

Memory settings for resource governance

There are three new memory settings to assist with resource governance. These memory settings are currently available for Azure Analysis Services:

- **Memory\QueryMemoryLimit**: The `QueryMemoryLimit` property is an advanced property that is used to control how much memory can be used by temporary results during a query. This only applies to DAX measures and queries and does not account for general memory allocations used by the query. The default value for this property is 0, which indicates that there is no limit specified. A value specified between 1 and 100 indicates a percentage of memory. Numbers larger than 100 are interpreted as numbers of bytes. This property can be set using the latest release of ssms to access the Analysis Server Properties dialog box.

- **DbpropMsmdRequestMemoryLimit**: This property is an XML for analysis property used to override the Memory\QueryMemoryLimit server property value for a given connection. The unit of measure is kilobytes. Here's a sample connection string utilizing the `DbpropMsmdRequestMemoryLimit` property:

```
Provider=MSOLAP.8;Integrated Security=SSPI;Persist
Security Info=True;Initial Catalog=Adventure
Works;Data Source=localhost;Extended
Properties="DbpropMsmdRequestMemoryLimit=10000";MDX
Compatibility=1;Safety Options=2;MDX Missing Member
Mode=Error;Update Isolation Level=2
```

- **OLAP\Query\RowsetSerializationLimit**: The RowsetSerializationLimit server property limits the number of rows returned in a rowset to clients. This property applies to both DAX and MDX and can be used to protect server resources from extensive data export usage. The default value for this property is -1, which indicates that no limit is applied. When a query is submitted that exceeds the defined value for RowsetSerializationLimit, the query is canceled and an error is returned. This property can be set using the latest release of SSMS to access the Server Properties dialog box.

Calculation groups

Calculation groups are an exciting new feature available in Azure Analysis Services and are new to SQL Server 2019 Analysis Services. Calculation groups are intended to address the issue of extensive measure proliferation in complex modeling scenarios involving common calculations such as time-intelligence calculations. Also, calculation groups will enable many organizations with existing multidimensional cubes featuring time-intelligence dimensions to migrate to tabular models. This way, they can take advantage of the latest tabular features and/or migrate to the cloud using Azure Analysis Services.

Many Analysis Services tabular models feature dozens or hundreds of base calculations. Calculation groups allow you to define a series of calculations via a calculation group, which can be applied to any number of base calculations. A calculation group is exposed to the end user as a table with a single column. Each value in the column represents a reusable calculation that can be applied to any base measure when applicable. Calculation groups reduce the number of calculations in a tabular model and provide a simple, uncluttered interface for the end user.

The following three new DAX functions are introduced to support calculation groups:

SELECTEDMEASURE()	Returns a reference to the measure currently in context
SELECTEDMEASURENAME()	Returns a string containing the name of the measure currently in context
ISSELECTEDMEASURE(M1, M2, ...)	Returns a Boolean indicating whether the measure currently in context is one of those specified as an argument

Table 12.3: New DAX functions

> **Note**
>
> Review the following documentation to learn more about calculation groups: https://docs.microsoft.com/en-us/sql/analysis-services/tabular-models/calculation-groups?view=sql-server-ver15.

Dynamic format strings

Dynamic format strings, when used with calculation groups, allow conditional formatting for measures. This is very useful in scenarios where the calculations in a calculation group should format measures differently based on the calculation. For example, a year-on-year growth calculation should be formatted as a currency, while a year-on-year growth percentage calculation should be formatted as a percentage.

To facilitate the dynamic formatting of measures used with a calculation group, the following DAX function is added:

SELECTEDMEASUREFORMATSTRING()	Returns a string holding the format string of the measure that is currently in context when the calculation item is evaluated

Table 12.4: The added DAX function

> **Note**
>
> For more information on format strings in Analysis Services, review the following documentation: https://docs.microsoft.com/en-us/sql/analysis-services/multidimensional-models/mdx/mdx-cell-properties-format-string-contents?view=sql-server-2017#numeric-values.

DirectQuery

By default, tabular models use an in-memory cache to store and query data. Typically, this ensures that simple and complex queries against a tabular model are very fast. But in certain scenarios with very large datasets, the available memory may not be enough to meet data volume and refresh requirements.

A tabular model with DirectQuery turned on does not store data in the in-memory cache. Instead, the dataset remains in the **Relational Database Management System (RDBMS)** and all queries against the tabular model are sent to the underlying RDBMS.

DirectQuery offers the following benefits to overcome limitations related to aggressive data volume and refresh requirements:

- Datasets can be larger than the available memory of the Analysis Services server.

- The data is always up to date because changes to the underlying dataset are immediately reflected in queries against the models without the need for processing the Analysis Services model.

- Security can be managed in the RDBMS.

- Analysis Services can perform optimization for complex formulas to ensure the query plan for the query executed against the RDBMS will be as efficient as possible.

In SQL Server 2019, the following data sources are supported for DirectQuery:

- SQL Server 2008 and later

- Azure SQL Database

- Azure SQL Data Warehouse

- Microsoft SQL **Analytics Platform System (APS)**

- Oracle 9i and later relational databases

- Teradata V2R6 and later relational databases

To enable a tabular model for DirectQuery using either SSDT or Visual Studio with the Analysis Services extension, select the **model.bim** file and navigate to the **Properties** window. Find the **DirectQuery Mode** property and set the value to **On**, as seen in the following screenshot. DirectQuery can also be enabled for a model after deployment by modifying the database properties in SSMS:

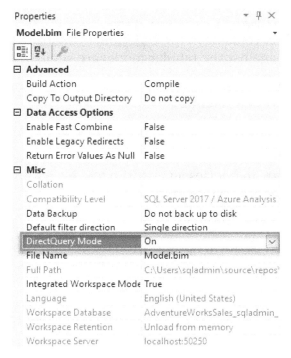

Figure 12.5: Enabling DirectQuery for a tabular model by setting the DirectQuery Mode property to On

DirectQuery models have the following functional restrictions:

- DirectQuery models can only use data from a single relational database. Tabular models including data from multiple sources cannot be enabled for DirectQuery.

- DirectQuery models cannot use a stored procedure as the specified SQL statement for a table definition when using the Data Import Wizard.

- Calculated tables are not supported in DirectQuery models.

- The default row limit is 1,000,000 rows, which can be increased by specifying the `MaxIntermediateRowSize` property in the `msmdsrv.ini` file.

- In DirectQuery mode, Analysis Services converts DAX formulas and calculated measure definitions to SQL statements. DAX formulas containing elements that cannot be converted into SQL syntax will return validation errors in the model. This could result in some calculation formulas needing to be rewritten to use a different function or to work around the limitation by using a derived column.

- In DirectQuery mode, only a single partition can be designated as the DirectQuery partition for a table.

- In specific cases, the query results may differ between a cached model compared to a DirectQuery model. The potential differences are related to the semantic difference between the cached model engine and the database engine.

Consider the following MDX limitations:

- All object names must be fully qualified.

- Session-scoped MDX statements are not supported although query-scoped constructs are supported.

- No user-defined hierarchies.

- No native SQL queries are supported.

- No tuples with members from different levels in MDX sub-select clauses.

Consider the following recommendations and best practices:

- Use DirectQuery mode when your users require real-time access to data, the data volume is larger than the available memory, or you are required to use row-level security in the database engine.

- Typically, the query performance of a cached model is very fast, which is ideal for business intelligence and analysis applications. A DirectQuery model, however, may have noticeably slower query performance since all queries are converted to SQL and sent to the underlying data source. Consider using columnstore indexes in SQL Server 2019 to ensure DirectQuery can leverage query optimizations provided by the database engine.

- Enable the **Rely on Referential Integrity** option on relationships in a model using DirectQuery. This will ensure that queries generated by Analysis Services use an inner join instead of an outer join.

- Because some features in the cached model are not supported with DirectQuery, it is generally recommended to decide before beginning model development whether your model will utilize DirectQuery. This way, you eliminate the risk of developing a cached model with features that are not compatible with DirectQuery.

- Always review the previously mentioned benefits and limitations of DirectQuery before making the decision to use DirectQuery mode. Review the following documentation to learn more about DirectQuery mode: https://docs.microsoft.com/en-us/sql/analysis-services/tabular-models/directquery-mode-ssas-tabular?view=sql-server-ver15.

- Read the following documentation to understand the DAX formula compatibility issues in DirectQuery mode: https://docs.microsoft.com/en-us/sql/analysis-services/tabular-models/dax-formula-compatibility-in-directquery-mode-ssas-2016?view=sql-server-ver15.

Bidirectional cross-filtering

Single-directional filters are the default filters in Analysis Services tabular models. Bidirectional cross-filters allow the filter context of a given relationship to be used as the filter context for another relationship, with one table being common to both relationships. This means that a filter context can be propagated to a second related table on the other side of a relationship.

Consider the following example. The `Customer` and Product tables each have a bidirectional relationship with `Internet Sales`. Because both relationships are set to bidirectional, meaning that filtering can occur in both directions, a filter context from the `Customer` table can propagate to the `Product` table.

Bidirectional cross-filtering allows filter contexts to propagate from one table to another table on the opposite side of a complementary relationship:

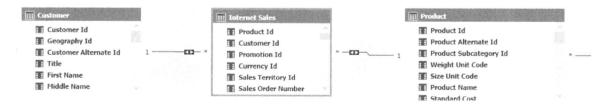

Figure 12.6: Bidirectional cross-filtering

To enable bidirectional cross-filtering, set the **Filter Direction** property to **<<To Both Tables>>**:

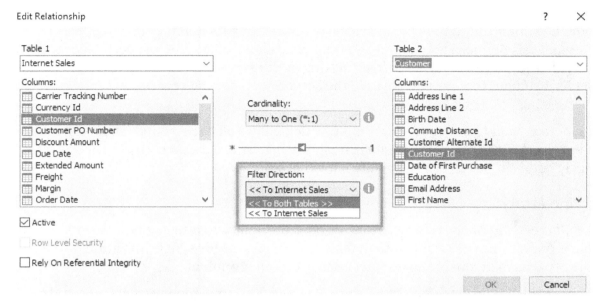

Figure 12.7: Setting the filter direction property

Many-to-many relationships

Another important feature new to SQL Server 2019 Analysis Services and available in Azure Analysis Services is many-to-many relationships. Many-to-many relationships in tabular models enable relationships between two tables with non-unique columns. For example, if the Sales Forecast table is specified at the monthly level, there is no need to normalize the Date table into a separate table at the month level because the many-to-many relationship at the month level can be created.

Governance settings for Power BI cache refreshes

Because the Power BI service in the cloud caches dashboard tile data and report data for the initial loading of Live Connect reports, an excessive number of cache queries could be submitted to Analysis Services. In Azure Analysis Services and SQL Server 2019 Analysis Services and later, the `ClientCacheRefreshPolicy` property allows you to override the `Schedule` cache refresh setting at the server level for all Power BI datasets. All Live Connect reports will observe the server-level setting regardless of the dataset-level setting.

The default value for this property is `-1`, which allows all background cache refreshes as specified in the `Schedule` cache refresh setting for the dataset. To discourage all background cache refreshes, specify `0` for this setting.

Online attach

SQL Server 2019 Analysis Services introduces the ability to attach a tabular model as an online operation. The Online attach feature can be used for synchronization of read-only replicas in an on-premises query scale-out environment.

Without this feature, administrators are first required to detach the database and then attach the new version of the database, which leads to downtime when the database is unavailable to users.

To perform an Online attach operation, use the `AllowOverwrite` option of the `Attach XMLA` command:

```
<Attach xmlns="http://schemas.microsoft.com/analysisservices/2003/
engine">

  <Folder>C:\Program Files\Microsoft SQL Server\MSAS15\OLAP\Data\
AdventureWorks.0.db\</Folder>

  <AllowOverwrite>True</AllowOverwrite>

</Attach>
```

Introducing DAX

The **DAX** language is the formula language used to create calculations in Analysis Services, Power BI Desktop, and Power Pivot for Excel. DAX formulas include functions, operators, and values to perform basic calculations on data in tables and columns. For tabular models authored using Visual Studio 2019, DAX formulas can be used to create calculated columns, measures, tables, and row filters. The flexibility and capability of the DAX formula language is one of the most powerful aspects of Analysis Services. A firm understanding of DAX will allow you to tackle any set of user requirements using an optimal approach.

> **Note**
>
> Review the following documentation for the complete guide to the extensive DAX functions reference library: https://docs.microsoft.com/en-us/dax/dax-function-reference.

The model author will define the DAX formula for a calculated column, measure, and table using the formula bar in Visual Studio. The formula for a row filter will be defined in the Role Manager window. The formula bar and the Role Manager window include the following features to assist the model author with writing DAX formulas:

- **Syntax coloring**: Functions are now displayed in a blue font, variables in a cyan font, and string constants in a red font to distinguish these expression elements more easily from fields and other elements.

- **IntelliSense**: Errors are now identified by a wavy red underscore, and typing a few characters displays a function, table, or column name that begins with matching characters.

- **Formatting**: You can persist tabs and multiple lines by pressing *Alt + Enter* in your expression to improve legibility. You can also include a comment line by typing // as a prefix to your comment.

- **Formula fixup**: In a model set to compatibility level 1,200 or higher, the model designer automatically updates measures that reference a renamed column or table. This does not apply to row filters defined in roles using the Role Manager dialog box.

- **Incomplete formula preservation**: In a model set to compatibility level 1,200 or higher, you can enter an incomplete formula, save and close the model, and then return to your work at a later time.

Calculated columns

Calculated columns in a tabular model allow the addition of new data to your model based on a DAX formula that the model author defines during the designing of the tabular model in Visual Studio. The formula for a calculated column can refer to other columns existing in the tabular model. A given calculated column can also depend on other calculated columns.

When you define a valid formula for a calculated column during the designing of the tabular model, the value for each row in the column is computed immediately. After the tabular model is deployed to the server, the row values for the calculated column are computed during the data refresh process.

Calculated columns can be used for a variety of purposes. For example, a calculated column could be used to concatenate values from other columns, manipulate string values, perform arithmetic on numeric values, manipulate date and time values, create conditional values, and much more.

The following example demonstrates a simple formula in a calculated column to concatenate the values from two other columns:

```
='Geography'[City] & ", " & 'Geography'[State Province Code]
```

> **Note**
>
> For a step-by-step example describing how to create a calculated column in an Analysis Services tabular model, see the following tutorial: https://docs.microsoft.com/en-us/sql/analysis-services/tabular-models/ssas-calculated-columns-create-a-calculated-column?view=sql-server-ver15.
>
> To learn more about calculated columns in Analysis Services tabular models, review the following article: https://docs.microsoft.com/en-us/sql/analysis-services/tabular-models/ssas-calculated-columns?view=sql-server-ver15.

Calculated measures

Calculated measures are formulas that are generally used to aggregate data automatically within the context of a query. Like calculated columns, calculated measures are defined by the model author using Visual Studio. Measures can be based on standard aggregation functions such as **SUM** or **AVG** or can be defined using a custom DAX formula.

Unlike calculated columns, calculated measures require a reporting client application, such as Excel or Power BI, to provide the context with which to evaluate the formula. The formula within the calculated measure is evaluated at query time for each cell within the result set.

To create a basic calculation using the **SUM**, **AVG**, **COUNT**, **DISTINCTCOUNT**, **MAX**, or **MIN** functions, first select the column you wish to aggregate. Then, click the **Column** menu, select **AutoSum**, and then select the aggregation method you'd like to use, as depicted in the following screenshot:

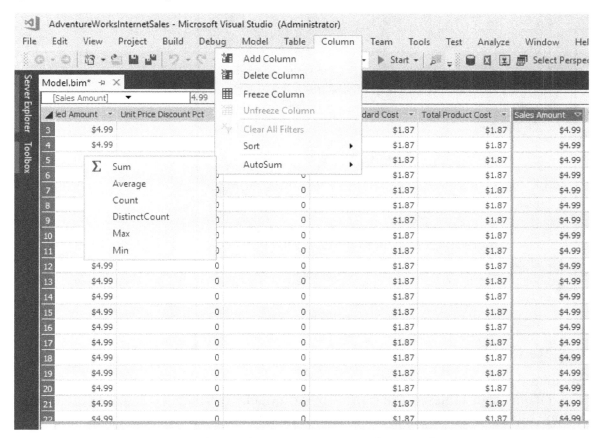

Figure 12.8: Creating a calculated measure automatically using the AutoSum option

Calculated measures can also use more complex formulas to create custom methods of aggregations. For example, the following formula creates a measure that calculates the running total for the `Sales Amount` column:

```
=CALCULATE(SUM('Internet Sales'[Sales Amount]),DATESYTD('Date'[Date]))
```

Calculated measures can be used to create **Key Performance Indicators** (**KPIs**). In Analysis Services, a KPI is a collection of calculated measures used to define a base value, a target value, and a status value. Before you can create a KPI, you must first define a calculated measure to use as the base value. To create a KPI, right click on the **measure** that will be used as the **base value** and then click **Create KPI**. To define the target value, select **Measure** and then select the **target measure** from the drop-down list or select **Absolute value** and then **type** a numeric value. Then, use the **slider bar** to define the status thresholds. Finally, select an **icon style** to display the KPI status graphically.

> **Note**
>
> For a step-by-step example describing how to create a calculated measure in an Analysis Services tabular model, see the following tutorial: https://docs.microsoft.com/en-us/sql/analysis-services/tabular-models/create-and-manage-measures-ssas-tabular?view=sql-server-ver15.
>
> For an example of how to create a KPI, see the following article: https://docs.microsoft.com/en-us/sql/analysis-services/tabular-models/create-and-manage-kpis-ssas-tabular?view=sql-server-ver15.
>
> To learn more about calculated measures in Analysis Services tabular models, including how to use calculated measures to create KPIs, see the following article. https://docs.microsoft.com/en-us/sql/analysis-services/tabular-models/measures-ssas-tabular?view=sql-server-ver15.

Calculated tables

A calculated table is a computed table based on either a DAX query or expression derived from other tables in the same tabular model. To create a calculated table, at least one table must first exist in the tabular model.

Calculated tables, for example, are useful for addressing the following scenarios:

- Creating a custom date table using the `CALENDAR()` or `CALENDARAUTO()` functions
- Creating separate tables based on a single table as a role-playing dimension table
- Creating a filtered row set with a subset or superset of columns from existing tables

To create a calculated table, click the **Create A New Table Calculated From A DAX Formula** tab at the bottom of the model designer, as shown in the following figure:

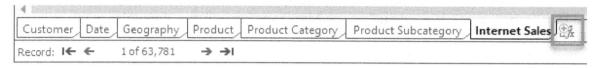

Figure 12.9: Creating a calculated table based on a DAX formula

Here's an example of a calculated table summing the sales amount for each state province name and calendar year:

```
=SUMMARIZECOLUMNS(Geography[State Province Name]
, 'Date'[Calendar Year]
, "Sales Amount" , SUM('Internet Sales'[Sales Amount])
```

> **Note**
>
> Review the following article for a step-by-step example of how to create a calculated column: https://docs.microsoft.com/en-us/sql/analysis-services/tabular-models/create-a-calculated-table-ssas-tabular?view=sql-server-ver15.

Row filters

Row filters define which rows in a table are accessible to members of a given security role and are defined via a DAX formula. When the model author defines a role by using the Role Manager in Visual Studio, row filters can be applied to ensure members of the role only have access to designated rows. Row filters can also be defined for a model currently deployed to the Analysis Services server using Role Properties in SSMS. A tabular model can have multiple roles for different groups of users, with each role having different row filters.

A row filter creates an allowed row set that does not deny access to other rows. Rows not returned as part of the allowed row set are simply excluded by the DAX formula. But because Analysis Services Security is additive, if a user is a member of a security role that allows access to a given row set but the user also a member of another security role that does not allow access to that row set, the user will be able to view the role set.

To create a security role with a row filter in Visual Studio, select the **Model** menu and select **Roles**. In the **Role Manager**, click **New** to create a new role. You must give the role a name and the level of permissions assigned to members of the role. You can assign membership to the role using the **Members** tab. On the **Row Filters** tab, enter a DAX formula to define which rows can be returned by members of the role. The DAX formula for a row filter must evaluate to a Boolean TRUE/FALSE condition, as seen in the following figure:

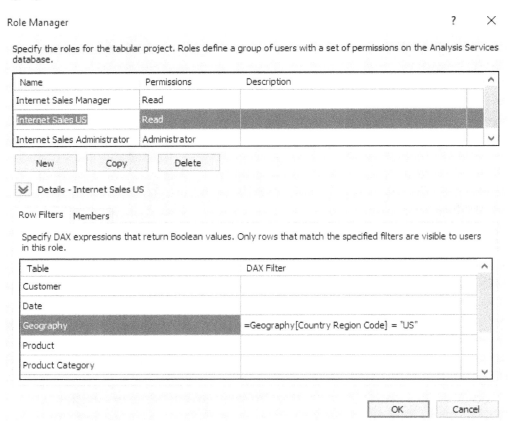

Figure 12.10: Creating a role with a row filter to restrict which rows are accessible to members of the role

> **Note**
>
> To learn more about roles and row filters in Analysis Services, see the following documentation: https://docs.microsoft.com/en-us/sql/analysis-services/tabular-models/roles-ssas-tabular?view=sql-server-ver15.
>
> Dynamic row-level security allows the model designer to apply row-level security to a group of users based on the username or login ID of the user at the time of accessing the Analysis Services model. To understand how to implement dynamic row-level security, see the following article and tutorial: https://docs.microsoft.com/en-us/sql/analysis-services/tutorial-tabular-1200/supplemental-lesson-implement-dynamic-security-by-using-row-filters?view=sql-server-ver15.
>
> Analysis Services also supports table-level and column-level security in addition to row-level security. To learn more about how to use object-level security, see the following article: https://docs.microsoft.com/en-us/sql/analysis-services/tabular-models/object-level-security?view=sql-server-ver15.

DAX calculation best practices

To avoid suboptimal performance with calculations, see the following recommended practices:

- Avoid creating large, complex DAX formulas when possible. Subdivide complex calculated columns into multiple calculated columns utilizing smaller, less complex formulas. This will ease troubleshooting and debugging.

- If you're experiencing poor performance when developing calculations in Visual Studio, you may benefit from setting recalculation mode to manual to prevent calculations from automatically being recalculated during development. To set recalculation mode to manual in Visual Studio, navigate to the **Model** menu, select **Calculation Options**, and then select **Manual Calculation**.

- Use variables whenever possible. Variables allow a given DAX expression to reuse logic within the same expression thus reducing execution time. We'll discuss variables in more detail later in this chapter.

Writing DAX queries

Once the tabular model has been deployed to the server, the model can be made available to users for use with client tool applications. Users who will connect to the tabular database must be a member of a security role that has read access.

Typically, an end user will use a client tool application such as Excel, Power BI, Power BI Report Server, or another third-party tool, for example, to connect to a tabular database and browse the model. These types of tools will write the DAX query against the tabular database on behalf of the user as the user adds a column, measure, or filter to the report. But DAX queries can also be created using SSMS or other tools such as DAX Studio. A query defined and executed using SSMS will return the result set as a table.

Analysis Services object names are case-insensitive, so referring to the `Internet Sales` table as `internet sales` would give you the same table. See the following table for examples of how to refer to Analysis Service objects within a DAX expression or query:

Object Type	Example	Description
Table name	Internet Sales	Table names must be unique in the context of a model.
Column name	Internet Sales[Sales Amount]	Column names must be unique in the context of a table. It is generally recommended to always fully qualify the column name.
Measure name	[Profit Margin]	Measure names must always be in brackets and the name must be unique in the context of the model. It is generally recommended to never fully qualify the measure name by including the table name so that the model author can easily recognize a measure reference from a column reference.

Table 12.11: DAX expressions and queries to refer to Analysis Service objects

In the following example, you will connect to an Analysis Services tabular database using SSMS and then issue several queries:

1. Open **SSMS**. In the **Connect to Server** dialog box, select **Analysis Services for Server Type** and enter the name for Server name. If connecting to SQL Server Analysis Services, select **Windows Authentication for Authentication method**. If connecting to Azure Analysis Services, select **Active Directory – Password or Active Directory – Universal with MFA support**. Click **Connect**.

2. In **Object Explorer**, expand the **Databases** folder, right-click on **Databases**, select **New Query**, and select **DAX**, as seen in the following figure. This will open a new query window to begin writing a DAX query:

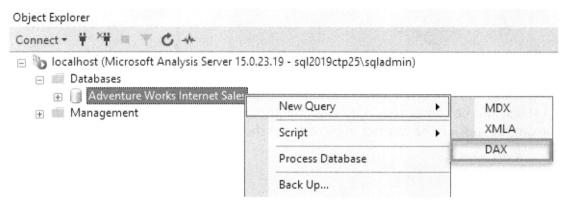

Figure 12.12: Writing a DAX query using SSMS

3. In the new query window, write a simple query using the **EVALUATE** function. The **EVALUATE** function requires a table reference, as seen here. The following query will return a result set including all columns and rows from the **Internet Sales** table:

```
EVALUATE(
    'Internet Sales'
    )
```

You should get the following output:

Internet Sales[Pr...	Internet Sales[C...	Internet Sales[Pr...	Internet Sales[C...	Internet Sales[S...	Internet Sales[S...	Internet Sales[S...	Internet Sales[R...	Internet Sales[Or...	Internet Sales[U...	Internet Sales[Ex...
528	14870	1	100	4	SO51900	1	1	1	4.99	4.99
528	15319	1	100	4	SO51948	1	1	1	4.99	4.99
528	16384	1	100	4	SO52043	1	1	1	4.99	4.99
528	15476	1	100	4	SO52045	1	1	1	4.99	4.99
528	15861	1	100	4	SO52094	1	1	1	4.99	4.99
528	26017	1	100	4	SO52175	1	1	1	4.99	4.99
528	14761	1	100	4	SO52190	1	1	1	4.99	4.99
528	22038	1	100	4	SO52232	1	1	1	4.99	4.99
528	22163	1	100	4	SO52234	1	1	1	4.99	4.99
528	16018	1	100	4	SO52245	1	1	1	4.99	4.99
528	25839	1	100	4	SO52301	1	1	1	4.99	4.99
528	11260	1	100	4	SO52314	1	1	1	4.99	4.99
528	23695	1	100	4	SO52342	1	1	1	4.99	4.99
528	15198	1	100	4	SO52387	1	1	1	4.99	4.99
528	15414	1	100	4	SO52499	1	1	1	4.99	4.99
528	15469	1	100	4	SO52500	1	1	1	4.99	4.99
528	14901	1	100	4	SO52545	1	1	1	4.99	4.99
528	17369	1	100	4	SO52593	1	1	1	4.99	4.99

Executing query...   localhost   sql2019ctp25\sqladmin   Adventure Works Intern...   00:00:05

Figure 12.13: The Evaluate function returns a table

4. To sort the results of the previous query, add an `ORDER BY` keyword and a fully qualified column reference to sort the query result set. As an example, this query sorts the results of the previous query using the `Sales Order Number` column:

```
EVALUATE(
   'Internet Sales'
   )
   ORDER BY 'Internet Sales'[Sales Order Number] ASC
```

5. The `DEFINE` keyword supports creating entities, such as variables, measures, tables, and columns, that only exist for the duration of a query. In the following example, notice the `DEFINE` keyword and the definitions of multiple measures:

```
DEFINE
MEASURE
    'Internet Sales'[SumCost] = SUM('Internet Sales'[Total Product
Cost])
MEASURE
    'Internet Sales'[SumSalesAmount] = SUM('Internet Sales'[Sales
Amount])
MEASURE
    'Internet Sales'[ProfitMargin] = [SumSalesAmount] - [SumCost]
MEASURE
   'Internet Sales'[ProfitMarginRatio] =
DIVIDE([ProfitMargin],[SumSalesAmount],BLANK())
EVALUATE(
   SUMMARIZECOLUMNS(
   'Internet Sales'[Sales Order Number],
   'Internet Sales'[Order Date],
   "Profit Margin",[ProfitMargin],
   "Profit Margin Ratio",[ProfitMarginRatio]
   )
   )
   ORDER BY 'Internet Sales'[Sales Order Number]
```

You should get the following output:

Internet Sales[S...	Internet Sales[Order Date]	[Profit Margin]	[Profit Margin Ra...
SO43697	12/29/2010 12:00:00 AM	1406.9758	0.39320001006...
SO43698	12/29/2010 12:00:00 AM	1487.8356	0.43759999294...
SO43699	12/29/2010 12:00:00 AM	1487.8356	0.43759999294...
SO43700	12/29/2010 12:00:00 AM	285.9519	0.40902966135...
SO43701	12/29/2010 12:00:00 AM	1487.8356	0.43759999294...
SO43702	12/30/2010 12:00:00 AM	1406.9758	0.39320001006...
SO43703	12/30/2010 12:00:00 AM	1406.9758	0.39320001006...
SO43704	12/30/2010 12:00:00 AM	1476.8956	0.43759999288...
SO43705	12/30/2010 12:00:00 AM	1487.8356	0.43759999294...
SO43706	12/31/2010 12:00:00 AM	1406.9758	0.39320001006...
SO43707	12/31/2010 12:00:00 AM	1406.9758	0.39320001006...
SO43708	12/31/2010 12:00:00 AM	285.9519	0.40902966135...
SO43709	12/31/2010 12:00:00 AM	1406.9758	0.39320001006...
SO43710	12/31/2010 12:00:00 AM	1406.9758	0.39320001006...
SO43711	1/1/2011 12:00:00 AM	1406.9758	0.39320001006...
SO43712	1/1/2011 12:00:00 AM	1406.9758	0.39320001006...
SO43713	1/2/2011 12:00:00 AM	1406.9758	0.39320001006...
SO43714	1/2/2011 12:00:00 AM	1406.9758	0.39320001006...
SO43715	1/2/2011 12:00:00 AM	1406.9758	0.39320001006...

Query executed successfully.

Figure 12.14: The DEFINE keyword supports defining objects that exist only during the duration of the query

Note

For more information on writing DAX queries, see the following article: https://docs.microsoft.com/en-us/dax/dax-queries.

Using variables in DAX

Analysis Services DAX expressions also support using variables to simplify complex expressions by separating a single expression into a series of more easily understood expressions. As previously mentioned, variables also allow a given DAX expression to reuse logic within the same expression, which could improve query performance.

Variables can be defined anywhere in a DAX expression and for any data type, including tables, using the following syntax:

```
VARIABLENAME = RETURNEDVALUE
```

To create a variable definition, use the **VAR** keyword, as seen in the following code sample:

```
= VAR
    SumQuantity = SUM('Internet Sales'[Order Quantity])
RETURN
    IF(
        SumQuantity > 1000,
        SumQuantity * 0.95,
        SumQuantity * 1.10
    )
```

A DAX expression can have as many variables as the model author needs. Each variable will have its own **VAR** definition, as seen here:

```
= VAR
    SumCost = SUM('Internet Sales'[Total Product Cost])
VAR
    SumSalesAmount = SUM('Internet Sales'[Sales Amount])
VAR
    ProfitMargin = SumSalesAmount - SumCost
RETURN
    DIVIDE(
        ProfitMargin,
        SumSalesAmount,
        BLANK()
    )
```

Introduction to Azure Analysis Services

AAS is a fully managed **Platform as a Service** (**PaaS**) based on SQL Server Analysis Services tabular models to provide enterprise-grade data models in the cloud. AAS uses the same advanced mashup and modeling engine built into SQL Server 2019 Analysis Services to supporting combining data from multiple sources, defining metrics, and securing your data in a tabular semantic data model.

AAS supports tabular models at the 1,200 compatibility level and higher. It is compatible with many great features that you may already be familiar with in SQL Server Analysis Services Enterprise Edition, including partitions, perspectives, row-level and object-level security, bidirectional and many-to-many relationships, calculation groups, DirectQuery mode, and more.

Selecting the right tier

AAS is available in three different tiers, with each tier offering different amounts of processing power, **Query Performance Units** (**QPUs**), and memory size:

- **Developer tier**: This tier is recommended for development and test scenarios. The Basic tier includes the same functionality of the Standard tier but is limited in processing power, QPUs, and memory. There is no service level agreement available for the Developer tier as this tier is intended only for development and test scenarios.

- **Basic tier**: The Basic tier is intended for production solutions that utilize smaller tabular models, have simple data refresh requirements, and have limited user concurrency. The Basic tier does not include the capability for query replica scale-out, perspectives, multiple partitions, and DirectQuery.

- **Standard tier**: The Standard tier is for mission-critical production applications that require elastic user concurrency and support for rapidly growing data models. The Standard tier also includes all the capabilities offered by AAS.

When you create a server, you must select a plan with a tier, although you can change the plan and/or tier later. You always have the flexibility to change plans within the same tier or upgrade to a higher tier, but you can't downgrade from a higher tier to a lower tier. All tiers support row-level and object-level security, in-memory storage, backup and restore, translations, and DAX calculations.

> **Note**
>
> Check out the pricing details documentation for more information on the features and pricing of AAS: https://azure.microsoft.com/en-us/pricing/details/analysis-services/.

Scale-up, down, pause, resume, and scale-out

In addition to the previously mentioned enterprise features, AAS also provides the ability for you to scale up, scale down, or even pause your Analysis Services server using the Azure portal or on the fly with PowerShell, meaning that you only pay for what you use. The ability to scale up, scale down, pause, and resume provides customers with the flexibility to scale based on user demand and get the right level of resources at the appropriate level when needed.

AAS scale-out allows queries to be distributed among multiple query replicas in a query pool. Query replicas include synchronized copies of your tabular models to support distributing query workloads to reduce query times for high query workloads. The query pool can contain up to seven additional query replicas depending on the selected plan and region.

> **Note**
>
> See the following documentation to learn how to configure AAS scale-out: https://docs.microsoft.com/en-us/azure/analysis-services/analysis-services-scale-out.

Connecting to your data where it lives

AAS supports a wide variety of data sources. AAS can directly connect to Azure data sources such as Azure SQL Database, Azure SQL Data Warehouse, Azure Blob Storage, and Azure Cosmos DB. To support connectivity to on-premises data sources or other data sources secured in Azure with an Azure virtual network, an on-premises data gateway is required to facilitate connectivity behind the firewall. The types of data sources supported depends on factors such as model compatibility level, available data connectors, authentication type, providers, and on-premises data gateway support.

> **Note**
>
> See the following documentation to learn more about supported data sources: https://docs.microsoft.com/en-us/azure/analysis-services/analysis-services-datasource.
>
> To learn more about installing and configuring the on-premises data gateway, see the following documentation: https://docs.microsoft.com/en-us/azure/analysis-services/analysis-services-gateway-install.

Securing your data

AAS also provides security for your sensitive data at multiple levels. At the server level, AAS provides firewall protection, Azure authentication based on Azure Active Directory, server-side encryption using Azure Blob server-side encryption, row-level and object-level security, and automation through service principals to perform unattended tasks.

As an Azure service, AAS also provides a basic level of protection from **Distributed Denial of Service** (**DDoS**) attacks automatically.

> **Note**
>
> To learn more about how AAS secures your data, see the following documentation: https://docs.microsoft.com/en-us/azure/analysis-services/analysis-services-overview#your-data-is-secure.
>
> To learn more about how Azure protects against DDoS attacks, see the following documentation: https://docs.microsoft.com/en-us/azure/virtual-network/ddos-protection-overview.

Using familiar tools

With AAS, you can continue to use the same tools you're already familiar with. Continue developing tabular models for AAS using SSDT for Visual Studio or Visual Studio with the Analysis Services extension.

Management of your servers through SSMS is also supported. Connect to your AAS server, execute DAX queries, run TMSL scripts, and automate tasks using TMSL scripts and PowerShell.

Connectivity with modern business intelligence tools such as Power BI, Excel, Power BI Report Server, and third-party tools is supported, providing users with the flexibility to continue to use tools that they're already familiar with to produce interactive visualizations based on tabular models.

Built-in monitoring and diagnostics

An important part of any Analysis Services solution is monitoring how your servers are performing. With Azure diagnostic logs, you can monitor and send logs to Azure Storage, stream logs to Azure Event Hubs, and export logs to Azure Monitor. Using **Extended Events** (**xEvents**), all Analysis Services events can be captured and targeted to specific consumers.

> **Note**
>
> Learn more about how to use Dynamic Management Views to monitor AAS by reading the following documentation: https://docs.microsoft.com/sql/analysis-services/instances/use-dynamic-management-views-dmvs-to-monitor-analysis-services.
>
> See the following article and tutorial to understand how to set up diagnostic logging for AAS: https://docs.microsoft.com/en-us/azure/analysis-services/analysis-services-logging.

Provisioning an Azure Analysis Services server and deploying a tabular model

In this example, we will walk through configuring an AAS server using the Azure portal and deploying an Analysis Services database using Visual Studio:

1. Log in to the Azure portal using https://portal.azure.com.

2. Click the **Create a resource** button at the top left. Search for **Analysis Services** and click **Create**.

3. In **Analysis Services**, fill in the required field and click **Create**. Typically, it only takes a minute or two to create the AAS server:

   Server name: A unique name used to reference your Analysis Services server.

   Subscription: The Azure subscription the server will be associated with.

   Resource Group: You can create a new resource group or use a previously existing resource group.

   Location: Select the Azure datacenter region where your Analysis Services server should exist.

Pricing tier: Select the pricing tier and plan.

Administrator: Define the server administrator using Azure Active Directory.

Backup Storage Setting: Optionally define the default storage account for holding Analysis Services database backups. This can also be specified later.

Storage key expiration: Optionally specify a storage key expiration period:

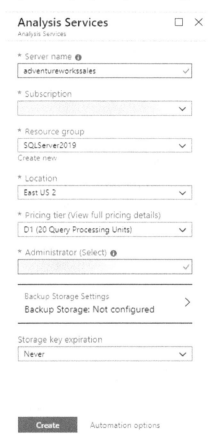

Figure 12.15: Use the Azure portal to create an AAS server

4. After the AAS server is created, navigate to the AAS resource using the Azure portal. In the **Analysis Services** blade, find the server name and copy the Server name to your clipboard by clicking the **Copy to clipboard** icon to the right of the Server name:

Figure 12.16: Copy the server name to your clipboard

5. Open your Analysis Services project in Visual Studio. In the **Solution Explorer**, right-click the project name and select **Properties**.

6. On the deployment property page, paste the AAS server name in the **Server** property box. Click **OK**:

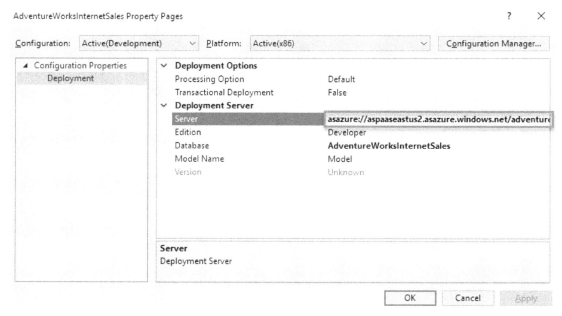

Figure 12.17: Paste the server name in the server property box in the deployment property page

7. Now you're ready to deploy the model. In Visual Studio, right-click the project file in the **Solution Explorer** and select **Deploy**. You'll be asked to authenticate to Azure using your Azure credentials. To deploy or modify an Analysis Services database, you need to be an administrator on the server. Once you have authenticated, the model will be deployed and ready for querying.

13

Power BI Report Server

Power BI Report Server is an enterprise **Business Intelligence** (**BI**) solution that supports displaying reports and **key performance indicators** (**KPIs**) and managing report distribution across desktop and mobile devices. Power BI Report Server includes all the features you may be familiar with in **SQL Server Reporting Services** (**SSRS**) as well as many of the features included with Power BI. In this chapter, we'll review the core capabilities of Power BI Report Server, the new features that are included in the latest releases of Power BI Report Server, as well as key differences between Power BI Report Server and SSRS.

SSRS versus Power BI Report Server

While SSRS was introduced with the release of SQL Server 2005, the first release of Power BI Report Server was made generally available in June 2017. Power BI Report Server includes a superset of the features of SSRS. This means that everything you can do in SSRS can be done with Power BI Report Server plus the additional capability of distributing interactive dashboard-style reports through the report web portal.

So, even though Power BI Report Server includes all the features of SSRS, Power BI Report Server offers several new capabilities that are unique to Power BI and Power BI Report Server.

With Power BI Report Server, organizations can now deploy interactive and highly flexible Power BI reports based on an integrated data model in their on-premises or cloud infrastructure environments alongside the traditional document-style, paginated reports introduced with SSRS. A Power BI report is a highly interactive report featuring one or more pages that supports browsing an integrated data model or a data model hosted in Analysis. Power BI reports are developed using Power BI Desktop optimized for the report server.

The Power BI mobile app is available at no cost for iOS, Android, and Windows mobile devices and is used to browse Power BI reports hosted in the Power BI service in the cloud or hosted on Power BI Report Server. A user authenticates using their own credentials and can browse their Power BI content in online and offline modes.

SSRS is licensed by purchasing SQL Server. Power BI Report Server, however, is available through two different licensing models:

1. **Power BI Premium**: Power BI Premium, previously covered in *Chapter 11, Data Warehousing*, of this book, includes dedicated capacity for running your Power BI workload in the cloud. By purchasing Power BI Premium, an organization automatically gains the rights to deploy Power BI Report Server on an equivalent number of cores on-premises or in Azure.

2. **SQL Server Enterprise edition with Software Assurance**: An organization can also obtain the rights to deploy Power BI Report Server by purchasing SQL Server Enterprise edition with Software Assurance.

> **Note**
>
> To learn more about licensing Power BI Report Server and finding your Power BI Report Server product key, you can refer to the following documentation: https://docs.microsoft.com/en-us/power-bi/report-server/find-product-key.

Report content types

Power BI Report Server includes the following report content types:

- **Power BI reports**: Power BI reports are multipage reports based on an integrated data model or an Analysis Services data model. Power BI reports are created using Power BI Desktop optimized for Power BI Report Server. Power BI Desktop is used to develop the data model and reports that are published to Power BI Report Server. Reports published to Power BI Report Server can be browsed using the Power BI mobile app. Power BI reports can include a custom layout optimized for a mobile device.

- **Paginated reports**: Paginated reports are the traditional content type that you may be familiar with if you have used SSRS. You use this content type when you need precise control over the layout, appearance, and behavior of each element in your report. Users can view a paginated report online, export it to another format, or receive it on a scheduled basis by subscribing to the report. A paginated report can consist of a single page or hundreds of pages, based on the dataset associated with the report. The need for this type of report continues to persist in most organizations, as well as the other report content types that are now available on the Microsoft reporting platform.

- **Mobile reports**: SSRS mobile reports are reports optimized for mobile devices and connected to your on-premises data. Mobile reports are developed using SQL Server Mobile Report Publisher. Once developed, the mobile reports are published and shared through the Power BI Report Server web portal and can be browsed through the web portal as well as via the Power BI mobile app on Android, iOS, and Windows mobile devices in online and offline modes. Mobile reports feature a variety of chart types, including time, category, totals, comparison, tree maps, custom maps, and more. Mobile reports can be configured to use shared datasets or local Excel files as a data source. Later in this chapter, we'll discuss the process for creating mobile reports using SQL Server Mobile Report Publisher in more detail.

- **KPIs**: A KPI is a visual indicator that communicates the amount of progress made toward a goal or illustrates the relationship between a given metric and a target value. In Power BI Report Server, a KPI is based on the first row of data from a shared dataset. Shared datasets can be created and published using Report Builder or Visual Studio with the SSRS extension. Once the shared dataset has been created, KPIs can be created in the Power BI Report Server web portal; we'll cover this in more detail later in this chapter:

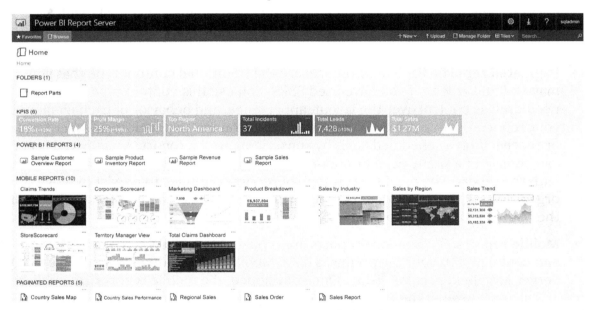

Figure 13.1: Power BI Report Server is an enterprise BI solution that supports displaying reports and KPIs and distributing data visualizations to users on multiple devices

Migrating existing paginated reports to Power BI Report Server

Because Power BI Report Server includes a superset of the capabilities of SSRS, migrating from SSRS to Power BI Report Server is a great option for allowing an organization to modernize their SSRS environment. There are several reasons why you may choose to migrate your SSRS environment(s) to Power BI Report Server:

- You wish to take advantage of functionality that is unique to Power BI Report Server, including interactive and flexible Power BI reports.

- You need to migrate from a legacy version of SSRS to Power BI Report Server to ensure your application is supported.

- You would like to take advantage of Power BI Report Server's frequent release cycle to take advantage of new features.

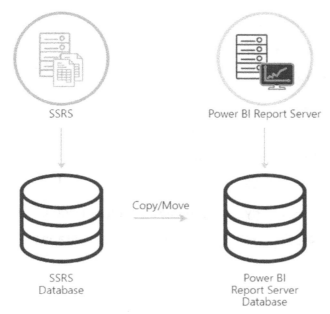

Figure 13.2: Migrating from SSRS (native mode) to Power BI Report Server requires a few simple steps

> **Note**
>
> SQL Server 2008 Report Services (and later) are supported for migration to Power BI Report Server.
>
> There is no in-place upgrade from SSRS to Power BI Report Server. Only a migration is supported.

To migrate from SSRS (native mode) to Power BI Report Server, complete the following steps.

1. Back up the `ReportServer` and `ReportServerTempdb` databases.

2. Back up the report server configuration files, including:

   - `Rsreportserver.config`.

   - `Rswebapplication.config`.

   - `Rssvrpolicy.config`.

   - `Rsmgrpolicy.config`.

   - `Reportingservicesservice.exe.config`.

   - `Web.config` for the report server ASP.NET application.

   - `Machine.config` for ASP.NET if you modified it for report server operations.

3. Back up the encryption key using the Reporting Service Configuration Manager.

4. Move the `ReportServer` and `ReportServerTempDb` databases to the new Database Engine instance.

> **Note**
>
> If your migration includes using a different Database Engine instance, you must move the report server database to the new Database Engine instance. If you are using the same Database Engine instance, then you can skip *Step 4*.
>
> You can review the following documentation to learn more about moving the report server databases to another instance: https://docs.microsoft.com/en-us/sql/reporting-services/report-server/moving-the-report-server-databases-to-another-computer-ssrs-native-mode?view=sql-server-ver15.

5. Install Power BI Report Server.

> **Note**
>
> If you're using the same hardware, you can install Power BI Report Server on the same server as the SSRS instance.
>
> You can review the following documentation to learn more about installing Power BI Report Server: https://docs.microsoft.com/en-us/power-bi/report-server/install-report-server.

6. Configure the report server using the Report Server Configuration Manager and connect to the cloned database.

7. Perform any cleanup needed for the SSRS (native mode) instance.

> **Note**
>
> You can review the following documentation to familiarize yourself with the detailed steps for migrating an SSRS (native mode) deployment to a Power BI Report Server instance: https://docs.microsoft.com/en-us/power-bi/report-server/migrate-report-server#migrating-to-power-bi-report-server-from-ssrs-native-mode.
>
> To learn more about migrating Reporting Services (SharePoint integrated mode) to Power BI Report Server, review the following documentation: https://docs.microsoft.com/en-us/power-bi/report-server/migrate-report-server#migration-to-power-bi-report-server-from-ssrs-sharepoint-integrated-mode.

Exploring new capabilities

While the features and visualizations available in previous versions of SSRS and Power BI Report Server continue to be available in the latest release of Power BI Report Server, there are many new and important features that have been introduced to Power BI Report Server during the last year. In this section, we'll focus on just a few of the dozens of important new features released over the past 12 months.

Performance Analyzer

Using the Performance Analyzer in Power BI Desktop, you can quickly and easily discover how each of your report elements, such as visualizations and DAX formulas, is performing. The Performance Analyzer inspects and displays the processing time necessary for updating and refreshing all the visuals that a user interaction initiates, and presents the information so that you can view, drill down, and export the results. This means that you can quickly identify the performance impact of specific visual elements.

To display the Performance Analyzer pane, select the **View** ribbon and then select the checkbox next to **Performance Analyzer** to display the Performance Analyzer panel:

Figure 13.3: Enable the Performance Analyzer to study the performance impact of visual elements within your Power BI report

To start using the Performance Analyzer, click on the **Start Recording** button. Then, simply create an interaction in the report, such as selecting a **slicer**, **visualization**, or **filter**, or click on **Refresh visuals** in the Performance Analyzer panel. The query durations generated by the interaction will be displayed visually.

Each interaction has a section identifier in the pane, describing the action that initiated the logged entries. In the following figure, the interaction was from a user cross-highlighting a visualization:

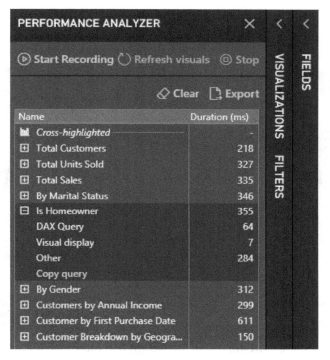

Figure 13.4: The Performance Analyzer is used to measure the performance of specific report elements and can be used to export the results

The log information includes the duration of the following tasks:

- **DAX query**: If a DAX query was required, the duration of the time between the visual sending the query and Analysis Services returning the results is displayed.

- **Visual display**: This is the time required for the visual to be drawn on the screen, including any time necessary for retrieving any web images or geocoding.

- **Other**: This includes the time required for preparing queries, waiting for other visuals to complete, or performing other background processing.

> **Note**
>
> You can review the following link to learn more about Performance Analyzer in Power BI Desktop: https://docs.microsoft.com/en-us/power-bi/desktop-performance-analyzer.

The new Modeling view

The new Modeling view in Power BI Desktop allows you to view and work with complex datasets that may contain many tables. The new Modeling view now supports multiple diagram perspectives and bulk editing of columns, measures, and tables:

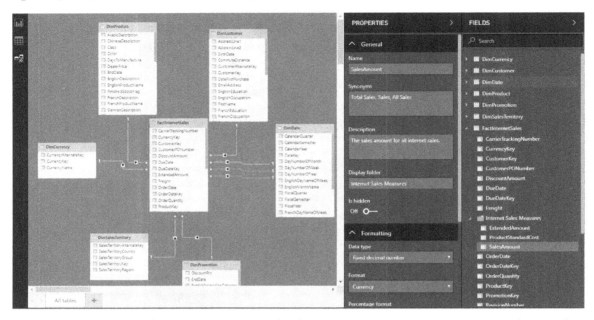

Figure 13.5: The new Modeling view improves the design and management experience when working with large and complex data models

> **Note**
>
> You can review the following link to learn more about using the Modeling view, creating separate diagrams, and setting common properties: https://docs.microsoft.com/en-us/power-bi/desktop-modeling-view.

Row-level security for Power BI data models

Row-level security (**RLS**) can now be configured for data models designed using Power BI Desktop. RLS allows you to restrict data access at the row level for given users using filters defined within security roles.

RLS can be configured for reports imported into Power BI with Power BI Desktop. You can also configure RLS for reports that use DirectQuery.

To create a security role, navigate to the **Modeling** ribbon in Power BI Desktop and select **Manage Roles**:

Figure 13.6: Select Manage Roles in the Modeling ribbon to create or modify security roles

Click on **Create** to create a new security role. Select the table you want to use to apply a DAX rule and enter the table filter DAX expression. Click on **Save**:

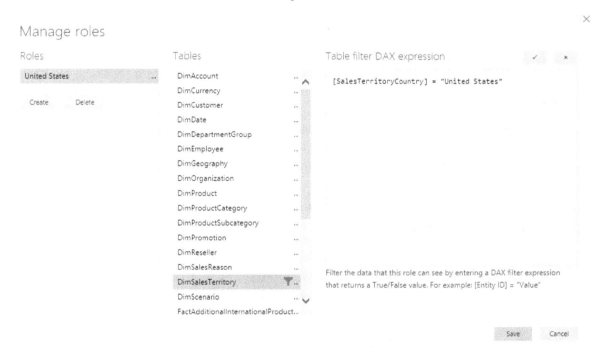

Figure 13.7: Security roles in Power BI use a DAX filter to restrict access to data at the row level

Once you've created the security role(s), you can use the **View as Roles** button in the **Modeling** ribbon of Power BI Desktop to test your security roles.

After you have saved the Power BI report to Power BI Report Server, you can assign members to the security roles. In Power BI Report Server, select the ellipsis (...) next to the report. Then, select **Manage**.

Select the **Row-level security** page and click on **Add Member**. You'll then be able to select security roles and add users or groups from Active Directory in the username format (**DOMAIN\user**).

> **Note**
>
> Learn more about RLS in Power BI Report Server by reviewing the documentation at https://docs.microsoft.com/en-us/power-bi/report-server/row-level-security-report-server.

Report theming

Report themes allow you to quickly color your entire report to match a theme or corporate branding. When you import a theme, each visualization is automatically updated to use the theme colors. You also have access to the theme colors from the color palette.

A theme file is a JSON file that includes all of the colors you want to use in your report along with any default formatting you want to apply to visuals:

```
{

        "name": "Valentine's Day",

        "dataColors": ["#990011", "#cc1144", "#ee7799", "#eebbcc",
 "#cc4477", "#cc5555", "#882222", "#A30E33"],

        "background":"#FFFFFF",

        "foreground": "#ee7799",          "tableAccent": "#990011"

    }
```

To apply a theme to a report in Power BI Desktop, navigate to the **Home** ribbon, select **Switch Theme**, and select **Import Theme**. Navigate to the ᴊsᴏɴ file containing your theme definition and select the theme. Next, click on **Open**.

> **Note**
>
> You can review the following documentation to learn more about how report themes work: https://docs.microsoft.com/en-us/power-bi/desktop-report-themes.
>
> New features are added to each release of Power BI Report Server every four months. For an extensive list of all the new features introduced in Power BI Report Server, review the following documentation: https://docs.microsoft.com/en-us/power-bi/report-server/whats-new.

Managing parameter layouts

The primary purpose of report parameters is to filter the data source and limit the data returned based on what the user needs. In Power BI Report Server, paginated reports support defining customized parameter layouts in the report design view in Report Builder and Visual Studio with the Reporting Services extension. You can drag a parameter to a specific column and row in the Parameters pane to organize the parameters based on your requirements or modify the size and shape of the parameter panel.

> **Note**
>
> When using report parameters, use a commonly used value for the parameter's default value so the report will load immediately when the user accesses the report.

To customize the report's parameter layout in Report Builder, open the report, and navigate to the **View** ribbon. Select the checkbox next to **Parameter**. This will expose the **Parameters** pane near the top of your report.

To add or delete columns and rows from the **Parameters** pane, right-click anywhere in the panel and then select the **Insert** or **Delete** command to modify the layout.

To move a parameter to a new location in the **Parameters** pane, simply drag the parameter to a different cell in the panel.

To add a new parameter to the pane, either right-click on an empty cell in the **Parameters** panel and click on **Add Parameter** or right-click on **Parameters** in the **Report Data** panel and then click on **Add Parameter**:

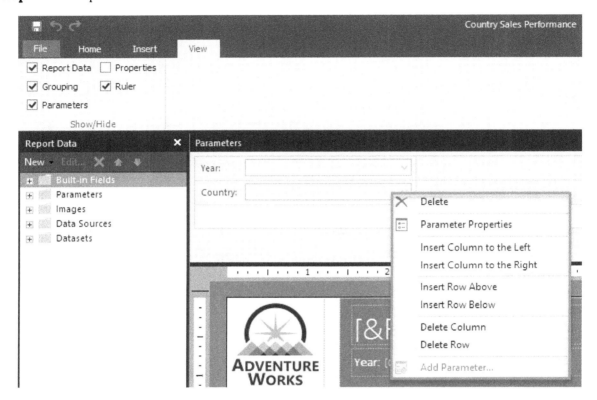

Figure 13.8: The Parameters panel can be modified by simply right-clicking anywhere in the panel

Developing KPIs

A KPI is an indicator that illustrates the progress made toward a goal. KPIs are great for users who wish to quickly evaluate and monitor the progress made toward a measurable goal.

> **Note**
>
> KPIs are only accessible with SSRS Enterprise edition and Power BI Report Server.

A KPI can be defined manually or based on the first row of a shared dataset. A shared dataset enables you to manage the settings for a dataset separately from reports and other report server items. In the following example, we will walk through the steps required to create a shared dataset using Report Builder. Then, we'll define the KPI in the Power BI Report Server portal:

1. First, open **Report Builder**.

2. Select **New Dataset** and browse to the data source you would like to use to create the new dataset. Then, click on **Create**:

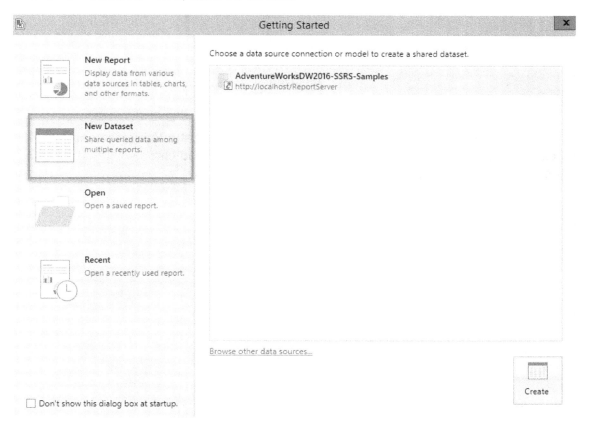

Figure 13.9: A shared dataset is the data source for a KPI in Power BI Report Server

3. Select a shared data source to use for your shared dataset.

4. You can use **Query Designer** to build your query or click on **Edit as text** to copy and paste in a previously written T-SQL select statement. Bear in mind that only the first row will be used to populate the KPI, so format your query results accordingly.

5. Click on **File** and select **Save As** to save the new dataset to the Report Server.

6. In the Power BI Report Server portal, navigate to the folder where you would like to create the KPI. Click on the **+New** button and select **KPI**:

Figure 13.10: Creating KPIs directly in the Power BI Report Server portal

7. In the **New KPI** screen, specify **KPI name**, then select the **Value format**, **Value**, **Goal**, **Status**, **Trend set**, and **Visualization** settings. You can also specify related content to link to from the KPI:

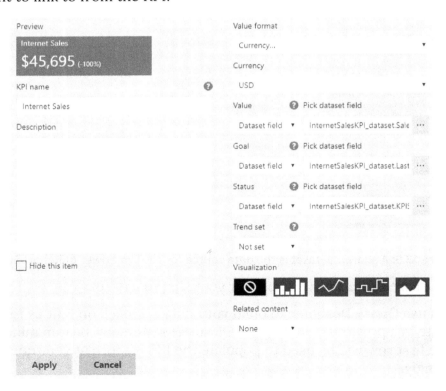

Figure 13.11: Creating a new KPI using Power BI Report Server

8. Click on **Create** when you're done.

> **Note**
>
> You can review the following documentation for more details on creating a KPI in Power BI Report Server: https://docs.microsoft.com/en-us/sql/reporting-services/working-with-kpis-in-reporting-services?view=sql-server-ver15.

Publishing reports

Power BI Desktop optimized for the report server is the development tool for Power BI reports. Users wishing to create and/or edit Power BI content should ensure they have installed the correct version of Power BI Desktop, which is compatible with their installation of Power BI Report Server. To download and install the compatible version of Power BI Desktop, navigate to the Power BI Report Server web portal, click on the **Download** button in the top-right corner, and select **Power BI Desktop**. This will open your web browser to the page with the link to download the correct version of Power BI Desktop optimized for the report server:

Figure 13.12: You must use the correct version of Power BI Desktop to ensure compatibility with your installation of Power BI Report Server

After installing Power BI Desktop optimized for report server, you're ready to begin developing Power BI content for Power BI Report Server.

Once you've created your Power BI content, you're ready to publish the Power BI report to the report server. In Power BI Desktop, click on **File**, select **Save as**, and then select **Power BI Report Server**, as shown in the following screenshot:

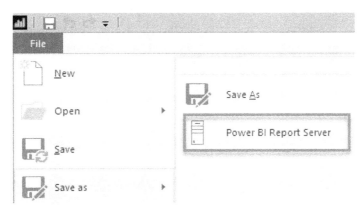

Figure 13.13: Publish your Power BI reports to Power BI Report Server by clicking on Save as

In the **Power BI Report Server** selection window, either select a recently used report server or enter a new report server address (for example, `http://reportserver/reports` or `https://reportserver/reports`). Then, click on **OK**.

Navigate to the folder on your report server where you would like to save the Power BI report. Specify the name of your report and then click on **OK** to save the report to Power BI Report Server.

Managing report access and security

Like SSRS, Power BI Report Server provides an authentication subsystem and role-based authorization model to determine which users can perform specific tasks and access items on the report server. Role-based authorization categorizes the set of tasks into roles that the user can perform.

Power BI Report Server installs with predefined roles that you can use to grant access to report server operations. Each predefined role aligns with a collection of tasks related to the role. Groups and user accounts can be assigned to the roles to provide immediate access to report server items and operations.

The following table describes the predefined scope of the roles:

Use case	Description
Email delivery of reports	Subscriptions can be used to email reports to a user or group.
View reports offline	Reports that need to be archived can be sent directly to a shared folder that is backed up on a recurring schedule. Reports that take too long to load in a browser can be sent to a shared folder for viewing in a desktop application.
Preload cache	A subscription can be used to preload the cache to improve report rendering performance in scenarios where many users are viewing a report with several different parameter value selections.
Data-driven report	Use a data-driven subscription to customize report output, delivery options, and report parameter values at runtime. The subscription uses a query to get input values from a data source at runtime. Data-driven subscriptions are useful for programmatically delivering a report to many users who need the reports with different parameter values and in different file formats.

Table 13.14: Roles and their descriptions

> **Note**
>
> The predefined roles can be modified or replaced with custom roles based on your requirements. To learn more about roles, review the following documentation: https://docs.microsoft.com/en-us/sql/reporting-services/security/role-definitions-predefined-roles?view=sql-server-ver15.

The following items in Power BI Report Server can be secured:

- Folders
- Reports (including Power BI reports, paginated reports, and mobile reports)
- Report models
- Resources
- Shared data sources
- Shared datasets

When you create a role assignment, you're creating a security policy that determines whether a user or group can access or modify a specific report server item or perform a task. Role assignments are scoped at the item level or system level.

To assign a user or group access to an item role, complete the following steps:

1. Navigate to the Power BI Report Server web portal and locate the report item you would like to add a user or group to. The report item could be a folder, report, or another resource.

2. Select the ... (ellipsis) on an item.

3. Select **Manage**.

4. Select the **Security** tab.

5. Select **Customize security** then select **Add group or user**.

6. Enter the user or group account in **Group or user** (for example, domain\user or domain\group).

7. Select the role definition(s), that define(s) how the user(s) should access the item. Then, click on **OK**:

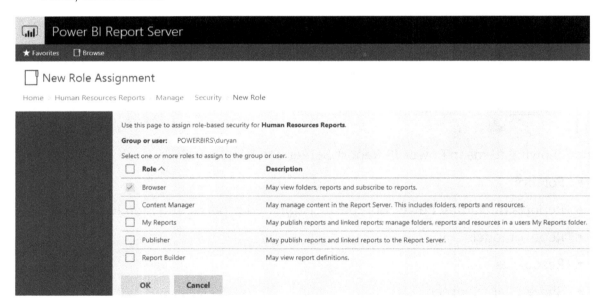

Figure 13.15: Creating a role assignment to grant a user or group of users access to a report item

> **Note**
>
> You can review the following documentation to learn more about granting permissions on Power BI Report Server: https://docs.microsoft.com/en-us/sql/reporting-services/security/granting-permissions-on-a-native-mode-report-server?view=sql-server-ver15.

Publishing mobile reports

Once you've developed a mobile report using SQL Server Mobile Report Publisher, click on the **Save Mobile Report As** button in the **Navigation** panel:

Figure 13.16: To publish a mobile report, click on the Save Mobile Report As button

Mobile reports can be saved locally or to the report server. When you select **Save to server**, you can specify the new report name, the server, and then browse to the location where the report should be saved. Click on **Save** to save the mobile report to the specified report server.

Viewing reports in modern browsers

The web portal for Power BI Report Server is a web-based experience. In the portal, you can view Power BI reports, paginated reports, mobile reports, and KPIs. The web portal is also used to administer a report server instance.

To access the web portal, type in the web portal URL in the address bar of the browser window. When you access the web portal, the folders, links, reports, and options you see will depend on the permissions you have on the Power BI Report Server. To perform a task on the report server, a user should be assigned to a role with the appropriate permissions depending on the task. For example, a user wishing to simply view reports and subscribe to reports should be assigned to the Browser Role.

The Power BI Report Server web portal groups content by the following categories:

- KPIs
- Mobile reports
- Paginated reports
- Power BI desktop reports

- Excel workbooks

- Datasets

- Data sources

- Resources

Power BI Report Server also allows you to search for report content based on your permissions. Use the search bar by entering a search term and then pressing Enter:

Figure 13.17: Searching for report content by entering a search term

The following browsers are supported for managing and viewing Power BI Report Server:

Browser	Microsoft Windows Windows 7, 8.1, 10; Windows Server 2008 R2, 2012, 2012 R2	macOS X OS X 10.9-10.11	Apple iOS iPhone and iPad with iOS 10	Google Android Phones and tablets with Android 4.4 (KitKat) or higher
Microsoft Edge*	X			
Microsoft Internet Explorer 11	X			
Google Chrome*	X	X	X	
Mozilla Firefox*	X	X		
Apple Safari*	X	X		

*Latest publicly released version

Table 13.18: Supported browsers

> **Note**
>
> You can learn about what browser versions are supported for managing and viewing Power BI Report Server and the Report Viewer controls here: https://docs.microsoft.com/en-us/power-bi/report-server/browser-support.

You can also add comments to Power BI reports, paginated reports, and mobile reports directly in the report server web portal.

To add or view a comment, open a report in the web portal. Click on the **Comments** button in the top-right corner and enter your comment. Click on **Post Comment** to post your comment. The comments live with the report and anyone with the right permissions can view the comments for the report:

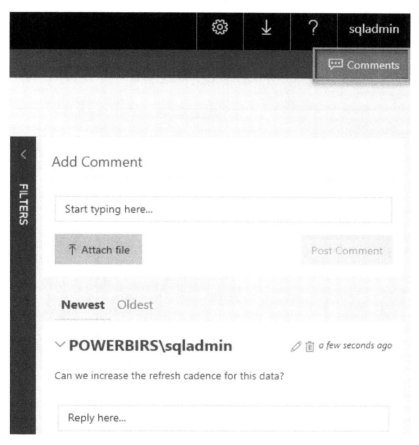

Figure 13.19: Using the Comments pane to view and add comments or to reply to existing comments

Viewing reports on mobile devices

The Power BI mobile app delivers live, touch-enabled access to your on-premises Power BI Report Server. You can connect up to five different Power BI Report Server instances at a time using the Power BI mobile app. The Power BI mobile app can be used to deliver three different types of content to mobile devices with Power BI Report Server:

- **Power BI reports**: Power BI reports can be specially optimized for viewing on a mobile device and via web browsers simultaneously. In **Power BI Desktop** on the **View** ribbon, use **Phone Layout** to customize how the report will appear on a mobile device. Use **Desktop Layout** to design how the report will look on your desktop:

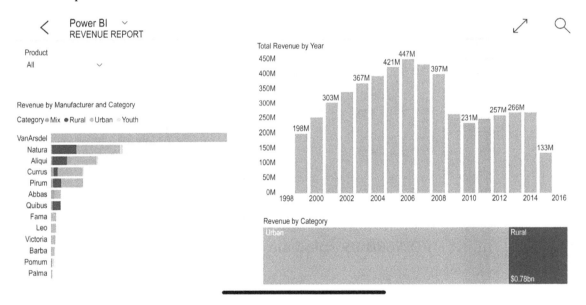

Figure 13.20: Power BI reports are developed using Power BI Desktop optimized for the report server and can also be optimized for viewing via mobile devices

> **Note**
>
> You can review the following documentation to learn more about using Power BI Desktop to optimize Power BI reports for a mobile device: https://docs.microsoft.com/en-us/power-bi/desktop-create-phone-report.

- **Mobile reports**: Mobile reports are specially optimized reports designed for viewing on a mobile device using the Power BI mobile app. Mobile reports are also able to be accessed via the web browser:

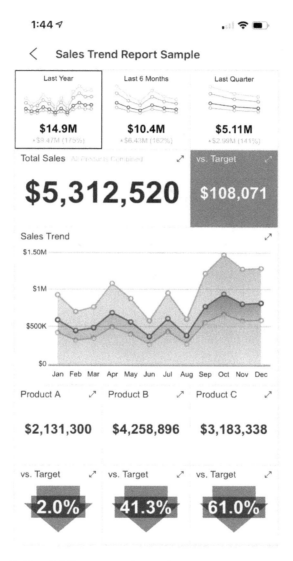

Figure 13.21: Mobile reports hosted on Power BI Report Server can be viewed using the Power BI mobile app

- **KPIs**: KPIs are great for tracking the performance of a given metric in relation to a specified goal or threshold. KPIs can be viewed through the Power BI mobile app as well as your web browser:

Figure 13.22: KPIs can be shared through the Power BI mobile app

Note

To learn more about viewing Power BI reports, mobile reports, and KPIs in the Power BI mobile app and connecting to an on-premises report server, review the following article and tutorials: https://docs.microsoft.com/en-us/power-bi/consumer/mobile/mobile-app-ssrs-kpis-mobile-on-premises-reports.

Exploring Power BI reports

Once you've published a Power BI report to your Power BI Report Server instance, a user can access the report by navigating to the report server using their browser:

Figure 13.23: To view a Power BI report, navigate to the report server portal in your browser, and click on the report you would like to view

Power BI reports can be viewed on a variety of device types with many different screen sizes and aspect ratios. To adjust the display options, use the **View** menu to optimize the report view. You can choose **Fit to page**, **Fit to width**, or **Actual size**. You can also choose to hide the Selection panel and Bookmarks panel to increase the screen real estate for the report.

Using the FILTERS panel

If the report includes filters, the **FILTERS** panel can be used to interact with the filters. Filters can be applied at the visual level, page level, and report level. To expose the visual-level filters in the **FILTERS** panel, select a visual in the Power BI report by clicking on the visual:

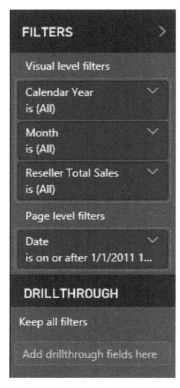

Figure 13.24: The FILTERS pane allows you to view and interact with filters in the Power BI report

Crossing-highlighting and cross-filtering

In a Power BI report, the visualizations are designed to interact with each other by default. By selecting one or more values in a visualization, other visualizations that use the same value will change based on the selection. This behavior is called cross-highlighting and cross-filtering.

Sorting a visualization

Visuals in a Power BI report can be sorted based on the visualization attributes. Visuals can be sorted into ascending or descending order using the fields included in the visualization. To expose the sorting controls, hover over the visual and select the ellipsis (…) in the top-right corner of the chart.

Displaying a visualization's underlying data

The underlying data for a given visualization can be displayed by selecting **Show data**. Select a visual, click on the ellipsis (…) in the top-right corner of the visual, and select **Show data**. This will display the dataset used to construct the following report next to the visualization:

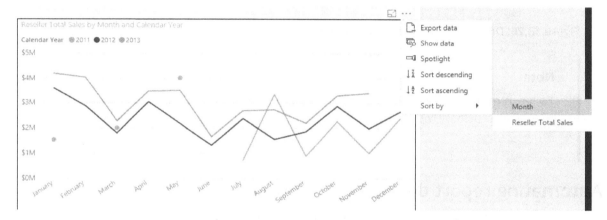

Figure 13.25: Exposing the more options menu by selecting the ellipsis (…) in the top-right corner of a visualization

Drill-down in a visualization

Power BI reports can also be configured to support drill-down behavior across hierarchies and other fields. To interact with a drill-down-enabled visualization, hover over the visual to expose the drill-down controls. The drill-down controls enable you to go to the next level of a hierarchy, expand all the data points to the next level in the hierarchy, or drill down to the next level of a hierarchy on a selected data point:

Figure 13.26: Drill down in a visualization to focus your analysis from a high level to a lower level

> **Note**
>
> To learn more about exploring and interacting with Power BI reports, review the following article: https://docs.microsoft.com/en-us/power-bi/consumer/end-user-reading-view.

Automating report delivery with subscriptions

Power BI Report Server allows you to create subscriptions to reports. A subscription is a standing request to deliver a report in a specified application file format at a specific time or in response to an event. As opposed to accessing a report on demand, subscriptions are used to schedule and automate the delivery of a report. Reports can be delivered to an email inbox or a file share.

There are two types of subscriptions in Power BI Report Server:

- **Standard subscriptions**

    Standard subscriptions are created and managed by individual users. Standard subscriptions are useful for users when they need a frequently viewed report delivered on a regular basis with a consistent file format and set of parameter values.

- **Data-driven subscriptions**

  Data-driven subscriptions are subscriptions that obtain subscription information at runtime by querying an external data source. The external data source provides information to specify a recipient, parameter values, and/or application format. Data-driven subscriptions are typically created and managed by the report server administrator.

Subscriptions can be delivered in the following formats:

- XML file with report data
- CSV file
- PDF file
- MHTML file
- Microsoft Excel file
- TIFF file
- Microsoft Word file

> **Note**
>
> If you plan to deliver your report as a subscription, test the subscription early on in the design process.
>
> Also, if you are required to deliver the report in a specific format, test the export format early on in the design process. Feature support varies based on the renderer you choose.

In the following table, you can find a few use cases related to Power BI Report Server subscriptions:

Use case	Description
Email delivery of reports	Subscriptions can be used to email reports to a user or group.
View reports offline	Reports that need to be archived can be sent directly to a shared folder that is backed up on a recurring schedule. Reports that take too long to load in a browser can be sent to a shared folder for viewing in a desktop application.
Preload cache	A subscription can be used to preload the cache to improve report rendering performance in scenarios where many users are viewing a report with several different parameter value selections.
Data-driven report	Use a data-driven subscription to customize report output, delivery options, and report parameter values at runtime. The subscription uses a query to get input values from a data source at runtime. Data-driven subscriptions are useful for programmatically delivering a report to many users who need the reports with different parameter values and in different file formats.

Table 13.27: Use cases related to Power BI Report Server

> **Note**
>
> You can review the following tutorial to learn how to create a data-driven subscription: https://docs.microsoft.com/en-us/sql/reporting-services/create-a-data-driven-subscription-ssrs-tutorial?view=sql-server-ver15.
>
> To learn more about subscriptions and automating the delivering of reports, review the following documentation: https://docs.microsoft.com/en-us/sql/reporting-services/working-with-subscriptions-web-portal?view=sql-server-ver15.

Pinning report items to the Power BI service

With Power BI Report Server, paginated report items can be pinned to the Power BI service in the cloud as a new tile. This capability allows you to integrate report items, such as charts, gauges, or maps, with Power BI dashboards you have deployed in the cloud.

To enable pinning paginated report items to the Power BI service, you must first complete the following steps:

1. Configure Power BI Report Server for Power BI integration using Report Server Configuration Manager.

2. Configure your browser to allow pop-up windows from your Power BI Report Server site.

3. The report should be configured for stored credentials if the pinned item should refresh on an automated schedule using a Reporting Services subscription.

> **Note**
>
> To learn more about configuring Power BI Report Server for Power BI integration, including troubleshooting common issues, you can review the following: https:// docs.microsoft.com/en-us/sql/reporting-services/pin-reporting-services-items-to-power-bi-dashboards?view=sql-server-ver15.

To pin the report item to Power BI, click on the Pin to Power BI button in the toolbar. If you're not signed into the Power BI service, you'll be prompted to sign in. Next, you'll be prompted to select the report item you'd like to pin. If there are no report items compatible for pinning to Power BI, a notification window will appear informing you:

Figure 13.28: Click on the Pin to Power BI button in the toolbar to select the report item you would like to pin to Power BI

After selecting the report item, the Pin to Power BI Dashboard window will appear. You will need to specify the **Group** (App Workspace), **Dashboard**, and **Frequency of updates** settings. Click on **Pin**.

14
Modernization to the Azure Cloud

No SQL Server 2019 book is complete without a discussion of Azure's role regarding modernization and the data platform. Research data puts the percentage of workloads in the cloud by 2020 at more than 80% (according to the Cloud Vision 2020 study carried out by LogicMonitor: https://www.logicmonitor.com/resource/the-future-of-the-cloud-a-cloud-influencers-survey/). The cloud's cost savings in a shorter time to market, the ability to scale without hardware limitations, and fewer resource demands on IT teams, all provide an opportunity that more and more businesses are taking advantage of. Just a decade ago, it was a common scenario for the database administrator to wait for a server to be made available by the infrastructure team before they could perform their work, and then there was a similar waiting period for developers waiting for other technical teams to complete their work. The cloud grants access to resources and allows the database administrator to create a database in a matter of minutes instead of days or weeks. The developer can gain access to their working environment with fewer roadblocks and more consistency between environments, eliminating the downtime that was once a common issue.

The SQL data platform in Azure

Azure is not only about services or acting as a **Platform as a Service** (**PaaS**). Azure's SQL data platform offerings help those who want to make the transition to the cloud but may have critical requirements that cause hesitation when considering Azure databases.

Azure SQL Database managed instance

Azure SQL Database Managed Instance offers the ability to "lift and shift" to a "managed" PaaS with only a few requirements, such as when moving a set of services to the cloud that are hosted on one or more isolated virtual machines inside a virtual network subnet. This general-purpose managed instance has shifted the management of the platform to the instance level, granting greater control over advanced features, and capabilities that are closer to on-premises functionality in SQL Server 2019, allowing for greater flexibility. A managed instance offers the cloud option for connectivity to Azure Analysis Services and Power BI for reporting.

Managed instance allows the user to always run on the latest release, eliminating the need to patch and upgrade. Currently, one managed instance can support:

- 1,000 user databases
- 4 TB of storage
- A virtual network for isolation
- SQL Server Agent and Agent Jobs
- Linked servers, for those who are using cross-database joins
- Azure Active Directory integration
- Database Mail
- **Common Language Runtime** (**CLR**)
- Filegroups

To simplify migration to Azure, managed instance offers the opportunity to migrate with fewer changes required.

When deploying a managed instance, there is a support infrastructure, including a **virtual network** (**VNet**) that contains a **Network Security Group** (**NSG**), with the managed instance deployed as part of a dedicated subnet. The subnet for a managed instance must have at least 16 dedicated IP addresses configured, but best practice recommends at least 32. This isolation offers a protected silo for your managed instance, but you must create inbound and outbound security rules before any other rules are deployed. The data endpoints to redirect traffic as part of port 1433 and 11000-11999 are part of the requirements for redirect connections. One of the differences between other PaaS offerings and a managed instance is that no service endpoint is configured as part of a managed instance due to the VNet configuration.

Deployment of a managed instance in Azure

There are a number of requirements for deploying a managed instance:

- A new or existing resource group
- A new or existing VNet
- A dedicated subnet
- A routing table with at least 16 dedicated IP addresses

Managed instance via the Azure portal

Once you've created the resource group that you wish to deploy to or have chosen to use an existing resource group, click on **Add**. Then, in the search bar, type in **Azure SQL Managed** to return the option to add a managed instance:

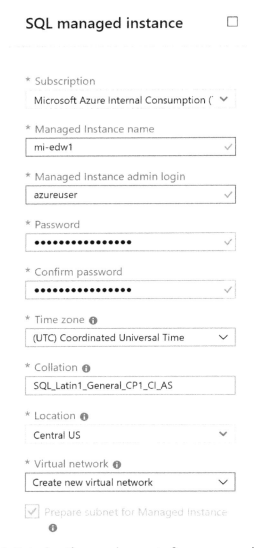

Figure 14.1: Entering the requirements for a managed instance

As you fill in the information for your managed instance, be sure to follow the requirements for passwords. Also, use collation matching if the managed instance will be used for migration from an existing database. You will also need to make a new VNet to create the subnet in if one doesn't already exist.

Managed instance via templates

To simplify the deployment of managed instances, you can utilize prebuilt templates available from Azure. The following command creates an **SQL Server Management Studio** (**SSMS**) jump box to ease management, along with the managed instance. If a new resource group is required, a simple command can create one:

PowerShell:

```
New-AzResourceGroup -Name <resource-group-name> -Location <resource-grouplocation>
```

Bash CLI:

```
az group create --name <resource-group-name> --location <resource-grouplocation>
```

You can also create the managed instance from the command line with direction to the available GitHub template:

PowerShell:

```
New-AzResourceGroupDeployment -ResourceGroupName <resource-group-name> -TemplateUri    https://raw.githubusercontent.com/Azure/azure-quickstarttemplates/master/201-sqlmi-new-vnet-w-jumpbox/azuredeploy.json
```

Bash CLI:

```
az group deployment create --resource-group <my-resource-group> --templateuri https://raw.githubusercontent.com/Azure/azure-quickstart-templates/ master/201-sqlmi-new-vnet-w-jumpbox/azuredeploy.json
```

As automation and DevOps become more central in the cloud administrator's world, more advanced build options in Azure become available. The deployment of a managed instance can be automated with an interactive script to make things simple, either in Bash (Linux) or PowerShell (Linux). As a virtual cluster is implemented as part of the managed instance (and more than one managed instance can be part of a virtual cluster), scripting from the command line reveals the layers in the architecture.

Using the Azure CLI with a Bash script, you can create a managed instance, passing in the variables for the required infrastructure as follows:

```
az sql mi create -n $instancename -u $username -p $password
\                         -g $groupname -l "$zone" \
        --vnet-name $vnet --subnet $snet
```

Notice in the Bash and Azure CLI versions that abbreviated arguments are used, such as -u instead of –user and -p instead of –password. Both full commands and abbreviations are acceptable, and mixed usage also has no impact on the success of deployment from the command line or a script.

In PowerShell, the same command to create the managed instance can be done, this time incorporating an **Azure Resource Manager** (**ARM**) template but still passing in variables for a Bash script to fulfill. PowerShell uses the `New-AzResourceGroupDeployment` command rather than the Azure CLI `az sql mi create` command:

```
New-AzResourceGroupDeployment   '
            -Name MyDeployment -ResourceGroupName $resourceGroup   '
            -TemplateFile './create-managed-instance.json' '
            -instance $name -user $user -pwd $secpasswd -subnetId
$subnetId
```

The ARM template could be used with either command, as could the simplified requirement variables without the template. The template, a JSON file, looks like the following:

```
{
    "$schema": "https://schema.management.azure.com/schemas/2014-04-
01preview/deploymentTemplate.json#",     "contentVersion": "1.0.0.1",
    "parameters": {
        "instance": {
            "type": "string"
        },
        "user": {
            "type": "string"
        },
        "pwd": {
            "type": "securestring"
        },
        "subnetId": {
            "type": "string"
        }
    },
```

```
    "resources": [
        {
            "name": "[parameters('instance')]",
            "location": "West Central US",
            "tags": {
                "Description":"GP Instance with custom instance
collation -
Serbian_Cyrillic_100_CS_AS"
            },
            "sku": {
                "name": "GP_Gen4",
                "tier": "GeneralPurpose"
            },
            "properties": {
                "administratorLogin": "[parameters('user')]",
                "administratorLoginPassword": "[parameters('pwd')]",
                "subnetId": "[parameters('subnetId')]",
                "storageSizeInGB": 256,
                "vCores": 8,
                "licenseType": "LicenseIncluded",
                "hardwareFamily": "Gen4",
                "collation": "Serbian_Cyrillic_100_CS_AS"
            },
            "type": "Microsoft.Sql/managedInstances",
            "identity": {
                "type": "SystemAssigned"
            },
            "apiVersion": "2015-05-01-preview"
        }
    ]
}
```

The ARM template ensures that all aspects of the deployment requirements are met, and that less is required at the command line. Sizes, the number of cores, the license type, and the collation are listed. This ensures that the configuration matches what will be required if and when migration of an existing database to the new managed instance is performed.

Migrating SQL Server to Managed Instance

Microsoft offers numerous options when migrating databases to Azure SQL Database Managed Instance. A migration project can be overwhelming. As such, it's important to choose the correct service model and service tier. There are a few, and your choice of them will depend on the use case for your managed instance:

- Cross-database joins
- CLR
- SQL Server Agent Jobs
- Log shipping
- Global temporary tables

These are some factors to consider when deciding on your managed instance. Additionally, unlike a virtual machine solution, managed instance is a **Platform-as-a-Service** (**PaaS**) solution, ensuring that you don't have to support the patching and upgrading of the database.

It is crucial before undertaking a migration to a Managed Instance that any compatibility issues due to deprecated versioning and features, such as 2008/R2/2012 are identified and resolved beforehand. SQL Server 2008/R2 contains a significant list of deprecated features to consider in multiple areas:

- Database Engine
- Integration Services
- Analysis Services
- Reporting Services

It is important to read a full assessment, no matter the tool chosen for the migration, ensuring all compatibility issues are identified before moving forward with a migration to Azure Managed Instance.

It's also a good idea to perform extensive workload testing and identify any high latency issues that can be addressed before the migration attempt. Although many on-premises features are supported as part of Azure managed instance, it's important to thoroughly understand the demands of your workloads, compatibility parameters, and latency when the database is hosted in the cloud. This includes any network latency that may not be quickly apparent in the day-to-day usage. Consider performing a proof-of-concept with a smaller workload of varying usage from your on-premises SQL Server databases and avoid those running at 100% utilization in their current environment. This allows you to focus on databases that are prepared to move to the cloud and address incompatible features that often are in place in multiple scenarios before commencing more complex migration opportunities.

The preferred methods provided by Microsoft for migration to a managed instance in Azure are:

* Azure Database Migration Service (DMS)
* Data Migration Assistant (DMA)
* Transactional Replication
* Bulk Load

Azure Database Migration Service (DMS)

Azure DMS is a convenient, robust, fully managed service for migrating multiple database platforms to Azure databases. As the DMS is a cloud-based service that allows for online migrations, it can lessen downtime involved with a migration. The DMS also has an offline option for a one-time migration option, able to handle database versions from SQL Server 2005 to 2017. Having a service in Azure removes the demands to install software on a server or workstation and places the resource demands squarely on the cloud, eliminating some of the demands required with other solutions.

Application Connectivity

As with any connection between on-prem and the Azure cloud, you can use a VPN or Azure Express Route configured with a secure virtual network from the Azure Resource Manager deployment model. Once this is set up, you must ensure rules are set up to not block the ports required for communication ports and the DMS can access the source databases you wish to migrate.

The Managed Instance to be migrated to will reside inside a **Virtual Network** (**Vnet**) and your cloud applications can connect to the database inside this VNet, connect through a different VNet than the Managed Instance, or if continuing to reside on-prem, the application can use a site-to-site VPN. If latency is an issue, this would be the reason to use an Express Route to gain additional bandwidth.

If an Azure App Service is to be used to connect to the Managed Instance, then a private IP address will be the only connection option and further configuration will be required once the Managed Instance migration is completed.

Requirements for the DMS

To use the Azure Data Migration Service, there is a requirement to set up an instance of the Azure Database in a secondary resource group from the virtual network you've configured to work with the DMS. This Azure database must have the CONTROL DATABASE permissions for it to use the DMS and allow it to perform the migration steps.

The Azure DMS uses the **Data Migration Assistant** (**DMA**) to provide assessment reports to get recommendations and guidance for the migration. Unlike other tools, DMS offers a very distinct set of migration use cases that can provide value to organizations that may not have realized that there are options for them to migrate to Azure:

- **PostgreSQL** to Azure SQL Database for PostgreSQL
- MySQL to Azure SQL Database for MySQL
- **Amazon Relational Database** (**RDS**) to Azure SQL or Azure SQL Managed Instance
- **MongoDB** to Azure Cosmos DB's API for MongoDB (either online or offline)

To remove roadblocks to a successful Azure Managed Instance migration, compatibility and resource usage of the on-prem SQL Server should be collected to ensure unique configurations, features and workloads have been identified.

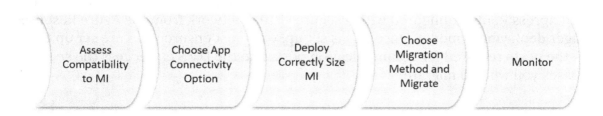

Figure 14.2: High-level migration steps from on-premises to Managed Instance

Data Migration Assistant

The **Data Migration Assistant**, (**DMA**), to be used in conjunction with the DMS, must be installed locally. A Managed Instance that the on-prem database will be migrated to must be created beforehand in the Azure portal.

Managed Instance Sizing

Before moving past the app connectivity step, a baseline should be gathered from the on-prem database to ensure that the correct size is chosen for the Azure Managed Instance to be deployed. Along with database size, critical information about CPU usage, IOPs, IO latency, memory, **TempDB** and top executions should be gathered. A Managed Instance, unlike an on-prem SQL Server or a PaaS Azure DB, isn't directly accessible through SQL Server Management Studio, (SSMS). The best way to work with the database as a DBA is to create a VM inside the same resource group and subnet as the Managed instance and use it as a jumpbox with the tools needed to work with the databases. You also won't have access to a Managed Instance with Remote Desktop, (RDP).

The best size estimates take the Managed Instance pricing model into consideration, ensuring to scale to the size and latency SLA requirements for the Managed Instance. Take the time necessary to understand Managed Instance VM characteristics and service tiers (i.e. general purpose vs. business critical).

Recent offers of 2 **vCore** Managed Instance also gives greater opportunity to choose this as an option where before greater requirements of **vCore** may have limited the choice.

Migration

Once you've selected and deployed the correctly sized Managed Instance, choose the best method for your database migration. An additional benefit of Managed Instance is that you can use a native backup from an on-premises database (.bak) file and restore via a URL. This method takes advantage of Azure storage as the go between for the on-prem to the Managed Instance for the backup file(s). There are some restrictions and added requirements depending on the database version or if you are using **Transparent Data Encryption** (**TDE**) so it's best to read through all documentation as part of Native Restore from URL to ensure success.

Following the steps to assess the migration and correct any issues, the next step is to perform the migration to Azure Managed Instance. If no issues are found and the migration is completed successfully, then the only step left is to monitor the new Managed Instance.

Monitoring Managed Instance

Unlike when issues arise on a regular basis, during this step-by-step migration, a baseline exists for comparison. This should be your first step and ongoing criteria as the new Managed Instance is under observation.

The same process of collecting memory, CPU and IO latency/IOPs should be followed and compared to the baseline. Acceptable variations in scoring should be decided and regular reviews should be held with users to avoid reactive challenges.

Just as with on-prem SQL Servers, the workload and application can benefit from optimization in code and database storage choices. The Query Store will also be able to identify where performance gains can be achieved. Azure Intelligent Insights uses artificial intelligence to compare database workloads, notifying of performance degradation and providing insight on issues and excessive wait times. For more, see the documentation here: https://docs.microsoft.com/en-us/azure/sql-database/ sql-database-intelligent-insights.

Monitoring and enforcing security is of the upmost importance. Although the topic is too complex to go into this high-level chapter, there are white papers and documents to help the cloud DBA implement a secure Managed Instance. See the documentation here: https://docs.microsoft.com/bs-latn-ba/azure/sql-database/sql-database-managed-instance-threat-detection and here: https://docs.microsoft.com/bs-latn-ba/ azure/sql-database/sql-database-advanced-data-security.

Secondary Options for Migration

There are two other options for migration from on-prem SQL Server to an Azure Managed Instance. **Transactional Replication** can be used to migrate from version SQL Server 2012, (SP2+)-2017 and offers the ability for ongoing synchronization of transactions until a desired cutoff point. **Bulk Load** is also still an option for any SQL Server version from 2005 on, to load data from an on-prem SQL Server to an Azure Managed Instance. Both options will benefit from an Azure Express Route connection to remove latency for ongoing traffic between the on-prem and cloud databases.

SQL Server in Azure virtual machines

For those databases that possess complex requirements not supported in Azure SQL Database or Azure Managed Instance, there is still the option to migrate to the cloud. This can be done by utilizing **Infrastructure as a Service** (**IaaS**) services such as virtual machines. SQL Server 2019 is no different, in that it can be deployed in an Azure VM, either with Windows, Linux, or a Docker image. This option grants incredible control to the business to build what they need, scale up as needed, and still have many of the benefits of the cloud:

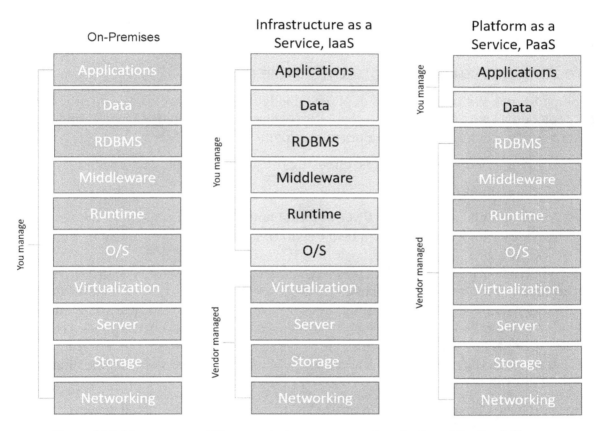

Figure 14.3: Management differences between on-premises, IaaS, and PaaS solutions

The added benefit of an Azure VM over an on-premises one is the ability to scale to larger VMs as needed without the purchase of on-premises hardware. The hardware is maintained by Azure, only requiring the operating system, up to the applications, to be managed by the user. For third-party applications that require a specific version of a database, or where an application isn't offered as a service inside Azure and should be moved to the cloud, Azure VM offers an option to solve this.

Virtually managed hosts make for simplified management from traditional server configuration and to use Azure VM. This removes another layer to the infrastructure support and purchasing that an on-premises VM solution would require. One of the ways that Azure VMs simplify management for the team is by offering automated patching, backups and diagnostics using the SQL Server IaaS Agent.

Creating an Azure VM from the Azure portal

When adding a VM to Azure, it is deployed inside a resource group. It can either be deployed as part of an existing group or to a new group. Inside the Azure portal resource group, you can start the portal deployment of a VM by:

- Clicking on **Resource Groups**, choosing the group to deploy to.

- Clicking on **Add**.

- In the search bar, typing in **VM** or **virtual machine** (note that there are several services and options that will be listed in the dropdown).

Once you've proceeded to this step, verify your requirements and type in **SQL Server** in the search window. The VM images for SQL Server 2019 will quickly display for the operating systems available, including Red Hat, Ubuntu, and Windows. Some images will include both the host operating system and database configured to support a relational database as part of the image. If a specific operating system version is required, the CLI (`az` commands) may provide the correct VM image to meet your needs. This will be covered later in the chapter.

Once you have chosen the version of the VM image you wish to install, the portal wizard will prompt you to either go through the configuration settings via the **Create** button or allow you to skip this by choosing the **Start with a pre-set configuration** option:

(RC1) SQL Server 2019 on Windows Server 2016
Microsoft

(RC1) SQL Server 2019 on Windows Server 2016 ♡ Save for later
Microsoft

Create   Start with a pre-set configuration
Deploy with Resource Manager (change to Classic)

SQL Server 2019 Developer image on Windows Server 2016

Useful Links
Documentation
SQL Server 2019 information
Support forum
Pricing details

Figure 14.4: Prompt for creating a VM in the Azure portal

In our example, we've chosen to create a VM with Windows Server 2016 and an SQL Server 2019 image. The first screen will ask you to name the VM and verify the resource group and other basic settings:

Create a virtual machine

Basics Disks Networking Management Advanced SQL Server settings Tags Review + create

Create a virtual machine that runs Linux or Windows. Select an image from Azure marketplace or use your own customized image.
Complete the Basics tab then Review + create to provision a virtual machine with default parameters or review each tab for full customization.
Looking for classic VMs? Create VM from Azure Marketplace

Project details

Select the subscription to manage deployed resources and costs. Use resource groups like folders to organize and manage all your resources.

* Subscription ❶   Microsoft Azure Internal Consumption (73aa270e-fffd-411a-b368-b44263f61deb) ∨

    * Resource group ❶   SQL2019_grp   ∨
                        Create new

Instance details

* Virtual machine name ❶ SQL2019vm1   ∨

* Region ❶   (US) East US 2   ∨

Availability options ❶   No infrastructure redundancy required   ∨

* Image ❶   Free SQL Server License: (CTP3.2) SQL 2019 Developer on Windows Server 2016 ∨
                        Browse all public and private images

* Size ❶   **Standard DS13 v2**
                        8 vcpus, 56 GiB memory
                        Change size

Azure resource names cannot contain special characters \/""[]:|<>+=;,?@& or begin with '_' or end with '.' or '-'*
Virtual machine name must be unique in the current resource group.
The value is in between 1 and 15 characters long.
All characters are valid for Windows OS computername.

Administrator account

Review + create   < Previous   Next : Disks >

Figure 14.5: Creating an Azure VM in the Azure portal interface

The name of the VM must be unique to the resource group. If, for some reason, you've chosen the incorrect VM image, you can update it using the Image dropdown menu. You can also change the size of the image if the default size isn't appropriate for your deployment and you need to scale up. Not all sizes are available for all VM images, but there is a wide array of sizes to suit almost any need. The **M Series** is great for memory intensive loads, with up to 4 TB of memory and 128 vCore. You can see some recommendations here: https://docs.microsoft.com/en-us/azure/virtual-machines/windows/sql/virtual-machines-windows-sql-performance.

Storage options for VMs

Once you have finished choosing these options, you will be asked to choose the type of disk you would like for storage on your VM. You have the options of a standard hard disk, **standard solid-state disk** (**SSD**), premium SSD, or even the new private preview of Ultra Disk. Ultra Disk is a new SSD made for IO-intensive loads that has sub-millisecond latency times. These new disks will autotune workloads without the requirement to restart a VM and will provide incredible performance for workloads on SQL Server and other database platforms. The disks will come in sizes from 4-64 TB and should be considered for any database that requires top IO performance:

Ultra SSD Managed Disk Offerings

Disk size (GiB)	4	8	16	32	64	128	256	512	1,024-65,536 (in increments of 1 TiB)
IOPS range	100-1,200	100-2,400	100-4,800	100-9,600	100-19,200	100-38,400	100-76,800	100-153,600	100-160,000
Throughput Cap (MBps)	300	600	1,200	2,000	2,000	2,000	2,000	2,000	2,000

Figure 14.6: IOPS ranges on Ultra Disk SSD from Azure

Diagnostics and advanced options

The **Advanced** tab lets you update to **Ephemeral OS disks**, which only save to the local VM storage and work great for stateless workloads, as they don't save to Azure cloud storage. Once you've made these decisions, you then progress to virtual networking. A VNet is then used to connect to the **network interface** (**NIC**) and the Azure cloud.

If a VNet already exists in the resource group, location, and subscription tenant, then a VM can use it. This will mean you won't have to deploy a new one just for the VM. Workload traffic should be discussed as part of the decision to use an existing VNet or deploy a new one as part of the VM.

The VNet will deploy public and private IP addresses to be used by the VM for access. These addresses must be associated with the VM by assigning them to the NIC. Inside each VNet, there is a subnet (or subnets) that follows rules for allocating traffic in and out of the VM. If a rule hasn't been set up to allow traffic through a subnet for a port or IP address, the traffic is blocked.

The next step in the wizard has options to turn on boot diagnostics, auto-shutdown, and security settings. The step following this is for advanced settings, including extensions that provide services such as backups, DevOps, and other extensions to automate management of the VM.

The SQL Server tab has the important settings to decide the port for the database to communicate on, the type of database authentication to be used, patching, and features:

Create a virtual machine

SQL Authentication 🛈	(Disable Enable)
Azure Key Vault integration 🛈	(Disable Enable)

Storage configuration

Select your desired performance, storage size, and workload to optimize the storage on your virtual machine.

Storage 🛈	**General** 5000 IOPS, 200 MBps Throughput, 1 TB Change configuration

SQL Server License

Save up to 43% with licenses you already own. Already have a SQL Server license? Learn more

SQL Server License 🛈	(◉) No ( ) Yes

Automated patching

Set a patching window during which all Windows and SQL patches will be applied.

Automated patching 🛈	**Enabled** Sunday at 2:00 Change configuration

Automated backup

Automated backup 🛈	(Disable Enable)

R Services(Advanced Analytics)

SQL Server Machine Learning Services (In-Database) 🛈	(Disable Enable)

Figure 14.7: SQL Server 2019 settings for a VM image in the Azure portal

Once you're satisfied with the settings you've chosen for the VM and your choices have passed the validation check from Azure, click on the **Create** button. The VM isn't as fast to create as it is for an Azure SQL database, but know that this is to do with all the networking going on behind the scenes. This process takes a bit longer to perform.

Creating a SQL Server 2019 VM from the command line in Azure

After all the steps taken in the previous section to create a VM in the Azure portal, it's time to realize the power of the command line. The Azure CLI can be accessed in numerous ways, including through the Azure CLI interface and through the Azure portal. However, directly using **Azure Cloud Shell** (https://shell.azure.com/) offers a full-screen experience that can offer dedicated cloud storage (when configured) to house scripts and automate common tasks.

The reason to use the command line becomes evident when performing a task multiple time. The command line simplifies the task into simple lines of code that are easier to manage and automate than the user interface-based solutions. The user interface, on the other hand, makes it simpler for those that may not be familiar with the syntax and requirements, offering them prompts and organizing steps.

The Azure CLI (also referred to as AZ CLI or AZ Commands) is a command-line tool that when accessed from Azure Cloud Shell can deploy a VM with just a small set of commands.

The Azure CLI command to create a VM is `az vm create`, and the arguments in the following list are used to complete the steps, just as you would in the user interface. Single-letter arguments have a single dash preceding them, whereas single words have a double dash. Arguments with more than one word are preceded by a double dash and separated by a single dash between words, as in `--admin-password`. The most common values used for SQL Server VM creation are the following:

- `-s` or `--subscription`, if you need to specify the subscription for the tenant to deploy the VM to a subscription different than the subscription you're currently logged in as.
- `-n` or `--name`, for the name of the VM.
- `-g` or `--group`, for the name of the resource group. This must exist or be created before you create the VM.

- `--image` specifies the operating system image.

- `--location`, for the location/zone in which the VM will reside.

- `--admin-username`, for the login of the administrator for the VM.

- `--admin-password`, for the password for the administrator login.

To begin, we need to know the name of the image we want to deploy from the command line. We can locate the image by querying the Azure catalog:

```
az vm image list --all \
--publisher MicrosoftSQLServer --output table
```

The output, formatted as a table rather than the default JSON, looks like this:

```
kellyn@Azure:~/MISC$ az vm image list --offer SQL2019-WS2016 --all --publisher MicrosoftSQLServer --output table
Offer            Publisher            Sku      Urn                                                          Version
---------------  -------------------  -------  -----------------------------------------------------------  ------------
SQL2019-WS2016   MicrosoftSQLServer   SQLDEV   MicrosoftSQLServer:SQL2019-WS2016:SQLDEV:15.0.181130         15.0.181130
SQL2019-WS2016   MicrosoftSQLServer   SQLDEV   MicrosoftSQLServer:SQL2019-WS2016:SQLDEV:15.0.190108         15.0.190108
SQL2019-WS2016   MicrosoftSQLServer   SQLDEV   MicrosoftSQLServer:SQL2019-WS2016:SQLDEV:15.0.190220         15.0.190220
SQL2019-WS2016   MicrosoftSQLServer   SQLDEV   MicrosoftSQLServer:SQL2019-WS2016:SQLDEV:15.0.190325         15.0.190325
SQL2019-WS2016   MicrosoftSQLServer   SQLDEV   MicrosoftSQLServer:SQL2019-WS2016:SQLDEV:15.0.190329         15.0.190329
SQL2019-WS2016   MicrosoftSQLServer   SQLDEV   MicrosoftSQLServer:SQL2019-WS2016:SQLDEV:15.0.190409         15.0.190409
SQL2019-WS2016   MicrosoftSQLServer   SQLDEV   MicrosoftSQLServer:SQL2019-WS2016:SQLDEV:15.0.190424         15.0.190424
SQL2019-WS2016   MicrosoftSQLServer   SQLDEV   MicrosoftSQLServer:SQL2019-WS2016:SQLDEV:15.0.190514         15.0.190514
SQL2019-WS2016   MicrosoftSQLServer   SQLDEV   MicrosoftSQLServer:SQL2019-WS2016:SQLDEV:15.0.190624         15.0.190624
SQL2019-WS2016   MicrosoftSQLServer   SQLDEV   MicrosoftSQLServer:SQL2019-WS2016:SQLDEV:15.0.190709         15.0.190709
SQL2019-WS2016   MicrosoftSQLServer   SQLDEV   MicrosoftSQLServer:SQL2019-WS2016:SQLDEV:15.0.190724         15.0.190724
SQL2019-WS2016   MicrosoftSQLServer   SQLDEV   MicrosoftSQLServer:SQL2019-WS2016:SQLDEV:15.0.190813         15.0.190813
```

Figure 14.8: Output from the az vm image list command

Armed with this information, we can choose the latest image **uniform resource name** (**URN**) and build our VM. We'll provide the last of the information from the list of arguments for a common Azure VM deployment:

```
az vm create -n SQL2019vm1 -g SQL2019_grp \
--image MicrosoftSQLServer:SQL2019-WS2016:SQLDEV:15.0.190813 \
--admin-username xxxx@contoso.com --admin-password <password> \
--location eastus --verbose
```

You can enter information onto proceeding lines by using a space and a backslash to notify the CLI that you are continuing. Once all parameters and values are entered, the Azure CLI will proceed to create your SQL Server VM from the image chosen, in the resource group listed, and with the resources from the information entered at the command line:

```
      "etag": "W/\"                                     \"",
      "id": "/subscriptions/                                    /resourceGroups/packt_grp/
urityGroups/sql2019vm1NSG/securityRules/open-port-22",
      "name": "open-port-22",
      "priority": 330,
      "protocol": "*",
      "provisioningState": "Succeeded",
      "resourceGroup": "packt_grp",
      "sourceAddressPrefix": "*",
      "sourceAddressPrefixes": [],
      "sourceApplicationSecurityGroups": null,
      "sourcePortRange": "*",
      "sourcePortRanges": [],
      "type": "Microsoft.Network/networkSecurityGroups/securityRules"
    }
  ],
  "subnets": null,
  "tags": {},
  "type": "Microsoft.Network/networkSecurityGroups"
}
Deployment of          sql2019vm1 in resource group packt_grp Complete
Keys generated for authentication
Admin name is azureuser
```

Figure 14.9: Successful deployment of an Azure VM from the command line

You can monitor the status of the VM creation in the Azure portal by going to the resource group you are deploying to and clicking the **Refresh** button in the ribbon in the **Resource Group Overview** pane.

Although the preceding Azure SQL VM deployment did require an existing resource group and VNet for support, it does demonstrate why it may be easier to deploy the script we used 20, 50, or hundreds of times with just a few changes instead of using the Azure portal user interface. With the addition of advanced scripting and DevOps automation, the process to deploy can be sped up massively, eliminating the need for manual steps to be performed.

Security for SQL Server on an Azure VM

VM support in the cloud may be new for those just migrating to Azure and knowing what to secure can be overwhelming. This can be simplified by enabling advanced data security on the VMs in your Azure tenant inside the Azure portal. This service will perform advanced threat protection. It uses the Azure Log Analytics agent to review and report on any security vulnerabilities. It then documents these vulnerabilities and suggests how to resolve them in Azure Security Center in the Azure portal. Along with accessing this information in the portal, notifications are recommended to keep you on top of any security vulnerabilities.

The Azure Security Center, upon a newly created VM, would detect if port 3389 for Remote Desktop connection, or if the default port for SQL Server, 1433, was configured open and report it as a possible security risk. The user could then update the configuration and secure the default ports.

When creating an Azure VM, the **Management** tab contains the step to turn on advanced data security as part of the VM creation process and it's highly advisable to do so:

Create a virtual machine

Basics   Disks   Networking   Management   Advanced   SQL Server settings   Tags   Review + create

Configure monitoring and management options for your VM.

Azure Security Center

Azure Security Center provides unified security management and advanced threat protection across hybrid cloud workloads.
Learn more

🛡   Your subscription is protected by Azure Security Center basic plan.

Monitoring

Boot diagnostics ⓘ	⦿ On ○ Off
OS guest diagnostics ⓘ	○ On ⦿ Off
* Diagnostics storage account ⓘ	(new) sql2019grpdiag ⌄
	Create new

Identity

System assigned managed identity ⓘ	○ On ⦿ Off

Auto-shutdown

Enable auto-shutdown ⓘ	○ On ⦿ Off

Figure 14.10: Management tab in the Create a virtual machine wizard in the Azure portal

As this service uses the agent from Log Analytics, this log data is available for querying for research and investigation. The portal dashboard contains considerable information even if you aren't into querying the log data, making this service very valuable to anyone managing VMs and wanting to ensure that the VM cloud environment is secure.

Backups of Azure VM SQL Server instances

There are numerous ways to back up a SQL Server 2019 instance deployed to an Azure IaaS VM, but automated backups via a service using the SQL Server IaaS agent is one of the best solutions. Along with configuring the service and agent, cloud storage to back up to must be configured before backups can be performed. The ease of this solution becomes apparent when the cloud database administrator finds that they are able to perform recoveries from SSMS and standard T-SQL commands, as they are accustomed to with on-premises solutions.

A second choice, no less viable, is the **volume snapshot service** (**VSS**) backup for IaaS VMs, which allows for two backup choices: VSS full backup or VSS copy backup. Where the full backup takes a one-time backup of the full VM (not just the database), it does truncate logs that may be required for application backups. The VSS copy backup takes both a VM snapshot and a full backup of the SQL Server database, which is a great solution for those still responsible for infrastructure.

Built-in security for Azure VMs

When a cloud migration project is initiated, one of the first topics of discussion is around cloud security. Azure incorporates numerous layers of security to create an ecosystem that blankets the cloud with security from end to end.

For Azure VMs with databases, this involves authentication through database logins, row-level permissions, database roles, Azure Active Directory, and firewall rules. There are more advanced data protection features, such static data masking, and **Transparent Data Encryption** (**TDE**).

Azure also makes it easy to set up advanced data security for SQL Server on Azure Virtual Machines, which is a package of security features that will provide assessment reports that can be viewed in the Azure portal (and/or emailed):

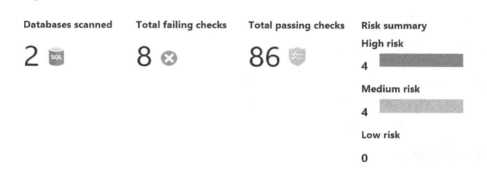

Microsoft Azure

A Vulnerability Assessment scan has completed on your server 'demoazuresql1'

Scan results

Databases scanned	Total failing checks	Total passing checks	Risk summary
2	8	86	High risk 4
			Medium risk 4
			Low risk 0

Database	Scan result	Failing checks	Passing checks	Details
HiEd_DW	Findings	4	43	View results
HiEd_Staging	Findings	4	43	View results

Figure 14.11: Vulnerability assessment email notification

These reports offer guidance on best practices around security, along with links to correct any possible threats.

SQL Server IaaS agent extension

Unlike the "Full" or "No Agent" options, the SQL Server IaaS agent extension offers you the ability to have a service agent to manage jobs on the VM, but without a requirement for SQL Server and must be granted sa privileges to enable.

Although more SQL Server database administrators are building out PowerShell/ shell scripts to address management tasks, the robust and capable agent was clearly an important feature to have. With the lightweight extension version, which requires no reboot or privilege requirements for the risk-averse, the agent can perform the following:

- Automatic SQL backups
- Automatic SQL patching
- Azure Key Vault integration

Installing the extension for lightweight mode in SQL Server 2019 on an Azure VM can be performed via PowerShell. The first step is to set the variable for the VM host name:

```
$vm = Get-AzVM -Name <vm_name> -ResourceGroupName <resource_group_name>
```

Once this is performed, PowerShell can install the extension to the VM host:

```
New-AzResource -Name $vm.Name -ResourceGroupName $vm.ResourceGroupName
-Location $vm.Location '
    -ResourceType Microsoft.SqlVirtualMachine/SqlVirtualMachines '
    -Properties @{virtualMachineResourceId=$vm.
Id;sqlServerLicenseType='AHUB';sqlManagement='LightWeight'}
```

Note that each return carriage is marked with a ' symbol. Without this delimiter, the execution call will fail due to required arguments.

Once installed, these features can be accessed in the Azure portal from the SQL Server blade.

Viewing the current mode of your SQL Server agent can be performed via PowerShell. If you are in the same command window as your installation, you won't need to set the VM variable again, but if you are in a new one, it will need to be set a second time:

```
$vm = Get-AzVM -Name <vm_name> -ResourceGroupName <resource_group_name>
$sqlvm = Get-AzResource -Name $vm.Name  -ResourceGroupName $vm.
ResourceGroupName  -ResourceType Microsoft.SqlVirtualMachine/
SqlVirtualMachines
$sqlvm.Properties.sqlManagement
```

Disaster Recovery environment in the cloud

One of the most common challenges when moving to the cloud is how often you need to rethink the way the business may have performed tasks or architected solutions. **Disaster Recovery** (**DR**) is no different.

Azure has numerous high-availability components built into it, but if you choose to build your environment with virtually managed hosts in the cloud, there are significant options for DR. Here, we'll discuss the Azure Site Recovery service.

Azure Site Recovery

Azure Site Recovery (**ASR**) is a versatile service for backing up, cloning, and recovering data. Considered Azure's **Disaster Recovery as a Service** (**DRaaS**), the service is a hybrid, connecting to both on-premises and cloud VMs, even connecting to VMware and AWS for migrations to Azure VMs.

The service has a critical role to play for VMs with SQL 2019 databases residing on them. Once the ASR resource is added to a resource group, VMs can be added and schedules can be added for all necessary DR functions via a simple wizard:

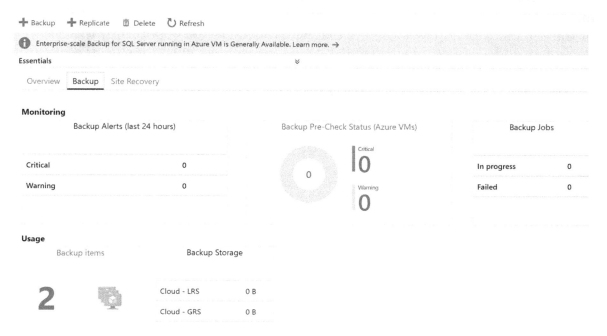

Figure 14.12: Azure ASR portal interface with backups displayed

Once all pertinent information about the VM is entered, the service builds all required resources to build a fully redundant and robust DR solution in Azure, even in separate location zones. The best practice would be to have ASR stored in a different location zone and replicated to a third location for a fully redundant DR solution.

The ASR service offers a simple interface to build backup jobs and replicate VMs, as well as providing site testing recommendations and failover testing. Although it's fully possible to build your own backup and DR solution in Azure, the ASR service is feature-rich and provides a single pane of glass to support an array of IaaS DR needs.

Extended support for SQL 2008 and 2008 R2

As of July 2019, SQL Server 2008 and 2008 R2 have reached the end of their support life cycle. This should signal for any business to upgrade to a newer version for sustainability. However, for some cases, due to vendor requirements, moving away from 2008 is not an option.

SQL Server 2008 and 2008 R2 databases can be migrated to an Azure VM with a simple backup and restore option rather than using a migration tool such as SSMA. The only way to use one of the existing migration tools, such as DMS, would be to agree to upgrade to SQL Server 2012 or higher. One of the added benefits of choosing this option for the end of life of 2008/2008 R2 is that with the Azure VM opportunity there is three years of extended support included. For more, see the documentation here: https://azure.microsoft.com/en-us/blog/announcing-new-options-for-sql-server-2008-and-windows-server-2008-end-of-support/.

For those customers that must remain on 2008 or 2008 R2, Azure Marketplace has a pay-as-you-go SQL Server 2008 R2 image that can be used to get them through this challenging time. The image has the SQL IaaS extension with it for automatic patching and licensing:

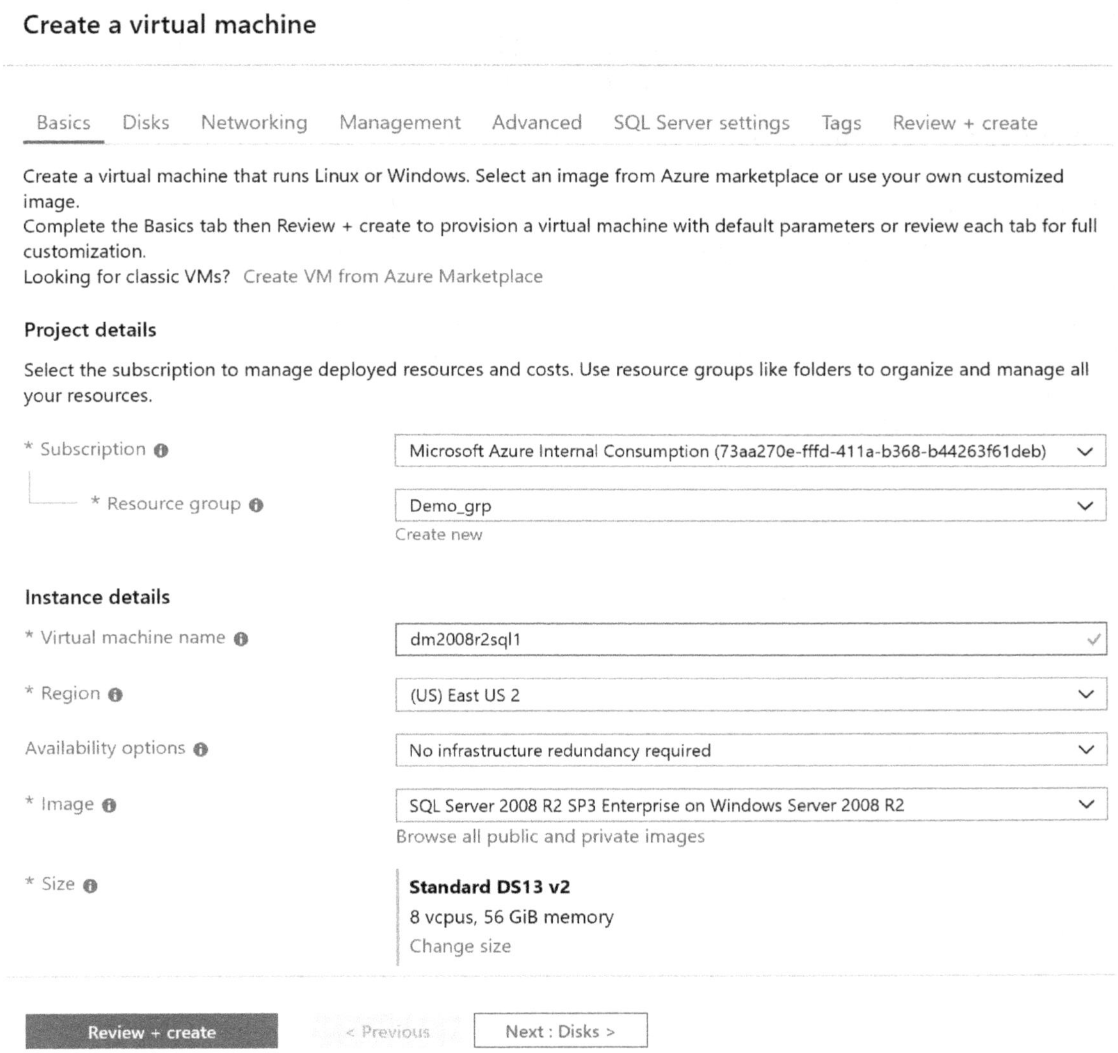

Create a virtual machine

| Basics | Disks | Networking | Management | Advanced | SQL Server settings | Tags | Review + create |

Create a virtual machine that runs Linux or Windows. Select an image from Azure marketplace or use your own customized image.
Complete the Basics tab then Review + create to provision a virtual machine with default parameters or review each tab for full customization.
Looking for classic VMs? Create VM from Azure Marketplace

Project details

Select the subscription to manage deployed resources and costs. Use resource groups like folders to organize and manage all your resources.

* Subscription ⓘ

[Microsoft Azure Internal Consumption (73aa270e-fffd-411a-b368-b44263f61deb) ⌄]

   * Resource group ⓘ

[Demo_grp ⌄]
Create new

Instance details

* Virtual machine name ⓘ

[dm2008r2sql1 ✓]

* Region ⓘ

[(US) East US 2 ⌄]

Availability options ⓘ

[No infrastructure redundancy required ⌄]

* Image ⓘ

[SQL Server 2008 R2 SP3 Enterprise on Windows Server 2008 R2 ⌄]
Browse all public and private images

* Size ⓘ

Standard DS13 v2
8 vcpus, 56 GiB memory
Change size

[Review + create] < Previous [Next : Disks >]

Figure 14.13: Creating a VM from the SQL Server 2008 R2 image

Customers that require 2008 can install the software on a VM, along with the SQL IaaS extension, as it's not part of the standard VM image.

The option to convert to the **Azure Hybrid Benefit** (**AHB**) for any SQL Server 2008 R2 image will provide savings over running in Azure without it.

The customer needs to manage their own backup and DR solution in Azure, as it's not part of the IaaS solution or SQL Server 2008 R2 image. This can be accomplished by backing up to separate storage or setting up ASR.

This chapter covered numerous topics around SQL Server 2019 in Azure around VMs, extended support for SQL Server 2008/2008 R2, and making intelligent choices as you migrate to the cloud. Having the opportunity to know what options and services exist when considering implementing to the cloud is essential to ensure you do it right the first time rather than doing it two, three, or four times. This chapter demonstrates that whether you go for Azure SQL Database, SQL Server 2019 on Azure VMs, or any other data platform, there are service tiers to support the Microsoft professional inside the Azure cloud.

Index

About

All major keywords used in this book are captured alphabetically in this section. Each one is accompanied by the page number of where they appear.

www.ingramcontent.com/pod-product-compliance
Lightning Source LLC
Chambersburg PA
CBHW060643060326
40690CB00020B/4495